Wisconsin

Wisconsin

Mollie Boutell-Butler
with photographs by the author

The Countryman Press ✳ Woodstock, Vermont

FIRST EDITION

ISBN: 978-0-88150-828-4

Interior photographs by the author unless otherwise specified
Maps by Moore Creative Designs, © The Countryman Press
Book design by Bodenweber Design
Composition by PerfecType, Nashville, TN

Published by The Countryman Press, P.O. Box 748, Woodstock, VT 05091

Distributed by W. W. Norton & Company, Inc., 500 Fifth Avenue, New York, NY 10110

Printed in the United States of America

10 9 8 7 6 5 4 3 2 1

To Jacques and Lucie–my favorite little cheeseheads,
dairy intolerances notwithstanding.

EXPLORE WITH US!

Among the things I learned as I worked on this first edition is that Wisconsin is a very big state. Of course, I knew that before—I've lived here all my life—but trying to cover all that ground during my research really drove it home. This guide is intended to get you to all corners (such as they are) of Wisconsin—not simply give you direction, but give you the impetus. There is so much more going on just beyond the highways here than many people realize. This guide, I hope, surprises a few people, who then discover a new, favorite spot.

Wisconsin: An Explorer's Guide is an easy-to-use and comprehensive guide to the state. I've arranged the chapters into generally accepted regions and titled them that way, too. That way both you and the locals will be on the same page. Subchapters are based strictly on proximity in some cases, but in others those chapters cover a lot more land, because the towns are smaller, and spread apart, but the attractions are considered as one. Here's a rundown of what's in each chapter.

WHAT'S WHERE

There's an alphabetical reference in the beginning of the book that highlights important information and Wisconsin trivia. It's a good place to peek for quick state park guidance and the definition of bubbler.

LODGING

The lodgings in this guide were chosen on their merits; nobody has to pay to get listed. Please don't hold us or the innkeepers responsible for the listed rates as of press time. Keep in mind that things can change, and always verify the information. Wisconsin sales tax at press time is 5–5.5 percent. Local room taxes range from 5–8 percent.

RESTAURANTS

Restaurants are grouped into two categories: *Dining Out* and *Eating Out*. Dining Out is meant for pricier, finer affairs, while Eating Out is for the less expensive. Keep in mind, though, that in Wisconsin there's a huge gray area of upscale casual, or casual fine dining, or the supper club—which offers pricey food but never demands you dress up.

KEY TO SYMBOLS

ℰ   The kids-alert symbol appears next to lodgings, restaurants, activities, and shops of special appeal to youngsters.

Ŷ   The martini glass symbol appears next to a restaurant or other venue that has a well-stocked bar and beer on tap.

♿ The wheelchair symbol appears next to lodgings, restaurants, activities, and shops that are partially or fully handicapped-accessible.

🐾 The dog paw symbol indicates pet–friendly lodging.

☂ The umbrella symbol suggests a good rainy day activity.

▼ The inverted triangle appears next to establishments that are particularly LGBT-friendly.

🎖 The blue ribbon symbol appears next to establishments and attractions that offer an exceptional value

"ı" The "WiFi" symbol indicates which establishments offer free WiFi Internet.

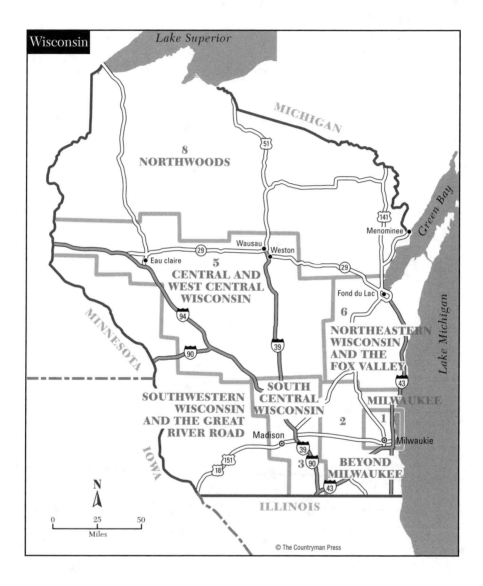

CONTENTS

8 Northwoods / 325

ACKNOWLEDGMENTS

Without a doubt, I will fail to thank everyone who ought to be thanked, but I'll give it a shot. Among the family, friends, and parents of Mom's coworkers who put me up for a night or two, gave tours, and offered wonderful recommendations are Jerry and Mary Butler, Carol and Gerald Boutell, Becky and Craig Filiatreaux, Leon and Betty Shellswick, and many others. I'm also very grateful for the folks at the convention and visitors' bureaus who went out of their way to make sure I had everything I needed, including Jean Galasinski at the Trempealeau Chamber of Commerce, Stephanie Sabo at the Greater Madison Convention Visitors Bureau, Becky Seiler and Melanie Platt-Gibson at the Wisconsin Dells Visitor and Convention Bureau, Grace C. Eckland at the Lake Geneva Area Convention and Visitors Bureau, and Jodi McMahon at the Manitowish Waters Chamber of Commerce. Finally, the many people involved in this project or my life who demonstrated seemingly limitless patience, including Kim Grant and the rest of the folks at Countryman Press, who provided encouragement at the roughest times; Sarah Bissen; my husband, Joel; and my kids, who celebrated when I completed the book.

INTRODUCTION

Wisconsin. The license plates may read "America's Dairyland," and there may be a cow on the state quarter, but in truth there is no one way to define Wisconsin. From world-class arts and exceptional dining in the urban centers of Milwaukee and Madison to the untouched majesty of the Northwoods, Wisconsin offers something for everyone. If it's "fly-over country" to some bicoastal travelers, folks around here know this: Wisconsin may just be the nation's best-kept travel secret. Of course, it's no secret in these parts; Wisconsin's tourism industry rakes in a whopping $13 billion annually, with 58 percent of those dollars coming from state residents themselves.

So, what do Wisconsinites know that other Americans don't? Simply put, Wisconsin is astonishingly rich in both land and culture. Sure, we like our cheese. We really do. But that guy on TV wearing a foam Cheesehead at a Packers game is a very small part of the picture. He is a part of it, just not the whole thing. A closer

LAKE MICHIGAN

look reveals land that's wilder and more varied than the farmland you expect. It reveals ethnic diversity and pride, a strong sense of history, and perhaps unexpected sophistication.

The Wisconsin landscape is remarkable. Advancing and retreating glaciers during the Ice Age left the state with stunning geography: Along with 15 million acres of forest (that's 46 percent of the land), Wisconsin boasts 15,000 lakes, 33,000 miles of river, bogs, marshes, moraines, and more. And in southwestern and south central Wisconsin you'll find the Driftless Area, so named because of its lack of glacial drift. Here, rolling hills, valleys, and striking rock formations that existed before the Ice Age mark the land. Small wonder Frank Lloyd Wright, a native of this area, designed his buildings to fit their environment so well.

Much of Wisconsin's border is shoreline, thanks to two Great Lakes—Lake Michigan and Lake Superior—and the Mississippi River forms a large part of the western border. This, along with all those interior lakes, makes water recreation a big part of Wisconsin tourism. Fishing, boating, and just hanging out on a lake, whether it's at Bradford Beach in Milwaukee or at a cabin in the Northwoods, are integral parts of experiencing Wisconsin.

Proud of its heritage and history, Wisconsin's regions are often culturally linked in some way to ethnic background. In Milwaukee, ethnic festivals draw millions of people to the lakefront all summer long, while museums around the state, such as Little Norway, the Swiss Historical Village, Old World Wisconsin, the Wisconsin Black Historical Society Museum, and others, honor some of Wisconsin's diverse immigrants. Home to 11 sovereign tribal nations, more than a half-million acres of Wisconsin's land is reservation. For visitors, the tribal communities offer educational opportunities, tours, arts, and special events as well as, yes, casinos. Many of Wisconsin's cities and towns have names with roots in Native American languages.

Then there's food. Perhaps the strongest sign that an ethnic group settled in one area is that region's signature foods. After all, beer and brats came to Milwaukee from Germany—the beers that gave Milwaukee the nickname Brew City include Pabst, Schlitz, Blatz, and Miller. In Racine, the locals enjoy Danish kringle; in Green Bay, the signature booyah—a somewhat phonetic spelling of bouillon—is courtesy of the Belgians.

Wisconsin, too, is home to some of the most unusual tourist attractions and local history a traveler could hope to find. From the House on the Rock to highway grottos to dozens of lighthouses dotting the shores, there is something here for everyone. Because of this abundance, few Wisconsin residents have seen it all. This guide, then, is for those fortunate residents who wish to see the beauty and culture Wisconsin has to offer.

It is my hope that more than a few lifelong Wisconsinites, reading through these pages, stop and marvel at all they didn't know about their home state. I also hope that folks traveling here from other states will find this guide and begin to understand the complexity of Wisconsin.

This guide is arranged roughly by geography, and largely by how any given region of the state defines itself. Wisconsin is not a square. Not even close. But the tradition is to refer to its regions in terms of direction, i.e., Northeastern Wisconsin, Southwestern Wisconsin. I have used these terms as well, and tried to group counties according to how area organizations and institutions group themselves.

As a lifelong Wisconsin resident who's made various cities along the Lake Michigan shore home, I'm excited to help you explore all the state has to offer. I've

FLOODED FARMLAND IN MADISON.

included things that are Wisconsin "musts," such as cheese shops and supper clubs, as well as the more unexpected, interesting finds around the state. Like many, I love feeling like I've discovered something—an out-of-the-way diner with home-cooked meals and friendly faces, or stunning scenery on a less-traveled road. But, I'll admit, I'm sometimes more than willing to take the bait of a tourist trap, and get sucked in with all the other camera-wielding gawkers. I believe it's the right way to be, because you'll miss out on some fun if you write off the famous places simply for their fame. Goats on the roof at Al Johnson's in Door County? Some do call it a tourist trap, but the food and service are fantastic and, well, they have goats on the roof.

I happened to write this first edition during a very tumultuous period, which made painfully evident to me the temporary nature of my carefully chosen entries. Record snowfall was followed by dramatic flooding, which at worst washed away businesses, and at best left some of us with a pile of garbage to toss out. As I traveled the state I saw farmland turned into lakes, and in the Wisconsin Dells' Lake Delton, a lake turned into a sandy pit. Winter came again, and again we had record snowfall, but this time the snow wasn't the big story; it was the economic downturn and the ensuing rash of store and restaurant closings around the state. My head was absolutely spinning as I wrapped up the last chapters. Surely there were businesses in chapters I'd completed that had closed, and if not, there would be by summer. With that, I ask the reader to keep in mind that any travel guide will have mistakes, businesses will close, and there will be changes that businesses and organizations make between the time a guide is written and the time it lands in a reader's hands. This book is your guide; it is what I found as I traveled my home state. But it's almost certainly imperfect, and many of my favorite establishments have shut their doors in recent months, while new ones have popped up; you'd be wise to call ahead.

The other thing I learned, though, is that traveling Wisconsin is a fantastic way to spend a vacation. As we tighten our pocketbooks, we still need leisure. Anyone looking for a getaway need not look far. Wisconsin really does have it all. Support the mom-and-pops I've found. Keep them around through these tough times, and have a great time yourself.

I'll be launching a Web site with the release of this book at wisconsinexplorer .com. It will parallel what you find in here, and then some. You can also follow me on Twitter @WISCguide.

WHAT'S WHERE IN WISCONSIN

AIRPORTS AND AIRLINES
General Mitchell International Airport (414-747-5300; mitchellair port.com) in Milwaukee is the state's largest airport, with direct service to around 90 cities. Thirteen airlines operate out of MKE, including **Air Canada** (800-247-2262; aircanada.com), **Air-Tran Airways** (800-247-8726; air-tran.com), **American Airlines** (800-433-7300; aa.com), **Continental Express** (800-523-3273; continental.com), **Delta** (800-221-1212; delta.com), **Frontier** (800-432-1359; frontierairlines.com), **Midwest Airlines** (800-452-2022; midwestairlines.com), **Southwest Airlines** (800-435-9792; southwest.com), **United Express** (800-241-6522; united.com), and **US Airways Express** (800-428-4322; usairways.com). The second largest airport in Wisconsin is **Dane County Regional Airport** (608-246-3380; msnairport.com) in Madison, with 15 direct flights to cities around the Midwest, followed by **Austin Straubel International Airport** (920-498-4800) in Green Bay.

There are more than 120 other municipal and regional airports and airfields throughout the state. **Wittman Regional Airport** (920-236-4930; wittmanairport.com) in Oshkosh is home to the **Experimental Aircraft**
Association's annual convention, which attracts more than 500,000 visitors.

AMUSEMENT PARKS **Bay Beach Amusement Park** in Green Bay is a nostalgic favorite, dating back to 1892. With free admission and rides costing as little as a quarter, a family can have a load of fun for very little cash. While there are no roller coasters, there are rides here for both the very young and the not-so-young. The Wisconsin Dells area is amusement-park central, though. While not as insanely cheap as Bay Beach (few things are), there's arguably more here. The Dells is home to Mount Olympus Theme Park and Riverview Park, along with a huge number of water parks.

ANTIQUES You'll find antiques throughout Wisconsin, with concentrations around Door County and the southwestern region of Wisconsin. Check with the **Wisconsin Antique Dealers Association** (wisconsin antiquedealers.com) for listings and show information. There's also a paid listing pamphlet called *Wisconsin Antiques Road Trip* with the locations of antiques dealers, flea markets, and malls. The state's largest antique mall is **Fox River Antiques** (920-731-9699; foxriverantiques.com) in Appleton.

APPLE ORCHARDS There are apple orchards in every part of the state, but they are concentrated in the area surrounding Milwaukee, the Southwestern part of the state, in Bayfield, and in Door County. Some are attached to wineries which produce fruit wines and ciders, and they're often home to pumpkin patches. Check with the **Wisconsin Apple Growers Association** (usagnet.com/waga) for listings and information.

AREA CODES Wisconsin has five area codes. Milwaukee is served entirely by 414, while the other four cover the rest of the state. Roughly, 262 covers Southeastern Wisconsin outside of Milwaukee; 608 covers South Central and Southwestern Wisconsin; 920 covers Northeastern Wisconsin, and 715 covers Central and West-Central Wisconsin as well as the Northwoods.

AQUARIUMS The newest and snazziest aquarium is at **Discovery World** in Milwaukee. Visitors walk through a clear tunnel under water and even get to touch de-armed stingrays at this impressive aquarium. **The Milwaukee County Zoo** also houses a small aquarium that's worth a look.

ARTISTS AND ART GALLERIES
Aside from Milwaukee and Madison, there are communities of artists and the art galleries that support them throughout the state. There is a distinct concentration of artists in the Spring Green area, with charming Mount Horeb home to a vibrant arts community. Door County is also especially abundant in art galleries and working studios, as is charming Bayfield. The **Wisconsin Arts Board** (608-266-0190; arts.state.wi.us/STATIC/default.htm) publishes the annual *Wisconsin Art Museum and Gallery Guide*, which includes a map and listings.

You'll find art fairs all summer long throughout the state. The best-known is Milwaukee's **Lakefront Festival of Arts**, held in front of the Milwaukee Art Museum, but don't discount the smaller guys—they often have more than 100 exhibiters. Check out **Art Street** in Green Bay; this free street festival spans three days and features more than 200 exhibitors, scheduled

performers as well as strolling musicians, arts activities, and, of course, food. Keep in mind, too, that a lot of summer festivals feature arts vendors, too. The Wisconsin Arts Board also publishes a guide to the state's arts and crafts fairs (arts.state.wi.us/static/fairs/directory.htm).

Be sure to check out the outdoor art environments around the state, among them the **Dickeyville Grotto**, **Evermor Sculpture Park**, and the **Wisconsin Concrete Park**. Most of these are covered in this book, but a good place to get more information is from the **Kohler Foundation** (kohler foundation.org), which has funded the restoration of many folk sculpture sites.

ART MUSEUMS While it's overshadowed by the **Milwaukee Art Museum** (414-224-3200; mam.org) an hour south, the **Kohler Arts Center** (920-458-6144; jmkac.org) in Sheboygan is a must-stop on any art lover's itinerary (be sure to check out the bathrooms). The **Madison Museum of Contemporary Art** (608-257-0158; mmoca .org) right near State Street is a small but worthy (and free) museum, and the **Chazen Museum of Art**

(chazen.wisc.edu) at the University of Wisconsin-Madison is home to broad and extensive collections. The **Racine Art Museum** (262-638-8300; ramart .org) in downtown Racine houses one of the nation's best collections of contemporary crafts, and the **Museum of Wisconsin Art** (262-334-9638; wiscon sinart.org) in West Bend features the state's most significant collection of Wisconsin art pieces and archives.

ATTIRE What should you wear? Well, it depends what you're doing, and when you're here, of course. It's true that Wisconsin is a casual place, and if you're out and about in a touristy area or the Northwoods, you won't get a second look for wearing jeans at a nice restaurant. It's an issue of practicality; nobody expects you dock your boat and change your clothes before heading into a supper club—that would be silly. But you won't get a second look for dressing nicely, either. My take? You can never be overdressed. Come as you are, or as you're comfortable. If you think you should wear your Sunday best, you probably should, but you can get by without a jacket, too.

Ⓨ BARS There are plenty of bars in Wisconsin, to be sure. The Ⓨ symbol lets you know a restaurant or venue has a well-stocked bar and beer on tap, or at least libations of some sort.

BEACHES You don't automatically think of lazy weekends on the beach when you think of Wisconsin, but the short summers and plentiful shoreline have created more than a few beach bums here. There are sandy beaches from Kenosha to Door County on Lake Michigan and all along Lake Superior, but don't forget the inland lakes. Geneva Lake is home to a handful (it's also one of the few places to charge a fee for beach use), and there are many more—check with parks departments in your area. Inland lakes tend to be warmer and calmer than Lake Michigan and Lake Superior.

BED & BREAKFASTS There are wonderful Bed & Breakfasts throughout the state, but they're particularly concentrated in high tourism areas, like Door County. Frequently housed in historic buildings, they add a personal touch to your vacation. You can find out more and order a directory from the **Wisconsin Bed & Breakfast Association** at wbba.org.

BEER We like to think we've got the market cornered on beer—after all, Milwaukee is nicknamed Brew City. But in truth, Wisconsin ranks a mere seventh nationally in per-capita beer consumption, and 12th in production. Those numbers aren't bad, but they hardly justify the state's reputation for insatiable guzzling. While Milwaukee once reigned as the "beer capital of the world" thanks to Miller, Pabst, Schlitz, and Blatz, today that's just not true. The city's last big brewery, Miller, isn't even headquartered here anymore; after merging with Colorado's Coors in 2008, the headquarters for both breweries were combined and moved to Chicago. Miller's not even Miller anymore, it's **MillerCoors** (414-931-2337; millercoors.com). You can still tour the brewery in Milwaukee, however, and learn the rich history of Miller while sampling the brewery's offerings. Better yet, check out the state's craft breweries, which not only produce some outstanding beers, but often take a place in Wisconsin's beer history. I recommend without hesitation the **Lakefront Brewery Tour** (414-372-8800; lakefrontbrewery.com) in Milwaukee, which gets you four 4-ounce pours, colorful history, and a chance to sing the *Laverne & Shirley* theme.

Come on a Friday night, and you can have one of the city's most popular fish fries, paired with polka. **New Glarus Brewing Company** in Southwestern Wisconsin offers a popular tour as well. I've included many craft breweries and brewpubs in each chapter's listings, but statewide directories are available from the **Wisconsin Brewer's Guild** (wibrewersguild.org). Also don't miss historic, erstwhile beer leaders **Stevens Point Brewery** (715-344-9310; pointbeer.com) in Stevens Point, **City Brewing Company** (608-785-4470; citybrewery.com) in La Crosse, and **Leinenkugel's** (888-534-6437; leinie.com) in Chippewa Falls. For even more beer background, there's a museum in Grant County housed in the historic **Potosi Brewing Company** (608-763-4002; potosibrewery.com) that's filled with memorabilia on loan from beer fanatics. Potosi cranked out beer from 1852 to 1972; in 2008 it started making craft brews again.

BICYCLING Wisconsin was a pioneer in the rails-to-trails movement and is currently home to 64 rail trails, with more than 1,200 miles of paths. The Elroy-Sparta State Trail was among the

first rail conversions in the country and remains a popular biking destination in Wisconsin. Many trails are free; some require day passes. The **Wisconsin Bicycle Federation** (608-251-4456; bfw.org) publishes the yearly *Ride Guide* and is a valuable source of information on biking throughout the state. Also check out more information from the state's **Department of Tourism** at travelwisconsin.com/Biking_in _Wisconsin.aspx, or visit the **Department of Transportation** for a complete list of local biking information organized by county, including phone numbers and downloadable guides at www.dot.wisconsin.gov/travel/bike-foot/countymaps.htm. State trail maps are available at www.dnr.state.wi.us/org/land/parks/maps. The **Wisconsin Department of Natural Resources** (608-266-2181; www.dnr.state.wi.us) has information on the more than 1,000 miles of mountain bike trails in Wisconsin state parks.

BIRDING Birding in Wisconsin has really taken flight. Every part of the state boasts at least one great location for spying our winged friends. Western Wisconsin is along the **Mississippi River Flyway**, and some 326 species travel along the Mississippi River and Wisconsin's **Great River Road** as they migrate each spring and fall. The Wisconsin Department of Natural Resources publishes a thorough, five-guide set called the *Great Wisconsin Birding and Nature Trail* (www.dnr .state.wi.us/Org/land/er/birds/trail.htm) that points visitors to state natural areas, refuges, and parks where the birding is good. The sites are linked by highways, making it an easy tour. There are 14 chapters of the **Audubon Society** (audubon.org) in Wisconsin.

BLACK BEARS Black bears aren't usually a bother; they don't really like to be around people. If you see one, it will probably run off.

BOOKS There's no shortage of books about Wisconsin. Something to check out for its historical value, if not tourist information, is the 1941 *Wisconsin: A Guide to the Badger State* by the Federal Writers' Project of the Works Progress Administration. It's a good read, and while it's obviously dated, much of the background information and geographical breakdowns remain accurate. Particularly interesting is the passage concerning Wisconsin's northern forests. Today, we call this region the Northwoods, but when this book was written, the forests that covered the state were "all but gone." The book describes in detail the reforestation project, as well as many other details about Wisconsin history (at least, before 1941). Many activity-specific guides exist, including those covering hiking, fishing, and camping—a browse through the regional section of almost any local bookstore is almost overwhelming. *The Wisconsin Atlas and Gazetteer* isn't just maps, but all kinds of useful state information. *Weird Wisconsin* by Linda Godfrey and Richard Hendricks is good for a laugh, and my favorite Wisconsin-themed kid's book is *W Is for Wisconsin* by Dori Hillestad Butler—it's beautiful and covers a lot of Wisconsin trivia. Anything put out by the **Wisconsin Historical Society Press** is worth a look; it's got titles such as *Fill 'er Up: The Glory Days of Wisconsin Gas Stations.*

BUS SERVICE Greyhound Bus Lines (800-231-2222; greyhound.com) operates in 32 cities and towns in Wisconsin, including Milwaukee, Madison, and many smaller communities. Badger Coaches (608-255-1511; badger bus.com) provides daily service between Milwaukee and Madison, with round-trip tickets running around $34. Wisconsin Coach Lines (877-324-7767; coachusa.com/wisconsincoach) serves the area as well. Folks on a budget should check out **Mega Bus** (877-462-6342; megabus.com), which has stops in Milwaukee and Madison and connects to Chicago and Minneapolis. The **Wisconsin Department of Transportation** has a very complete guide to public transit around Wisconsin at dot.wisconsin.gov/modes/bus.htm.

CAMPING Close to half Wisconsin is covered in forest, so camping is a no-brainer here. There are 99 state parks and areas for woodsy recreation, plus two national forests (well, one really big one, actually), county parks, and many private campgrounds, and I've covered a lot of these. Contact the **Department of Natural Resources** (www.dnr.state.wi.us) for more information on state areas, including reservations and permit requirements—most require a state park vehicle sticker, but some do not. The **Chequamegon-Nicolet National Forest** is covered in this book, but you can check with the **U.S. Department of Agriculture/Forest Service** (http://www.fs.fed.us/r9/cnnf/) for more info. The **Wisconsin Department of Tourism** (1-800-432-8747; travelwisconsin.com) can hook you up with campground and state parks directories. Note that you cannot move firewood within the state of Wisconsin—see the entry on firewood for more information about the emerald ash borer.

CANOEING/KAYAKING There is no part of the state that doesn't have an option for canoeing and kayaking. Wisconsin's watery landscape means that opportunities for paddling abound. In Wausau, there's a championship kayak

course on the Wisconsin River running right through downtown, and on the Great River Road, kayakers head out on the backwaters of the Mississippi. There are many, many more opportunities.

CHEESE There are Wisconsin stereotypes that don't hold water, and then there's cheese. Sure, there are some vegans here, and the lactose-intolerant, but on the whole we really like our cheese. We have a proud history and many claims to cheese fame: Colby cheese, for example, was developed in the Wisconsin town of Colby, and tiny Monroe is home to the nation's only makers of stinky Limburger cheese, but Wisconsin produces more mozzarella than anything else.

And while the state may be in constant competition with California over which makes more (currently it's Wisconsin, but the lead is narrow), cheese is serious business here. More than 1,200 cheesemakers—some dating back four generations—produce 600 varieties, and the cheese they make wins more awards than any other *nation*, let alone state, in the world. Wisconsin was the first American state to host a dairy school, and that school at the University of Wisconsin-Madison continues to graduate students. In 1921, Wisconsin became the first state to grade cheese quality. Most recently, in 1994, UW-Madison developed a Master Cheesemaker Program within its Center for Dairy Research, and as of 2009, there are 44 companies with this lofty distinction. That emphasis on quality has also given rise to the growth of artisan cheesemakers: specialty (and often organic) cheeses, made in small batches right where the cows are, now comprise 16 percent of Wisconsin's cheese output, and that's likely to grow. To find out more about both the artisans and the big guys, check out the **Wisconsin Milk Marketing Board** (608-836-8820; eat wisconsincheese.com). It publishes a number of directories, travel guides, and maps to factory tours and specialty cheese shops you can get for the asking.

No discussion of Wisconsin cheese is complete without mention of cheese curds, those squeaky byproducts of cheddar cheese-making that we like to munch on, oh, whenever. The fresher the better, so your best bet is to pick up some of these cheesy little nuggets right at the source, then eat them right away. You know they're fresh if they squeak when you bite into them.

CHERRIES Door County cherry orchards produce 7–10 million pounds of cherries each year, making Wisconsin the fourth largest cherry-producing area in the country. Most of the cherries grown here are the tart, Montmorency variety, perfect for all those pies and jams you'll find at markets and on menus throughout the peninsula. Recently identified as a super-food, the Montmorency cherry is credited with all sorts of disease-fighting abilities, and many people swear by the *highly* tart juice. Around the middle of May, people flock to see the blossoms, but from mid-July to early August, the cherry picking is in full swing. Head to an orchard and load up on these beauties, which practically fall off the trees into your hands. Check with the **Wisconsin Cherry Growers** (wisconsin cherries.org) for more information.

CHILDREN, ESPECIALLY FOR Throughout this book, when you see the crayon ✐ symbol, it indicates a business that caters to kids, or tends to be very family friendly.

CLIMATE It's a tired old joke, but painfully true: Don't like the weather? Wait 10 minutes, it'll change. Typically, it's cold in winter and hot in summer. Winters are long, resulting in the excessive number of events you'll find here in summer. You'd do well to travel ready for any type of weather at any time of year, though. Winters have been known to dump 20 inches of snow or more in the course of a day, and summers can heat up to more than 100 degrees. On the other hand, we've had 70-degree Christmases and 30-degree June festivals. It's possible that you cannot over-pack for a trip in Wisconsin. Even when Mother Nature is cooperating, lakeside evenings can be cool, and lakeside days unbearably muggy. I always bring at least one jacket or sweater and a pair of jeans along with my shorts and tank tops, even in August, because there's nothing worse than shivering on vacation, and you never know when the temperature will drop. If you're traveling in winter, pack an emergency kit and wear extra layers of clothing—multiple thin layers are better than a single heavy layer. I know I sound like your mom, but it's important, particularly if you're going up north. The remote roads can get narrow and winding; if you break down in the forest, it could be a wait. You'll want a blanket, for sure, a flashlight, and maybe something to eat. For information on Wisconsin weather events such as tornadoes, see *Weather Events* in this section.

CRANBERRIES The red-dotted bogs offset by fall's yellow and orange foliage make central Wisconsin a popular spot when September rolls around.

Wisconsin is the nation's top producer of cranberries, with more than 18,000 acres of cranberry farms, and central Wisconsin pulls most of that weight. There are marshes up north, too—everywhere from Manitowish Waters to Superior—but the area stretching from Wisconsin Rapids all the way west to Tomah is the prime cranberry region. Visit this area in autumn for a stunning peek at the cranberry harvest. Tours are offered by **Glacial Lake Cranberry Tours** (715-887-2095) and **Splash of Red Cranberry Tours** (715-884-6412; psd.pittsville.k12 .wi.us/Cranberry/). The **Cranberry Highway and Cranberry Bike Trail** follows a 50-mile path between Wisconsin Rapids and Warrens, past marshes and farms, and hits many of the area's major attractions. On the bike trail, the 29-mile route takes you right through the marshes and hits important sites, as well. Contact the **Wisconsin Rapids Area Convention and Visitors Bureau** (715-422-4650; visitwisrapids.com), 841 Goodnow Avenue, Wisconsin Rapids, for a map of these self-guided tours. Also check out the **Wisconsin Cranberry Discovery Center** (608-378-4878; discovercranberries.com), in Tomah. Be sure to watch for cranberry festivals and special events in this part of the state, including **Wisconsin Rapids Cranberry Blossom Festival** in June, **Warrens Cranfest** in September, and **Wetherby Cranberry Harvest Day** in October. Check with the **Wisconsin State Cranberry Growers Association** (715-423-2070; wiscran.org) for more information on the crop, including recipes, regions, and more festivals.

DINING There's great food all over Wisconsin, but what you can get depends on your location. In Milwaukee and Madison, there are all kinds of ethnic, vegetarian, and contemporary options, plus the usual assortment of chains and fast-food spots. As you move more to the Southwestern part of the state, there's an increasing emphasis on local, seasonal, and organic foods. Although the concentration of restaurants isn't high, you should be able to find something for everybody. Headed north, things get a bit more about seafood, meat, and potatoes, although that's starting to change. If you have dietary restrictions, it's best to plan ahead.

EMERGENCIES Call 911 from anywhere in Wisconsin.

FARMERS' MARKETS It certainly isn't hard to find a market or stand here in summer. Most cities and towns have one, many have more. And in rural areas, farmers operate stands— sometimes they're only selling a few tomatoes and ears of corn, sometimes the stand is more like a store—that are usually marked by a wooden sign along the road with a painted list of offerings. Hands down, the best farmers' market in the state is the **Dane County Farmers' Market** (608-455-1999; dcfm.org) held each Saturday in Madison. The market's 150 vendors are not allowed to resell any agricultural products from other places, making it the largest producer-only farmers' market in the country. Most visitors'

bureaus will have information on area farmers' markets, or consult the **Farm Fresh Atlases** (farmfreshatlas.org) and **Savor Wisconsin** (savorwisconsin.com) to find one.

FESTIVALS Milwaukee gets all the press for its continuous summertime lakefront festivals, but you'll find them all around the state. Some are ethnic festivals—there are Scandinavian festivals, Polish festivals, and Oktoberfests in every part of Wisconsin—and some are simple county fairs, agricultural throwbacks to bygone days. Those feature carnival rides, tractors, and animals, plus cotton candy and other goodies. There are plenty of offbeat ones, too. Try **Beef-a-Rama** in Minocqua, or the **National Mustard Day** festival in Monroe. Like those, many of Wisconsin's festivals are centered on foods—the **Cedarburg Strawberry Festival**, the **Warrens Cranberry Festival**, and the **Bratfest** in Madison are good examples. And, of course, there's **Summerfest** in Milwaukee, the famous 11-day blowout that features hundreds of musical acts. Milwaukee is home to ethnic festivals on the lakefront, too, plus many neighborhood and church festivals nearly every weekend in summer.

FIREWOOD AND THE EMERALD ASH BORER The state is doing all it can to keep the invasive emerald ash borer away. This beetle has already killed millions of trees in the Great Lakes region; in August 2008, it showed up in Wisconsin. As a result, it is now illegal to bring firewood from more than 50 miles away into any state parks or forests in Wisconsin, and many private campgrounds have rules against it as well. More, you can't move firewood any distance from Ozaukee, Sheboygan, Fond du Lac, and Washington counties onto state property—

those counties are under federal quarantine because the insect has been positively identified there. Visitors from the quarantined areas of Illinois, Indiana, Ohio, and lower Michigan should note that if you bring firewood into Wisconsin, you risk a $1,000 fine (and the loss of your wood). Best for everyone just to leave the firewood at home; almost every state park in Wisconsin sells it.

FISH FRY Friday night fish fries are a Wisconsin tradition, and one that's almost impossible to miss. You can find a good version just about anywhere, from restaurants to churches and even parks—and the great versions are just too good to miss.

FISHING Wisconsin's many lakes and rivers certainly make for good fishing. You can angle for musky in the north, catfish in the west, trout in the center, salmon on Lake Michigan, plus walleye, bass, and more. On Washington Island, unique fish referred to as "lawyers" are the catch of the day. The **Department of Natural Resources** (dnr.wi.gov/fish) has all the information you need, including licensing information (you need a license to fish), fishing reports, and complete information on places to fish.

GOLF There are more than 400 golf courses in Wisconsin, including public, private, and municipal. Some are nationally recognized, some are best for beginners, but all take advantage of the state's beautiful natural resources. Contact the **Wisconsin Department of Tourism** (608-266-2161; travel wisconsin.com) for a free golf guide, which describes in detail each of the state's courses. Get info from the **Wisconsin State Golf Association** (wsga .org) as well.

HISTORY The last glacier retreated from Wisconsin more than 10,000 years ago, and the land was occupied long before records were kept, as evidenced by what remains of scattered effigy mounds and other archeological sites around the state. It was home to the Ho-Chunk and Menominee people since the glacial retreat, but Wisconsin first saw European settlers in the 1600s. French fur trade posts were set up at Green Bay and Prairie du Chien, making these among the oldest settlements in the state. It wasn't long before Native Americans were pushed off their territory; by 1854, the United States had control of the land in Wisconsin. European settlement in the southwestern part of the state grew in the 1800s, when lead mining was big. Logging was also a major industry at this time, concentrated in the north, and farming, of course, was big business, too. By the end of the 19th century, the economic landscape began to resemble what we know today (although it could easily be argued that we are at the end of this era)—dairy farming was the leading agricultural activity, and manufacturing became the backbone of the economy. It was

during the second half of the 19th century, too, that Wisconsin saw a huge influx of European immigrants, including those from Germany, Ireland, and Scandinavia—more than a million people made their way to Wisconsin during this time.

Politically, Wisconsin has a rich, and liberal, past. The Republican Party—Abraham Lincoln's party—was formed in Ripon, Wisconsin; as an important part of the Underground Railroad, residents here helped more than 100 slaves reach freedom in Canada, and the state's abolitionists actively fought against slavery, even breaking into a Milwaukee jail and freeing fugitive slave Joshua Glover. Glover had run away from his Missouri master and settled in Racine; when his master discovered where he was, he had Glover arrested under the federal Fugitive Slave Act and thrown in a Milwaukee jail. Glover eventually made it to Canada. Not long after, Progressivism was born, thanks to "Fighting" Bob La Follette. La Follette saw government corruption and fought for change, and during his career held a number of state and national offices; from 1900–1905, he was Wisconsin's governor. Among the Progressives' credits are increased regulation of the railroad industry, worker's compensation, and the creation of a state park system. La Follette was denouncing corporate influence on government about 100 years before it was fashionable. At about the same time, the Socialists in Milwaukee were gaining steam—they just took the Progressives' platform a little further left. Socialists reigned in Milwaukee for the better part of the 20th century, electing three Socialist mayors, one as recently as 1960. Today, Wisconsin nearly always leans blue in state and national elections, and La Follette's magazine, *The Progressive* (progressive.org), is still published in

Madison. It celebrated its 100th anniversary in 2009.

The Wisconsin Historical Society (wisconsinhistory.org), 816 State Street, Madison, was founded before Wisconsin was even a state. The society maintains archives and operates museums and historical sites throughout the state.

HOURS OF OPERATION Where practical, I've given the actual business hours as of press time for establishments listed. When hours vary more than twice throughout the week, the hours given are more general (for example, a restaurant's hours may list only the meals, or a store's hours may simply say "daily"). In all cases—whether specific hours are listed or not—it's a good idea to verify the hours by calling ahead. Things change: Businesses close, restaurants stop serving lunch, and museums shift their hours around. You just never know.

INFORMATION ON WISCONSIN, OFFICIAL Wisconsin Department of Tourism (608-266-2161; travelwisconsin.com), 201 West Washington Avenue, Madison, is the state's official tourism board, and you can get a free road map here, plus useful guides and directories on topics such as camping, lodging, birding trails, and more. As of early 2009, the state still operated welcome centers in Beloit, Grant County, Hudson, Hurley, Kenosha, La Crosse, Marinette, and Superior, but it's possible they will not be manned by the time you read this; they've been targeted for budget cuts.

LAKES With 15,000 lakes, you'll find more than a few opportunities to get out on the water. Swim, fish, sail, kayak, water ski, parasail, take a pontoon ride, riverboat cruise, lake cruise, or laze on a sunny beach—there's no

reason not to enjoy some water fun while you're in Wisconsin. Lakes are everywhere. The largest inland lake is **Lake Winnebago**, at 137,708 acres, but **Geneva Lake** at half its size is certainly not tiny. In Northern Wisconsin there's the **Chain of Lakes**, which with 28 interconnected lakes is the largest such chain in the world.

LIGHTHOUSES Home to more than 30 lighthouses, Wisconsin's lakefront cities and towns proudly preserve these beautiful monuments to their maritime heritage. Lighthouses dot the Lake Michigan shoreline from Kenosha to Washington Island, and on Lake Superior, the Apostle Islands boast six lovely, historic beacons. Door County, with its 300 miles of shoreline, is home to 10 lights—more than any other county in the U.S.

MUSEUMS Milwaukee and Madison are obvious places to find museums; in addition to the art museums, you'll find the **Milwaukee Public Museum**, **Discovery World**, and **Black Holocaust Museum** in Milwaukee, and the **Geology Museum** in Madison. But head south to Kenosha, and you'll find an impressive threesome on the lakeshore, including the **Dinosaur Discovery Museum**, the **Civil War Museum**, and the **Kenosha Public Museum**. Head north, and there's the **Wisconsin Maritime Museum** in Manitowoc. Don't forget about the **Mount Horeb Mustard Museum**— possibly the silliest museum in the state. Then again, there's **A World of Accordions Museum** (715-395-2787; museum.accordionworld.org) in Superior. Check with the **Wisconsin Federation of Museums** (wisconsin museums.org), which has information and events listings.

NATIVE AMERICAN COMMUNITIES Wisconsin is home to 11 Native American tribes—more than any other state east of the Mississippi. These include the **Ho-Chunk Nation** (715-284-9343; ho-chunknation.com); the **Forest County Potawatomi** (715-478-2903; fcpotawatomi.com); the **Lac Courtes Oreilles** (715-634-8934; wojb.org), **Lac du Flambeau** (715-588-3303; lacduflambeauchamber .com), **Bad River** (715-682-7111; badriver.com), and **Red Cliff** (800-226-8478; redcliff-nsn.gov) bands of the Lake Superior Chippewa; the **Sokaogon Chippewa Community** (715-478-7500; sokaogonchippewa .com); the **St. Croix Chippewa Community** (800-236-2195; stcroixcasino .com); the **Menominee Nation** (715-799-5114; menominee-nsn.gov); the **Oneida Nation** (800-236-2214; oneidanation.org); and the **Stockbridge-Munsee Band of Mohicans**

(715-793-4111; mohican.com). Of these, the Ho-Chunk and the Menominee have been in Wisconsin 10,000 years or more; the others have been in the area a couple of hundred years. Despite their roots in Wisconsin, the Ho-Chunk have no reservation land here; after 11 rounds of removal, during which members of the tribe always returned to Wisconsin, the Ho-Chunk Nation was eventually able to secure scattered plots of land throughout the state, mostly concentrated in the central region.

The highest-profile Native American enterprises—and often the most attractive to travelers—are, without question, the casinos. But there's much more going on. The Lac Courtes Oreilles Band of Lake Superior Chippewa, Lac du Flambeau, Oneida Nation, Menominee Nation, and the Forest County Potawatomi all operate museums and cultural centers that the public can tour. And as stewards of the land, Wisconsin's Native American communities are responsible for maintaining some of the state's wildest areas, including a sizeable chunk of Lake Superior wetland, numerous wildlife refuges, and almost all of the Great Lakes region's remaining pre-logging stands of pines and other trees. Many of the communities hold annual festivals and powwows, so keep an eye out. When in Hayward, tune the FM dial to 88.9 and listen to indie radio operated by the Lac Courte Oreilles Band of Lake Superior Chippewa—the music ranges from punk to jazz. For more information on Native American heritage travel, check with the individual tribes. The **Great Lakes Intertribal Council** (natow.org) publishes a comprehensive guide to Native American tourism, events, and attractions in Wisconsin.

Chequamegon-Nicolet National Forest (715-362-1371; www.fs.fed.us/r9/cnnf/index.html). In all, the Chequamegon-Nicolet National Forest stretches over more than a million and a half acres in 11 northern Wisconsin counties. It's actually two forests combined into one; before 1993, there was the Chequamegon National Forest and the Nicolet National Forest. Today, the two are managed as a single entity, but it's still considered in terms of the Chequamegon side and the Nicolet side. The Chequamegon side spans Ashland, Bayfield, Sawyer, Price, Taylor, and Vilas counties, covering 858,400 acres. The Nicolet side includes Florence, Forest, Langlade, Oconto, Oneida, and Vilas counties, covering 661,400. Enjoy camping, hiking, skiing, kayaking, fishing, wildlife viewing—just about everything. The official visitor's center on the Nicolet side is at the **Florence Wild Rivers Interpretive Center** (888-889-0049; northerngreatlakescenter.org), 4818 Forestry Drive, Florence, and the visitor's center on the Chequamegon side is in Ashland at the **Northern Great Lakes Visitor Center** (715-685-9983; northerngreatlakescenter.org), 29270 County Highway G. Open 9–5 daily. Not just a place to pick up brochures, this visitors' center offers an introduction to the entire area through interactive exhibits, archives, and programs. There's an observation tower here, too, as well as nature trails. The Apostle Islands National Lakeshore in Bayfield is operated by the National Park Service, as well as the Ice Age Trail.

PARKS AND FORESTS, STATE

The state operates close to 80 parks and forests, and most include campgrounds and hiking trails, at the very least. The **Brule River State Forest** (715-372-5678), 6250 S Ranger Road,

Brule, is a popular spot for kayaking and trout fishing. The **Flambeau River State Forest** (715-332-5271), W1613 County Road W, Winter, is huge at 90,000 acres. **Kettle Moraine State Forest** is also enormous and is divided into several units. The **Peshtigo River State Forest** (715-757-3965), N10008 Paust Lane, Crivitz, butts up against Governor Thompson State Park and offers good kayaking and canoeing. The **Northern Highland-American Legion State Forest** (715-385-2727), 4125 County Road M, Boulder Junction, covers three counties in Northern Wisconsin. In Milwaukee, the budding **Havenswood State Forest** (414-527-0232) offers education and hiking.

POPULATION 5,627,967

RAIL SERVICE Two Amtrak routes serve Wisconsin; the Hiawatha offers daily service between Milwaukee and Chicago, while the Empire Builder travels through Wisconsin from Chicago on its way to the Pacific Northwest. Wisconsin is also served minimally by the Chicago Metra, which offers inexpensive commuter rail between Kenosha and the Chicago area. The Wisconsin Department of Transportation has a very complete guide to public transit around Wisconsin at dot .wisconsin.gov/modes/bus.htm. Plans are being worked out to establish high-speed rail service from Chicago to Minneapolis, which would include stops in Milwaukee and Madison, at least. And talk continues regarding the long-discussed Kenosha-Racine-Milwaukee connector which, combined with the Chicago Metra, would provide another interstate rail option. Keep your fingers crossed.

RATES In most cases, rates listed are summer or high season rates based on double occupancy. Keep in mind, however, that things change. Please don't consider the rates information as definitive; always check with hotels and attractions to get the most current prices.

SCENIC DRIVES It's not hard to find a scenic drive in Wisconsin, especially in the north and the west. But here are a few of the official ones. **Great Divide National Scenic Byway** WI 77 cuts through the Chequamegon-Nicolet National Forest, offering you a look at these majestic woods from the comfort of your auto. **Kettle Moraine Scenic Drive** (262-626-2116) is a 115-mile drive through Kettle Moraine State Forest. And the **Great River Road**, along the Mississippi, is my favorite.

SKIING Almost anywhere with hiking trails is home to ski trails once the snow flies—it's a simple conversion. Some downhill skiing spots in Wisconsin include **Rib Mountain** at Wausau, **Alpine Valley** in East Troy, **Tyrol Basin** in Mount Horeb, **Mount Ashwabay** in Bayfield, **Christmas Mountain** in Wisconsin Dells, and **Mount La Crosse** in La Crosse. The **Wisconsin Department**

of Tourism (608-266-2161; travelwisconsin.com/snow_report.aspx) maintains listings and snow reports for ski areas.

SMOKING Legislation passed in 2009 to outlaw smoking in public places throughout Wisconsin, which will take effect in July 2010. Until then, chances are you can smoke in a bar at night, but increasingly not in restaurants. Check with the business on its policy.

SNOWMOBILING There are 25,000 miles of groomed snowmobile trails in Wisconsin, mostly in the north, but all around the state, too. Check with the **Department of Natural Resources** (888-936-7463; www.dnr.state.wi .us/Org/caer/cs/registrations/snow.htm) for information on certification, registration, and trail conditions. The **Wisconsin Department of Tourism** (608-266-2161; travelwisconsin.com) publishes a free guide to snowmobile trails.

SUPPER CLUBS Although it's a dying genre, the supper club is among Wisconsin's most fabled cultural institutions. Originally, they were meant as complete destinations—dining and dancing all in one. As time went on, the dancing faded away, but the restaurants remained dinner-only establishments, with menus focused on seafood and steaks. Traditionally, you wait for a table at a large bar where you knock back a few Brandy Old Fashioneds. When seated, you get a relish tray to snack on before dinner, with carrots, celery, and radishes. There's a salad bar included, and the potato choice includes hash browns. And that's about it; just simple, classic American fare, such as surf and turf and shrimp cocktail, plus a Friday night fish fry. These days, most clubs have changed a bit, ditching the relish tray and salad bar,

and adding a few more menu options, but largely, they're still about simple, meat-based dishes. Most, however, retain the nostalgic decor—including '60s-style lamps, stone fireplaces, and mounted deer heads—from the supper clubs' heyday. You'll find supper clubs all over the state, but they're most common in the northern section, where a day of hunting and fishing can really work up an appetite.

TRAVEL GREEN WISCONSIN **Travel Green Wisconsin** is a voluntary certification program created through a partnership between the Wisconsin Department of Tourism and the Wisconsin Environmental Initiative. Businesses and organizations in the tourism industry can participate by meeting the requirements of a checklist covering areas such as conservation, education, land use, purchasing, and waste reduction. New businesses are getting on board all the time; check with Travel Green Wisconsin (travelgreenwisconsin.com) for listings.

WEATHER EVENTS Wisconsin weather can be eventful, all right, and extreme. You should keep an eye on the weather at all times of year. In June 2008, vast portions of the state were declared federal disaster areas after four days of torrential downpours flooded rivers and lakes; in the Wisconsin Dells, catastrophic flooding broke a dam and drained Lake Delton. (Quick to act, the state repaired the breach and filled the lake in time for the 2009 summer season.) The rainy spring of 2008 was sandwiched between remarkably **snowy winters**— upwards of 14 inches fell on single days, repeatedly, in some parts of the state each season—not just in the north, but in Milwaukee and Madison, too. That kind of snow can be hazardous, for sure, and if you don't know how to drive in it, you shouldn't. Really, no one should drive if they don't have a need; best to hunker down and wait it out. An even greater winter threat is the arctic **wind chill** that sometimes plunges Wisconsin's functional temperature into the double-digits-below-zero range: in January 2009, some days felt as cold as 40 below. The thermometer won't say it's that cold outside, but the winds tell your skin it is. It doesn't happen often, but when it does, be aware: frostbite can happen in as little as five minutes, and hypothermia sets in quickly, too. When spring rolls around, we're still not out of the woods. With heavy rainfalls can come wild thunderstorms and their accompanying tornadoes. It's true they rarely touch down here, but there's no way to predict when one will, or where. **Tornado watches** are issued by the National Weather Service when conditions are right to produce a twister, while a **tornado warning** means a funnel cloud has been spotted, or an active tornado is on the ground. You'll know there's a tornado warning when the Emergency Broadcast System

blares its shrill alarm on your radio and the air-raid sirens sound outside. When this happens, you're supposed to get to a basement, or at least an interior room on the lowest level of the building, and quick; in reality, almost nobody does. I don't condone this cavalier attitude, but if you hear sirens and notice no one reacting, don't be surprised. Also note: a vehicle is among the most dangerous places to be during a tornado. If you're driving and spot a twister nearby, FEMA recommends you get out of the car and lie down in a ditch. Summer has lovely days, to be sure, but lakeside it can get muggy, and the heat index pushes temperatures into the hundreds. We have warnings for this, too—**heat advisories** and **excessive heat warnings**. Don't go mountain biking on these days, and be sure to drink lots of water.

WHEELCHAIR ACCESS The wheelchair symbol ♿ is used throughout this book to indicate restaurants and lodging that are wheelchair accessible.

WINERIES While not always thought of as a wine destination, Wisconsin is home to dozens of wineries—Door County, in particular, is a popular spot for wine tours, but they're also found to the north and west. Most houses specialize in fruit wines that take advantage of the delicious apples, cherries, strawberries, and cranberries here. As a result, the wines are often light and sweet, but some wineries do use grapes from California. Check with the **Wisconsin Winery Association** (wiswine.com) for guides and information. The **Wisconsin Department of Tourism** (608-266-2161; travelwisconsin.com) publishes a free guide to the state's wineries as well.

WISCONSIN WORDS We don't sound nearly as funny as everyone thinks, but we do have a few linguistic quirks. For instance; we say "bubbler"; if you ask for a water fountain or drinking fountain, you'll get directed to a garden centerpiece or tagged as an outsider.

We call sugary, carbonated beverages "soda," while most everyone else says "pop." And have you asked a Wisconsinite where you can get cash? If you asked for an ATM, they probably told you where to find a time machine. We're not sending you back in time, and we're not crazy. It's just that the first ATM to show up in these parts was called a TYME machine, which stood for "take your money everywhere." Decades on, we're still referring to ATMs that way.

WISCONSIN-MADE There's an increasing interest in keeping things local. If you'd like to know where to get Wisconsin products, check with Wisconsinmade.com, which sells everything you could think of that might be made in Milwaukee, or savor wisconsin.com, which will direct you to local foods.

WISCONSIN PUBLIC RADIO Wisconsin Public Radio is broadcast on 31 stations throughout the state. The *Ideas Network* is a talk-based format, and four of its programs are nationally syndicated: Michael Feldman's *Whad'Ya Know, Zorba Pastor on Your Health, To the Best of Our Knowledge,* and *Tent Show Radio.*

Milwaukee Area

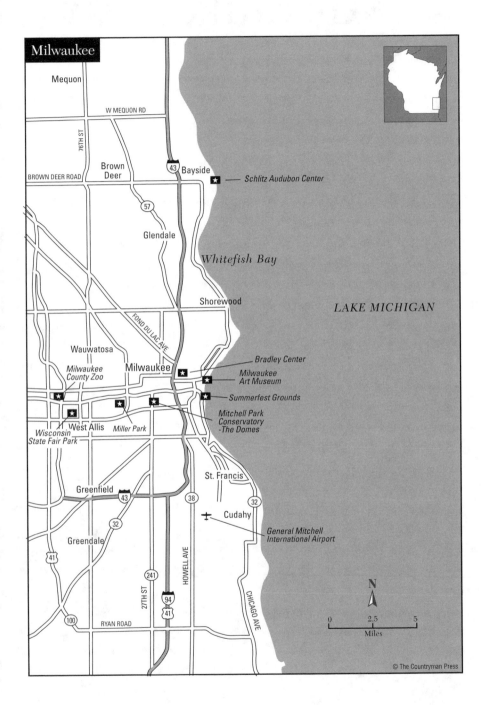

MILWAUKEE AREA

Milwaukee sure has an image problem—or maybe it's a self-image problem. For every beer, brat, and blue-collar shirt in this city, there are two people complaining about that industrial reputation. I suppose there's some validity to that complaint; Milwaukee is so much more than German cuisine and factories, but denying its history (which does include beer, brats, and manufacturing) is dishonest and a little curmudgeonly. The concern, largely, is that by focusing on its history, Milwaukee risks not moving forward. That's not unfounded, but there's room for a healthy enjoyment of the city's past as it makes steps into the future.

Milwaukee, just like, well, the rest of the United States, was originally inhabited by Native American tribes, including Menomonee, Ojibwe, Ottawa, and Potawatomi, and, like many towns in Wisconsin, it gets its name from a tribal language. Which one is debatable—it means either "beautiful land" or "gathering place by the water." In either case, the original meaning remains true—Milwaukee is indeed a beautiful gathering spot, with plenty of water. Lake Michigan gets all the attention, but the Milwaukee River provides endless entertainment, and many restaurants along the riverwalk have great patio dining.

Founded by not one but three settlers, the bizarre layout of Milwaukee's downtown bridges can be traced to the struggles between two of these men. The story, greatly simplified, goes like this: In the early 1800s, Solomon Juneau, a French Canadian, founded Juneautown. (This area is now known as the East Side, and a proud statue of Juneau, who eventually became Milwaukee's first mayor, now stands in Juneau Park on Lincoln Memorial Drive.) West of the Milwaukee River, a man named Byron Kilbourn established Kilbourntown, and out of rivalry (and an attempt to isolate Juneau), he deliberately caused the streets on his side of the river to not line up with the streets on Juneau's side. Somehow, Wisconsin officials managed to order a bridge built between these two communities. That bridge was promptly destroyed by Kilbourn, violence ensued, and the Bridge War officially broke out in 1845. In the end, everybody made up and joined forces with the guy to the south, George Walker (his area is now called Walker's Point), to create the city of Milwaukee. Modern-day visitors are left with a handful of angled bridges zigzagging across the river.

But that has nothing to do with beer and brats, does it? Shortly after Milwaukee was granted a charter in 1846, political refugees from Germany began flooding the city. Here, they opened 24 breweries and lively beer halls, and by 1860 the Germans were the majority population in Milwaukee. Over the next several decades,

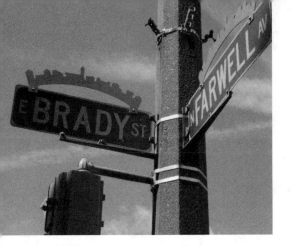

BRADY AND FARWELL ON MILWAUKEE'S
EAST SIDE

other immigrant groups, mostly Polish and Irish, moved in, but Germans remained in the majority for some time, and another product of German influence flourished. Not bratwurst—that had already happened. The next major contribution Milwaukee's German population made to the city was Socialism. An Austrian immigrant named Victor Berger is largely credited with organizing the Socialist party here, and he was the first Socialist elected to the U.S. Congress. In 1904, under Berger's leadership, nine Socialists were elected to the Milwaukee Common Council, and in 1910, Milwaukee elected its first Socialist mayor, Emil Seidel. This may seem like distant history now, but Milwaukee has had three Socialist mayors, one as recently as 1960, and the Socialist politicians of the past are credited with, among other things, building an impressive parks system that includes the beautiful park along the lakefront. That's no small contribution; Milwaukee's lakefront is an outstanding example of well-used green space. It's a destination in itself, made for people to simply enjoy.

Today, Milwaukee is much more ethnically diverse than those early German roots would suggest, with sizable black and Hispanic populations. At the same time, unfortunately, it remains among the most racially and economically segregated cities in the nation. Still, this diversity is responsible for much of the cultural landscape today—Milwaukee's performing and fine arts are clearly influenced by a rich ethnic heritage, as are all those ethnic festivals on the lakefront.

And ahh, those festivals. If you're here in summer, you'll have a hard time missing one. Even if it's not a major festival at the Summerfest grounds, there are street festivals, church festivals, and any other reason for a festival all summer long. Even when there isn't an actual festival, Milwaukeeans love dining and drinking alfresco so much that every restaurant and bar that can find a chair and a piece of sidewalk declares it an outdoor patio (maybe there's some German beer garden influence here). In more bustling areas, like the East Side, there's a festive atmosphere all summer long. It's probably because summers are so short here; Milwaukee definitely lives it up when the sun finally comes out.

GUIDANCE **Visit Milwaukee** (800-554-1448; milwaukee.org), 500 North Harbor Drive. Open 9–5 daily. The main information center is located at Discovery World at Pier Wisconsin, although there is another located at the Midwest Airlines Center with hours based on events.

Milwaukee Downtown (414-220-4700; milwaukeedowntown.com) has public service ambassadors who roam the streets, offering assistance with everything from car trouble to dining recommendations. They staff traveling information kiosks, walks, and ride bikes. You'll recognize these approachable folks by their blue shirts and quick smiles.

Milwaukee's main alt-weekly, ***The Shepherd Express***, has a sizable dining guide along with a large arts and entertainment section to clue you into what's going on around town, as does *The Onion's Decider Milwaukee* (milwaukee.decider.com), which publishes both a print arts and entertainment section in the weekly and more content and dining information online. *OnMilwaukee.com* is an online-only resource with a wealth of information about all things Milwaukee. Both *Decider* and *OnMilwaukee* are updated daily. Milwaukee's only daily newspaper, the *Milwaukee Journal-Sentinel,* can be found around town and online at jsonline.com.

GETTING THERE *By Air:* **Mitchell International Airport** (414-747-5300; mitchellairport.com) is served by a number of airlines, including **Air Canada** (800-247-2262; aircanada.com), **AirTran Airways** (800-247-8726; airtran.com), **American Airlines** (800-433-7300; aa.com), **Continental Express** (800-523-3273; continental.com), **Delta** (800-221-1212; delta.com), **Frontier** (800-432-1359; frontierairlines.com), **Midwest Airlines** (800-452-2022; midwestairlines.com), **Southwest Airlines** (800-435-9792; southwest.com), **United Express** (800-241-6522; united.com), and **US Airways Express** (800-428-4322; usairways.com). Car rentals are available. The **Go Airport Connection** (414-769-2444; mkelimo.com) offers shuttle service to and from the airport. The airport is also served by the **Milwaukee County Transit System** (414-344-6711; ridemcts.com), **Badger Coaches** (414-276-7490; badgerbus.com), and **Wisconsin Coach Lines** (877-324-7767; coachusa.com), as well as **Amtrak** (800-872-7245; amtrak.com).

By Bus: **Greyhound Lines** (800-231-2222; greyhound.com), serves Milwaukee with a 24 hour station downtown, and makes stops in cities throughout Wisconsin. The bus station is combined with the Amtrak station downtown at the **Milwaukee Intermodal Station** (433 West St. Paul Avenue). Folks on a budget should check out **Mega Bus** (877-462-6342; megabus.com), which has stops in Milwaukee and Madison and connects to Chicago and Minneapolis.

By Car: Interstate 94 and I-43 intersect in Milwaukee, which makes it fairly easy to find by car. Which exit you take depends on where you're going in the city. The path to the lakefront is clearly marked, and you'll find your way to Summerfest by following the smiley face logo on road signs.

By Ferry: Folks coming from Michigan can avoid the Chicago traffic snarl and hop on the **Lake Express** (866-914-1010; lake-express.com). This high-speed ferry takes just 2½ hours to travel between Milwaukee and Muskegon, Michigan—a considerable time saver if you consider you could easily spend that time sitting on the Illinois Tollway waiting for the cars to move! The ferry operates from May to October, with three trips daily in spring and summer, and two in fall.

By Train: **Amtrak** (800-872-7245;amtrak.com) operates two services to Milwaukee. The Hiawatha runs daily between Milwaukee and Chicago, while the Empire Builder stops in Milwaukee on trips between Chicago and the Pacific Northwest.

GETTING AROUND Milwaukee's public transit options leave something to be desired; there's only a bus system serving the city. Once a top-rated bus system in the country, budget reductions have resulted in higher fares and route cuts. Still, for trips around the East Side and downtown, the bus is great. Getting to other areas can be time-consuming and mean more than one transfer, but the **Milwaukee County Transit System** (414-344-6711; ridemcts.com) does tend to run on time. MCTS also runs fantastic shuttle services to some of Milwaukee's major summer festivals as well as Brewers games, and in summer the trolley runs from the Third Ward to the East Side and can be a lot of fun. Taxi service is available, but expensive, and you're unlikely to hail a cab on the street—you need to place a call. Bartenders favor **Yellow Cab Co-op** (414-271-1800), but other options are good and include **American United Taxi** (414-220-5000) and Veteran Taxi Cab Cooperative (414-220-5000). Look for more transit options in the future: After 17 years of political deadlock, a downtown streetcar loop is on the horizon.

Milwaukee's effort toward making more bike-friendly streets is commendable, but that doesn't mean it's perfect. The newer bike lanes are great—when the cars stay out of them—and a program to put free bike racks in front of businesses around the city has been successful. Just be sure to lock your bike up with a high-quality lock. And new in 2009, some city buses now have bike racks.

Milwaukee's Third Ward neighborhood and the East Side are by far the most walkable, although the commercial districts in some of the suburbs are surprisingly pedestrian-friendly as well. Still, to get from one neighborhood to another, you're going to want wheels of some sort.

MEDICAL EMERGENCY Call 911.

Columbia St. Mary's (414-291-1000), 2323 North Lake Drive.

Froedtert and The Medical College of Wisconsin (414-805-3000), 9200 West Wisconsin Avenue.

Children's Hospital of Wisconsin (414-266-2000), 9000 West Wisconsin Avenue.

Aurora West Allis Medical Center (414-328-6000), 8901 West Lincoln Avenue, West Allis.

Aurora St. Luke's Medical Center (414-647-3000), 2900 West Oklahoma Avenue.

Wheaton Franciscan Healthcare—St. Francis (414-647-5000), 3237 South 16th Street.

Wheaton Franciscan Healthcare—St. Joseph (414-447-2000),5000 West Chambers Street.

Aurora Sinai Medical Center (414-219-2000), 945 North Twelfth Street.

✳ To See and Do

ART MUSEUMS AND GALLERIES ✍ ✦ ☂ **Milwaukee Art Museum** (414-224-3200; mam.org), 700 North Art Museum Drive. Open 10–5 daily, 10–8 Thursday. With around 20,000 works of art ranging from antiquity to contemporary times, the museum's collection is impressive enough. These days, though, plenty of people come to look at the building itself. Unveiled in 2001, the Santiago Calatrava-designed addition is beautiful and dramatic. Inside, a 90-foot high, glass-walled reception hall overlooks Lake Michigan and is enclosed by a moving sunscreen, known as the Burke Brise Soleil, which looks like a pair of wings. If it's windy or storming, the wings will be closed, otherwise they are open when the museum is open. The museum also hosts special events and exhibits, has a store selling local art along with gift shop items, and a cafe that's open until 4 PM. Adults $8; seniors $6; students $4; children younger than 12, free.

GALLERY NIGHT

Four times a year, somewhere around 50 galleries, museums, and other business participate in the wildly popular Gallery Night and Day. Museums and galleries coordinate openings, offer cheese and wine, and ditch any cover charges. The best one is in summer, when the weather is conducive to wandering around the Third Ward and hopping on the free shuttle. There's no need to stick to the official Gallery Night participant list, though—everyone gets in on the game, and recently smaller galleries have pushed to get noticed on these nights as well. The Milwaukee Independent Gallery Association (migaonline.com) brings together a handful of smaller galleries that don't quite make enough money to buy space in the official Gallery Night brochure. Sadly, these smaller, contemporary art galleries tend to shut down as quickly as they crop up quickly, so the Web site is a good way to keep tabs on the spots that fly below the radar.

✇ ৬ ⳨ The Eisner American Museum of Advertising and Design (414-847-3290; eisnermuseum.org), 208 North Water Street. Open 11–5 Wednesday and Friday; 11–8 Thursday; noon–5 Saturday; 1–5 Sunday. This interactive museum in the Third Ward focuses on advertising and design as art, as well as its place in society, both now and through history. A must for anyone interested in advertising, it's also a lot of fun for the curious of all ages. Adults $5; seniors and youth $3; children 12 and younger, free.

⳨ **Charles Allis Art Museum** (414-278-8295; cavtmuseums.org/ca/home.html), 1801 North Prospect Avenue. Open 1–5 Wednesday through Sunday. This Tudor-style mansion holds an impressive collection of international art and antiques in each of its rooms, along with a changing exhibit of Wisconsin artists in the adjacent gallery. Once the home of Charles and Sarah Allis, the couple donated the museum along with the collection to the people of Milwaukee. It is currently part of the Milwaukee County War Memorial Corporation, which also operates the Villa Terrace Decorative Arts Museum (see below). Adults $5; seniors, students, and military members $3; children 12 and younger, free.

⳨ **Villa Terrace Decorative Arts Museum** (414-271-3656; cavtmuseums.org/vt/home.html), 2220 North Terrace Avenue. Open 1–5 Wednesday through Sunday. This museum is an Italian Renaissance-style villa housing decorative arts and furnishings from the 15th to 18th centuries. Outside, the dramatic, sloped Renaissance garden faces Lake Michigan and is visible from Lincoln Memorial Drive. It's a popular spot for weddings and photos. Adults $5; seniors, students, and military members $3; children 12 and younger, free.

৬ ⳨ **Haggerty Museum of Art** (414-288-1669; mu.edu/haggerty), 13th Street and West Clybourn Avenue on the Marquette University campus. Open daily. This small but fantastic museum features a permanent salon-style gallery of Old Masters, as well as contemporary art and a changing exhibit. The museum has a gift shop and hosts educational events. No art lover should miss a trip to this find in downtown Milwaukee. Free admission.

&. ↑ **Grohmann Museum** (414-277-2300; msoe.edu/about_msoe/manatwork), 1000 North Broadway Avenue. Open daily. With around 700 pieces of art depicting all manner of labor, the Man at Work Collection at the Milwaukee School of Engineering is an unusually specific collection. Gifted to the museum in 2007, the art spans 400 years and is housed in a three-floor gallery on the MSOE campus. Adults $5.

&. ↑ **Galleries at the Milwaukee Institute of Art and Design: The Layton Gallery and the Brooks Stevens Gallery of Industrial Design** (414-847-3200; miad.edu), 273 East Erie Street. Open 10–5 Tuesday through Saturday. MIAD's galleries feature both student works and curated shows that often focus on design and offer great learning opportunities. The art school's location in the Third Ward makes it a perfect side trip when shopping in this district. Free.

&. ↑ **Green Gallery East** (414-226-1978; thegreengallery.biz), 1500 North Farwell Avenue. Open 4–8 Thursday and Friday, 2–6 Saturday and Sunday. New in 2009, this second location opened after four years of success with Riverwest's Green Gallery West (thegreengallery.tk), 631 East Center Street. Both locations are focused on brainy, contemporary art.

&. ↑ **Portrait Society Gallery** (414-870-9930; portraitsocietygallery.wordpress .com), 207 East Buffalo Street, Suite 526. Open 1–4 Friday and Saturday. As the name suggests, this Third Ward gallery is focused on portraiture, both historical and contemporary. The works are impressive; sometimes straightforward, sometimes challenging, but always worth a look.

&. ↑ **Tory Folliard Gallery** (414-273-7311; toryfolliard.com), 233 North Milwaukee Street. Open 11–5 Tuesday through Friday, 11–4 on Saturday. Opened in 1988, the Tory Folliard has become a major spot for contemporary art in Wisconsin. The works here don't qualify as cutting edge, but the gallery isn't stodgy either. In the heart of the Third Ward gallery district, it's a great place to start a day of art viewing.

&. ↑ **Dean Jensen Gallery** (414-278-7100; deanjensengallery.com), 759 North Water Street. Open 10–6 Tuesday through Friday, 10–4 Saturday. A leading gallery in Milwaukee, Dean Jensen features contemporary art as well as outsider art, and hosts shows with a little more edge than the typical Third Ward Gallery.

&. ↑ **Walker's Point Center for the Arts** (414-672-2787; wpca-milwaukee.org), 911 West National Avenue. Open noon–5 Tuesday through Saturday. Providing space for visual and performing artists in the Walker's Point neighborhood, the WPCA consistently shows excellent local and regional works.

&. ↑ **Elaine Erickson Gallery** (414-221-0613; eericksongallery.com), 207 East Buffalo Street. Showing art since 1994, the Elaine Erickson Gallery is a well-rooted space for contemporary art and shows both emerging and established artists.

&. ↑ **Underwood Art Gallery** (414-476-1255; underwoodgallery.com), 1430 Underwood Avenue, Wauwatosa. Open Tuesday through Saturday. Head west to this Wauwatosa gallery, housed in an 1889 firehouse. The works span a diverse lineup of arts and crafts, including pottery, paintings, prints, and jewelry.

OTHER MUSEUMS ✐ &. ↑ **Milwaukee Public Museum** (888-700-9069; mpm.edu), 800 West Wells Street. Open daily. This museum of human and natural history has permanent and changing exhibits in 150,000 square feet of space. The museum is home to an Imax theatre, which doubles as the state's largest planetarium, and an indoor butterfly wing. Chartered in 1882, the Milwaukee Public Museum is a favorite family stop, but the curious at any age will be delighted. Adults $11.

✍ ᕱ ᐪ **Discovery World** at Pier Wisconsin (414-765-9966; discoveryworld.org), 500 North Harbor Drive. Open 9–5 Tuesday through Sunday. Discovery World is Wisconsin's only science and technology museum. Featuring interactive exhibits, an aquarium, labs and studios, films, weekend workshops, and more, grade-school kids will have a ton of fun here, and so will their parents. Adults $16.95; children 3–17 $12.95; children younger than 3, free.

✍ ᕱ ᐪ **Betty Brinn Children's Museum** (414-390-5437; bbcmkids.org), 929 East Wisconsin Avenue. Open 9– 5 Tuesday through Sunday in winter, plus 9–5 Monday, June through August. Aimed at children ages 10 and younger, the Betty Brinn is a great way for kids to learn while they burn off some excess energy. Permanent exhibits offer hands-on fun with music and art, and there are interactive galleries which allow kids to crawl through a huge human heart, work on a car, grocery shop, and more. There's also a soft, enclosed toddler area with slides and a sandbox. Weekends tend to be crazy, but it's still a lot of fun. $6.

✍ ᕱ ᐪ **Harley-Davidson Museum** (877-436-8738; harley-davidson.com), 400 Canal Street. Open daily. Brand new in 2008, the H-D Museum is a worthy celebration of both the company's fiercely loyal riders and its contributions to Milwaukee. Explore the 100-plus year history of the Harley-Davidson in this modern building. There is, of course, plenty of motorcycle parking. Adults $16.

✍ ᕱ ᐪ **Pabst Mansion** (414-931-0808; pabstmansion.com), 2000 West Wisconsin Avenue. Open 10–4 Monday through Saturday, noon–4 Sunday. Closed Mondays in winter and on holidays. The historic home of one of Milwaukee's original beer barons, Captain Frederick Pabst, this Flemish Renaissance Revival mansion was built in 1892. After Pabst's death in 1904, the mansion was home to five archbishops over the years. These days, you can tour the rooms, stunningly decked out in Victorian treasures. The mansion also hosts temporary exhibits of Victorian objects. Adults $8; ages 6–17, $4; children younger than 6, free. Add $1 during the Christmas season.

✍ ᕱ ᐪ **Mitchell Park Horticultural Conservatory—The Domes** (414-649-9800), 524 South Layton Boulevard. Open 9–5 daily. You'll only hear it called "The Domes." Marked by three somewhat conical glass domes that stand 85 feet high, if you get in the general area, it's hard to miss. This conservatory is operated by the Milwaukee County Parks and houses thousands of plants from around the world. The Arid Dome features succulents and other dry-land plants from Madagascar, Africa, the Canary Islands, and the Americas, while the Tropical Dome is home to some 1,200 species of tropical plants and a few birds. The Floral Show Dome changes seasonally and each show has a theme, including plant changes and props. Special events are held throughout the year. Adults $6; children ages 6–17, $3.50; children younger than 6, free.

ᐪ **Milwaukee County Historical Society** (414-273-8288; milwaukeecountyhist soc.org), 910 North Old World Third Street. Open 9:30–5 Monday through Friday, 10–5 Saturday, 1–5 Sunday. History buffs and fans of Milwaukee will find plenty of interest in the museum's collections and records. The society publishes a quarterly magazine, *Milwaukee History*, as well as books, and conducts entertaining walking tours and visits to historic sites around Milwaukee. Admission $3.

BREWERY TOURS ⍓ 🍺 **Miller Brewing Company Tour** (414-931-BEER), 4251 West State Street. Tours run 10:30–4;30, Memorial Day to Labor Day; 10:30–3:30, Labor Day to Memorial Day. Miller's Milwaukee operations still stand on the land Fredrick J. Miller purchased in 1855, making this the oldest brewery in the U.S. This guided walking tour takes about an hour and can be tiring for some—if you need to, skip ahead to the free samples at the end. Otherwise, this is a fun and educational tour steeped in Milwaukee history. Adults get free beer at the end of the tour; anyone younger than 21 gets soda. Free.

⍓ 🍺 **Lakefront Brewery Tour** (414-273-8300; lakefrontbrewery.com), 1872 North Commerce Street. Tours usually start at 3 PM during the week and 1 PM on Saturdays, but check to be sure. Visit one of Milwaukee's favorite microbreweries, where you'll get to sample beer at the start of the tour, as well as the middle and the end (teetotalers get root beer). Opened in 1987, this local brewery has found a following through its award-winning specialty brews, many of them named for Milwaukee neighborhoods or other places, such as Riverwest Stein, East Side Lager, and Fuel Cafe Stout. This tour is entertaining and largely at the whim of the guides, who ad lib their way through the brewery. The Palm Garden is also here, and features one of Milwaukee's favorite Friday fish fries. For tours, you must be 21 or accompanied by a parent or legal guardian. Tours $6.

⍓ 🍺 **Sprecher Brewery Tour** (414-964-2739; sprecherbrewery.com), 701 West Glendale Avenue, Glendale. Tour hours vary; call ahead. Perhaps as famous for its soda as its award-winning beer, Sprecher is another darling on the microbrew scene. The end of the tour gets adults four beer samples, and everyone gets to try all the soda they can drink. The root beer is delicious, but make sure you try Orange Dream. Tours $3.

HISTORIC AND ARCHITECTURAL SITES Many of Milwaukee's museums and other places of interest are housed in wonderfully historic or architecturally significant buildings. Where appropriate, I've noted that in individual entries, but I've added a few additional Milwaukee buildings and landmarks to check out here.

Annunciation Greek Orthodox Church (414-461-9400; annunciationwi.com), 9400 West Congress Street. Designed by Frank Lloyd Wright, this church looks a little bit like a spaceship. They don't give tours, but if you want to attend a Sunday service, you're welcome inside.

Allen-Bradley Clock Tower, 1201 South Second Street. This clock tower is the largest four-faced clock in the world—its faces are nearly twice the size of Big Ben's, but it does not chime.

City Hall, 200 East Wells Street. Before it was ousted by the Calatrava addition to the Milwaukee Art Museum, City Hall was the architectural landmark most associated with Milwaukee. Built in 1895, its style is German Renaissance Revival, and a complete renovation was finished in 2009. City Hall might not seem like a fun place to go, but it's worth marveling at outside and in.

Wisconsin Gas Building, 626 East Wisconsin Avenue. An art deco building finished in 1930, perhaps the most interesting part is the weather light up top, shaped like a flame and 21 feet tall. It was added in the '50s and signals a forecast nightly. There's a poem to go along with it, but I'll just break it down: red means warm, yellow means cold, blue means the weather will be the same, and if it's flashing, it's going to rain or snow. There. Who needs the Weather Channel?

The Basilica of St. Josaphat, 2333 South Sixth Street. Built in 1929 at the direction of Pope Pius XI, this minor basilica was modeled after St. Peter's in Rome. Tours are offered on Sundays, after Mass.

BOWLING ⍨ Milwaukee is home to lots of bowling alleys, but a few stand out. **Holler House** (414-647-9284), 2042 West Lincoln Avenue, couldn't be called family friendly, but if you're looking for something a little different, this is it.

THE BRONZE FONZ

You wouldn't think a simple little statue based on a character from *Happy Days* (which was set in Milwaukee) could cause a lot of controversy, but in Milwaukee, it did. When Visit Milwaukee announced it would raise the $85,000 needed to create and place the statue, a few local art gallery owners contended that money would be better spent on the arts in the city, and shut down their galleries in protest. Soon, pro-"Bronzie" and anti-"Bronzie" camps emerged, and the controversy made national news. At the heart of the squabble was Milwaukee's notoriously uneasy relationship with public art—although it would be a stretch to call this statue art, really—and concern over whether it would really generate tourism dollars. Of course, all this outcry just makes it a more appealing attraction, doesn't it? See it for yourself along the Milwaukee River just south of Wells Street.

THE CONTROVERSIAL BRONZE FONZ, ALONG THE RIVERWALK.

Opened in 1908, Holler House is primarily just a bar, but it's got the oldest certified bowling lanes in the nation, and bras on the ceiling left by patrons. In the basement, two lanes and a real, live, pinsetter await. **Koz's Mini Bowl** (414-383-0560), 2078 South Seventh Street, is another old bar/bowling alley with human pinsetters. The difference here is that it's done with miniature balls and shortened lanes. More traditional, but still classic, bowling can be found at **Bay View Bowl** (414-483-0950), 2416 South Kinnickinnic Avenue. This neighborhood alley has glow bowling on Fridays and Saturdays, and is popular for its cheap drinks and games. On the east side, **Landmark Lanes** (414-278-8770), 2220 North Farwell Avenue, has been around since 1927. Today it features automated lanes, three bars, an arcade, and more.

SPORTS Major League Baseball team the Milwaukee Brewers play home games at **Miller Park** (414-902-4400), 1 Brewers Way, a high-tech ballpark with a retractable roof that means games never get rained out (unless the roof happens to be broken that day).

The Milwaukee Bucks professional basketball team shoots hoops at the **Bradley Center** (414-227-0400; bradleycenter.com), 1001 North Fourth Street, as does the Marquette University men's basketball team. The American Hockey League's Milwaukee Admirals play games here as well.

Milwaukee's professional indoor soccer team, the Milwaukee Wave, plays home games at the **U.S. Cellular Arena** (414-276-4545; uscellulararena.com), 400 West Kilbourn Avenue.

The city's roller derby girls, the Brew City Bruisers (brewcitybruisers.com), skate home bouts at the **Milwaukee County Sports Complex** (414-423-9267), 6000 West Ryan Road, Franklin. You can frequently catch a shuttle to the bout at bars around Bay View and the East Side.

✳ Green Space and Outdoors

The **Milwaukee County Parks Department** (414-257-7275; countyparks.com) operates numerous parks throughout the county, but some stand out for their beauty and frequent activity. Likewise, there are 15 public golf courses run by the parks department—check online for details. Here are a few of the most popular spots to relax and enjoy the scenery.

♈ ✿ **Bradford Beach** (414-967-9531; bradfordbeachjam.com), 2400 North Lincoln Memorial Drive. Long a sadly abandoned natural beauty, Bradford Beach was revived in 2008 when the owners of some popular East Side restaurants stepped in and started running the concessions. A little extra private funding, and overnight the beach was a hit again. Catch some rays and enjoy a beer or snack at the pavilion—it's worth a visit in itself. The pavilion was designed by Gilbert Grunwald in 1950, and its simple, curved shapes stand as a fine example of Art Moderne architecture. Most would say it looks really cool, and it's great to see it back in business.

Veteran's Park (414-275-7275), 1010 North Lincoln Memorial Drive. Veteran's Park, along the lakefront, is the basis for lakefront activities. Just south is the Milwaukee Art Museum; just north is Bradford Beach. From here you can catch the Oak Leaf Trail, rent bikes, paddle boat in the lagoon, fly a kite, or just mill about on a sunny day and enjoy the lake and trees. Events are held here regularly in summer, and it's the prime viewing spot for Milwaukee's Fourth of July fireworks.

Oak Leaf Trail (414-275-7275). The Oak Leaf Trail consists of more than 100 miles of multi-use paths, connecting parks and parkways as it loops around Milwaukee County. Fifty of those miles are paved bike paths running along old rail lines. The most popular portion runs along the lakefront from the **Milwaukee Art Museum** to **Estabrook Park** in Glendale. This portion is well signed and remarkable for its ability to make you feel like you're out of the city. If you stay along the lake, you'll end up in Lake Park. It doesn't feel as remote, but it's a shorter ride and you'll remain closer to all the lakefront activity. Bike, walk, or skate, and in winter, cross-country ski.

Lakeshore State Park (414-274-4281; friendslsp.org), North Harbor Drive. A constructed island in Lake Michigan, just off the shore from downtown, near Discovery World at Pier Wisconsin (414-765-9966; discoveryworld.org), 500 North Harbor Drive, there's not much to it, but you can camp here or dock your boat, take in views of the lake and the city, or—best of all—follow the bike path all along the lake. Lakeshore State Park connects the Hank Aaron State Trail with the Oak Leaf Trail, so bikers can follow an uninterrupted route.

✇ **South Shore Park** (414-257-7230), 2900 South Shore Drive. Home to the South Shore Frolics (see Special Events) and the popular **South Shore Farmers Market**, this park along the lake offers plenty of opportunities to relax and catch some rays.

Lake Park (414-257-7275), 3233 East Kenwood Boulevard. At the north end of the city, and (as you might guess) along Lake Michigan, Lake Park is a sprawling green space connected to the Oak Leaf Trail, with tennis courts, footbridges, trails, golf, ice skating, and more. Bartolotta's Lake Park Bistro is here, and free live concerts are held in the park throughout summer.

✇ **Atwater Park**, Beach East Capitol Drive, Shorewood. Just north of the city, this park is a little break from busy Bradford on a hot Milwaukee day. Perched on a

LAKE PARK

bluff overlooking Lake Michigan, Atwater Park has great views, spots to picnic, and a playground. Head down the many steps to a clean beach, where you can dig your to toes in the sand and enjoy the lake.

Boerner Botanical Gardens (Whitnall Park) (414-525-5600; boernerbotanical gardens.org), 9400 Boerner Drive, Hales Corners. Formal gardens and buildings open from 8 AM–dusk April through October. Another fantastic member of the Milwaukee County Parks system, there are 11 separate gardens and trails on 600 acres, along with an education center, gift shop, and more. The gardens were created during the Depression by WPA and CCC workers, who carved statuary and built buildings. Spaces include the Annual Garden, the Perennial Garden, Herb Garden, Rose Garden, and the Trial Garden, an official test garden for All-America selections. Along with kids' programs and guided tours, there's a Sunday brunch and Friday night fish fry in the gardens. Adults $4.50; seniors $3.50; children 6–17 $2.50; children younger than 6, free.

*Schlitz Audubon Nature Center** (414-352-2880; sanc.org), 1111 East Brown Deer Road, Bayside. Open 9–5 daily. Just 15 minutes north of downtown Milwaukee, the Schlitz Audubon Nature Center boasts 185 acres along the shores of Lake Michigan. Once farmland used to feed and house brewery horses, the land was given to the National Audubon Society in 1971. There are 6 miles of hiking trails here (you can showshoe or ski them in winter) along with an observation tower. In 2003, the award-winning Dorothy K. Vallier Environmental Learning Center opened, bringing much-needed space for the center's educational programs. The building is considered one of the greenest in the country, using natural light and a geothermal heating system. Adults $4, children $2.

*Red Arrow Park** "Slice of Ice" (414-289-8791; county.milwaukee.gov/ RedArrow11930.htm), 920 North Water Street. Open daily from December to February or March. When the weather's cold, but not too cold, nothing beats skating in the city, as evidenced by the popularity of this park. Bring your own skates and get on the rink for free, or rent them for a small fee. When you get too chilly and need hot chocolate or a latte, there's a Starbucks and a fireplace in the warming house. Skate rentals $6.

*Pettit National Ice Center** (414-266-0100; thepettit.com), 500 South 84th Street. Public skating hours vary. Here's your chance to take a spin on the ice at an Olympic training facility; more than a few Olympic speed skaters have practiced here. One of 12 indoor skating ovals in the world, the center offers classes and events throughout the year. Adults $7, children and seniors $5.

*Milwaukee County Zoo** (414-256-5412; milwaukeezoo.org), 10001 West Bluemound Road. With a history dating back more than 100 years and over one million visitors annually, the Milwaukee County Zoo is worthy of its reputation as one of the finest in the country. More than 2,000 animals on 200 acres of land mean you'll tire out long before you've seen everything. Adults $12.25, ages 3–12, $9.95.

*Urban Ecology Center** (414-964-8505; urbanecologycenter.org), 1500 East Park Place. Located on 12 acres of wooded land and connected to the Oak Leaf Trail, the Urban Ecology Center is a wonderful green space right inside the city. The center has a classroom and laboratory and offers programs for adults and school kids alike. Aside from being a great park and place to explore nature, the center has way more programs and things to do to list. Check out the weekend family activities.

℣ **Edelweiss Cruises** (414-276-3625; edelweissboats.com), 205 West Highland Avenue. Cruises run April through December. Offering all manner of cruises on the Milwaukee River, from Sunday brunch to a beer and brat cruise, one focused on martinis, a hip-hop margarita cruise, and of course, historic sightseeing, there must be a cruise here for you. Tickets $14-75, depending on the extras.

Milwaukee Boat Line (414-294-9450; mkeboat.com), 101 West Michigan Street. Tours run May through September. The outfit offers a variety of cruises, including special events with live bands, and happy hour cruises.

✳ Lodging

Downtown and East Side

℣ ⅌ **The Pfister Hotel** (414-273-8222; pfisterhotel.com), 424 East Wisconsin Avenue. Restored and updated to include modern amenities, The Pfister is Milwaukee's favorite and most well-known hotel. If you're worried it's overrated, fear not: It's every bit as lovely as the hype, and the downtown site is close to many attractions. Opened in 1893, this hotel was among the most lavish of its time, and to this day maintains its reputation as among the finest. The Pfister houses a sizable collection of late Victorian art, interesting for its value both as art and as historical objects—the collection was contemporary when the hotel opened. Services include salon and spa, fitness, shopping, and concierge. There are five bars and restaurants in the Pfister, but my favorite is the martini bar, Blu. On the 23rd floor, Blu offers breathtaking views of the city. $170–380.

℣ ⅌ **Hilton Milwaukee City Center** (414-271-7250; hiltonmilwaukee.com), 509 West Wisconsin Avenue. Located in downtown Milwaukee, this 1920s building is elegant enough, but the real reasons to stay here have nothing to do with ambiance. First, there's Paradise Landing Indoor Waterpark, sure to entertain the kids (there is no lap pool, though). This hotel is very kid-friendly, offering family entertainment packages year-round, including New Year's Eve. You'll not find a better place for families to stay in downtown Milwaukee. Second, a skywalk connects this hotel directly to the Midwest Airlines Convention Center, which is a huge bonus if you're attending events there in winter. $150–250.

🐾 ℣ ⅌ **Hotel Metro** (414-272-1937; hotelmetro.com), 411 East Mason Street. Clearly Milwaukee's swankiest, Hotel Metro has it all: It's a historic, luxury hotel that happens to be eco-friendly. There's a rooftop spa with a full menu of services, a great bar and cafe onsite, wonderful rooms with luxurious beds, and a broad range of business services. Hotel Metro is also pet-friendly, so you don't have to leave your pooch at home. Travel Green Wisconsin Certified. Suites $200–400.

℣ ⅌ **Milwaukee InterContinental** (414-276-8686; ichotelsgroup.com), 139 East Kilbourn Avenue. Right next to the Marcus Center, the InterContinental is a great downtown choice, especially if you're here to enjoy the theater. It offers a full range of business amenities as well as a spa. Try the popular onsite restaurant, Kil@wat, for dinner. $160–250.

℣ ⅌ **The Iron Horse Hotel** (888-543-4766; theironhorsehotel.com), 500 West Florida Street. A boutique hotel catering to Harley-Davidson riders visiting the nearby Harley museum, it sports modern decor and motorcycle amenities—yes, features just for your bike—plus spa services, 42-inch LCD televisions, an onsite bar and restaurant, and lots more. Without question, this hotel, which opened in 2008, stands out. Not quite like pulling your Harley over to the side of the road and pitching a tent, but we all have to make compromises, don't we? Guest rooms start at $169.

♈ ♿ **Residence Inn Downtown** (414-224-7890; marriott.com), 648 North Plankinton Avenue. Sure, it's a chain, but it's a chain housed in a historic Marshall Fields building that's connected to a downtown mall, which makes it perfect for not only for business travelers, but for people who have come to Milwaukee to shop. A friendly staff and clean rooms are the icing on the cake. $109–$209.

♂ ♿ **The Astor Hotel** (414-271-4220; theastorhotel.com), 924 East Juneau Avenue. Built in 1920, the Astor functions as a combination hotel and apartment building, and like its near twin a block away, The Knickerbocker, it was designed as such. This makes it perfect for extended stays on the East Side. There's an onsite restaurant, a beauty salon, and typical business traveler amenities. Its location on the East Side is perfect for enjoying many of the city's activities. Full of charm. $99–159.

♣ ♿ **The Plaza Hotel** (414-271-5575; shorelinerealestate.com/plaza), 1007 North Cass Street. Another charming, historic East Side hotel, this one also has apartment dwellers and an onsite restaurant (see Cafe at the Plaza in Dining Out). Rooms have complete kitchens. $99–159.

♈ ♿ **The Knickerbocker on the Lake** (414-276-8500; knickerbocker onthelake.com), 1028 East Juneau Avenue. Built in 1929, the Knickerbocker is known for its historic charm, catering to both short- and extended-stay guests. It's probably better known

locally for its onsite restaurant, The Knick (see Eating Out), which has gained a reputation locally as both a great brunch spot (well, okay, lunch, dinner, and dessert too), and a great people-watching spot. The more upscale Osteria del Mondo is here, too, and features homemade pastas and entrees such as Strauss veal scaloppini. $129–199.

♈ ♿ **County Clare Guesthouse** (414-272-5273; countyclare-inn.com), 1234 North Astor Street. Locals know County Clare as a great place to drink a pint of Guinness while listening to traditional Irish music, but their out-of-town guests get to enjoy the charming accommodations above the pub and a big breakfast in the morning. The East Town location makes parking a little rough, but it also makes it a great spot from which to enjoy Milwaukee. $109–149.

Brumder Mansion (414-342-9767; brumdermansion.com), 3046 West Wisconsin Avenue. West of downtown, the Brumder Mansion is about as Victorian as it gets, inside and out—except for those whirlpools in the suites. Creative breakfast by candlelight is offered in the morning. Suites $179–259, Blue Room $149.

Schuster Mansion (414-342-3210; schustermansion.com), 3209 West Wells Street. Another huge Victorian just west of downtown, the Schuster offers three rooms and three suites, most with private bathrooms. Suites offer extra seating room. Decor ranges from country to a little bit frilly, but in all cases it's romantic and in keeping with the mansion's grandeur. WiFi is available. Rooms $120–130, suites $150–190.

Northeast Milwaukee
If you don't want to spend the money on a hotel downtown, the North Shore area is a good option. Right near the

highway and minutes from all the action of downtown and the East Side, you're also within spitting distance of Bayshore Town Center, so if shopping is on your agenda, you're in the right area. These hotels work well for families.

☀ ⚕ ♪ La Quinta Inns & Suites (414-962-6767; lq.com), 5423 North Port Washington Road, Glendale. There are two La Quinta hotels on Port Washington Road; this one is on the west side of the street (take note). While there's nothing outstanding or unique about a chain hotel, this one is newer, clean, has large rooms, a swimming pool, and a pet-friendly policy, along with standard La Quinta amenities such as free breakfast and WiFi. In short, you could do a lot worse. $105–145.

♪ ⚕ Radisson Hotel North Shore (414-351-6960; radisson.com), 7065 North Port Washington Road. Another chain, but it does the job. With large rooms and suites, plus a great pool room, there's more than enough to keep you rested and content. It's a bit more north of the action than La Quinta, but you're still right near the highway when you're ready to hit the town. $100–205.

Airport
Y ♪ Sheridan House (414-747-9800; sheridanhouseandcafe.com), 5133 South Lake Drive, Cudahy. This boutique hotel is a welcome change of pace from all the chains you'll find in the area. Renovated in 2007, each room's theme is based on a different wine-producing part of the world. The onsite cafe features contemporary cuisine in art deco surroundings. Modern amenities, including flat-screen televisions and WiFi, round it out, but it's the massaging shower that will make you wish you could stay longer. $139–269.

✳ Where to Eat

Milwaukee is home to a wide and delicious array of dining choices, the variety apparent in cuisine as well as price range. While you'll find a lot of chains in the western suburbs, the communities along the lakeshore tend to have the best choices in local dining. Of these, the East Side neighborhood takes the crown. Here you'll find fantastic dining, ranging from $4 falafel at Abu's to local fine-dining darling Sanford (which was recently named one of *Gourmet Magazine's* top 50 restaurants in the country), all in one compact and bustling neighborhood. But good options exist in up-and-coming Bay View, the Third Ward, and in ethnically diverse Riverwest, as well, and there are bright spots all around the area.

As with all food entries in this book, restaurants are split between "Dining Out" and "Eating Out," with the latter including more casual choices. That said, keep in mind that Milwaukee has an overwhelming number of fantastic restaurants in that gray area between the two. Because of this, "Eating Out" lists everything from legendary dirt-cheap diners to upscale casual options in town, where you can have a terrific meal, with great wine and service, in a more relaxed atmosphere than your white tablecloth options.

DINING OUT

East Side
Y The Pasta Tree (414-276-8867), 1503 North Farwell Avenue. Open for lunch Tuesday through Saturday, daily for dinner. Known for almost 30 years as the East Side's most romantic restaurant, there's a lot to fall in love with here. From the charming decor to the homemade pasta and fairly complete wine selection, this intimate restaurant is perfect for couples or small groups. You sit very close to

fellow diners, so bringing the kids is probably not the best idea. Located in Milwaukee's hip East Side neighborhood, you might miss the sign, as the outside is very unassuming. Parking in this neighborhood can be a chore, so plan accordingly as there is no lot. Arrive early to ensure they haven't run out of any menu items. Entrees $13–32.

Y **Sanford** (414-276-9608; sanford restaurant.com), 1547 North Jackson Street. Open for dinner Monday through Saturday. The state's most highly acclaimed restaurant sits in an unassuming East Side building that once was home to the family business—a grocery store. Now an intimate and modern dining space, Sanford has the remarkable distinction of being top-rated by both Zagat and *Gourmet Magazine.* Never stuffy or aloof, Sanford offers a welcoming and elegant dining experience. Entrees $30–50.

Y & **Roots** (414-374-8480; rootsmil waukee.com), 1818 North Hubbard Street. Open for dinner daily, Sunday brunch. Among the first businesses in the growing Brewer's Hill neighborhood, Roots focuses on locally grown and organic ingredients as much as possible, with a farmer as one of its owners. Don't confuse this for vegetarian; dinner options are overwhelmingly (though not entirely) meat-based, and offer a contemporary twist on traditional favorites. The atmosphere is equally contemporary and the location offers a great city view. Dishes $15–30.

Y & **Pitch's Lounge and Restaurant** (414-272-9313; pitchsribs.com), 1801 North Humboldt Avenue. Open daily for dinner. Tucked away in a residential part of the East Side, Pitch's is the neighborhood's own Wisconsin supper club, with a popular fish fry and a huge choice of steaks. It's most known, however, for its ribs. Dishes $12.95–18.95.

Y & **Lake Park Bistro** (414-962-6300; lakeparkbistro.com), 3133 East Newberry Boulevard. Open Monday through Friday for lunch, daily for dinner, Sunday brunch. With fantastic French cuisine in a beautiful park setting, this Bartolotta Group restaurant remains a Milwaukee favorite for special occasions and romantic nights out. The main dining room offers a stunning view of Lake Michigan. Dishes $20–30.

Y & **Mimma's** (414-271-7337; mim mas.com), 1307 East Brady Street. Open for daily for dinner. Mimma's is among Milwaukee's most beloved restaurants. Holding its own on Brady Street since 1989, Mimma's offers traditional Italian dishes in an elegant atmosphere, with one big bonus: you can people-watch out the big windows and take in the East Side activity. The holiday season, when the restaurant is decorated with countless white Christmas lights, is especially delightful. $11.95–17.95.

Y & **Osteria del Mondo** (414-291-3770; getosteria.com), 1028 East Juneau Avenue. Open for dinner Monday through Saturday. Located in the Knickerbocker Hotel (see Lodging), Osteria del Mondo is popular with locals as well as national critics. Featuring contemporary Italian cuisine in an elegant setting, it's perfect for a nice, but unstuffy, night out. Dishes $9–29.

Downtown/Third Ward

Y & **Mader's** (414-271-3377; maders restaurant.com), 1041 North Old World Third Street. Open for lunch Monday through Saturday, daily for dinner, Sunday brunch. A Milwaukee institution since 1902, Mader's isn't simply great German food. With the largest Hummel collection in the U.S., beer steins for sale, and a huge collection of art and antiques to enjoy,

BARTOLOTTA'S LAKE PARK BISTRO

Mader's is a historical Milwaukee experience. Dine on sauerbraten and schnitzel, and wash it down with a beer. Lunch $8–15, dinner $20–30, brunch $20.

🍸 ♿ **Karl Ratzsch's** (414-276-2720; karlratzsch.com), 320 East Mason Street. Open for lunch Wednesday through Saturday, dinner Monday through Saturday. Another Milwaukee haven for German food, Karl Ratzsch's has been around since 1904. It might get a little less of the spotlight than Mader's, but don't dare overlook it. With all the traditional German favorites and then some, including a kid's menu, lighter fare with a few vegetarian options, an early dining menu, and more, you can find something for everyone in your group and still get a taste of old German dining in Milwaukee. Lunch $7.95–14.95, dinner $14.95–30.50

🍸 ♿ **Bacchus** (414-765-1166; bacchusmke.com), 925 East Wells Street. Open daily for dinner. It's changed hands a few times, but this restaurant in Cudahy Tower is now in the hands of the successful Bartolotta Group, and with its varied wine list, lives up to its name. The sophisticated ambiance and incredible lake views (if you're in the right spot) make it a perfect place to woo a lover or impress friends. Contemporary American dishes dominate the menu, with options such as sautéed Scottish salmon and veal ravioli. Dishes $26–37.

🍸 ♿ **Carnevor** (414-223-2200; carnevor.com), 724 North Milwaukee Street. Open for dinner Monday through Saturday. In a state with no dearth of steakhouses, Carnevor stands out for its modern take on this traditional cuisine. The interior is contemporary and comfortable—decidedly unstuffy—but it doesn't lack sophistication. As the name suggests, this place is about steak, but there are modern alternatives here as well, like organic salmon and free-range chicken. $18–38.

🍸 ♿ **Five O'Clock Steakhouse** (414-342-3553; fiveoclocksteakhouse.com), 2413 West State Street. Open for dinner Tuesday through Sunday. Consistently winning awards and accolades from diners and national press alike, Five O'Clock maintains its true supper-club roots, right down to the relish tray. Opened in 1948, the decor now passes for retro, but the prices do not. Entrees $21–38.

Y & **Mason Street Grill** (4141-298-3131; masonstreetgrill.com), 425 East Mason Street. Open for lunch Monday through Friday, dinner daily. Located in the Pfister, the Mason Street Grill stands out as an upscale but unstuffy option for a more sophisticated meal out. Dinner features everything from burgers to filet mignon plus a host of seafood options, but lunch has a tempting array of sandwiches and other lighter dishes. Get the popular fried surf clams as an appetizer or a snack while you're sitting at the bar, and remember there's a Friday fish fry here, too. Don't skip dessert—whether you choose creme brulée or carrot cake, it's worth the calories. Lunch $10–20, dinner $30–40.

Suburbs/Elsewhere

Y ✿ & **Bavarian Inn** (414-964-0300; bavarianinnmilw.com), 700 West Lexington Boulevard, Glendale. Open for lunch and dinner Tuesday through Friday, Sunday brunch. Another traditional German restaurant, Bavarian Inn has great service and food. Like the others, the atmosphere is very German, with a beer-hall feel and lots of dark wood and steins. You'll find traditional German dishes, such as sauerbraten and schnitzel, but there are lighter options, too, and pasta. Sunday brunch offers a huge buffet plus champagne. Dinner $11–20, fish fry $11.50–13.95, brunch $12.95–17.95.

Y & **Ristorante Bartolotta** (414-771-7910; ristorantebartolotta.com), West State Street, Wauwatosa. Open daily for dinner. The Bartolotta Restaurant Group is known around the area for its excellent food and attention to detail. This one whips up some of the best Italian food in Milwaukee in a warm, charming atmosphere. The menus—there's a regular menu as well as a seasonal tasting menu—feature recipes from various regions in Italy, and the

wine list is extensive. Dishes $19.95–35.95.

Y & **Dream Dance** (414-847-7883; paysbig.com/dining/dreamdance), 1721 West Canal Street. Open for dinner Tuesday through Saturday. It might be surprising that one of the most highly regarded restaurants in the city is located at Potawatomi Bingo Casino, but it's true. Even more, Dream Dance features traditional (and not so traditional) Wisconsin foods in an elegant atmosphere. I don't mean beer and cheese—I mean items such as lobsterwurst, cannibal sandwiches (these are raw ground beef sandwiches akin to beef tartare, served with slices of onion on rye bread. The concept is not unique to Wisconsin, but it's particularly embraced here), root beer venison rossini (made with Milwaukee's Sprecher), butternut squash pancakes, and other highly creative dishes. $20–50.

EATING OUT

East Side and Riverwest

Y & **Comet Cafe** (414-273-7677; the cometcafe.com), 1947 North Farwell Avenue. Open 10:30 AM–bar time Monday through Friday, 9 AM–bar time Saturday and Sunday. Once a smoky little coffee shop filled with artists and local characters nursing cheap cups of coffee and munching on the best sandwiches around, Comet's grown up, both in size and focus. Now half family friendly cafe, half bar, the Comet (as locals like to call it) offers an outstanding menu of home-cooked comfort foods, more than half of which are available vegan. Everyone will be pleased here, including kids (although there's no kid's menu)—the meat versions delight carnivores, while vegetarians swoon over the likes of vegan meatloaf and vegan gyros. Entrees $10–15.

♂ & ❦ **Beans and Barley** (414-278-7878; beansandbarley.com), 1901 East North Avenue. Open daily for all three meals. In the health-food game long before it was cool, Beans and Barley offers delicious, heart-healthy meals at very reasonable prices. Burritos, including meat, bean, and vegan varieties, are extremely popular, but everything on the menu is worth a try. Weekend brunch fills up fast; get here early or you'll be waiting. Not to worry, though, you can browse the market and deli until your name is called. If you just can't wait, try the tofu scrambler or an omelet during the week. Entrees $6–10.

❦ **Abu's** (414-277-0485), 1978 North Farwell Avenue. Open 11:30—9 Monday through Saturday. Wisconsin's oldest and most beloved Middle Eastern restaurant, Abu's is tiny, but that adds to the charm. You get to watch your food being prepared and maybe even chat with the ever-interesting employees. There's a broad range of choices for both vegetarians and meat-eaters, but it must be said Abu's does vegetarian especially well. Choose from tasty

APOLLO CAFÉ

falafel or the savory lentil and rice-based mojadras. There are wonderful combination plates for those who can't decide. Abu's stands out for its great food and very low prices. Make sure to try the rosewater lemonade. Dishes $3.50–10.

& **Apollo Cafe** (414-272-2233; apollo cafe.com), 1310 Brady Street. Open daily with late-night hours on weekends. A step up from typical fast-food Greek cuisine, Apollo offers the reasonable prices and self-service speed of its lesser cousins, but the atmosphere and quality are fantastic. With higher-end menu options in a cafe designed to evoke mythical Greece, and right in the center of Brady Street, Apollo's my favorite place to grab spanakopita and dolmathes. Dishes $5–8.

Ⴤ & **County Clare Irish Inn** (414-272-5273; countyclare-inn.com), 1234 North Astor Street. Open daily for lunch and dinner. County Clare is a great place to drink a pint of Guinness while listening to traditional Irish music, certainly, but they've got a huge menu featuring authentic Irish dishes, such as bangers and mash or Irish stew, and then some—there's hummus

BEANS AND BARLEY

FISH FRY

As a native of Wisconsin, it surprised me a little when I realized that not everyone is familiar with the phenomenon of the fish fry. Naive, sure, but fish fry is such a part of Wisconsin's cultural landscape that it's as familiar as air to a Milwaukeean. Local media outlets scramble, year after year, to get their lists of the top fish fries in print before Lent, and sometimes these lists top 50 or so restaurants. It can get a little ridiculous—it's probably harder to find a restaurant not serving fish on a Friday night than it is to find a good one. Even churches, bars, diners, county parks, and Mexican, Japanese, and Polish restaurants get in on the game. Typically, the fish fry includes breaded cod, lake perch, or haddock, served with coleslaw, bread, French fries or potato pancakes, and tartar sauce, of course.

So what's the deal with fish fries in Wisconsin? It's really not that hard to figure out. What first lead to their popularity was the abundance and availability of fish in the area—Wisconsin is practically surrounded by water. The second was strong Catholic tradition, particularly in the Milwaukee area, which still means that many people won't eat meat on Fridays (vegetarians take note: to Catholics, fish is not meat). The third was Prohibition—bars, eager to get customers in the door, began serving up a Friday fish fry to cash in on working-class paydays. Mix all this together, and you've got an unstoppable culinary tradition. As I mentioned before, you won't have a hard time finding one on a Friday night, but if you've somehow gotten through life without attending a proper Milwaukee fish fry, here are but a few suggestions. Be sure to make a reservation, because it's not hype: Fish fry is really popular.

Y & **Lakefront Brewery Palm Garden** (414-273-8300; cafevec-chio.com/palmgarden/fishfry), 1872 North Commerce Street. Open 4–9 Friday. I am loath to bestow the distinction of best in Milwaukee on any establishment because, among the good ones, there are different reasons people love them. However, if forced to offer only one suggestion, I'd pick this one, and here's why: It's fun, and full of as much Milwaukee kitsch as you can stand. The fish gets rave reviews (though if you don't like fish, there

here as well. Inside it's as warm and welcoming as you'd expect an Irish inn to be. Dishes $7.95–17.95.

Y & **Balzac** (414-755-0099; balzacwine bar.com), 1716 North Arlington Place. Open daily for dinner. The fact that it's a wine bar causes people to forget it

has a full menu of contemporary cuisine available nightly, and it's not simply cheese plates. Yes, there are cheese plates, but there are also pizzas, pasta, and sandwiches, too. If you're not into wine, you can still enjoy Balzac's modern and cozy ambiance: It serves cock-

are burgers, veggie burgers, and grilled cheese options), you might dine with strangers, and there's a polka band playing from 6 PM on. More, special Friday night brewery tours offer a keepsake pint glass and a coupon for dinner. Fish fry $9.95–12.95, other dishes $5.50–8.95.

Y & **Historic Turner Restaurant** (414-276-4844; historicturner.com), 1034 North Fourth Street. Open for fish fry nightly. A favorite for its Friday fish fry, the restaurant also serves pasta dishes, burgers, and German specialties in its large dining room. Right downtown, it's a good location from which to take in the city's entertainment options—some of which might be right there in the Historic Turner Ballroom. Dishes $9–20.

Y & **Bavarian Inn** (414-964-0300; bavarianinnmilw.com), 700 West Lexington Boulevard, Glendale. Open for lunch and dinner Tuesday through Friday, Sunday brunch. The popular Friday fish fry features a choice of potato pancakes, German potato salad, dumplings, or fries. Dinner $11–20, fish fry $11.50–13.95, brunch $12.95–17.95.

Y & **Karl Ratzsch's Restaurant** (414-276-2720; karlratzsch.com), 320 East Mason Street. Open for fish fry Fridays at 4:30. On Fridays, the Sprecher Beer Battered Haddock is a hit, served with your choice of potato pancakes or German potato salad. Fish fry $13.95.

& **Bartolotta Fish Fry at Boerner Botanical Gardens** (414-525-5635; boerner botanicalgardens.org), 9400 Boerner Drive, Hales Corners. Serving fish fry 4:30–8:30 Fridays. Catered by the esteemed Bartolotta Group, this is a unique way to enjoy a great fish fry and sightsee at the same time. Okay, of course you're dining indoors, but it's by candlelight, and there's all-you-can-eat soup, salad, and bread to start you off. Live music starts at 6 PM. Come early in summer and tour the gardens, that way you'll work up an appetite. $14.95–18.95.

Y **Kegel's Inn** (414-257-9999), 5599 West National Avenue. Open at 4 PM for fish fry Friday nights. A traditional German restaurant that's a little off the radar, except for its well-loved Friday fish fry, Kegel's Inn is thick with dark wood and nostalgia. It serves old-fashioned German fare, including hasenpfeffer, which means you'll be thinking about Laverne and Shirley all night long. Dishes $9.95–17.95.

tails as well as a decent array of imported and craft beers. Dishes $8–16.

Y & **Izumi's** (414-271-5278; izumis .com), 2150 North Prospect Avenue. Open daily for lunch and dinner. It seems sushi bars pop up in Milwaukee, then quickly close. Izumi's has apparently not been touched by any competition; it's a favorite on the East Side and has only grown larger over the years, moving in 2005 to its present location. It could be the lengthy menu, or that the food is consistently good.

Whatever the reason, locals love it. Here's a bonus: It offers delivery in the evenings. Dinner $13–38, sushi and sashimi $5–12.

☙ ও **EE Sane** (414-224-8284), 1896 North Farwell Avenue. Open for lunch and dinner Monday through Saturday. There are higher-profile and nicer-looking Thai restaurants around, but they can't match EE Sane's quality and freshness. What's more, the prices are very reasonable; if you're willing to sacrifice a little ambiance, this place is for you. Okay, you'll sacrifice a lot of ambiance, but you won't be alone— EE Sane is very popular with East Siders. The curries and pad Thai are delicious, but use caution with the spiciness scale—a 10 is crazy hot. Dishes $7–12.

☙ ও **Pizza Man** (414-272-1745; pizza man.org), 1800 East North Avenue. Open for dinner daily, lunch and dinner Saturday and Sunday. Pizza Man has a great atmosphere for a nice meal out, but it's casual enough to pop in for pizza, too. Offering an award-winning wine menu and creative pasta dishes in addition to its pizza, you can't really go wrong here. Be sure to get an onion loaf for your appetizer. Pizza starts at $12.75; dinners $13–19.

☙ ও **Cafe Hollander** (414-963-6342; cafehollander.com), 2608 North Downer Avenue. Open daily for all three meals. A creative mix of Belgian- and Dutch-influenced food and beer offerings, Cafe Hollander is a great place to go for something a little different. The menu is decidedly eclectic, ranging from mussels to burgers and mac and cheese. Don't skip that cone of fries—it comes with your choice among 13 dipping sauces. Dishes $10–15.

☙ ও **Casablanca** (414-271-6000; casablancaonbrady.com), 728 East Brady Street. Open for lunch and din-

ner daily. Casablanca is easily one of Milwaukee's favorite Middle Eastern restaurants. The atmosphere is a step up from most of the others in town, and the food is, too. If you can't make it for dinner, you're in luck—Casablanca's weekday vegetarian lunch buffet is huge and satisfying, not to mention affordable. $4.95–12.95.

☙ ও **Hi-Hat Garage** (414-225-9330; hihatlounge.com), 1701 North Arlington Avenue. Open for lunch and dinner daily, brunch on Saturday and Sunday. A popular bar in the Brady Street neighborhood, the Hi-Hat should not be overlooked for dinner or weekend brunch. Offering a creative menu that matches the woodsy atmosphere, Hi-Hat's great for something casual, but not too casual. With dishes such as the Haute Dog (a hot dog with the works), burgers, salads, and vegetarian dishes, there's something for everyone. Dishes $6–12.

☙ ☙ ও **Maharaja** (414-276-2250), 1550 North Farwell Avenue. Open daily for lunch and dinner. Others come and go, but Maharaja remains a consistently good option for Indian food on the East Side. Offering a well-priced lunch buffet and fabulous dinner options, this is a great spot to stop for malai kofta or any other Indian favorite. The restaurant is generous with the rice and naan, so don't come here on a low-carb diet. Dishes $10–15.

☙ ও **Cempazuchi Comida Brava** (414-291-5233; cempazuchi.com), 1205 East Brady Street. Open for lunch and dinner Tuesday through Saturday, dinner Sunday. Cempazuchi has seen a lot of restaurants come and go on Brady Street, but its contemporary, authentic Mexican cuisine and reputation for mixing up a mean margarita keep fans coming back. House specialties include the enchilada suiza—a veggie enchilada packed with spinach, zucchini, and more—and salmon tacos. It's so sunny inside and brightly decorated that even if the weather outside is gloomy, you'll feel a little happier here. Dishes $8.95–17.95.

Y & **Bayou** (414-431-1511; bayou milwaukee.com), 2060 North Humboldt Boulevard. Open for lunch and dinner Tuesday through Sunday, Monday for dinner, weekends for brunch. Bayou offers a creative Cajun menu in contemporary surroundings perched on the river. Milwaukee doesn't have a lot of Cajun options, but this one's got the perfect spot. Dishes $10–15.

Y ✍ & **Carini's la Conca d'Oro** (414-963-9623; carinislaconcadoro.com), 3468 North Oakland Avenue. Open daily for lunch and dinner. You might miss it if you're not looking, despite its location on busy Oakland Avenue. Great food, including a reasonably priced, fantastic vegetarian lunch buffet, is what this place is about. Dishes $10–15.

Y & **Emperor of China** (414-271-8889), 1010 East Brady Street. Open daily for lunch and dinner. There are a lot of options for Chinese food in Milwaukee, but this one never disappoints. Inside, it's typical of a sit-down Chinese place, and the service is friendly. No surprises on the menu, but the food is consistently good, and the restaurant regularly wins popularity contests. If you're short on time or cash, the lunch specials are great. Dishes $8.95–15.95.

Y ✍ & **Ethiopian Cottage** (414-224-5226; ethiopiancottage.com), 1824 North Farwell Avenue. Open for lunch and dinner Tuesday through Saturday, dinner on Sunday. Housed in what had been some sort of tragic mini-mall on the East Side, Ethiopian Cottage does a good job of disguising the location's past once you get inside, with warm

tones and African accents adding a cozy touch. Ethiopian tradition means dining communally and using your fingers and injera bread as utensils, but you can have a fork, if you need one. Dishes $10–15.

& **Fuel Cafe** (414-374-3835; fuel cafe.com), 818 East Center Street, Riverwest. Open daily for all three meals. For a very casual sandwich in the company of artists, students, and other colorful neighborhood characters, Fuel offers a great coffee-shop atmosphere. The sandwich menu is extensive and creative, and Fuel has other goodies like soup and bakery items. You can, of course, fuel up on espresso drinks here, as well. Sandwiches $6–8.

Y & **The Good Life** (414-271-5375), 1935 North Water Street. Open for dinner Tuesday through Sunday, Sunday brunch. Featuring Caribbean cuisine in a lively atmosphere, the Good Life lives up to its name. The Jerk Wrap, yucca fritters, pulled pork, and plenty of vegetarian options mean everyone in your party will be happy—which is what the good life is all about, isn't it? Dishes $9–16.

Y & **The Knick** (414-272-0011; theknickrestaurant.com), 1030 East Juneau Avenue. Open for dinner daily, brunch on weekends. Snazzy but casual, the Knick is well loved for its brunch, especially when the weather lets diners can sit on the patio and people-watch. With options such as drunken shrimp and penne pasta, plus a host of burgers and sandwiches, you'll find something you like. Brunch $8–12, sandwiches $9.99–12.99, dinner $16.99–28.99.

✍ **Riverwest Co-op Cafe** (414-264-7933; riverwestcoop.org), 733 East Clark Street, Riverwest. Open daily for all three meals. Tucked away in the edgy and diverse Riverwest neighborhood, the Co-op Cafe features satisfying vegetarian and vegan dishes in a tiny space next to the grocery. It's worth going out of your way for the Seitan Philly, but breakfast is such a hit with the neighborhood you might have a hard time getting a table. Dishes $4–7.50.

✿ **Shiraz Persian Grill** (414-763-1925; shirazpersiangrill.com), 2921 North Oakland Avenue. Open 11–10 daily. A great place to sample Persian and Middle Eastern fare, Shiraz has fast food/deli counter-style service, but the variety and quality does its sit-down-style sister in Wauwatosa proud. It's a great alternative to run-of-the-mill fast food. Dishes $5–8.

✵ & **Twisted Fork** (414-431-1080; twisted-fork.com), 2238 North Farwell Avenue. Open daily for lunch and dinner, brunch on Saturday and Sunday. It took East Siders a little adjustment when this somewhat commercial-looking restaurant took over the space once occupied by the Oriental Pharmacy, but the neighborhood learned it to love the Twisted Fork. Your options range from burgers and sandwiches to pasta and seafood, so there's something for everyone. Dishes $8–24.

& **Koppa's Fulbeli Deli** (414-273-1273; koppas.com), 1940 North Farwell Avenue. Open 11–6 daily. If you're on the run, or looking for a quick bite to bring to the lakefront, you could do a lot worse than Koppa's. This neighborhood family owned grocer has served the East Side for decades, and shows no sign of slowing down. Grab a sandwich in the deli—you can play Atari while you wait—and enjoy the character of this homespun mom-and-pop. Sandwiches include one named for each planet, the Lunklunk, the Bread Favre, the Obi-wan Bologna, and the Deli Lama, to name a few. Koppa's consistently wins "best

sandwich" in media polls. Be sure to get a souvenir tee-shirt on your way out. Sandwiches $3.29–4.99.

✵ & **Zaffiro's Pizza** (414-289-8776; zaffirospizza.com), 1724 North Farwell Avenue. Open daily for lunch and dinner. The building's not much to look at, but the thin-crust pizza is consistently voted a favorite among locals. Just don't go looking for atmosphere; it's more like a dive bar than anything, but that doesn't stop everyone from college students to Milwaukee's most notable residents from crowding Zaffiro's for dinner. Pizza $10–20, entrees $7–10.

Downtown/Third Ward

✵ & **Elsa's on the Park** (414-765-0615; elsas.com), 833 North Jefferson Street. Open daily for dinner, Monday through Friday for lunch. This is classy pub grub in a trendy, modern setting. Burgers are the standout here, and they're anything but ordinary. Try the Burger Alfredo or any of five porkchop sandwiches. My favorite appetizer is called Just Broccoli, but I my obsessive love of broccoli may bias me. There are tons of other great appetizers that serve as great munchies to sip wine with late at night. Dishes $10–15.

✵ & **Coquette Cafe** (414-291-2655; coquettecafe.com), 316 North Milwaukee Street. Open Monday through Friday for lunch and dinner, Saturday dinner. As cute and as French as its name, the Coquette Cafe is owned by Sandy D'Amato, owner of the award-winning **Sanford**. Blending casual dining with upscale menu options at reasonable prices, Coquette Cafe is popular with lunchtime and evening diners alike, offering sandwiches, stews, seafood, and more. Dishes $10–20.

✵ ✿ **Safe House** (414-271-2007; safe-house.com), 779 North Front Street. Open Thursday through Saturday for lunch and daily for dinner, bar hours later. This bar and restaurant is more about drinking and entertaining than dining, but the menu is broad, featuring burgers, vegetable dishes, and a host of chicken and steak options, and there's even a kid's menu for spies-in-training. Dishes $8–22.

Y & **Historic Turner Restaurant** (414-276-4844; historicturner.com), 1034 North Fourth Street. Open daily for lunch and dinner. A favorite for its Friday fish fry, the menu also features pasta dishes, burgers, and German specialties in its large dining room. Right downtown, it's a good location from which to take in the city's entertainment options. Dishes $9–20.

Y & **Water Street Brewery** (414-646-7878; waterstreetbrewery.com), 1101 North Water Street. Open daily for lunch and dinner, Saturday and Sunday for brunch. A cornerstone of the Water Street bar district, it's a microbrewery offering a great dining menu and casual atmosphere. The focus is on sandwiches and casual fare that complements the handful of house beers, and the atmosphere is casual and bright. Dishes $9–15.

Y & **Milwaukee Ale House** (414-226-2337; ale-house.com/alehouse), 233 North Water Street. Open for lunch and dinner daily, until bar time for drinks. The spacious but comfortable interior means a lot of people can pack into this riverfront favorite, which also has boat slips if that's how you get here. Serving craft beer and tasty sandwiches in the Third Ward since 1997, the Milwaukee Ale House has everything from tenderloin steak sandwiches to pizza and pasta, with plenty of seafood and vegetarian options mixed in. Around 10 house-brewed ales and lagers are on tap, and live music is offered on weekends. Dishes $8.95–18.95.

Y & **Alem Ethiopian Village** (414-224-5324; http://alemethiopianvillage

.com/), 307 East Wisconsin Avenue. Open for lunch and dinner Monday through Saturday, dinner on Sunday. The downtown location makes it convenient, but there's not a lot going on around this restaurant. No matter, the food's great and the inside sunny and clean. Ethiopian food involves eating communally and with your fingers (with the help of a spongy bread called injera), but if you really need a fork, they'll give you one. Dishes $10–15

♪ & **Cafe at the Plaza** (414-272-0515), 1007 North Cass Street. Open daily for breakfast and lunch. The onsite restaurant for the **Plaza Hotel and Apartments**, the cafe is more diner than anything, but with a charming, historic flair. The breakfast potatoes are locally famous, and therefore worth the trip. Inside is a lunch counter, which is fun, but if you can get a seat out on the patio when the weather cooperates, it's a perfect way to spend your morning. Dishes $5.75–7.75.

♪ **The Soup House** (414-277-7687; tlcsoup.com), 324 East Michigan Street. Open daily for lunch, Saturday and Sunday for dinner. Downtown worker bees line up at lunchtime for a bowl of bisque or chowder, even if it means standing outside in winter. The restaurant offers six or seven soups each day, accompanied by a sizable chunk of warm bread, and you can check the weekly soup schedule online. Each day's offering includes vegan and gluten-free options, so if your diet's restricted, this is a good choice. Soup prices depend on size, $5–10.

Y & **Palms Bistro** (414-298-3000; palmsbistrobar.com), 221 North Broadway Street. Open daily for lunch and dinner, Sunday for brunch. Palms is fun and casual yet a little upscale, with a jungle theme that isn't corny or overdone. The menu is huge and qualifies as contemporary American, with everything from sandwiches to pizza and pasta—try the chipotle mac and cheese or curried shrimp tempura. Lunch $9–15, dinner $10–24.

Bay View

Y **Palomino** (414-747-1007), 2491 South Superior Street, Bay View. Open for dinner daily, "hangover brunch" 10–3 Saturday and Sunday. The Palomino fries just about everything, including pickles and tofu. It's a bar, plain and simple, with decor that crosses Southern U.S. with Northern Wisconsin kitsch. Offering a popular Friday fish fry along with chicken-fried tofu, hush puppies, real and veggie brats, butter burgers (a Milwaukee favorite—same as a regular burger, but with generous slabs of butter melted between the meat and the bun), and more, your taste buds will be happy, but don't even think about your waistline here. Dishes $10–15.

♿ **Classic Slice Pizza** (414-238-2406), 2797 South Kinnickinnic Avenue, Bay View. Open for lunch and dinner daily. At home in Milwaukee's burgeoning Bay View neighborhood, casual Classic Slice is frequented by neighborhood cool kids and families alike. The slices are so big they don't fit on the paper plate, and the options are wild, though you can get a run-of-the-mill cheese and sausage slice if you'd like. Vegans will be pleased to know there are options for them, too. Groups can order an entire pie, but will probably have a hard time agreeing on toppings. $3.50–$6.

Y ♿ **LuLu** (414-294-5858; lulubayview.com), 2261 South Howell Avenue, Bay View. Open daily for lunch and dinner, Sunday brunch. Lulu is half cafe, half bar, thanks to a 2004 expansion that was heartily welcomed by the neighborhood. The food's the same on both sides, so it all depends on your choice of atmosphere. The menu is focused squarely on sandwiches—they come on pita, buns, baguettes, and plain old bread—and you get your choice of house-made chips or the popular Asian slaw. If you can't decide, they'll give you both. Sandwiches $7–9.25.

♿ **Soup Otzie's** (414-747-9670), 3950 South Howell Avenue, Bay View. Open for lunch Monday through Saturday. Considered by many to be the best soup joint in town, Soup Otzie's offers six soups daily with tasty bread. This cozy spot is friendly and fun, and will leave plenty of dough for shopping. $3–5.

Y ♿ **Three Brothers** (414-481-7530), 2414 Saint Clair Street, Bay View. Open for dinner Tuesday through Sunday. The charming eclectic atmosphere, cozy and heartwarming, is only the beginning. This is a favorite for Serbian food in Milwaukee, offering specialties such as paprikash and burek, plus other rarities like roast goose. Relaxing and friendly, if you're in the mood for something different, this is it. Dishes $10–20.

Y ♿ **Cafe Centraal** (414-755-0377; thecafecentraal.com), 2306 South Kinnickinnic Avenue, Bay View. Open for lunch and dinner daily, Saturday and Sunday brunch. Like its Eastside cousin, Café Hollander, this Bay View restaurant offers Belgian- and Dutch-influenced food and beer. Dishes include diverse items such as mussels, burgers. and mac and cheese. Fries come with one of 13 dipping sauces. Kid's menu available. Dishes $10–15.

♿ **Hi-Fi Cafe** (414-486-0504; hificafe.com), 2640 South Kinnickinnic Avenue, Bay View. Open daily for all three meals. Bright, clean, and a little bit retro, Hi-Fi offers great sandwiches and breakfast to soak up that espresso. Dishes $5–10.

Walker's Point

Y & **La Merenda** (414-389-0125; lamerenda125.com), 125 East National Avenue, Walker's Point. Open for dinner daily, lunch Monday through Friday. Housed in a renovated wood-working shop, La Merenda is a modern, bright tapas bar featuring small-plate dishes from around the world. Somewhere in the neighborhood of 15 countries are represented on the menu; the U.S. is represented by dishes from Wisconsin, such as the roasted beet salad. Tapas plates $4–9.25.

Y & **Chez Jacques** (414-672-1040; chezjacques.com), 1022 South First Street, Walker's Point. Open for all three meals Tuesday through Sunday. There are a number of French-themed restaurants in town, but this one's the real deal. Owned by someone whose name actually is Jacques, the menu features classic French dishes, and is remarkably complete. There are plenty of crepes to choose from, as well as quiche, cheese plates, sandwiches, and all manner of entrees. Dishes $11.95–21.95.

Y & **La Fuente** (414-271-8595; megustalafuente.com), 625 South Fifth Street, Walker's Point. Open for lunch and dinner daily. It's impossible not to find a fantastic Mexican restaurant in this neighborhood, and everyone's got their favorite. La Fuente is huge and extremely busy on weekends, which makes it remarkable that it can maintain good service and food consistently. Dishes $10–20.

Y & **Botanas** (414-672-3755; www .botanasrestaurant.com), 816 South Fifth Street, Walker's Point. Open for lunch and dinner daily. Another Milwaukee favorite for Mexican dining, Botanas has authentic Mexican dishes with extra options such as vegetarian dishes and a huge seafood offering.

The interior is sunny, and the service, with, oh, a million employees doing the job, is usually good. Indoor and outdoor dining is available. Dishes $8.50–16.50.

Suburbs/Elsewhere

& ❧ **Bombay Sweets** (414-383-3553), 3401 South Thirteenth Street. Open 11–9 daily. Okay, it's in a kind of depressed-looking strip mall, completely out of the way, and you order at the counter and eat off paper plates. Not usually how I start a rave review, but this is delicious Indian food on the cheap. Each of the 57 items offered is vegetarian, and displayed on a huge wall menu with photos. It's hard to decide, but everything here is so inexpensive, you can order more than one if you want. Dishes $4–5.

& **Benji's Deli** (414-332-7777; food spot.com/benjisdeli), 4156 North Oakland Avenue, Shorewood. Open daily for all three meals. Benji's is part grungy diner, part traditional Jewish deli, with key items such as its well-loved corned beef, potato pancakes, and my favorite, the Hoppel Poppel. With everything from ratatouille to fried matzo, there are great options here not found elsewhere in Milwaukee. Do try the corned beef. Dishes $5–10.

& **City Market** (414-962-0100; thecitymarketcafe.com), 2205 East Capitol Drive, Shorewood. Open daily for all three meals. Sunny and comfortable, City Market is extremely casual—more like a coffee shop—but it offers a wide variety of sandwiches and breakfast options. What you really want here, though, is dessert. With tempting cakes and other yummy baked goods, dessert makes this cafe a destination all by itself. $5–10.

& **Anaba Tea Room** (414-963-9510; anabatearoom.com), 2107 East Capitol Drive, Shorewood. Open 11–3 Tuesday through Sunday, 3–5 Tuesday through Friday. Anaba Tea Room calls itself, "A little known but pleasing spot." I'm not going to argue with that. Combine the uniqueness of an honest-to-goodness tea room with the pleasant atmosphere of Anaba's co-business, the Garden Room (see Selective Shopping), and you've got the makings for one relaxing lunch. Offering salads, tea sandwiches, crumpets, and sweets, Anaba Tea room was made for, well, tea-time. Sunday brunch features live music. Dishes $4–8.

Y & **East Garden Chinese Restaurant** (414-962-7460; eastgarden restaurant.com), 3600 North Oakland Avenue, Shorewood. Open for lunch and dinner daily. This popular Chinese restaurant just north of the city limits offers a pleasant, upscale atmosphere with reasonable prices. The menu includes standard Chinese fare, but there are vegetarian options as well. Try the weekday lunch buffet for only $5.95. Dishes $8.95–12.95.

Y & & **Organ Piper Pizza** (414-529-1177; organpiperpizza.com), 4353 South 108 Street, Greenfield. Open for dinner Tuesday through Saturday, lunch on weekends. Forget the big-name kiddie casinos—Organ Piper is an entertaining pizza joint even adults can stand. The pizza's all right, and there are pasta options, too, but it's the live organ music—performed on a 1929 Wurlitzer by staff musicians—that's the real draw here. Toys and percussive instruments—including a row of wooden ducks—are played by the organist and come to life while you eat. Pizza $10–15, dishes $4–10.

Y & **Crawdaddy's** (414-778-2228; crawdaddysrestaurant.com), 6414 West Greenfield Avenue, West Allis. Open for lunch and dinner Tuesday through Friday, dinner only Saturday and Sunday. A popular Cajun restaurant, and

the first in Milwaukee, Crawdaddy's serves up the expected dishes—catfish, paella, po' boys—but the menu is huge and creative, and even features a couple of vegetarian options. Entrees $15–20.

BURGER AND CUSTARD STANDS

& & **Kopp's Frozen Custard** (414-282-4080; kopps.com), 7631 West Layton Avenue, Greenfield; (262-789-1393), 18880 West Bluemound Road, Brookfield; (414-961-2006), 5373 Port Washington Road, Glendale. Open 10:30–11 daily. Kopp's is an amazing stainless-steel operation with a huge crew of aproned and paper-hatted workers buzzing about scooping custard, blending malts, frying burgers and grilling cheeses for its hungry line of loyal customers. The building is enormous, but there's not really a seating area inside. There are, however, plenty of benches and other spots to sit outside, and there's always your car. Dishes $3–5.

& & **Leon's** (414-383-1784; foodspot .com/leons), 3131 South 27th Street. Open 11 AM–midnight daily. Leon's been around since the '50s, in case the round, neon-encased building doesn't clue you in. Many Milwaukeeans name Leon's as their favorite custard, and it's certainly worthy. This is a walk-up operation, you eat outside or in your car, and you can get the full array of custard-stand burger options. There's nearly always a line in summer, and sometimes in winter, too. Dishes $3–5.

& & **Bella's Fat Cat** (414-747-9746; bellascustard.com), 2737 South Kinnickinnic Avenue, Bayview; or (414-431-8480), 2974 North Oakland Avenue. Open daily for lunch and dinner. Like its venerable competitors, Bella's serves a full range of yummy burgers and sandwiches fast-food style in a shiny stainless-steel atmosphere, with the requisite frozen custard and malts to remind you this is Milwaukee! What sets this custard stand apart is the locations—oddly, the East Side and Bayview were lacking proper custard and burger joints for years before Bella's opened up. It fills the role well, and also offers veggie dogs and burgers suit its progressive neighborhoods. Dishes $3–5.

COFFEE SHOPS Like any proper U.S. city, Milwaukee's landscape is dotted with Starbucks stores, at the ready and easy to find when you need them. But the city is home to a number of independently run coffeehouses and roasters. Here's a sampling.

& **Alterra** (414-292-3320; alterra coffeepro.com), multiple locations. Open daily. Alterra sure has grown up since 1997, when its first location on the East Side (2211 North Prospect Avenue) began offering fresh-roasted coffees to a neighborhood that became quickly addicted. By 2009, Alterra was roasting more than 60 coffees and operating 16 cafes. Alterra on the Lake (414-223-4551), 1701 North Lincoln Memorial Drive, has great views, but it gets outrageously busy in summer. All locations around Milwaukee are slightly different, but feature exposed brick, warm tones, and great music.

& ✐ **Anodyne Cafe** (414-489-0765; anodynecoffee.com), 2920 South Kinnickinnic Avenue, Bay View. Open daily until 9 PM. Anodyne roasts its own coffee with good results, and the cafe is comfortable. Sit at the counter, or at a table. Kids are more than welcome here, and the owners even supply toys.

& ✐ **Hi-Fi Cafe** (414-486-0504; hifi cafe.com), 2640 South Kinnickinnic Avenue, Bay View. Open daily for all three meals. Bright, clean, and a little bit retro, Hi-Fi offers great sandwiches

and breakfast to soak up that espresso. Dishes $5–10.

& ✐ **Fuel Cafe** (414-374-3835; fuel cafe.com), 818 East Center Street, Riverwest. See the listing under Eating Out. Sandwiches $6–8.

✳ Entertainment

Y & **Potawatomi Bingo Casino** (800-729-7244; paysbig.com), 1721 West Canal Street. Aside from slots, poker, and bingo in a smoke-free game room, this casino offers a huge theater featuring national acts, some of them free, and three restaurants, including the highly regarded Dreamdance restaurant (see Dining Out).

& **The Milwaukee Ballet** (414-902-2103; milwaukeeballet.org). Performances are held at The Pabst Theatre, 144 East Wells Street, and at the Marcus Center for the Performing Arts, 929 North Water Street. Both venues are located in downtown Milwaukee's theater district. Ranked one of the top 12 ballet companies in the nation, the Milwaukee Ballet performs for more than 70,000 people each year. Offering evening-length works as well as world premieres of the more experimental variety, the Milwaukee Ballet is surprisingly accessible. More modern concerts are held at The Pabst, which is an intimate and beautiful setting.

& **The Rep—Milwaukee Repertory Theatre** (414-224-9490; milwaukee rep.com), 108 East Wells Street. The Rep, running since 1954, offers 16 productions each season with a resident acting company. It's the largest company in Wisconsin, and a favorite in Milwaukee. Productions run the gamut at this very versatile theatre.

✐ & **First Stage Children's Theatre** (414-267-2929; firststage.org), 325 West Walnut Street. Presenting around eight productions a year, First Stage offers exceptional opportunities for families to enjoy live theatre. It offers an age guide for each play, along with the recommendation that you not bring children younger than 3.

& **The Broadway Theatre Centre** (414-291-7800; skylightopera.com), 158 North Broadway Avenue, is the Third Ward venue for three companies: the Skylight Opera Theatre, which offers light opera and musicals, the Milwaukee Chamber Theater, and Renaissance Theatreworks.

Danceworks (414-277-8480; dance worksmke.org), 1661 North Water Street. Danceworks quickly moved from up-and-comer to perhaps the city's premiere modern dance company. Productions are sophisticated and professional, but often display a sly sense of humor.

Ko-Thi Dance Company (414-273-0676; ko-thi.org). Formed in 1969, the Ko-Thi Dance Company performs traditional African American and Caribbean dance at various locations throughout the city and internationally.

Milwaukee Symphony Orchestra (414-291-6010; mso.org), 700 North Water Street. Since 1959, the highly acclaimed MSO has been performing concerts and providing education and outreach to the community. Performances are held at the Marcus Center (414-273-7121; marcuscenter.org), 929 North Water Street, as well as other locations around Milwaukee.

Y & **J. D.'s Comedy Cafe** (414-271-5653; jdscomedycafe.com), 615 Brady Street. Shows run Thursday through Saturday. Bringing in national acts to make Milwaukee audiences bust a gut for years, the Comedy Cafe is at home on the East Side.

& **The Oriental Theatre** (414-276-8711; landmarktheatres.com), 2230 North Farwell Avenue. Hailed by local

and national media alike as one of the best places in the U.S. to see a film, the Oriental is a sentimental favorite among locals. Getting a look at the inside of this magnificent movie house is worth the price of a ticket alone. One of only a handful of movie palaces remaining in America today, the Oriental has shown films for 75 years straight. Decorated in an East Indian theme complete with six Buddha statues and hundreds of elephants, this theater is ornate to say the least. The main auditorium houses a Kimball theatre pipe organ—the third-largest in the world, in fact—and Friday and Saturday evening shows are preceded by a brief concert. Having gone through a number of different incarnations (including a short stint as an adult theater), these days the Oriental is owned by Landmark Theatres and shows arthouse films.

& **Downer Theatre** (414-276-8711; landmarktheatres.com), 2589 North Downer Avenue. This is one of two East Side cinemas owned by Landmark Theatres, and both show arthouse flicks. Like the Oriental Theatre, the Downer is historic (in fact, it's the oldest operating theatre in Milwaukee), but it's not nearly as impressive as the Oriental. Still, great movies play here, and it's a far cry from bland.

Y & **Rosebud Cinema Drafthouse** (414-607-9446; rosebudcinema.com), 6823 West Avenue, Wauwatosa. The Rosebud offers current, classic, and art-house films in a historic, but renovated, theater. The bonus here is you can get dinner and beer, too. Okay, dinner equals pizza and fried appetizers, but that's what you want with a movie, isn't it? A handful of domestic and craft beers are on tap, as well.

Y & **The Times Cinema** (414-453-3128; rosebudcinema.com), 5906 West

Vliet Street. Run by the same people who own the Rosebud Cinema Drafthouse, the Times doesn't have dinner, but it does feature even more arthouse films and a midnight movie on Fridays. Beer and wine are available, as are typical movie snacks.

🍸 ✄ ♿ **Fox Bay Cinema** (414-906-9994; foxbaycinemagrill.com), 334 East Silver Spring Drive. This cinema offers dinner while you watch a flick, and features mainstream movies, as well as films you can take the kids to. Menu includes sandwiches and pizza, plus a special kid's menu.

♿ **Pabst Theatre** (414-286-3205; pabsttheater.org), 144 East Wells Street. The Pabst isn't simply a great venue to see a show, it's also a beautiful, historic building. Built in 1895, it's been carefully restored and preserved to reflect its original charm, although some concessions to modern comfort have been made. It's easily my favorite venue, and it's the heart of the downtown theater district. Local and nationally touring acts perform here, so if you can find any reason to get inside, do it.

☀ Nightlife

In Milwaukee, of course, by nightlife I mean bars. It would take remarkable effort to avoid finding bars in Brew City, and while there are watering holes all over the county, some neighborhoods are just better for sipping a pint. Because I don't want you bar hopping all over town (well, maybe if you're taking a cab), I've grouped some favorites into the neighborhoods most known for weeknight revelry. In Milwaukee, bar time is 2 AM Sunday through Thursday and 2:30 AM Friday and Saturday. When hours are listed, they are for the kitchen; bars usually stay open as long as the law allows and someone is willing to buy a drink. The Water Street bar district, just north of downtown, is not represented by individual bars here; there are just so many of them, one next to another, that if you're in the mood for college-style partying, head straight there. Otherwise, avoid it.

East Side

A little bit college, a little bit professional, the East Side was once considered a haven for artists and hippies. These days it's a little more polished, and the bohemian torch has somewhat been passed to Riverwest. Credit or blame it on all the condo development (depending on how you feel about polish). One thing remains, to be sure: It's a great neighborhood for a night out. Just make sure you find a legal parking spot. On the East Side, two streets contain the bulk of the fun—Brady Street and North Avenue. The bars on and around North Avenue tend to be more of the college sort, while the Brady Street bars skew slightly older. That's not a hard-and-fast rule, though.

🍸 ♿ **Hi Hat Lounge and Garage** (414-225-9330; hihatlounge.com), 1701 North Arlington Place. Open nightly. Standing proudly at the corner of

PABST THEATER

Arlington and Brady, the Hi Hat offers a mix of martini–lounge atmosphere and great drink specials. Next door is the more casual Garage, which once was, yes, a garage. Both use the same kitchen to serve up casual meals and perfect munchies while you share a drink with friends.

Y & **Balzac** (414-755-0099; balzac winebar.com), 1716 North Arlington Place. Open nightly. If you're not into wine, you can still enjoy Balzac's modern and cozy ambiance: It serves cocktail as well as a decent array of imported and craft beers, and evenings are packed. There are nice options for sipping outdoors, too, which is great for people–watching.

Y & **Von Trier** (414-272-1775), 2235 North Farwell Avenue. Open nightly. This is the East Side's German beer garden, extremely popular in summer, but serving hot drinks inside when winter comes along. Dark wood, steins, and friendly service are the hallmarks, along with a good selection of draft beer. Another plus is it tends to miss the North Avenue college crowd, who spend weekends hopping the nearby bars.

Y & **Paddy's Pub** (414-223-3496; paddyspub.net), 2339 North Murray Avenue. Open nights Tuesday through Saturday. There are many Irish pubs in Milwaukee, but this one's a little extra homey. Maybe it's that you feel like you're in someone's living room, or maybe it's the owners, Woody (Orlen) Wood and Patty Phillips-Wood, who might be the friendliest people on Earth. They'll strike up a conversation, and genuinely want you to have a good time. No food here, but the pub does have an apparently unlimited supply of Chex Mix and Peanut M&Ms for you to munch on. Paddy's can get uncomfortably packed on the weekends; if you want to really enjoy the atmos-

phere, try going a little early or during the week. There's live music, ranging from traditional Irish to jazz, on Fridays and Saturdays.

Y & **County Clare Irish Inn** (414-272-5273; countyclare-inn.com), 1234 North Astor Street. Open daily. County Clare is a great place to drink a pint of Guinness while listening to traditional Irish music, which is featured several nights a week. Inside it's as warm and welcoming as you'd expect an Irish inn to be.

Y & **The Jazz Estate** (414-964-9923; jazzestate.com), 2423 North Murray Avenue. Open nightly. A favorite for live jazz since 1976, the Jazz Estate is a large bar with a retro lounge atmosphere. It's got live music five nights a week, ranging from popular local acts to nationally known musicians. It's a friendly, relaxing place to listen to jazz and sip a drink.

Y & **Up and Under** (414-276-2677), 1216 East Brady Street. Open nightly. The Up and Under is a Brady Street institution featuring live music ranging from blues to reggae Thursday through Saturday, as well as running a popular open mic night on Mondays and karaoke on Wednesdays. The atmosphere is typical tavern, but the room is big enough to make it a popular venue.

Y & **The Good Life** (414-271-5375; goodlifemilwaukee.com), 1935 North Water Street. Open nightly. This full-menu eatery has a hot bar scene at night, with DJs spinning Wednesday, Friday, and Saturday.

Y & **Angelo's Piano Bar** (414-347-4144), 1686 North Van Buren Street. Open nightly Wednesday through Saturday. Among the most unique finds in Milwaukee, Angelo's is a true piano bar, and a holdout from the neighborhood's Italian origins. Grab a cocktail, and watch the musicians go to town singing Sinatra tunes for a very diverse crowd that spans multiple generations.

Downtown/Third Ward

There are a lot of bars in the downtown and Third Ward areas, but the sad (or annoying) fact is that, for some reason, they close as fast as they open, and it sometimes defies logic. Many popular and great places have shut down, but at least they've been replaced by equally popular and great places. You can be sure you'll find a good time in this area—and it's highly walkable—but what the name and theme of the bars will be, I can't say. With that caveat, I've listed some area favorites which have stood the test of time, and don't appear to be going anywhere soon.

Y & **The Wicked Hop and Jackalope Lounj** (414-223-0345; thewicked hop.com), 345 North Broadway Street. Open nightly. Following the trend of day-into-night establishments, the Wicked Hop serves up great sandwiches and entrees during kitchen hours, and offers a relaxing bar atmosphere at night, with DJs spinning in the Jackalope Lounj several nights a week. The bartenders make a popular Bloody Mary, but if that's not your thing, there are plenty of craft beers, martinis, mojitos, and more.

Y & **Milwaukee Ale House** (414-226-2337; ale-house.com/alehouse), 233 North Water Street. Open nightly. The spacious but comfortable interior means a lot of people can pack into this riverfront favorite, which also has boat slips if that's how you get here. Serving craft beer and tasty sandwiches in the Third Ward since 1997, the Milwaukee Ale House serves everything from tenderloin steak sandwiches to pizza and pasta, with plenty of seafood and vegetarian options mixed in. Around 10 house-brewed ales and lagers are on tap, and live music is offered on weekends. Dishes $8.95–18.95.

THE WICKED HOP

Y & **Blu** (414-298-3196; pfisterhotel
.com/dining_cocktails/blu.asp), 424
East Wisconsin Avenue in the Pfister
Hotel. Open nightly Monday through
Saturday. On the 23rd floor of the Pfister Hotel, Blu's attraction is obvious:
Enjoying a breathtaking view of the city
while sipping a martini is a wonderful
night out, indeed, and the atmosphere
is sophisticated. Wine flights and jazz
are just the icing on the cake.

Y & **Elsa's on the Park** (414-765-
0615; elsas.com), 833 North Jefferson
Street. Open nightly. See the entry
under Eating Out.

Y & **Safe House** (414-271-2007; safe
-house.com), 779 North Front Street.
Open nightly Thursday through Saturday. This famous Milwaukee institution
is a fun spy-themed bar and restaurant
that's hard to find but well worth the
trouble. You'll likely need the password
to get in, but if you don't know it (and
I'm sure not telling you what it is, lest
Control disappear me) you can still get
in, albeit not with your dignity intact.
You'll first have to do silly dances on-
camera for everyone inside to enjoy.
Inside, trap doors and other spy props
are a delight.

Bay View
Y ♂ & **Sugar Maple** (414-481-2393),
441 East Lincoln Avenue, Bay View.
Open 4–bar time Monday through Friday, 2–bar time Saturday and Sunday.
New in 2008, Sugar Maple features
more than 60 craft beers on tap in a
non-smoking environment. In fact,
it's not only non-smoking, but it sometimes offers kid-friendly events on
weekend days. Inside, it's bright, modern, and clean—a pleasant change of
pace—and the bar is huge. Live music,
craft sessions, workshops, and other
events are offered regularly.

Y & **Cactus Club** (414-897-0663;
cactusclubmilwaukee.com), 2496
South Wentworth Avenue, Bay View.
Open 3–bar time. A popular venue for
local and national touring bands, the
Cactus Club has hosted the likes of the
White Stripes and Bright Eyes over
the years. Up front is a bar; in back the
room is just right for a small show.

Y & **Palomino** (414-747-1007), 2491
South Superior Street, Bay View. Open
for dinner daily, "hangover brunch"
10–3 Saturday and Sunday. See the
entry under Bay View restaurants.

Y & **LuLu** (414-294-5858; lulubayview
.com), 2261 South Howell Avenue, Bay
View. Open daily for lunch and dinner,
Sunday brunch. LuLu is half cafe, half
bar, thanks to a 2004 expansion that
was heartily welcomed by the neighborhood. The bar side is spacious and
features special events and live music
on an irregular basis.

Y **At Random** (414-481-8030), 2501
South Delaware Avenue, Bay View.
Open 7–bar time Tuesday through Saturday. A novelty bar, straight out of the
'60s, where the staff does not serve
beer or wine, but only specialty ice-
cream drinks or beverages they set on
fire—that sort of thing. Booths are
cozy, the room is dark, and At Random
only takes cash, so come prepared.
And don't eat too much before you
come, because a giant Grasshopper is
kind of like a meal.

Walker's Point
Walker's Point is the latest neighborhood touched by the condo building
craze, which means it's also seen a
blooming of businesses, including bars.
The variety of bars here has always
been great—while not a gay district
per se, because there have always been
plenty of, well, non-gay bars here, it's
been home to the city's gay and lesbian
bars for ages. New hotspots of all ori-
entations pop up all the time, these are
but a few.

Y & ▼ **Walker's Pint** (414-643-7468;
walkerspint.com), 818 South Second

Street. Open nightly. This is one of Milwaukee's only lesbian bars—there's not much else. With the sassy tagline "Lock up your daughters," Walker's Pint has a sense of humor but is in no way exclusionary—everyone is welcome, but this neighborhood pub is an especially safe spot for lesbians. There's frequent live music, plus karaoke on Wednesdays.

Y & ▼ **La Cage** (414-383-8330; lacagemke.com), 801 South Second Street. Open nights Wednesday through Saturday. Known as Wisconsin's largest and oldest gay dance club, it's fun for anybody who likes to boogie down. Friday nights feature fish fry and a drag show.

Y **Bryant's Cocktail Lounge** (414-383-2620; bryantscocktaillounge.com), 1579 South Ninth Street. Open 5–2 Tuesday through Saturday, 8–2 Sunday. This retro lounge prides itself on a huge list of cocktails, none of them written down. You don't get to look at a drink menu, because it doesn't have one. Instead, the staff happily helps you figure out what you want, even if you've never heard of the drink before. These are old-fashioned drinks, to be sure, and maybe you'll find a new favorite.

Y **Holler House** (414-647-9284), 2042 West Lincoln Avenue. Open nightly. There are a lot of places to bowl in Milwaukee, many of them more family friendly than this, but if you're looking for something a little different, this is it. Opened in 1908, Holler House is primarily just a bar, but it's got the oldest certified bowling lanes in the nation, and bras on the ceiling left by patrons. In the basement, two lanes and a real, live, pinsetter await.

✳ Selective Shopping

& **The Spice House** (414-272-0977; thespicehouse.com), 1031 North Old

World Third Street. Open 9–6 Monday through Friday, 9–5 Saturday, noon–4 Sunday. Old World Third Street might be called a little slice of culinary heaven, and the Spice House is certainly at home here. You can smell this store from down the block. With spices you never even knew existed, serious cooks and amateurs alike delight in the variety available. The folks who work here are happy to educate, and the spices are ground fresh. If you never dreamed you could find five kinds of paprika or 23 kinds of salt in one place, stop in. The Spice House holds cooking classes and special events as well.

& **Usinger's Famous Sausage** (414-276-9105; usinger.com), 1030 North Old World Street. Open 8:30–5 Monday through Saturday. You didn't think I'd skip the sausage, did you? While Milwaukeeans tire of being associated with brats and wieners, it's an undeniable fact that sausage plays a part in the city's cultural background. It's also true that a beer-soaked brat grilled on a sunny day and washed down with more beer will please your tummy and make you root for the Brewers. Stop in Usinger's historic downtown store, where they've made the famous sausage since 1880. You can't tour the factory, but you can leave with knackwurst, yachtwurst, pork butt, and headcheese, plus tamer varieties of sausage and brats.

Hot Pop (414-273-1301; hotpopshop .com), 213 North Broadway Street. Open 11–7 Tuesday through Saturday, noon–5 Sunday. This is the best place in town to pick up urban vinyl toys, skater apparel, design books, and other fun stuff. The shop also functions as an art gallery, showing work by local artists and regularly hosting events.

Sparrow Collective Gallery (414-747-9229; sparrowcollective.etsy.com). 2224 South Kinnickinnic Avenue.

Open noon–7 Tuesday through Saturday, noon–5 Sunday. This is the retail outlet of a local fashion collective. You'll find the coolest, most unique gifts here—all handmade by local and national artists. While the collective focuses on apparel, the shop carries other arts and crafts, such as pottery and home decor.

Fashion Ninja (481-3865; fashion ninja.com), 315 North Plankinton Drive. Open Thursday through Sunday. In 2003, owner/designer Areka Ikeler opened a little sewing school and boutique in Bay View, cementing her place among Milwaukee's DIY pioneers. These days she's got a bigger shop in the Third Ward, and also hosts a market for fashion designers of all types several times a year. Her style is unique and her handmade, one-of-a-kind clothing is surprisingly affordable.

Garden Room (414-963-1657; www .gardenroomonline.com), 2107 East Capitol Drive, Shorewood. Open 10–6 Tuesday through Friday, 10–5 Saturday and Sunday. Shorewood's "urban garden center" offers plenty of unique gifts and garden accessories to please any homebody. It's the perfect place to

find a special present, or just browse. When you're done shopping, head downstairs to the Anaba Tea Room (see Eating Out) for a sandwich.

&. ☂ **Green Gallery East** (414-226-1978; thegreengallery.biz), 1500 North Farwell Avenue. Open 4–8 Thursday and Friday, 2–6 Saturday and Sunday. New in 2009, this second location opened after four years of success with Riverwest's Green Gallery West (the-greengallery.tk), 631 East Center Street. Both locations are focused on brainy, contemporary art.

&. ☂ **Portrait Society Gallery** (414-870-9930; portraitsocietygallery.word press.com), 207 East Buffalo Street, Suite 526. Open 1–4 Friday and Saturday. As the name suggests, this Third Ward Gallery is focused on portraiture, both historical and contemporary. The works are impressive; sometimes straightforward, sometimes challenging, but always worth a look.

Moda3 (414-273-3333; moda3.com), 320 East Buffalo Street. Open 10–8 Monday through Friday. Billing itself as a "lifestyle shop," Moda3 is really a super hip skate/snowboarder's shop with clothing, winter gear, and trinkets to match. The staff is friendly and knowledgeable, and they won't call you out for being a poseur.

Goldi (414-961-9200), 4114 North Oakland Avenue, Shorewood. Open 10–6 Monday through Friday, noon–5 Saturday and Sunday. At 10,000 square feet, Goldi is bigger than your typical boutique, but every item in the store is just as unique and exceptional as those at smaller specialty shops. Girly to the core, Goldi is known for its fabulous selection of shoes and handbags, but the designer clothing will suit fashion-conscious girls and women. There's a wonderful selection of gifts and trinkets, plus plenty of jewelry and cosmetics to boot. There's a lot of

HOT POP BOUTIQUE AND GALLERY

boutique shopping on this strip in Shorewood, but Goldi should kick off your spree.

Chartreuse (414-747-8434), 2227 South Kinnickinnic Avenue. Open 11–7 Wednesday through Saturday, noon–5 Sunday. Focusing squarely on eco-friendly items, this Bay View shop carries everything from bamboo skirts to recycled laptop bags. The style is hip and friendly, with designer-level price tags and quality.

Olive Fine Organic Living (262-241-8068; oliveorganic.org), 10910 North Port Washington Road, Mequon. Open 10–8 Monday through Friday, 10–7 Saturday and Sunday. Offering a complete upscale boutique focused on organic clothing, Olive is a unique green shopping experience. The construction materials were repurposed, even, and the focus of the entire business is environmentally friendly, but don't mistake it for a hippie shop—this is upscale organic clothing.

Milwaukee Public Market (414-289-3107; milwaukeepublicmarket.org), 400 North Water Street. Open 10–8 Monday through Friday, 8–6 Saturday, 10–6 Sunday. A welcome and fun addition to Milwaukee's Third Ward, the Milwaukee Public Market is a great shopping and dining hotspot year-round. Featuring loads of Milwaukee- and Wisconsin-made products, the market serves the downtown area, but offers visitors a great opportunity to load up on local foods.

U.S. Science and Surplus (414-541-7777; sciplus.com), 6901 West Oklahoma Avenue. Open daily. This store, with bin after bin of unusual science-related item, is bizarre and fun. Get buzzers, electrical parts, beakers, tiny bottles, corks, obsolete flashbulbs—really, what are you looking for? Perfect for off-the-deep-end science

projects, kids will go crazy here, as will certain adults.

Art Smart's Dart Mart & Juggling Emporium (414-273-3278; juggling supplies.net), 1695 North Humboldt Avenue. Open 10–6 Monday through Friday, 9–5 Saturday, 11–5 Sunday. Maybe you've never wondered where to go for juggling supplies, but if you have, this is the place. Sitting proudly on the corner of Humboldt and Brady since 1985, Art Smart's has all manner of juggling goodies, including fire staffs in case you're that good, plus a variety of novelties ranging from whoopie cushions to rubber chickens. It also stocks ultimate Frisbee discs and more.

George Watts & Son (414-290-5700; georgewatts.com), 761 North Jefferson Street. Open 9–5:30 Monday through Friday, 9–5 Saturday. Selling china, tableware, and crystal you just won't find in area department stores, it's the perfect place to shop for a wedding gift or browse for yourself. Selling gifts since 1870, George Watts is a Milwaukee institution.

Loop Yarn Shop (414-265-2312; loopyarnshop.com), 2963 North Humboldt Boulevard. Open 10–7 Tuesday through Friday, 10–5 Saturday and Sunday. A knitters' heaven in Riverwest, Loop is a friendly, young store for the local DIY crowd, carrying more yarn than a cat would know what to do with.

✍ **Sprout** (414-289-0844; sproutmilwaukee.com), 320 East Buffalo Street. Open daily. Sprout offers a selection of adorable, designer kid's clothing and unique toys, including many European and hard-to-find items. Worth a visit if you've got little ones to shop for.

✍ **Freckle Face** (414-298-1488; frecklefaceboutique.com), 244 North Broadway. Open 10–6 Tuesday through Saturday, noon–4 Sunday. This

Third Ward shop carries all manner of adorable—and pricy—kid's clothing. It's hard to get away without dropping some cash.

Crate and Barrel (414-258-9500; crateandbarrel.com), 2450 North Mayfair Road. Open daily. Wisconsin's only Crate and Barrel is just outside the Mayfair Mall. It's fun to browse the modern furniture and all the stylish home furnishings and knickknacks in this bit of shopping heaven.

Artasia (414-220-4292; artasiagallery .com), 181 North Broadway Avenue. Open daily. With a huge selection of Asian imports from Tibet, Southeast Asia, Mongolia, Nepal, and China, Artasia crams countless items into its 14,000-square-foot shop. The museum here features more than 1,200 Chinese folk statues.

Broadway Paper (414-277-7699; broadwaypaper.com), 191 North Broadway Avenue. Open 11–7 Monday through Friday, 10–5 Saturday. This is a surprisingly huge store stocking nothing but specialty paper—great for brides and crafters. The selection ranges from designer stationery to eco-friendly papers and just about every paper good you can think of.

BOOKSTORES Woodland Pattern (414-263-5001; woodlandpattern.org), 720 East Locust Street. Open 11–8 Tuesday through Friday, noon–5 Saturday and Sunday. Not your typical bookstore, Woodland Pattern specializes in small press offerings, poetry, and contemporary literature. Priding itself on being able to find any book a customer didn't even know he wanted, Woodland Pattern is, hands down, the place to go for edgier reading material. The bookstore also has a large number of authors in for readings (over the years it's hosted Allen Ginsberg, Laurie Anderson, and Amiri Baraka, to name

a few), and features contemporary art in the gallery.

Boswell Books (414-332-1181; boswellandbooks.blogspot.com), 2559 North Downer Avenue. Open 10–9 Monday through Saturday, 10–5 Sunday. When Harry Schwartz Book Shops closed for good in March 2009, it sent a shockwave through the community. Even non-readers were stunned that all four stores in the chain were gone; after all, the bookshop had been around since 1927, and no one had seen it coming. There was a collective sigh of relief, however when it was announced that two of the stores would reopen under new management. Boswell Books jumped right in, opening mere days after Schwartz shut down, and it has been hosting events left and right. The store offers general titles, kid's books, regional works, and more.

Next Chapter Books (262-241-6220; nextchapterbookshop.com), 10976 North Port Washington Road, Mequon. Open 10–8 Monday through Friday, 9–8 Saturday, 10–5 Sunday. Next Chapter Books is another one that picked up where Harry Schwartz left off, carrying general titles, kid's books, and more.

Downtown Books (414-276-5330; downtownbooksonline.com), 327 East Wisconsin Avenue. Open daily. Three floors of used books, comics, magazines, and more will keep you busy for quite a while. It's huge, labyrinthine, patchwork, and a little off, just the way a used bookstore should be.

SHOPPING MALLS There are numerous malls around Milwaukee, but my favorite is the **Bayshore Town Center** (414-332-5304; bayshoretown center.com), 5900 North Port Washington Road, Glendale. Newly rehabbed and built as its own little community, Bayshore sort of has the feel of shopping in a downtown area. Mayfair Mall and Brookfield Square are good options, too, with some of the better stores (like Macy's at Mayfair). Downtown's Shops of Grand Avenue is cool because of its location and use of rehabbed buildings, but the store selection leaves something to be desired and it closes early. Still, it's worth a walk through.

✳ Special Events

Among Milwaukee's many nicknames is "City of Festivals," and with good reason: The lakefront is home to a different festival each weekend throughout the summer. Those are the really big ones; there are countless other festivals scattered throughout the area, including popular church festivals, neighborhood street festivals, and other smaller events. The Wisconsin State Fair is held in Milwaukee, as is the celebration of Harley-Davidson's anniversary, punctuated by the motorcycles' famous rumbling sound throughout the city. Most of the major ethnic festivals are held at Henry Maier Festival Park (200 North Harbor Drive) on the lakefront, more commonly known as the Summerfest Grounds. Follow the smiley faces on highway signs, or jump on a shuttle running for the largest fests.

February: **Greater Milwaukee Auto Show**, Midwest Airlines Center. Check out hundreds of cars at this popular annual event.

March: **Indian Summer Festivals Winter Pow Wow** (414-604-1000; indiansummer.org), Wisconsin State Fair Park. See a powwow and enjoy traditional foods and the Indian market.

Annual St. Patrick's Day Parade Milwaukee's got a rich Irish heritage, which means it does like to party on St. Patrick's Day. That doesn't mean, however, that the parade is held on the 17th—be sure to check for the exact date. More than 100 participants make this a great parade.

May: **RiverSplash!** (414-297-9855; riversplash.com), Pere Marquette Park. This free three-day festival has long marked the unofficial start of summer in Milwaukee. From here on out, there's a major festival almost every weekend until fall.

June: **PrideFest** (414-645-3378; pridefest.com), Henry Maier Festival Park. The state's largest LGBT festival is fun for everyone, and the festival routinely brings in big-name acts to entertain the crowds.

Lakefront Festival of Arts (414-224-3854; mam.org/lfoa), Milwaukee Art Museum Grounds. Nearly 200 artists participate in this spectacular juried art show outside the Milwaukee Art Museum. A bonus is free admission to the museum with your ticket.

SUMMERTIME TUNES

While Summerfest and the other major festivals on the lakefront may get all the attention, Milwaukee's got fabulous—and free—outdoor music events all summer long. You'll find free concerts in various parks, coffee shops, and other venues, but the most celebrated free summer events are River Rhythms, held Wednesdays at 6:30 PM throughout summer in Pere Marquette Park, and Jazz in the Park, held Thursdays at 6:30 PM June through August in Cathedral Square Park. Don't stop at these, though. There's a free concert every summer night somewhere at a Milwaukee County park.

Polish Fest (414-529-2140; polishfest
.org), Henry Maier Festival Park. The
largest Polish festival in the U.S. features everything you'd want—polka
dancing, peirogis, and sausage!

Summerfest (414-273-FEST; summer
fest.com), Henry Maier Festival Park.
Held late June and early July, Summerfest is billed as the world's largest
music festival. With hundreds of acts
on 11 stages over 11 days, it's no wonder the city goes bonkers this time
each year.

July: **U.S. Bank Fireworks** (800-231-
0903; county.milwaukee.gov), Veteran's
Park. Milwaukee's official Fourth of
July fireworks are always held on the
3rd of July, unless the weather doesn't
cooperate. Get your spot early—half a
million people head toward the lakefront each year to watch the display.
Bastille Days (414-271-1416; east
town.com), Cathedral Square. Bastille
Days, celebrating French culture, benefits from the fact that it's an actual
street festival and it's free. Enjoy wandering mimes, accordion players, giant
puppets on stilts, and fresh beignets in
downtown Milwaukee. **Greek Fest**
(800-884-FAIR annunciationwi.com),
Wisconsin State Fair Park. Once held
on the grounds of Annunciation Greek
Orthodox Church, the popular, and
free, festival moved to State Fair Park
in 2006 to better accommodate the
crowds. **South Shore Frolics** (414-
671-4712; countyparks.com), South
Shore Park. Spanning three days, this
festival is fun and small—more on the
order of a neighborhood festival. **Festa
Italiana** (414-223-2193; festaitaliana
.com), Henry Maier Festival Park.
Sample Italian foods, take a gondola
ride, and enjoy live music at one of
Milwaukee's favorite ethnic festivals.
The nightly fireworks are the best of
the summer. **German Fest** (414-464-
9444; germanfest.com), Henry Maier

Festival Park. German beer, schnitzel,
polka, and guys in lederhosen make
the experience. Milwaukee's proud
German heritage comes to life for four
days every July.

August: **Wisconsin State Fair** (414-
266-7000; wistatefair.com), Wisconsin
State Fair Park. The state fair is a great
place to learn more about Wisconsin's
agricultural heritage. It's also a great
place to people watch, and stuff your
face with the fair's famous cream puffs,
as well as the countless foodstuffs on
sticks. There's live music throughout
the 11- day fair, and countless other
entertainment options.

Arab World Festival (414-727-5517;
arabworldfest.com), Henry Maier Festival Park. When else will you get to
ride a camel in Milwaukee? Arab
World Festival is a little under-attend-
ed, but it's a dream come true for fans
of falafel and baklava. Traditional
music and dancing, as is customary at
all the city's ethnic festivals, make this
one fun.

Irish Fest (414-476-3378; irishfest
.com), Henry Maier Festival Park.
Another extremely popular event, this
four-day festival is full of red hair and
freckles, and plenty of Irish dancing
music—including lessons. Irish food
isn't typically festival-friendly, but
you'll find stew, shepherd's pie, corned
beef, and many, many potatoes.

Mexican Fiesta (414-383-7066;
mexicanfiesta.org), Henry Maier Festival Park. This celebration of Mexican
culture began as a street festival in the
'70s, but grew so large it needed to
move to its present location.

September: **Indian Summer Festival**
(414-774-6810; indiansummer.org),
Henry Maier Festival Park. A celebration of Wisconsin's Native American
culture, there's everything you'd expect
in a festival, plus traditional foods, a

powwow, and more at this three-day festival.

Oktoberfest (414-964-0300; bavarian innmilw.com/events/Oktoberfest.htm), Heidelburg Park, Glendale. This three-day festival has been held at Heidelburg Park, next to the **Bavarian Inn**, for years, and features everything you'd expect: sausage, beer, and polka. Following German tradition, Oktoberfest in Wisconsin takes place in September.

November: **Holiday Lights Festival** (414-220-4700; milwaukeedowntown .com), downtown Milwaukee. Three downtown parks light up with a dazzling display and a new theme each year.

Holiday Folk Fair International (414-225-6225; wiexpocenter.com), Wisconsin State Fair Park. More than 50 cultures are represented at this fair, which features food, crafts, and music from around the world.

Holiday Parade (414-262-377-5935; milwaukeeparade.com), downtown Milwaukee. Bundle up and head downtown to see this annual parade, featuring dozens of bands, huge balloons, local personalities, and the big guy—Santa.

Beyond Milwaukee

LAKE COUNTRY AND
NORTH OF MILWAUKEE

Waukesha, Washington, Dodge, Ozaukee,
and Jefferson Counties

RACINE AND KENOSHA

WALWORTH COUNTY

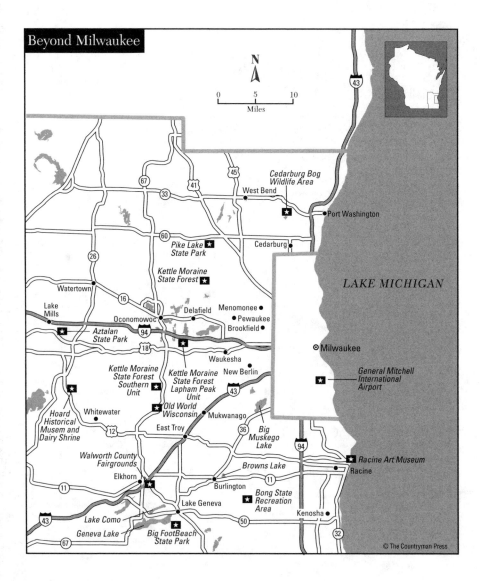

Beyond Milwaukee

N

0   5   10
Miles

Cedarburg Bog
Wildlife Area

West Bend

Port Washington

Cedarburg

Pike Lake
State Park

Kettle Moraine
State Forest

LAKE MICHIGAN

Watertown

Lake
Mills

Delafield

Menomonee

Oconomowoc

Pewaukee
Brookfield

Aztalan
State Park

Milwaukee

Waukesha

Kettle Moraine
State Forest
Southern
Unit

Kettle Moraine
State Forest
Lapham Peak
Unit

New Berlin

General Mitchell
International
Airport

Old World
Wisconsin

Mukwanago

Hoard
Historical
Musem and
Dairy Shrine

Whitewater

East Troy

Big
Muskego
Lake

Walworth County
Fairgrounds

Browns Lake

Racine Art Museum

Elkhorn

Burlington

Bong State
Recreation
Area

Racine

Lake Geneva

Kenosha

Lake Como

Geneva Lake

Big FootBeach
State Park

© The Countryman Press

LAKE COUNTRY AND
NORTH OF MILWAUKEE

WAUKESHA, WASHINGTON, DODGE, OZAUKEE AND JEFFERSON COUNTIES

While Milwaukee may be the cultural and economic hub of Southeastern Wisconsin, its surrounding areas, rich with forestland, glacial lakes, hiking trails, and ubiquitous farmland, provide a much more typical look at the state. The counties outside Milwaukee that make up the Southeastern Wisconsin area are home to a wide range of functions; industrial Kenosha and Racine are cities in their own right, Lake Geneva is a storied resort town minutes from Milwaukee, and the remaining counties—Waukesha, Washington, Dodge, Ozaukee, and Jefferson—at once provide rural escape, historic charm, and abundant outdoor activities. The difference is stark, so remember this: A visit to Milwaukee does not mean sacrificing the small-town appeal of Wisconsin. Indeed, you can have it all, and on a single tank of gas to boot.

There are so many things that make Southeastern Wisconsin a unique place to visit. Here, the mark of the Ice Age is clearly visible; this corner of the state lies in the glaciated area, home to varied geography and plentiful lakes, which sit in kettles left behind by the melting Green Bay Lobe when the Ice Age ended. Kettle Moraine State Forest is in this region, as is the Horicon Marsh, and both are wonderful examples of the wildly differing local landscape, courtesy of the glaciers. Geneva Lake (as it is properly called, rather than Lake Geneva, which we call the town) is among the area's largest inland lakes.

Beyond Milwaukee, too, the footprint of Wisconsin's many native cultures is more readily apparent. Aside from the Native American names given to many towns and counties in this area, such as Oconomowoc, Kenosha, Ozaukee, Pewaukee, and, of course, Milwaukee, there are visible reminders of the region's roots, too. In Milwaukee, this history has been somewhat obscured by development and post-settlement heritage; as you head away from the city, you'll find effigy mounds and some archeological preservation, although it's nothing compared to the tribal lands Northern Wisconsin. In fact, the only tribal land in Southeastern Wisconsin is Potawatomi Casino in Milwaukee. But head to Washington County, and you'll find the largest collection of preserved effigy mounds in the state, built during the

Woodland period. In Jefferson, Aztalan State Park, with its pyramid-shaped mounds, is a reminder of Mississippian culture here. What remains in this area is token, at best, when you consider the rich cultures of Wisconsin's native people, who hunted, fished, and farmed the land long before European settlers arrived. But the history is there, and you'll find stories in each town you visit.

Driving to the country, there are numerous historic districts, with buildings dating back to the 1800s and plenty of small-town charm. You'll also be able to get your hands on farm-fresh foods, pick strawberries, take hay-rides, and generally enjoy what rural Wisconsin is all about.

Lake Country and North of Milwaukee: Waukesha, Washington, Dodge, Ozaukee and Jefferson Counties

Sometimes considered suburbs of Milwaukee, these counties are perfect for short day trips while visiting Brew City, but the abundance of parks, historical sites, and charming shopping districts make them great destinations on their own (if you need a little more concrete, you can always make the short trip into Milwaukee). You get state forests and parks, many small lakes, and an abundance of rural charm without leaving the city far behind.

Just west of Milwaukee, Waukesha in many ways functions as part of the metro area, but its reach into more rural regions (or what used to be more rural regions—the metro area continues to creep outward) keeps it distinct from the city. Muskego, here, is home to three lakes, while Oconomowoc, once largely farmland, is quickly growing, but still retains its small-town atmosphere. Waukesha can be confusing to navigate; its suburban setup circling a historic downtown district can head you off in wrong directions if you're not paying close attention.

WISCONSIN WELCOMES YOU

Cedarburg, north of Milwaukee in Ozaukee County, is perhaps the region's
favorite little shopping destination. Close to 150 shops crowd the scenic downtown
area, the entirety of which is listed on the National Register of Historic Places.
The 19th—century buildings alone are a draw, but the shops and restaurants keep
you occupied all day long. Several times a year, Washington Avenue gets crowded
as lively festivals get underway.

Shopping, though, is good in any of the towns' historic districts; they are packed
full of art galleries, antique stores, boutiques, and other indie shops that will have
your wallet empty in no time. Throughout the entire Southeastern Wisconsin
region, there are stunning parks, forests, and unique attractions that beckon travelers to venture beyond the 'burbs and more.

GUIDANCE The **Waukesha and Pewaukee Convention and Visitors Bureau**
(262-542-0330; visitwaukesha.org), N14 W23755 Stone Ridge Drive, Suite 225,
Waukesha, publishes a visitor's guide annually, available at kiosks throughout the
area as well as online, as does the **Washington County Convention and Visitors
Bureau** (262-677-5069; www.visitwashingtoncounty.com), 3000 Highway County
Highway PV, West Bend. **Ozaukee County Tourism** (800-403-9898; www
.ozaukeetourism.com) offers information on the county, but the **Cedarburg
Chamber of Commerce** (262-377-5856; cedarburg.org), W61 N480 Washington
Avenue, right downtown in the General Store Museum, offers up detailed infor-
mation on the shopping district.

GETTING THERE Waukesha lies right on Interstate 94, just west of Milwaukee,
and is an easy find once you're on the highway. Jefferson County is just west of
Waukesha on I-94. US 151 heads north into Dodge County from the west, from
there take WI 33 east to get into Horicon. If you're traveling to Horicon from
Green Bay or Milwaukee, take US 41, then head east on WI 33. US 45 and US 41
run through Washington County. To get to Cedarburg from the south, take I-43 to
County Highway C (Exit 89), then turn north on Washington Avenue. From the
north, take I-43 south to WI 60, then travel west to the "five corners" intersection;
this becomes Washington Avenue. To reach Port Washington, take I-43.

GETTING AROUND Your best bet for getting around is in a car, but if you're
without wheels, the **Waukesha County Transit** (262-524-3636; www.waukesha
metro.org) operates limited service in Waukesha. There is no bus service to Cedarburg, though the **Ozaukee County Express** (414-344-6711; ozaukeetransit.com)
does travel between Milwaukee and a handful of commuter park-and-ride lots
along I-43 in Ozaukee County. You can connect up with the likes of **Amtrak** and
Greyhound in downtown Milwaukee. The historic downtown districts are made
for walking.

MEDICAL EMERGENCY Call 911.

Waukesha Memorial Hospital (262-928-1000), 725 American Avenue.

Oconomowoc Memorial Hospital (262-569-9400), 791 Summit Avenue,
Oconomowoc.

Community Memorial Hospital (262-251-1000), W180 N8085 Town Hall Road,
Menomonee Falls.

Aurora Medical Center (262-673-2300), 1032 East Sumner Street, Hartford.

Watertown Memorial Hospital (920-261-4210), 125 Hospital Drive, Watertown.

Fort Memorial Hospital (920-568-5000), 611 Sherman Avenue East, Fort Atkinson.

Columbia-St. Mary's Ozaukee Campus (262-243-7300), 13111 North Port Washington Road, Mequon.

✳ To See and Do

In Waukesha

✑ ♿ **Old World Wisconsin** (262-594-6300; oldworldwisconsin.org), S103 W37890 WI 67, Eagle. Open daily May through October. Each year, travelers, locals, families, and school groups make the trip to Eagle to see what is called the world's largest rural history museum. More than 60 historic buildings from around the state were moved here to create the museum, which celebrates the ethnic backgrounds of the state's settlers. Your onsite dining option fits right in with the museum—it's a cafeteria in the octagonal Clausing Barn serving rustic foods such as Yankee pot roast. Adults $16, children 5–17 $9, children younger than 5 free.

♿ ☂ **Ten Chimneys** (262-968-4110; tenchimneys.org), S43 W31575 Depot Road, Genessee Depot. Tours Tuesday through Saturday, May through November. Once the home of theater actors Alfred Lunt and Lynn Fontaine, here the couple welcomed guests such as Katherine Hepburn and Laurence Olivier into the 1960s. These days, you don't need a special invitation to tour this national landmark, and trained docents guide you through. Built in the 1920s, the estate has been carefully restored and retains the Lunts' personal furnishings and artifacts. The name Ten Chimneys comes from the number of chimneys on the estate; there are six on the main house. Admission $28–35.

In Washington

♿ **Holy Hill National Shrine of Mary, Help of Christians** (262-628-1838; holyhill.com), 1525 Carmel Road, Hubertus. Located atop the highest point in Southeastern Wisconsin, Holy Hill draws not only Catholics, but all manner of visitors who want to gaze out at the Milwaukee skyline as well as all points around the area from the observation tower. Like all national shrines, there's a place of worship here (the basilica), stations of the cross, a gift shop, restaurant, and more, all in a tranquil setting.

Lizard Mound County Park, 2121 County Highway A, Farmington. Just north of West Bend, this park contains the largest group of effigy mounds in the state. Of an original 60, 28 remain intact. Built between 500 and 1000 A.D., the mounds depict animals and mythical creatures; the largest is the lizard mound for which the park is named. A footpath travels most of them, and markers describe what is known of the history of the builders, who were long gone by the time European settlers arrived.

♿ ☂ **Wisconsin Automotive Museum** (262-673-7999; wisconsinautomuseum .com), 147 North Rural Street, Hartford. Open 10–5 Monday through Friday, noon–5 Saturday; closed Monday and Tuesday in winter. Featuring cars and other artifacts exploring the auto industry in Wisconsin, plus around 90 old-timey cars, this is a museum for every car buff. An added attraction is the foray into trains: There's a 250-ton locomotive on display here, as well as a Lionel Train set up. Free.

♂ & ♈ ❀ **Museum of Wisconsin Art** (262-334-1151; wisconsinart.org), 300 South Sixth Street, West Bend. Open 10–4:30 Wednesday, 1–4:30 Saturday. This museum is dedicated to the preservation and display of Wisconsin-made art, from 1800 to the present, and has an archive of more than 6,000 files, and a rotating exhibit of current Wisconsin artists. The museum also features special events, including the works of local filmmakers, classes, and more. In 2010, it gets new digs—a modern, 32,000-square-foot building in its present spot. Adults $5, children younger than 12 free.

In Jefferson

♈ & ♈ **Tyranena Brewing Company** (920-648-8699; tyranena.com), 1025 Owen Street, Lake Mills. Tasting room open Wednesday through Sunday, tour hours are irregular, but generally happen on Saturday. One of Wisconsin's many beloved microbreweries, you won't get these craft brews anywhere outside Wisconsin and Minnesota. Stop by the tasting room and try the Bitter Woman IPA.

& ❀ **Fort Atkinson Hoard Historical Museum and National Dairy Shrine** (920-563-7769; hoardmuseum.org), 401 Whitewater Avenue, Fort Atkinson. Open 9:30–4:30 Tuesday through Saturday, 11–3 Sunday. Closed Sunday in winter. It sounds like you'll bow down to a heifer goddess here, but really it's a dairy museum outlining the history of, well, dairy production. It's housed in the Hoard Historical Museum, which itself is interesting. Exhibits include more than 130 quilts and a bird room with more than 500 stuffed and mounted birds. Free admission.

The Octagon House (920-261-2796; watertownhistory.org), 919 Charles Street, Watertown. Open daily. Completed in 1854, this five-story brick home is a perfect example of the octagonal houses popular in the mid-19th century. Part of the Watertown Historical Society, visitors can also visit other buildings on the grounds, including the first kindergarten in the U.S. Adults $7, children 6–17 $4.

In Ozaukee

& **Cedar Creek Winery** (262-377-8020; cedarcreekwinery.com), N70 W6340 Bridge Road, Cedarburg. See Selective Shopping.

& **Wisconsin Museum of Quilts and Fiber Arts** (262-546-0300; wiquilt museum.org), N50 W5050 Portland Road, Cedarburg. Open 11–3 Wednesday through Saturday, 1–4 Sunday (call ahead to be sure.) A quilter's heaven, the museum exhibits the works of Wisconsin artists and sells fabrics and handmade goods in its boutique.

& ❀ **Cedarburg General Store Museum** (262-377-9620; cedarburgcultural center.org), W61 N480 Washington Avenue, Cedarburg. Call ahead for hours. Perhaps the most interesting location for a visitor's bureau I've found, you can grab information on the area here, but the best part is the collection of consumer artifacts, displayed to recreate the feeling of an old general store. All that nostalgic design and packaging provides a great, amusing way to kick off a day of shopping.

✳ Green Space

In Waukesha

Idle Isle Park, W182 S6666 Hardtke Drive, Muskego. This park set on a small island in Little Muskego Lake has a public beach, boat launches, and playgrounds for the kids. This park can get crowded on the weekends, so don't come here

KETTLE MORAINE STATE FOREST

Comprised of five separate units throughout southeast Wisconsin, the Southern Unit is only 37 miles from Milwaukee, and the Northern Unit is only 45 miles away. Kettle Moraine is sort of a pretty name, but it's really just very literal. Kettle and moraine are geological terms which, if you know what they mean, describe this area perfectly. Very simply put, a kettle is a hole carved out by a glacier, while a moraine is the deposit of sediment left behind. The result is a wildly varied landscape, with deposits and till left by the glacier, and kettle lakes formed when it melted. Most lakes in Southeastern Wisconsin are the result of kettles.

Lapham Peak State Park (262-646-3025; laphampeakfriends.org), W329 N846 County Highway C, Delafield. Lapham Peak was formed by glacial movement, and is the highest point in Waukesha County. Today, visitors can hike, bike, ski, and bird watch, or climb atop the 45-foot observation tower. **Kettle Moraine State Forest—Southern Unit** (414-594-6200), S91 W39091 WI 59, Eagle. Full of camps, including three family camps, a horse rider's camp, and two group camps, plus swimming beaches and trails totaling 160 miles, there's enough to do for a day or more. **Kettle Moraine State Forest—Northern Unit** (262-626-2116; www.dnr.state.wi.us/org/LAND/parks/specific/kmn/), N1765 County Highway G, Campbellsport. The Northern Unit is partially contained in Washington County, but spreads into Fond du Lac (where it's headquartered) and Sheboygan. This unit has plenty of campgrounds, swimming beaches, and hiking trails, and an observation tower. **The Pike Lake Unit** (262-670-3400; dnr.wi.gov/org/land/parks/specific/pikelake/), 3544 Kettle Moraine Road, Hartford, is smack in the middle of the kettle. It offers no campgrounds, but it's beautiful and interesting for its glacial topography; the glacial lake here (Pike Lake) is great for swimming and fishing; and a nearby kame provides opportunity for hiking, plus a great view. Nearby, the **Loew Lake Unit** offers similar opportunity. A state sticker is required. **The Ice Age National Scenic Trail** (262-691-2776; iceagetrail.org), WI 83, Delafield, runs through 30 counties in the state, following the path of the last glacier to recede. This hiking trail will cover more than 1,000 miles when complete. The trail runs through all five units of Kettle Moraine, providing both another opportunity for recreation, as well as another chance to take in the amazing mark the Ice Age made on Wisconsin.

looking for solitude. A local waterskiing club, the Muskego Waterbugs, performs here weekly during the summer.

& **Glacial Drumlin Trail** (262-646-3025; www.dnr.state.wi.us/Org/land/parks/specific/glacialdrumlin), W329 N846, County Highway C, Delafield. Running 52 miles between Waukesha County and Cottage Grove, this state trail features 13 miles of paved path, and lots of opportunity for biking and hiking. The trail is split in two sections, west and east, and there is a 1½-mile gap between the two where users must travel on public roads. Highway signs along I-94 mark entrance points to the trail. Traveling through moraines, it's another opportunity to see up close the impact of glaciation on the land. Daily state trail pass $4 (pass not needed if children younger than 16).

✆ ♿ **Retzer Nature Center** (262- 896-8007), S14 W28167 Madison Street, Waukesha. Part of the Waukesha County Park System, this park is home to trails, an education center, and the Charles Z. Horwitz Planetarium, which offers public programs regularly. In winter, ski the small trail, or rent snowshoes here and explore. Daily fee $3–5.

In Jefferson

Aztalan State Park and Museum (920-648-4632; www.dnr.state.wi.us/org/ LAND/parks/specific/aztalan/), County Highway B, Lake Mills. Considered to be Wisconsin's most important archeological site, this 172-acre park features mostly prairie land, and highlights the 12th- century Aztalan culture that once had a village here. Many of the original mounds remain; many have been restored, and parts of the stockade that surrounded the village have been reconstructed. You can panfish in the Crawfish River, but there's no boat launch.

In Ozaukee

Covered Bridge Park, 7600 Cedar Creek Road, Cedarburg. The park is a pretty place for a picnic, but it's also the location of Wisconsin's last historical covered bridge. Built in 1887, it crosses Cedar Creek and is listed on the National Register of Historic Places.

Cedarburg Bog State Natural Area, Cedar-Sauk Road. A unique wetland in this area, the bog contains six lakes and wildly varied flora and fauna. You'll see orchids and arrow-grass here, along with a great deal of peace. It's accessible by foot trails, but you'll need a canoe or kayak to get further in.

✳ Lodging

In Waukesha

♿ **The Delafield Hotel** (262-646-1600; thedelafieldhotel.com), 415 Genesee Street, Delafield. Located in historic (if sleepy) downtown Delafield, this boutique hotel modeled after turn-of-the-century architecture is at once a luxurious escape and a quiet retreat. The rooms are spacious and warmly decorated, and the king beds made up with soft linens, but the bathrooms—outfitted with Kohler multi-jet showers and televisions—are what you'll be talking about later. If you need to get work done, the business amenities are complete, but why not just come here with your sweetie? Suites $209–449.

♿ **The Clarke Hotel** (262-549-3800; theclarkehotel.com), 314 West Main Street, Waukesha. New in 2008, the Clarke Hotel occupies a city block of downtown Waukesha, itself a cute, historic part of the town. A section of the hotel once held an opera house, and today guests can stay in the six–bedroom suite there. The 21 guest rooms include a wide range of sizes, but all are luxurious and feature spa showers and soft linens. Onsite dining

HORICON MARSH

Horicon Marsh—Southern Unit (920-387-7860; dnr.wi.gov/org/land/wildlife/ wildlife_areas/horicon), N7728 Hgwy. 28, Horicon, Dodge.

Located about 45 miles northwest of Milwaukee (and, at the same time, about 45 miles northeast of Madison), Horicon Marsh is the largest freshwater cattail marsh in the United States, providing habitat for more than 290 species of birds and a rest stop for migrating birds, including Canada geese. Numbers swell into the hundreds of thousands around October as they prepare to head south, and again around April 21 as they get ready to fly north each year.

The southern third of Horicon Marsh is under the jurisdiction of the Wisconsin Department of Natural Resources, while the United States Fish and Wildlife Service manages the northern two-thirds as a National Wildlife Refuge. It is also part of the Ice Age National Scientific Reserve, which consists of nine units across the state meant to protect the glacial landscapes formed here during the Ice Age. The nine parks are connected by the Ice Age National Scenic Trail, which traces the outline of the last glacier to recede from Wisconsin. More than 1,000 miles long, this footpath serves somewhat as the boundary between the Driftless area in Southwest Wisconsin and the rest of the state.

Officially designated as a Wetland of International Importance, many visitors come here to catch a glimpse of the Canada geese, but there are plenty of other recreational and educational opportunities. Hiking, canoeing, and snowshoeing are all possibilities in the state-owned southern unit, and the northern unit features many paths for autos as well as multiple viewing areas and footpaths. The Horicon Marsh Parkway makes a 50-mile circle around the marsh and is great for a leisurely, scenic drive, or book a boat tour with Blue Heron Landing (920-485-4663; horiconmarsh.com), 311B Mill Street, to get a little closer.

includes The Black Trumpet (see Dining Out), featuring New American cuisine. Rooms $170–219.

♂ & **Country Springs Hotel** (262-547-0201; countryinnhotel.com), 2810 Golf Road, Waukesha. With a 45,000-square-foot indoor water park, this hotel is great for families (or playful adults). The decor isn't remarkable, but the rooms are clean and the suites give everyone enough room to spread

out. Free breakfast in the morning will keep everyone quiet until you're ready to explore the area. $129–189.

& **Westphal Mansion Inn** (262-673-7938; westphalmansioninn.com), 90 South Main Street, Hartford. Built in 1913, this mansion was originally the home of August Westphal, known in his day as the "cheese king." There's nothing cheesy about this bed & breakfast, though. Unfussy but charming, the rooms do suggest you're a guest in someone's home. $97–228

& **Hilton Garden Inn** (262-200-2222; hiltongardeninn.hilton.com), 1443 Pabst Farm Circle, Oconomowoc. Opened in 2007, this Hilton was one of the first businesses to open in the Pabst Farms planned community, which is still in development. Warmly decorated rooms and features such as spa tubs and onsite breakfast make this a safe choice. Nearby, there's currently a grocery store and a Starbucks, among other chains; as the development continues there should be more retail. Rooms $179–202.

In Dodge

Ⴘ & **Audubon Inn** (920-387-5858; auduboninn.jamhospitality.com), 45 North Main Street, Mayville. A winner of national awards, this historic inn is the place to stay if you're looking for a spot near Horicon Marsh. Housed on the second floor of a corner downtown building, the Audubon Inn was constructed in 1896 and functioned as a hotel until the 1970s, when it briefly became an apartment building. Nearing the 1990s, the inn was renovated, the corner turret was restored, and the building was given National Historic Landmark status. Today, the inn features 17 rooms and suites, each warm with Shaker decor, whirlpool tubs, and handmade quilts. Downstairs, the Audubon Restaurant serves dinner five days a week, and guests enjoy complimentary breakfast, while the pub offers a cozy place to relax. Rooms $120–160, suites $150–210.

& **Honeybee Inn Bed & Breakfast** (920-485-4855; honeybeeinn.com), 611 East Walnut Street, Horicon. A Victorian mansion located right in Horicon, this bed & breakfast has four rooms to choose from, each decorated in a different style, but each has a fireplace, and the Queen Bee and Country Nec-

tar both have spa tubs. Modern and romantic, you can play the piano in the common area, or surf the Web anywhere in the inn. Rooms $139–219.

In Ozaukee

& **The Washington House Inn** (262-375-3550; washingtonhouseinn.com), W62 N573 Washington Avenue, Cedarburg. Few other places in the state are so well suited to a night in a historic, antique-filled bed & breakfast, and this B&B is unique. The building, which houses 32 rooms, is a cream city brick beauty built in 1884. Each room is named after an early Cedarburg settler. The decor of most rooms runs between flowery Victorian and a calmer country style, but all of it is tasteful, and many rooms include a spa tub. For a little more legroom, try the Dr. Frederick A. Luening suite, room 222, with two rooms on different levels, connected by a spiral staircase. Located right in the historic downtown, grab breakfast first, then head out to the shops on foot. Rooms $95–275.

✳ Where to Eat

In Waukesha

& **Hartford Bistro** (262-670-9988; hartfordbistro.com), 3461 High Road, Hartford. Open for dinner Tuesday through Sunday, brunch Sunday. An authentic French bistro, owner and chef Pierre Briere cooks up everything from frog legs and snails to quiche and crepes, but the menu also offers quesadillas and burgers. Rustic and charming, it's an affordable yet classy option for dinner or brunch. $7.45–18.95.

Ⴘ & **Andrew's Bar and Restaurant** (262-646-1620; thedelafieldhotel.com/ dining/andrews.html), 415 Genesee Street, Delafield. Open for breakfast and dinner daily, lunch Monday through Saturday. A great fine-dining option in Delafield, lunch features casual options such as Thai basil chicken and Andrew's jalapeno bacon burger, but dinner is more upscale. The setting is elegant and charming. Lunch $10–20, dinner $20–40.

Ⴑ ৬ **The Black Trumpet** (262-549-3800; theclarkehotel.com), 314 West Main Street, Waukesha. Open for lunch Monday through Saturday, dinner daily, Sunday brunch. Features New American and other cuisines, with dishes such as organic Irish salmon and roasted vegetable strudel. New in 2008, this restaurant offers a unique dining experience in Waukesha. Dishes $15–30.

In Dodge

Ⴑ ৬ **The Audubon Restaurant** (262-387-5858; auduboninn.com), 45 North Main Street, Horicon. Open 5–9 Tuesday through Saturday. Although the menu tops out around $20, the options are more upscale than you might expect with dishes like lobster ravioli and grilled salmon, but don't worry about dressing up. White tablecloths and beautiful stained glass aside, you can come after a day at the Horicon Marsh. Dishes $13–22.

In Washington

৬ **Cafe Soeurette** (262-338-2233; cafe-soeurette.com), 111 North Main Street, West Bend. A charming French bistro in downtown West Bend, the menu has many creative and unique dishes, such as the maple beet salad or pecan tilapia. There are French standards here (like the croque monsieur), as well as more American dishes. In summer, dine outside on the garden patio. Lunch $7–11, dinner $14–24.

EATING OUT

In Waukesha

৬ **Machine Shed Restaurant** (262-523-1322; machineshed.com/

restaurants/pewaukee.asp), N14 W24145 Tower Road, Pewaukee. Open daily for all three meals. This small Midwestern chain has six restaurants in five states; two of those are in Wisconsin (the other is in Appleton). A farm-themed restaurant, it's not as kitschy as you might think, but it's certainly kitschy enough. The menu offers a huge selection of standard pancakes and eggs for breakfast, and lunch and dinner feature every imaginable down-home meat dish, from the Plowman's Meatloaf to the Full Pound Chicken Liver Dinner. Breakfast and lunch $7–10, $10–15.

✍ ৬ **Cafe Manna** (262-790-2340; cafemanna.com), 3815 North Brookfield Road, Brookfield. Open for lunch and dinner Monday through Saturday. A rare find in these parts, Cafe Manna is a completely vegetarian restaurant. Opened in 2007, Cafe Manna has been well received by local media and diners. Serving substantial, vegetarian food that satisfies carnivores is a feat, and Cafe Manna accomplishes it in their bright, cafe setting. Start off with the vegan pecan paté, then try the lentil loaf or Crunchy Nutty Sandwich (which comes on raw, sprouted bread) for something different. Eco-friendly serveware and fresh, organic ingredients are just the icing on the cake. Dishes $10–15.

৬ ✿ **Jimmy's Grotto** (262-542-1500; jimmysgrottopizza.com), 314 East Main Street, Waukesha. Open for lunch and dinner daily. This cash-only, casual pizza spot features loads of cheap sandwiches and tons of fried munchies, but what brings people in from near and far is the ponza rotta—a huge, greasy, deep-fried calzone. If you want to get really crazy, try the taco ponza rotta, stuffed with cheese, salsa, ground beef, and veggies. In business since 1946 (though not always at its current location), Jimmy's Grotto is one of those local places the locals wish so many people didn't know about. Dishes less than $5.

La Estacion (262-521-1986; laestacionrestaurant.com), 319 East Williams Street, Waukesha. Open 10 AM–11 PM Sunday through Thursday, 10 AM–midnight Friday and Saturday. Housed in an old train station in downtown Waukesha, La Estacion's Mexican food holds its own against Milwaukee's many well-loved spots for south-of-the-border cuisine. Festive and busy, the huge menu and unique atmosphere make this a great place for a fun dinner. Dishes $7–15.

Albanese's Roadhouse (262-785-1930; albanesesroadhouse.com), 2301 Bluemound Road, Waukesha. Open for dinner Monday through Saturday. Italian restaurant chains try to mimic the ideal of a family owned eatery that's been serving up traditional foods for generations. It's a place like Albanese's Roadhouse they're trying to emulate. This family has operated area restaurants since 1940 (the first, located on a corner in Milwaukee's Riverwest neighborhood, closed in 2008), and offers up traditional favorites in a casual, red-checkered tablecloth atmosphere. Dishes $10–20.

Delafield Brewhaus (262-646-7821; delafield-brewhaus.com), 3832 Hillside Drive, Delafield. Open for dinner Monday, lunch and dinner Tuesday through Sunday, brunch Sunday. This popular brewpub has a huge menu that includes everything anyone in your group might crave: pizza, sandwiches, pasta, steak, burgers, seafood, rotisserie chicken, ribs, German dishes—you get the idea. But don't forget why you really came here, which is beer. The restaurant always has around eight of its own craft beers on tap, and the offerings change roughly every two weeks at the whim of the brewmaster.

There's also a kid's menu available (no beer on that one, though). Lunch $8–12, dinner $8–20.

Stonefire Pizza Co. (262-970-8800; stonefirepizzaco.com), 5320 South Moorland Road, New Berlin. Open for lunch and dinner daily. It's a kiddie casino, but it's not nearly as crazy-making as some. Yes, there are arcades and play areas everywhere, and some of the dining rooms play movies—loudly—but if your children demand a day of their own, this is the place to go. They'll find plenty to do here, and the pizza buffet is much more than just 16 different kinds of tasty pizza—there's also pasta, stir fry, a salad bar, and lots of desserts. Kids $4.89–6.89, adults $9.29–12.79.

Water Street Brewery (262-646-7878; waterstreetbrewery.com), 3191 Golf Road, Delafield. Open for lunch and dinner daily, Sunday brunch. This Milwaukee brewpub brings its craft beers and casual menu to the suburbs. Like the Milwaukee location, this one features tons of beer memorabilia and a pub atmosphere, with plenty of sandwiches and American entrées to choose from. Dishes $9.95–14.95.

Sprizzo Gallery Caffé (262-513-5640; sprizzo.net), 363 West Main Street, Waukesha. Open for all three meals Monday through Saturday, breakfast and lunch Sunday. Sprizzo's looks a little like an upscale cafe, but the menu, which is quite large, keeps everything less than $10. Sandwiches rule the menu here, although there are good appetizer and salad options as well. Options run the gamut from meatloaf and braunschweiger sandwiches to the hummus veggie. Grab a cup of Alterra coffee or an Italian soda, or relax and choose from the small but decent menu of craft beers. Dishes less than $10.

SHOPPING HISTORIC DOWNTOWN CEDARBURG

The most interesting shopping in the area happens in Cedarburg, whose entire downtown is listed on the National Historic Register. The main shopping district is on Washington Avenue, which is home to more than 100 shops. Anchoring the district is Cedar Creek Settlement—a mall of sorts, but not in the traditional sense. It's the site of an old grist mill, and now contains shops, restaurants, art galleries, a winery, and more. Here is just a small sampling of what's in store for you in downtown Cedarburg.

Cedar Creek Winery (262-377-8020; cedarcreekwinery.com), N70 W6340 Bridge Road, Cedarburg. Open daily. Housed in Cedar Creek Settlement, this winery offers a popular tour and, of course, shop. Grapes are grown both at the winery's own vineyard in Wisconsin as well as out of state, allowing the house to produce a wide variety of award-winning wines.

Beerntsen's Confectionary (262-377-9512; beerntsens.com), W61 N520 Washington Avenue. Open daily. Attention, chocolate lovers: This little company, based in Manitowoc, makes fabulous chocolates and candies in all shapes and sizes. This store does not serve ice cream like the original in Manitowoc, but you should be able to find something to satisfy your sweet tooth here.

Amy's Candy Kitchen (262-376-0884; amyscandykitchen.com), W62 N579 Washington Avenue. Open 10–8 Monday through Saturday, 11–6 Sunday. The fudge is award-winning and the Belgian chocolates melty, but Amy's Gourmet Apples are what get everyone excited. The candy apples come in much more than just a simple caramel, and some are so pretty you'll have a hard time taking that first bite (but after that, you'll be fine). What's more,

In Ozaukee
Cream and Crepe Cafe (262-377-0900), N70 W6340 Bridge Road, Cedarburg. Housed in the old wool mill of Cedar Creek Settlement, this cafe has rustic charm and an outstanding selection of crepes. Lunch crepes include the Garden Bounty, loaded with veggies and cheese, and the Mill's Delight, an unusual corned beef and sauerkraut concoction. When you're done, have another crepe for dessert—some of them come with frozen custard. If for some reason you don't want a crepe, there are soups, salads, and sandwiches, too. Dishes less than $10.

COFFEE SHOPS & SWEETS

In Waukesha
& **Brewers Two Cafe** (262-513-1883; brewerstwocafe.com), 821 Meadowbrook Road, Waukesha; (262-701-4902), 203 West Wisconsin Avenue, Pewaukee. Open daily for breakfast and lunch. A cute and cozy cafe offering standard espresso drinks and bakery items, plus a few sandwiches, soups and snacks like granola and fruit, and many items are available organic. Dishes less than $10.

Amy's has an ongoing commitment to protect the environment, and all the products are certified kosher.

The Pagoda Fine Jewelry (262-376-8730), N58 W6189 Columbia Road. 10:15–6 Tuesday through Saturday, 10:15–6 Sunday. Just off Washington Avenue, and near the old mill, the Pagoda is worth a stop even if you're not interested jewelry—although you really should take a look at their one-of-a-kind offerings. Housed in a very unique, pagoda-style building constructed in 1926, it was originally used by the now-defunct Wadham's Oil and Grease Company of Milwaukee. Another such building remains in West Allis, where it functions as a very tiny museum.

Creekside Books (262-546-0004), W62 N596 Washington Avenue. Open daily. Stocking a small but complete selection of new and used books for adults and kids, this bookstore is an easy find on the main strip. Frequently hosting author events, you might find more to do here than you thought.

Downtown Dough (262-387-0311; downtowndough.com), W63 N658 Washington Avenue. Open 10–5 Monday through Saturday, noon–5 Sunday. They sell all things cookie-related here, including the dough, but what's amazing is the selection of more than 1,400 cookie-cutter shapes. If for some reason you can't find the right one, they custom-make cutters, as well.

Wisconsin Museum of Quilts and Fiber Arts (262-546-0300; wiquiltmuseum .org), N50 W5050 Portland Road, Cedarburg. Open 11–3 Wednesday through Saturday, 1–4 Sunday (call ahead to be sure). A quilter's heaven, the museum exhibits the works of Wisconsin artists and sells fabrics and handmade goods in its boutique.

&. **Divino Gelato Cafe** (262-446-9490; divinogelatocafe.com), 227 West Main Street, Waukesha. Open 11–9 Monday through Saturday, noon–9 Sunday. While hot summer days send most Milwaukeeans to a custard stand, the residents of Waukesha have artisan gelato served in a sunny downtown cafe. While the gelato is the obvious draw (for who can deny this icy Italian treat?), Divino also serves pizza, Italian beef sandwiches, espresso drinks, and more. Dishes less than $10.

Murf's Frozen Custard and Jumbo Burgers (262-547-7944), 1345 South West Avenue, Waukesha. A typical custard stand, you can get burgers, sandwiches, and all manner of fried foods here, but for a real treat, grab a couple of scoops of frozen custard. Malts, shakes, and sundaes come in more than 20 flavors. Sandwiches and custard, less than $5.

&. **The Steaming Cup** (262-522-3605; steamingcupwaukesha.com), 340 West Main Street, Waukesha. Open for breakfast and lunch daily, dinner Wednesday through Saturday. As the name suggests, this colorful cafe in downtown Waukesha specializes in piping-hot drinks from espresso to loose-leaf teas, but if you show up hungry, you won't be disappointed. It offers around 20 sandwiches, the most interesting of which is the Noodles Wrap (noodles on a sandwich? Brilliant!), which is like veggie pesto pasta you can hold in your hand. Dishes less than $10.

In Ozaukee

& **Amy's Candy Kitchen** (262-376-0884; amyscandykitchen.com), W62 N579 Washington Avenue. Open 10–9 Monday through Saturday, 11–8 Sunday. See Selective Shopping.

✳ Entertainment

In Waukesha

♪ & **Sharon Lynne Wilson Center for the Arts** (262-781-9470; wilson -center.com), 19805 West Capitol Drive, Brookfield. When it opened in 2002, this performing arts center filled a need for a major venue between Milwaukee and Madison. More than just a theater drawing national acts, there is an art gallery here, classes for kids and adults, special events throughout the year, and more.

♪ & **Sunset Playhouse** (262-782-4430; sunsetplayhouse.com), 800 North Elm Grove Road, Elm Grove. This community theatre draws an audience from Milwaukee and around the area. Running an active schedule throughout the year, the resident troupes perform for adults as well as offering children's productions. The playhouse features musical shows as well.

In Jefferson

& **Fireside Theatre** (800-477-9505; firesidetheatre.com), 1131 Janesville Avenue, Fort Atkinson. Opened in 1964, the Fireside has become one of

the area's most unique and well-loved entertainment options. Serving multi-course meals and featuring productions that target everyone from kids to baby boomers, it's an all-in-one night. Dinner choices vary, but you can always get fish fry on Friday. Tickets and dinner, $63.95 per person.

In Dodge

& **Schauer Arts and Activities Center** (262-670-0937; schauercenter.org), 147 North Rural Street, Hartford. Housed in a 1917 canning factory, this building is now home to a 571-seat theater and art gallery. The schedule is always full, with local and national acts as well as community theater and symphony.

In Ozaukee

⊤ **Cedarburg Cultural Center** (262-375-3676; cedarburgculturalcenter .org), W62 546 Washington Avenue, Cedarburg. Located right in historic downtown Cedarburg, this center includes four art galleries and a small theater that hosts local and national acts and special events throughout the year. Additionally, the center curates exhibits at local museums, including the General Store Museum (see To See and Do).

& **Cedarburg Performing Arts Center** (262-376-6162; www.cedar burgpac.com), W68 N611 Evergreen Boulevard, Cedarburg. Bringing in local and national theatrical productions, as well as music and comedy, this modern, 600-seat theater also provides space for community and school productions.

& **Silver Creek Brewing Company** (262-375-4444; silvercreekbrewing .com), N57 W6172 Portland Road, Cedarburg. Housed in the old Cedarburg Grist Mill, built in 1855 and today the heart of Cedarburg's downtown shopping district, this brewpub offers live music regularly, a heated outdoor beer garden, and a list of beers—both the pub's own and others'—that goes on and on. No food here, except for snacks like cheese and beef sticks, so make sure you have your dinner elsewhere. Open evenings Wednesday through Saturday, noon–5 Sunday.

✳ Selective Shopping

In Waukesha

✐ ও **The Elegant Farmer** (262-363-6770; elegantfarmer.com), 1545 Main Street, Mukwonago. Open 8–8 daily in summer, 8–6 daily September through May. Get all manner of muffins, jams, cookies, and more here, plus the famous apple pie, which is baked in a paper bag. It sounds dangerous, but it's good—so good, it's been called the best pie in America by the *Wall Street Journal* and *Gourmet Magazine*. Family-friendly events such as hayrides and hoedowns take place throughout the year.

ও **Books and Company** (262-567-0106; www.booksco.com), 1039 Summit Avenue, Oconomowoc. Open 9 AM–11 PM Monday through Saturday, 9–9 Sunday. An independent bookshop located in a strip mall, there's a good selection of new titles here, along with children's books and more. It's small, but complete.

ও **Half-Price Books** (262-789-0280; halfpricebooks.com), 16750 West Bluemound Road, Brookfield. Open 9 AM–10 PM Monday through Saturday, 10–8 Sunday. In a corner of a strip mall, this store's books really are half price. You can find nearly anything here, and not just books—they've got used records, DVDs, CDs, and more, plus games and gifts. The stock is always rotating, so you'll always find something new.

In Jefferson

ও **Johnson Creek Premium Outlets** (920-699-4111; premiumoutlets.com), Johnson Creek. Open 10–9 Monday through Saturday, 10–6 Sunday. Located right between Milwaukee and Madison on I-94, this outlet mall is a rare, sprawling commercial construction between fields and farmland just north of the highway. You can't miss it, nor do you want to. Sixty stores offering discounts await.

ও ✐ **Widmer's Cheese Cellars** (920-488-2503; widmerscheese.com), 214 West Henni Street, Theresa. Open 6:30–5 Monday through Friday, 7–5 Saturday. You can buy handcrafted cheese here, ranging from six-year aged cheddar to Colby and brick (they use actual bricks to make it), but the best part is the viewing area, where you can watch as the cheese is made. Don't forget to get some cheese curds.

✳ Special Events

February: **Winter Festival**, Washington Avenue, Cedarburg. About as much fun as a person can have on a cold day in February, there's a snowball tournament, ice-carving contest, chili cook-off, live music, and more.

June: **Strawberry Festival**, Washington Avenue, Cedarburg. Does it get better than a strawberry festival? If you come expecting juicy red berries in large numbers, you'll be happy. Along with strawberry wine, strawberry ice cream, and anything else that goes well with a strawberry, there's also an arts component and a plein-air painting competition. You'll more likely find me in the strawberry shortcake-eating contest, however.

July: **Port Washington Fish Day**, downtown Port Washington. Held right on the lakefront, this festival lays claim to the world's largest single-day fish fry. Port Washington pays tribute to its heritage as a once-bustling commercial fishing spot.

Gathering on the Green, Rotary Park, Cedarburg. A two-day festival celebrating music and the performing arts, this event draws people from around the area.

German Festival, Washington Avenue, Cedarburg. Newest among the Cedarburg festivals, this one's got German food, polka dancing, a lederhosen competition, a wife-carrying contest, live music and, um, outhouse races.

August: **Hartford Balloon Rally**, Hartford Airport, Hartford. A free, family friendly event features a hot-air balloon launch just before dusk.

Oconomowoc Festival of the Arts, Fowler Park, Oconomowoc. With 135 artists from around the nation showing here, this arts festival holds its own against the bigger ones. Plenty of kids' activities and fun.

September: **Wine and Harvest Festival**, Washington Avenue, Cedarburg. Mmmm . . . fall festivals always mean lots of apples, but this one's also got wine!

RACINE AND KENOSHA

There was a time when Racine suffered from a problem common in the Midwest: Rust-Belt decline combined with the unfortunate decision to abandon downtowns in favor of suburban shopping malls and office parks. After years of careful planning, though, Racine has transformed itself into a charming city, and maintained its industry at a remarkable rate. It doesn't hurt that S.C. Johnson keeps its corporate headquarters here—the company's mark is all over Racine, and it's hard to find a local who doesn't know someone who works there. That's not to say it's the only industry here; there are a number of international manufacturing companies based in Racine. But Johnson's influence is undeniable.

Reinventing itself as a tourist locale was natural for Racine. With its ideal location on Lake Michigan, 30 miles south of Milwaukee and about an hour north of Chicago, it's is a natural summer vacation spot. The downtown these days is cute and walkable, and Racine is home to one of the country's cleanest beaches and a large, beautiful marina. But it's more than just water. History buffs and Frank Lloyd Wright fans will delight in the architecture and historical buildings. Shoppers will find plenty to buy in the many boutiques the revitalized downtown now boasts, and foodies will find some of the best pizza and sinful baked goods right in the city.

The focus has turned from downtown revitalization to the arts, which makes Racine that much more special. It's not just the beautiful Racine Art Museum on the lakefront, or the annual art fairs. At present, there's a push to create an artists' community in one of the city's urban areas that's suffered from decline, where many historical buildings have been standing vacant and boarded up for years. Active recruitment of artists, with a relocation assistance program that provides help with funding through Johnson Bank and a facade grant, is underway. It's an interesting and heavily traveled place, between downtown and West Racine, with surprisingly well-preserved buildings. Watch this area over the coming years; it could be very exciting.

Immediately south of Racine is Kenosha, also an industrial town. Well, actually, it's more and more a post-industrial town. These days, it's looking more and more like a Chicago suburb. I don't think that's a bad thing, but it has really changed the cultural and physical landscape. Where once was a decaying brownfield left behind by a closed auto plant, museums, a park, shops, and new condo development now stand. The nearby downtown is flourishing with trendy restaurants and boutiques—and it's pedestrian-friendly. In many ways, Kenosha outpaces the rest of the state with its progress; increasingly, transit and smart development is becoming the norm here. Like Racine, Kenosha, too, looks very promising.

GUIDANCE **Racine County Convention and Visitors Bureau** (262-884-6400; racine.org), 14015 Washington Avenue, Sturtevant. Located at the intersection of I-94 and County Highway 20, this Frank Lloyd Wright-inspired building opened in 2000 and provides free WiFi to visitors. Racine's *Journal Times* (262-634-3322; journaltimes.com) is a typical medium-sized city newspaper, and you'll quickly find out what's concerning the locals by scanning the front section. The Web site is fairly good, and it's a good place to find things to do. Otherwise, Racine largely relies on Milwaukee television, radio, and alternative papers for information.

The Kenosha Convention and Visitors Bureau (262-654-7303; kenoshacvb .com), 812 56th Street, is just west of downtown adjacent to the library, on the streetcar route.

GETTING THERE *By Car:* Racine is located just south of Milwaukee on the shores of Lake Michigan. Take I-94 to exit 333. Just south on I-94 is Kenosha.

By Bus: Greyhound (greyhound.com) makes a stop in Racine along I-94, but you'll need some other transit to get into town. In Kenosha, it stops at the Metra station, 5414 13th Avenue, where you can pick up a streetcar or city bus.

By Train: Like Greyhound, Amtrak stops in Racine, but there's no ticketing office or actual station, and from there you'll need transportation into town. The Chicago Metra Union Pacific North Line (metrarail.com) makes its last stop in Kenosha, and from there you can hop on a streetcar to get to the lakefront, a city bus, or a Greyhound. On the horizon are connector trains and high-speed rail for the Kenosha-Racine-Milwaukee corridor, but it's not a sure bet yet.

GETTING AROUND Downtown Racine is a doable walking area, but to get there you'll want a car. There is a local bus called the **Belle Urban System** (262-

KENOSHA ELECTRIC STREETCAR

637-9000; racinetransit.com), but it's by no means exceptional. When you're traveling in Racine, it's good to know both the state highway name and street name for main routes, as locals use them interchangeably. Here's your translation: Washington Avenue is WI 20; Northwestern Avenue is WI 38; Douglas Avenue is WI 32; Green Bay Road is WI 31; Durand Avenue is WI 11.

Functionally, the communities in Racine County east of I-94 comprise a unified metro area. This includes the city of Racine, Sturtevant, Mount Pleasant, Caledonia, Franksville, North Bay, and Wind Point. These communities share a school system, bus system, and are simply, physically, closer to one another. I don't generally make a distinction between these communities as they are very much tied together, and when someone says, "Racine," this is the area they mean.

Kenosha's bus system is operated by the city (262-653-4290; kenosha.org/depart ments/transportation/index.html), and runs 10 routes, including two that travel to the universities. For a fun trip around the downtown, hop on a refurbished vintage streetcar. They loop through the Harbor Park area and, while they won't get you very far, it's a lot of fun for a quarter. If you're driving in Kenosha, you'll be happy to learn that the city's layout is on a grid—none of the crazy winding streets and one-ways you'll find in Racine and Milwaukee. More, the streets are all numbered. All you need to know is that numbered streets go east-west, and numbered avenues go north-south. Keep that straight, and you'll never get lost.

MEDICAL EMERGENCY Call 911.

Wheaton Franciscan All Saints (262-687-4011), 3801 Spring Street, Racine. You might hear locals refer to this as St. Mary's Hospital; in any case, it's the only hospital in Racine that handles emergencies.

United Hospital System Kenosha Medical Center Campus (262-656-2202), 6308 Eighth Avenue.

✳ To See and Do

ART MUSEUMS

In Racine

&. **Racine Art Museum** (262-638-8300; ramart.org), 441 Main Street. Tuesday through Saturday 10–5; Sunday noon–5. Located along the lakefront in downtown, the Racine Art Museum is home to a fabulous collection of contemporary crafts. The building is the stunning result of architectural repurposing—it was once American Bank and Trust, robbed in 1933 by John Dillinger—and is a cultural anchor downtown. If you're here the first Friday of the month, you'll get in free. Otherwise, admission is $5; free for children younger than 12.

&. ❧ **Charles A. Wustum Museum** (262-636-9177; ramart.org), 2519 Northwestern Avenue. Open Tuesday through Saturday 10–5. An arm of the Racine Art Museum, Wustum actually came first, and for years served as the primary visual arts center in Racine. When the museum's permanent collection grew so large it could only display about 10 percent of its pieces, the RAM opened up. These days, Wustum displays works by local artists and offers classes for adults and kids. A popular spot for weddings, the 13-acre grounds includes a one-acre formal garden designed by Wisconsin's Alfred Boerner. Tour the park or the museum; it's all free.

FRANK LLOYD WRIGHT S.C. Johnson Administration Building and Research Tower (262-260-2154), 1525 Howe Street. One of Frank Lloyd Wright's many famous buildings, the Johnson administration building remains the company's international headquarters, and although the three-legged chairs are gone (they encouraged good posture, but people fell off!), the building still functions much the way Wright intended. Designed with both workflow and corporate hierarchy in mind, the clerical workers on the main floor are treated to loads of natural light and space, but can be peered down upon by the suits in the offices upstairs. Tours begin at the Golden Rondelle and admission is free, but you should call for reservations.

Wingspread (262-681-3353; johnsonfdn.org/tour.html), 33 East Four Mile Road. Tours are run Tuesday through Friday 9–3 except during conferences. Call ahead to schedule. Built as a 14,000-square-foot residence for Herbert Fisk Johnson in 1939, this Frank Lloyd Wright-designed building now serves as an educational conference center. Tours are free.

The Golden Rondelle Theater (262-260-2154), 1525 Howe Street. Though not designed by Frank Lloyd Wright, the Golden Rondelle was moved to Racine after the 1964 World's Fair and ultimately redesigned by Taliesen architects to compliment the S.C. Johnson Administration Building, which was, in fact, designed by Wright. The building looks like a 1960s idea of a spaceship, and it's still used as a conference center and as the guest-relations hub by the Johnson company. It's also used by community organizations for a variety of programs.

HISTORIC

In Racine

Wind Point Lighthouse (262-639-3777), 4725 Lighthouse Drive, Wind Point. Among the oldest and tallest functioning lighthouses on the Great Lakes—and the oldest and tallest on Lake Michigan—the Wind Point Lighthouse is a favorite among local residents and lighthouse enthusiasts alike. Built in 1880 with $100,000 from Congress, the building has National Historic Site status. While the grounds are open daily from sunrise to 11 PM, the tower and building are normally closed to the public. Four times a year, however, the Friends of the Wind Point Lighthouse organization holds a "Tour to the Top" event, held the first Sunday in July, August, September, and October. These tours are held from 10–5 and cost $10 per person. Reservations are required.

DeKoven Center (262-633-6401; www.dekovencenter.org), 600 21st Street. Originally founded as Racine College in 1852, this lakefront conference and retreat center hosts events such as weddings and reunions as well as retreats of all sorts, including spiritual and creative, and is frequently the site of historical reenactments and large-scale role-play. The campus is also home to a number of organizations, such as the Original Root Zen Center and Spectrum School of the Arts. Tour the 20 wooded acres and enjoy the gardens, including the Quiet Garden, the Bishop's Garden, and the Zen Garden. All eight buildings are built in English Gothic Revival style and all are listed in the National Register of Historic Places.

Mound Cemetery (262-636-9188), 1147 West Boulevard. Anyone interested in Racine history needs to take a walk through Mound Cemetery. It officially became a public cemetery in 1851, but the Native American effigy mounds, from which the cemetery gets its name, date back thousands of years. Aside from the mounds, many important figures in Racine's history are buried or memorialized here, including Herbert Fisk Johnson, S. C. Johnson, J. I. Case, Olympia Brown, Charles Wustum, and three Revolutionary War soldiers, among others. There is also a soldier's cemetery and a heartbreaking "baby cemetery" here, with rows of tiny markers. The Mound Cemetery office has walking tour books available.

✏ ✿ **Racine Heritage Museum** (262-636-3926; racineheritagemuseum.org), 701 South Main Street. Open Tuesday through Friday 9–5; Saturday 10–3; Sunday noon–4. Located in downtown Racine, this museum focuses on the heritage of the community and features exhibits that include the history of local personalities and companies as well as information about Frank Lloyd Wright's influence on Racine's architecture, particularly the S.C. Johnson buildings. Free.

✏ ✿ **Racine Zoological Gardens** (262-636-9189; racinezoo.org), 200 Goold Street. Open 9–7 daily in summer; 9–4 daily from Labor Day to Memorial Day. The Racine zoo has a fabulous location right on Lake Michigan, which makes a visit about much more than the animals. More leisurely than bigger zoos, there are beautiful spots to picnic or relax on the beach, and with around 15 exhibits, a kiddy train, and a gift shop, it's a complete zoo experience. Wednesday nights in summer, the acclaimed Animal Crackers jazz series is held here. Adults $4; seniors $3; children ages 3–15 $2; children younger than 3 free.

BOWLING ⛳ ⛳ Like any good Wisconsin town, Racine has plenty of bowling alleys. Try **Castle Lanes** (262-633-1199), 5615 Castle Court, which offers a pro shop, pizza, beach volleyball in the summer, and pool tables. Similarly, **Paradise West** (262-886-5151), 6501 Washington Avenue, has live music on Saturdays and karaoke a few times a week. Check out racinebowling.org for more options.

GOLF There are six public golf courses in the Racine area, as well as a couple of country clubs. In the city, the nine-hole **Shoop Park** (262-681-9714), 4510 Lighthouse Drive, offers the best scenery, located right on Lake Michigan, near the lighthouse. Another nine-hole course, **Washington Park** (262-635-0118), 2801 12th Street, is the state's oldest remaining city course. Finally, **Johnson Park** (262-637-2840), 6200 Northwestern Avenue, has 18 holes and is a championship course for the Junior Masters. In Burlington, **Browns Lake Golf Course** (262-763-6065), 3110 South Browns Lake Drive, is another pretty spot, perched on Browns Lake, with lots of trees and the Fox River running through the course.

✳ Even More to See and Do

In Racine
✏ **Spinning Top & Yo-Yo Museum, Logic Puzzle Museum** (262-763-3946; topmuseum.org), 533 Milwaukee Ave, Burlington. Two whimsical museums in one, located in downtown Burlington. Both have interactive displays featuring thousands of these favorite toys. Tour times vary; call ahead to make reservations.

✏ **Aquaducks Ski Show** (262-763-2603; aquaducks.org), Fischer Park on Browns Lake, 30326 Durand Avenue, Burlington. Shows are held on Thursdays at 6 PM, Memorial Day to Labor Day. Show and stunt water skiing performances weekly to thrill and delight you. Okay, it's not Tommy Bartlett, but it's pretty good, and it's free.

KENOSHA'S MUSEUMS

Small- and medium-size cities tend to have cute little museums, housed in old schoolhouses or other historical buildings, which focus on the area's past and include objects donated over the years—a piece of clothing, somebody's old typewriter, that sort of thing. While these museums are fun and nearly always teach you something about the area, they rarely serve as a singular destination. Knowing this, you might be surprised to learn that Kenosha has not one but three sizeable public museums downtown, all with a different focus. The three are Smithsonian affiliates, a unique distinction bestowed upon only one other Wisconsin museum—the Wisconsin Maritime Museum in Manitowoc. The downtown triad provides an inexpensive, education-packed day for kids and adults alike.

 ✆ ⚐ **Civil War Museum** (262-653-4140; thecivilwarmuseum.org), 5400 First Avenue. Open 9–5 Tuesday through Saturday, noon–5 Sunday and Monday. New in 2008, the 57,000-square-foot Civil War Museum explores the role men and women from the upper Midwest had in the war. Unique in its focus, the museum is part of the city's lakefront harbor revitalization. Adults $5, children younger than 17 free.

 ✎ ✆ ⚐ **Kenosha Public Museum** (262-262-653-4140; kenosha.org/museum), 5500 First Avenue. Open 9–5 Tuesday through Saturday, noon–5 Sunday and Monday. Right next door to the Civil War Museum, the Kenosha Public Museum is housed in a modern two-story building. Its collection holds more than 70,000 pieces ranging from fine and decorative arts to natural science. Free.

 ✆ ⚐ ✎ **Dinosaur Discovery Museum** (262-653-4450; kenosha.org/dinosaurdiscovery), 5608 Tenth Avenue. Open noon–5 Tuesday through Saturday. Another unique museum, this one focuses on, well, dinosaurs. In association with the Carthage College Institute of Paleontology, the museum offers one of the best displays on meat-eating dinosaurs and primitive birds around. Free.

 ✆ ⚐ **Kenosha History Center** (262-654-5770; kenoshahistorycenter.org), 221 51st Place. Open Tuesday through Sunday. Housed in a picturesque historic lighthouse and its adjacent keeper's home, this museum explores the area's rich history in its four exhibits. In summer, tours to the top of the top of the lighthouse are offered for a fee. Museum admission is free.

Lakefront Trolley Rides (262-637-9000). Trolleys run from Memorial Day to Labor Day; the daytime trolley runs 10–4 Tuesday-Sunday and hits all the downtown spots. A weekend Pub and Grub trolley runs Friday and Saturday 4–midnight and stops at around 15 restaurants and pubs downtown. The fare is 25 cents.

✓ ↑ **Skatetown** (262-633-8333; skatetownracine.com), 1825 Sycamore Avenue. Hours and sessions vary, call ahead. Not just for kids, Skatetown offers live organ music sessions for adults, as well as jam skating and more. Times are reserved on weekends for the little ones. Skatetown's been around since the '70s, and remains one of the better rinks in the area. Public skating hours, sessions, and prices vary, so call ahead.

In Kenosha

✓ ও ↑ **Jelly Belly Center Tour** (866-868-7522; jellybelly.com), 10100 Jelly Belly Lane, Pleasant Prairie. Open daily. It's not really a factory tour, because this site is just a distribution location, but it's still a tour, and you still get free Jelly Bellies at the end. Kids love the short ride on a mini train through the endless amounts of jelly beans. Free.

Bristol Renaissance Faire (847-395-7773; renfair.com/bristol), 12550 120th Avenue. Open weekends July through September. A fair set in 1579, you'll meet minstrels and Robin Hood as you wander the grounds, seeking out a turkey leg to gnaw on. Everyone working here is an actor, including the people at the concession stands, and they're dressed in costume. Everything from the music and food to the games is based on the 16th century. Adults $18.95, children younger than 12 $13.95.

ALONG LAKE MICHIGAN

※ Green Space

In Racine

⚓ **North Beach** (northbeachoasis.com),100 Kewaunee Street. Concessions open, weather permitting, 9 AM–10 PM daily. This is likely the best beach in Wisconsin, and among the best in the Midwest, with 50 acres of pristine sand on Lake Michigan. It is the only beach in Wisconsin to receive the Certified Clean Beach designation by the Blue Wave Committee, which means the beach is actively kept environmentally sound and healthy for visitors. There are only around 50 beaches in the country with this distinction, and only one other in the Midwest. In addition to being squeaky clean, North Beach features concessions, including burgers and beer, and a giant playground for kids.

⚓ **River Bend Nature Center** (262-639-0930; riverbendracine.org), 3600 North Green Bay Road. Open 8:30–4:30 Monday through Friday, 12:30–4:30 Saturday and Sunday. Closed on major holidays. River Bend has 80 acres of preservation land along the Root River, including tons of trails for hiking in summer or skiing in winter, and offers numerous educational and family programs. Visiting the trails is free, but special programs have registrations fees.

⚓ ♿ **Bong Recreation Area** (262-878-5600), 26313 Burlington Road, Kansasville. The name has long been a source of giggles for area teenagers on field trips, but this state recreation area really is a beautiful place to spend some time with nature. It was originally meant to be a jet-fighter base and gets its name from Wisconsin native Richard I. Bong, a World War II fighter pilot. It's more than a campground: The state employs a naturalist here, runs educational programs, and allows activities ranging from hang gliding to horseback riding. There's also a boat launch, a beach, a ball field, and more, plus more than 200 campsites for overnight stays.

RACINE'S NORTH BEACH

You'll need a state park vehicle sticker to get in and a reservation through the DNR to camp.

In Kenosha

& **Harborpark**, near Second Avenue and Fifty–Sixth Street. One of Wisconsin's most stunning examples of brownfield reuse, Harborpark has all the markings of smart growth done well. The land sat idle after Chrysler closed its auto plant here in 1988, and in 2000 redevelopment began. Now home to open space, a sitting area for fishing, separate bike and pedestrian paths, an electric streetcar route, and a plaza that plays host to a weekly local foods market on Lake Michigan, this is perhaps the best public space in the area.

Petrifying Springs Park (262-857-1869), County Highway A, just east of WI 31, near UW-Parkside. This beautiful park is home to a hardwood forest, but there's plenty of recreational activity here. Picnic, ski, bike the 14-mile trail, swim, and more. Known locally as "Pets Park," this one is truly beautiful.

✳ Lodging

Hughes House (888-633-3401; racinebedandbreakfast.com), 1500 Main Street. This beautiful, historic Federal Revival home on Racine's lakefront has four guest rooms with private bathrooms, each suiting a slightly different taste. In summer, lounge on the porch and gaze at the lake. Full breakfast is served in a formal dining room. Rooms $110–210.

& **Radisson Hotel Harbourwalk** (262-632-7777; radisson.com/hotels/ wiracine), 223 Gaslight Circle. This is the only Racine hotel on the lake, and its downtown location makes it perfect for enjoying some of Racine's biggest attractions. Get a room overlooking the lake, if you can. $127–209.

& **Racine Marriott** (262-886-6100; marriott.com), 7111 Washington Avenue. Among the few nicer options in Racine, the beds here are comfortable and the staff is friendly. The hotel features a whole range of business services, a well-kept indoor pool and Jacuzzi, onsite restaurant, and bar. $129–250.

& **Fairfield Inn** (262-886-5000; marriott.com), 6421 Washington Avenue. Located along Washington Avenue, where most of Racine's hotels are, the

Fairfield Inn has clean rooms and basic amenities for all kinds of travelers at a reasonable price. It has a pool, continental breakfast, and some basic business services. $84–104.

BOATS AT GASLIGHT POINTE MARINA IN RACINE.

✳ Where to Eat

DINING OUT

In Racine

& Ϋ **The Corner House** (262-637-1295; foodspot.com/cornerhouse/), 1521 Washington Avenue. Open for dinner daily. Award-winning and acclaimed by local critics and diners alike, the Corner House is your best choice if you're in the mood for prime rib. You'll find your usual fine dining

BOATHOUSE PUB AND EATERY

fare of meats and seafood, along with a few locally flavored surprises, such as wiener schnitzel. The "lighter" menu includes fettuccine Alfredo and there's a tempting array of desserts, so don't come planning to watch your waistline. Dinner $10–30.

& Ϋ **The Summit** (262-886-9866; summitrestaurant.com), 6825 Washington Avenue. Open for lunch Monday through Friday 11:30–2, dinner daily, brunch on Sunday. With contemporary decor and typical white-tablecloth American fare, the Summit also offers a very popular Sunday brunch and a fantastic Friday fish fry, all at surprisingly reasonable prices. Kid's menu available. Dinner $10–30.

& Ϋ **The HobNob** (262-552-8008; thehobnob.com), 277 South Sheridan Road. Open for dinner nightly. A longtime favorite for finer dining in southeastern Wisconsin, the HobNob is known for great food, but the real appeal is the lakefront location and untarnished '50s ambiance. It's essentially a classic Wisconsin supper club, offering steaks and seafood. $10–30.

In Kenosha

& Ϋ **Ray Radigan's** (262-694-0455), 11712 Sheridan Road, Pleasant Prairie. Open daily for lunch and dinner. With its traditional relish tray and steak and seafood focus, Ray Radigan's certainly deserves the title of supper club. Lunch $7–10, dinner $15–30.

& Ϋ **Boathouse Pub and Eatery** (262-654-9922), 4917 Seventh Avenue. Open daily for lunch and dinner, Sunday for brunch. This is a typical steak and seafood joint, with the menu tending toward the fish. Great views of Lake Michigan and a nautical theme give this place a nice, authentic porttown feel. Boaters can dock for free. Sandwiches $5–8, dinners $9–22.

THE COFFEE POT

EATING OUT

In Racine

& **Kewpee** (262-634-9601; kewpee
.com); 520 Wisconsin Avenue. Open
7–6 Monday through Friday; 7–5 Saturday. This little diner is a Racine
landmark and worth a stop for its
charm as well as its insanely low
prices—the menu tops out at two
bucks and some change. Voted locally
to have the best burger around, lunches are packed as upwards of 1,000 customers visit each day. The root beer
and malts are delicious as well, and its
downtown location makes Kewpee a
natural choice for a day in Racine. The
restaurant got new digs in 1997 after
the parking structure it was in—or
under, really—was deemed unsafe, but
it's been on the same piece of land for
70 years. Pick up a tee-shirt before you
leave; it just might be your favorite
Racine memento. Entire menu, $2 or
so.

& **Red Onion Cafe** (262-637-4122),
555 North Main Street. Open daily for

breakfast and lunch. Located downtown in the Johnson Financial Building, this cafe offers simple but
excellent fare from breakfast to dinner
in simple, contemporary surroundings.
Award-winning chef John Oakland
runs the cafe with his sons, and his
passion for excellent food shines
through. It's a rare treat to have a
quick, reasonably priced breakfast prepared by an accomplished chef, and he
just might stop by to say hello. The
family also runs an outstanding catering service. Dishes $7–15.

& ⛾ **The Chancery** (262-635-0533;
thechancery.com), 207 Gas Light
Drive. Open for lunch and dinner daily.
In a city where so much great dining
happens in pubs, it's no surprise this
"family pub" began here. Back in the
day and at a different Racine location,
you'd get a basket of peanuts and were
encouraged to throw the shells on the
floor. Things are a little more upscale

KEWPEE HAMBURGERS

now, but it's still a fun place to go, with or without kids. There are six locations throughout Wisconsin, but the lake view here makes this one special. Kid's menu available. Dinner $9–20.

&. ☿ **Henry and Wanda's** (262-632-1772), 501 Sixth Street. Open for lunch and dinner Monday through Friday, dinner Saturday. With good food in a clean bar atmosphere, Henry and Wanda's is a little pricey for what you get by Racine standards, but would fit right in a little north in Milwaukee. Inside, it looks like a basic bar, but it's among the rare spots in Racine where you can get a cosmopolitan and snack on contemporary cuisine. If you're craving something a little more sophisticated but not white-tablecloth, this is it. Dishes $10–15.

&. ☿ **JavaVino** (262-633-0660), 424 Main Street. Open Tuesday through Saturday for all three meals, Sunday and Monday for breakfast and lunch. As the name suggests, coffee and wine are the delightful mainstays, but JavaVino also offers a complete cafe-style menu, including sandwiches and wraps, appetizers, and breakfast. It's a comfortable space and unique in Racine, with live music on Fridays. Dishes $8–13.

&. ☿ **The Ivanhoe** (262-637-4730; theivanhoepub.com), 231 Main Street. This pub, serving everything from shepherd's pie to burgers and wraps, steaks, seafood, and more than 300 drinks at the bar, is housed in a historic building on Main Street. A careful restoration of both the facade and interior in 2002 make it one of the more charming places in which to grab a beer and dinner in town. Entrees $8–10.

PIZZA Racine has an unusual abundance of excellent pizza, and every resident will eagerly tell you about his or her favorite. Kenosha, Racine's southerly neighbor, is more known for its Italian heritage, but for some reason Racine has the market cornered on mouthwatering Italian cuisine and perfect pizzas. Thin crust reigns here, and if you spend a few days sampling the city's options, you'll soon find yourself comparing crusts and sauces like a regular foodie. It's pretty hard to find a bad pizza in Racine as long as you stay out of the chain establishments.

&. ☿ **Infusino's** (262-633-3173; infusinos.com), 3325 Rapids Drive. Open for lunch and dinner daily. The atmosphere in this large restaurant is pleasant and clean, and the prices are almost unbelievable. Inexpensive dinners come with salad and bread, but the pizza is what's really outstanding. Options range from thick to thin; all are great. Try the virgin crust if you can't decide—it's in between thick and thin. Fourteen-inch pies $8.45–11.95, dishes $6.95–15.95.

&. **DeRango The Pizza King and Steakhouse** (262-639-0864; derango thepizzaking.com), 4621 6 Mile Road. Open for dinner daily. You will see other DeRango restaurants around town, including one just down Highway 32 at 3 Mile Road. If you see any of these, keep driving. The DeRango on 6 Mile is the one you want to check out. It has delicious pizza and amazing Italian dishes at remarkably low prices, and the portions are more than most can handle. The interior is comfortable and overall it's family friendly, complete with a kid's menu. DeRango's is also a good option for groups whose members can't agree; in addition to a lengthy Italian menu, there are stir fries, sandwiches, American dinners, and more. Weekends fill up fast and the restaurant doesn't take reservations, so be prepared to wait. Fourteen-inch pie $9–11.

& ⍦ **Wells Brothers Italian Restaurant** (262-632-4408), 2148 Mead Street. Open 11–9 Tuesday through Saturday. It's hard to believe you could weed out one pie in Racine and call it the best, but that's just what Chicago dining critics Penny Pollack and Jeff Ruby did when they named Wells Brothers pizza among the top 10 pizzas in the nation. That's quite a distinction, and the pizza is the reason this little dive is absolutely packed on weekends. Fourteen-inch pies $8.25–11.

BAKERIES **O&H Danish Bakery** (262-637-8895; ohdanishbakery.com), 1841 Douglas Avenue. Open Monday through Friday 5:30 AM–6 PM, Saturday 5–5. Nothing beats getting up early on a Saturday morning and picking up a kringle or a box full of danishes at this Racine institution. Things are crazy in the morning; take a number, figure out what you want, and move quickly when

they call you. The smell of all those fresh-baked goods will have you ready stuff a poppyseed danish in your mouth before you're out the door. Make sure to get more than you think you want, because you'll probably eat more than you care to admit. There's another location at 4006 Durand Avenue, which is open on Sundays from 7–1, but I'm partial to the Douglas Avenue location, which has more energy and a little more chaos.

Bendtsen's Bakery (262-633-0365; bendtsensbakery.com), 3200 Washington Avenue. Open Monday through Saturday from 5:30–5:30. You might think it's hard to live in the shadow of rock star kringle slinger O&H, which seems to get all the attention, but there's room in this town for more than one bakery. Bendtsen's could hardly be called overlooked, having been featured on the Food Network and other national TV channels for its delicious

---

KRINGLE: RACINE'S DANISH HERITAGE

Racine once boasted the largest Danish population outside of Copenhagen, and the heirloom these immigrants left Racine is kringle, a sinful pastry made with layers of flaky dough filled with fruit or nuts, then topped with icing. The ones made in Racine are shaped like a ring, although originally kringles were pretzel-shaped ("kringle" actually means "pretzel" in Danish), and they still are in Denmark. Danish bakeries, even in Racine, are often denoted by a pretzel shape on the sign (although the name can usually clue you in). You can't find a wedding, funeral, brunch, or meeting in Racine that doesn't have a tray of kringle slices somewhere in the room. Racine natives travel with them, carefully packed in boxes, and deliver them as offerings to out-of-town hosts, whom they pity for not having direct access to the delicious treat. Nothing quite compares to an authentic kringle made in Racine; it takes three days to make one, and an unthinkable amount of butter. Be careful, though—there are many impostors. To truly enjoy this Danish treat, stick to local family owned bakeries with storefronts. These kringles are made by hand in the traditional manner. Your taste buds will approve, even if your waistline doesn't. See the *Bakeries* listing for my favorites.

handmade kringle and other goodies. Bendtsen's is in West Racine, which was once known as "Kringleville" due to its large Danish population. The building is charming and comes complete with a cafe where you can have a cup of coffee and enjoy some of the finest Danish baked goods around.

Larsen Bakery (262-633-4298; larsen-skringle.com), 3311 Washington Avenue. Open Monday through Friday 6–5:30; Saturday 6–4:30. Closed Sunday. One of the shops in my holy trinity of delightful sweet rolls and kringles, Larsen is another longstanding, family-owned Danish bakery in West Racine. You'll know it buy the traditional pretzel sign, although its kringles are round, in the Racine fashion. They claim to be home to the "original" Racine kringle, and whether that's true or not, the kringle is worthy and delicious.

COFFEE SHOPS ఉ **Grounds Keeper Cafe** (262-638-8336), 327 Main Street. Open daily for breakfast and lunch. Cute and typical, this cafe offers all the usual espresso suspects plus a welcoming variety of sandwiches, gelato, and more.

ఉ **Mocha Lisa Coffeehouse** (262-681-2644; mochalisacoffeehouse.com), 2829 4½ Mile Road. Open early–2 PM daily. It's not downtown, but Mocha Lisa serves Alterra coffee and sells a variety of the Milwaukee roaster's beans by the pound. An array of baked goods is available.

ఉ **Wilson's Coffee & Tea** (262-634-6611; wilsonscoffee.com), 3306 Washington Avenue. Open Monday through Friday 6:30–6:30; Saturday 7–6. Wilson's is more about the coffee and tea and less about hanging out in a coffee shop. The list of available beans and teas is impressive, and anyone who likes to join in a coffee cupping should keep an eye out for monthly coffee tastings. No food here, but great chocolates for pairing.

ఉ **Milaeger's Java Garden Cafe** (262-639-2040; milaegers.com), 4838 Douglas Avenue, or (262-886-2117), 8717 Durand Avenue, Sturtevant. Open Monday through Friday 8–8; Saturday 8–6; Sunday 9:30–5. Located in Racine's favorite garden store, because yard work makes the locals thirsty! The cafe offers your usual coffeehouse drinks, juices, smoothies, and

---

A LEGENDARY KENOSHA DINER

🍴 **Franks Diner** (262-657-1017; franksdinerkenosha.com), 598 58th Street. Open daily for breakfast and lunch. You can't beat Franks for diner ambiance. In operation since 1926, it's an honest-to-goodness train car diner, although you wouldn't know it from the outside. Additions in the '40s increased the size a bit and now the original is encased in brick, but step inside and it's undeniable that this is the real deal. Franks is more than a pretty face, though; the service is sassy yet spectacular and the food is a creative, yummy step above diner grub. It's amazing considering the intensity of their rushes (no joke—get there early or you'll be waiting) and the small kitchen area. They've got a system down, to be sure, and it's impressive to watch. Everything's good, but be sure to check out the Garbage Plate (it's got five eggs!) and the pancakes, which are the largest I've seen. Dishes $5–10.

sandwiches ranging from hummus wraps and panini to brats and chicken salad, as well as plenty of vegetarian options.

In Kenosha

& **The Coffee Pot** (262-653-8849), 4914 Seventh Avenue. Open daily. Another great diner option; like Franks, this one's an original but offers updated diner fair. Breakfast is the main attraction, but the sandwich menu has all the standards, too. Try the stuffed french toast made with Kenosha's own outstanding Paielli's Italian bread. Breakfast $3–8, sandwiches $4–7.

& **The Nook** (262-657-6665; nookcafe .com), 5703 Sixth Avenue. Open Monday through Saturday for all three meals, 8–3 Sunday. The Nook, with its exposed brick walls and wood furniture, is a pleasant cafe in which to hang out or grab a bite to eat. The menu has cafe-style options, but it tends toward Mediterranean, with tons of vegetarian options. Bakery items include gelato and vegan chocolate cake. Sandwiches $7.

& **Jack's Cafe** (262-657-7732; andreas gifts.com/jacks.html) 2401 60th Street. Open for breakfast and lunch Monday through Saturday, 11–2:30 for Sunday brunch. Dishes $4–6.

Y & **The Brat Stop** (262-857-2011; bratstop.com), 12304 75th Street, at WI 50 and I-94. Open daily for all three meals. The Brat Stop is huge and the dining area has a sports bar atmosphere, but families are welcome and it's certainly a must for anyone looking for a stereotypical Wisconsin culinary experience. The menu, as you might imagine, is full of brats and other sausages, along with other options, and there's a gift shop and deli where you can purchase the requisite cheese curds and cow figurines. Dishes $5–15.

& **Carolyn's Coffee Connection** (262-653-1478; carolynscoffee.com), 1351 Fifty–Second Street. Open daily. Cute and spacious, Carolyn's offers typical coffee-shop options, with a build-your-own sandwich menu and a kid's menu, too. Dishes $7.

✳ Entertainment

In Racine

& **Racine Theatre Guild** (262-633-4218; racinetheatre.org), 2519 Northwestern Avenue. This all-volunteer community theatre has been around for more than 70 years, and stages eight plays a year in an auditorium on the Wustum Museum grounds. The Theatre Guild also runs a children's theatre, workshops, a comedy series, and a jazz series. That's a lot of activity under one roof.

Racine Symphony Orchestra (262-636-9285; racinesymphony.org). Racine's community orchestra has the distinction of being the state's longest continuously running orchestra. Concerts are held throughout the year at various locations, including Memorial Hall, the DeKoven Center, and Festival Hall.

Racine Concert Band (262-636-9109; rcb.addr.com). Racine's excellent concert band has an 85-year history in the area. The award-winning ensemble gives free concerts on Sundays throughout summer at the Racine Zoo amphitheater.

In Kenosha

Keno Drive-In (262-694-8855; keno drivein.net), 9102 Sheridan Road, Pleasant Prairie. Open evenings April through October. This is one of only 10 working drive-in theaters in Wisconsin. Like the others, the Keno shows second-run films under the cover of starlight to be enjoyed in the comfort of your vehicle. Built in 1949 and running continuously ever since, the drive-in can accomodate 800 cars. Adults $7.50, children $3.50.

 ♿ **Rhode Center for the Arts** (262-657-7529; rhodeopera.org), 514 56th Street. Staging plays throughout the year with its resident company, The Lakeside Players, this historic theatre is worth a trip.

✻ Selective Shopping

In Racine

♪ **Moxie Child** (262-898-9141; moxie child.net), 304 Sixth Street. Open daily. In business since 2006, Moxie Child stands alone in Racine for high-fashion children's clothing and accessories. So adorable you'll want to scream. Offering brands such as Tea and Greggy Girl in sizes up to 14 for girls and 10 for boys, it's hard to leave here without something for the little one in your life. The store also has swimwear, toys, diaper bags, nursing covers, and more. Moxie Child is owned by Racine native Cherri Cape and her daughters, Charity Chiappetta and Heidi Peterson, and they're all very welcoming and knowledgeable.

Elegant Pauper (262-632-3131; shopelegantpauper.com), 433 Main Street. Open daily. This is an adorable boutique has all sorts of gift items, from candles to stationery and more, that are sure to satisfy the insatiable girly shopper.

Sheepish (262-635-3244; sheepishin racine.com), 326 Main Street. Open 10–6 Monday through Saturday, 1–4 Sunday. Offering traditional medicines and organic teas along with new-agey stuff and world gifts, Sheepish is fun to browse.

Plumb Gold (262-632-5022; plumb goldltd.com), 322 Main Street. Open daily. Plumb Gold has been crafting custom fine jewelry since the '70s, and works with leading designers from around the country.

Gold Bear Trading Co. (262-637-6840), 3316 Washington Avenue. 10–5:30 Monday through Friday, 10–5 Saturday. This longtime West Racine gallery has a great selection of Native American arts and crafts to buy.

Nelson's Variety Store (262-633-3912; nelsonsvarietystores.com), 3220 Washington Avenue. Open Monday through Wednesday 9–6; Thursday 9–5:30; Friday 9–8:30; Saturday 9–5. A classic old-fashioned dime store, among the very last of a dying breed. Stop in for just about anything, or at least to look. There's wood flooring

MOXIE CHILD CHILDRENS BOUTIQUE

throughout the store, and the sound it makes beneath your feet really forms the experience.

Ye Olde Cheese Box (262-633-9427; yeoldecheesebox.com), 3315 Washington Avenue. Open 10–5:30 Tuesday through Friday, Saturday 10–4. It's a cheese shop with a Scandinavian twist. Yes, it has cheese, but also unusual Scandinavian gifts such as paper cutouts and gnomes, Racine gifts, chocolates, and other treats.

⊤ Porter's of Racine (262-633-6363; www.portersofracine.com), 301 Sixth Street. Open 10–6:30 Tuesday through Friday, 10–5:30 Saturday. Porter's has been in downtown Racine since 1857, and it's been in its current building since the '30s, evidenced by the art deco styling on the facade. This store is huge and full of high-end furnishings, with showrooms that make it look more like an art gallery or museum. In fact, touring the season's new showrooms was once a popular Racine pastime, and people would line up down the block to get in. These days, there are other things to do, but checking out Porter's showroom is always fun. Staff members are happy to hand you a map and let you browse, even if it's clear you're just looking.

In Kenosha

⊤ Mars' Cheese Castle (800-655-6147; marscheese.com), 2800 120th Avenue. Open 9–7 daily. Aside from having a great name, Mars' Cheese Castle has every quintessentially Wisconsin thing under one roof. It's amazing, especially if you're searching for Wisconsin kitsch. Sure, there's a lot of cheese (although not much you can't find at any sizeable Wisconsin grocery store), but it's about more than football-shaped cheddar. There's a gift shop with all sorts of cow figures, a bakery, a sandwich counter with brats and sandwiches with a German potato

salad side, and a bar. Tons of cheese and bread samples throughout the shop will keep your energy up and help you decide. And it has squeaky cheese curds. Welcome to Wisconsin!

Tenuta's Deli (262-657-9001; tenutasdeli.com), 3203 52nd Street. Open daily. What started in 1950 as a tiny ice-cream shop and deli has grown into a large store featuring specialty Italian foods, spices, and kitchen tools such as ravioli presses and sausage grinders. In summer, Tenuta's has an outdoor cafe where you can enjoy an Italian sausage and a beer.

⌀ Heim's Downtown Toy Store (262-652-8697; downtowntoystore .com), 5819 Sixth Avenue. Open 9–9 Monday through Saturday, 11–7 Sunday. This specialty toy shop has the coolest playthings for your little ones. With brands such as Haba and Plan, there are tons of safe, creative options to choose from. The friendly staff and huge selection of great toys make it hard to leave empty-handed. Heim's has opened an ice-cream shop next door that includes regular and vegan flavors. Look out.

✳ Special Events

March: **Quilters Land Cruise**, Radisson Inn Harbourwalk. This weekend-long event features quilting classes and quilt shows.

Sugarin' Off Pancake Sundays, Riverbend Nature Center (262-639-0930. Learn how maple syrup is made and enjoy an all-you-can-eat pancake breakfast served with—you guessed it—real maple syrup.

Early May: **Lakefront Artist Show**, Festival Park. This regional art event features around 100 artists from the area, one day only.

Kiwanis Pancake Day, Festival Hall. A true Racine tradition, this all-day, all-you-can-eat pancakes and sausage feast with a low price tag benefits youth programs in the area. Aside from stuffing your face, there's entertainment and you'll rub elbows with state politicians and local celebrities.

June: **Monument Square Art Fair on the Lake**, Festival Hall. This juried art fair brings in artists from around the U.S. each summer.

Late June: **Armenian Picnic**, Johnson Park. The annual event features delicious Armenian food and treats, along with music and dancing.

July: **Fourth of July Parade** 9–noon. It's the largest such parade in the Midwest, and a major event in Racine. Around 100,000 people head downtown to watch this three-hour spectacle, which includes marching bands from around the country, local organizations, elaborate floats, old cars, and lots of hometown pride. A pre-parade starts at 8:30 AM and runs for about 30 minutes before the parade officially starts. From the side of the road, it seems like every fire engine in the county participates. They all sound their sirens and let me tell you, it's loud.

Mid-July: **The Big Fish Bash** (formerly Salmon-a-Rama). Eight days of fishing and a four-day festival along Racine's lakefront. It's not just about salmon, which may account for the name change; prizes are awarded for a variety of the lake's fish. The festival on land features all the usual suspects of a proper Wisconsin festival: music, beer, fried cheese curds. The festival is a bargain, charging at most $5.

August: **Taste of Racine**, DeKoven Center. Spend all day sampling Racine's finest fare in one of the city's prettiest settings.

WALWORTH COUNTY

H ands down, the biggest draw to Walworth County is beautiful Lake Geneva, a sleepy resort town of around 7,000 that swells in numbers each summer and takes on a festive atmosphere.

Modern-day Lake Geneva developed as a summer playground for wealthy Chicagoans, and Chicago's influence is clearly evident here. Look around—the mansions you see on a Geneva Lake tour were largely built by big-name Chicagoans, William Wrigley among them. After the Great Chicago Fire, Lake Geneva became a more permanent home for these families, at least for a while, and their daily presence meant even more Chicago influence. These days, it's reflected largely in the Chicago pizza eateries and Chicago Bears headwear (this may be the only place in Wisconsin where those outnumber Green Bay Packers hats), and of course, all those Illinois license plates.

The towns around Geneva Lake include Fontana and Williams Bay, and can be considered a part of the Lake Geneva tourist area, but the main dining and shopping strip is downtown, along Main Street and Broad Street. Once you're in town, it's hard to miss, and Lake Geneva is pretty easy to navigate. Try to stay right downtown, so you can wander at will.

GENEVA LAKE

GUIDANCE The **Lake Geneva Area Convention and Visitors Bureau** (262-248-4416; lakegenevawi.com), 201 Wrigley Drive, has a little lakefront shop, but they do a good job of getting their very complete guides all over the place. The Walworth County Visitors' Bureau (262-723-3980; visitwalworthcounty.com) publishes a guide to the whole area.

GETTING THERE *By Car:* WI 50 heads right into Lake Geneva; catch it from I-94 coming from the south, or from Milwaukee, take I-43 south to US 12, which connects up with US 50. WI 11 runs straight to Elkhorn, and the exit from I-43 is clearly marked.

GETTING AROUND If you're staying in downtown Lake Geneva, you can walk to all the shops and restaurants, but to get further out, you'll need a car.

MEDICAL EMERGENCY Call 911.

Mercy Walworth Hospital and Medical Center (262-245-0535), N2950 State Road 67, Lake Geneva.

Aurora Lakeland Medical Center (262-741-2000), W3985 County Road NN, Elkhorn.

✳ To See and Do

Yerkes Observatory (262-245-5555; astro.uchicago.edu/yerkes), 373 West Geneva Street, Williams Bay. Open for tours Saturdays year-round except near Christmas and New Year's Day; tours start at 10, 11, and noon. Part of the University of Chicago, the world's largest refracting telescope is here, along with four other research telescopes. The building itself is something to see; built in 1897, the observatory is an impressive, domed Romanesque building set in a 77-acre park. In 2005, the University of Chicago began accepting bids to sell the property, but the threat of the land being turned into luxury housing resulted in public outcry. Free, $5 donation.

✐ ♿ ✝ **Geneva Lake Museum of History** (262-248-6060; genevalakemuseum .org), 255 Mill Street. Open Thursday through Sunday in summer, Friday through Sunday in winter. This small museum explores the history of the area, with particular focus on its development and architecture. Learn about all the area landmarks and the history of the lake. Adults $5.

✐ **Lake Geneva Cruise Line** (262-248-6206; cruiselakegeneva.com), 812 Wrigley Drive. Cruises run daily May through October. There are a variety of options, from champagne brunch to sunset cocktails, and all sorts of scenic and dining tours in between. It's the best—sometimes the only—way to see the historic mansions built by Chicago bigwigs around the lake. Other interesting options include the Black Point estate tour, which allows you to hop off the boat and tour the mansion, and the mailboat tour, where you ride along as brave mail carriers leap off the moving boat to deliver the mail, then leap back aboard—and hopefully don't fall in the water (see sidebar). Prices vary.

Lake Geneva Balloon (262-581-4302; www.lakegenevaballoon.com), meets at the **Lake Geneva Pie Company** (262-248-5100; lgpie.com), 150 East Geneva

WALWORTH U.S. MAILBOAT TOURS

There are plenty of opportunities to get on the lake, but how often can you ride along while the mail is delivered? **Lake Geneva Cruise Line** (262-248-6206; cruiselakegeneva.com), 812 Wrigley Drive, operates the mailboat tour in conjunction with the U.S. Postal Service, delivering mail to Geneva Lake's residents seven days a week. It's a 2½-hour cruise that not only gets you astoundingly close to the lakefront properties, but also features a carrier, called a mail jumper, who leaps off and back onto the vessel to deliver the mail. That doesn't sound so exciting until you realize the boat never stops, and sometimes the carrier falls in the water or nearly misses the boat on her way back (the carriers are frequently young women). What's more, the driver and mail carrier narrate the tour, giving historical facts and information about the houses' current owners and residents. Marine mail is delivered June 15 through September 15 each year, and has been done this way for 90 years.

LAKE GENEVA CRUISE LINE U.S. MAIL CARRIER BOAT TRIP. THIS TIME, THE MAILPERSON DID NOT FALL INTO THE WATER.

Square, Lake Geneva. Offers hot air balloon rides throughout the summer, depending on the weather that day. Tickets never expire.

✨ **Valley View Farm** (262-248-1398; valleyviewberryfarm.com), W3246 Springfield Road, Lake Geneva. Berry stand open 7:30–5 Monday through Saturday, 9–5. Pick your own strawberries and raspberries during June and July, depending on conditions. Call ahead to see if it's a good day to pick.

♪ **East Troy Electric Railroad** (262-642-3263; easttroyrr.org), 2002 Church Street, East Troy. Operates normally April through October. Among the last of Wisconsin electric railroads, the train runs from the East Troy station to a depot located at the Elegant Farmer in Mukwanago (see Selective Shopping in Waukesha) and back, but you can hop on the train in Mukwanago and purchase your ticket in East Troy on normal runs. Aside from plain old train rides, there are weekly dinner trains, featuring a different menu each week, brew trains (sip local craft beers aboard the train), and special events throughout the year. Tickets $12 adults, $7 children, brew train $35, dinner train $68.

♪ **Paradise Golf Park Miniature Golf** (262-248-3456; paradisegolfpark.com), 511 Wells Street, Lake Geneva. Open daily past dark. Less tacky than most, or even not tacky at all, this mini-golf park has attractive landscaping. Right near downtown, it's an easy trip with the kids. At night, the grounds are lit so you can keep playing. Eleven and older $6.75, 4–10 $5.75, children younger than 4 free.

GOLFING Golfing is a big deal in Lake Geneva. There are eight public courses here, and two private. None are municipal courses, but instead are attached to clubs and resorts; all offer 18 holes. The best is likely at the Grand Geneva, which has two award-winning championship courses. The Brute is considered among the most difficult in the Midwest, and the Highlands is a Scottish-style course. You'll pay for all this magnificence, though—high-season rates run upwards of $150. The Hawk's View Golf Club has two courses as well; one is five-star rated, the other, Barn Hollow, is geared toward families and beginners, and the prices reflect this, with 18 holes topping out at $25. In addition to the golf courses in Lake Geneva, there are many more throughout Walworth County.

BOAT RENTALS **Marina Bay Boat Rentals** (262-248-4477; lakegenevaboats .com), 300 Wrigley Drive, Lake Geneva.

Gordy's Lakefront Marine (262-275-2163; gordysboats.com), 320 Lake Avenue, Fontana.

✳ Green Space

♪ **Geneva Lake Shore Path**, Lake Geneva. Amid all the fancy homes, well-heeled tourists, endless shopping, and expensive restaurants, there is something very special and free. If so inclined, you can walk the 21-mile loop around the lake, even if that takes you through private property. The law here requires that the public have access to this path, and that the property owners maintain it. The result is a hodgepodge of terrain and materials—some owners take very good care of their portion, while others do not. It simply adds to the charm and keeps you going. Aside from the peace and solitude you'll find strolling this trail, you get as close to the lakefront mansions as anyone without an invitation ever will, and an equally good view of the lake. Pick up a copy of *Walk, Talk, and Gawk* (walktalk gawk.com), which contains seven guided walks and details the history of the properties you'll see, at many stores around town.

Kettle Moraine State Forest—Southern Unit (414-594-6200), S91 W39091 WI 59, Eagle. Comprised of five separate units throughout southeast Wisconsin, the Southern Unit lies partly in Walworth County. Full of camps, including three family camps, a horse rider's camp, and two group camps, plus swimming beaches and trails totaling 160 miles, there's enough to do for a day or more. Most lakes in Southeastern Wisconsin are the result of kettles, including Geneva Lake. State sticker required.

Fontana Fen, Dewey Avenue, Fontana. This 10-acre park is a wetland that is home to calcareous fen, a rare and endangered plant. There are three walks you can take through the conservation area. Free.

✍ **Lake Geneva Beach** (262-248-4416), Wrigley Drive, Lake Geneva. Open 9:30–7 daily. Right near the center of the action, this public beach is a popular spot on sunny days, and offers welcome respite from non-stop shopping. Admission $5, children younger than 6 free.

✍ **Fontana Beach** (262-275-6136), Fontana Boulevard, Fontana. Open 9:30–7 daily. Across the lake from the shopping madness, this beach features a sizable sandy area to catch some rays. Admission $5, children younger than 6 free.

✍ **Williams Bay Beach** (262-245-2700), Geneva Street, Williams Bay. Open 9:30–7 daily. Another lovely beach on Geneva Lake, this one has shady spots if the sun gets to be too much. Admission $5, children younger than 6 free.

✍ **Big Foot Beach State Park** (262-248-2528), WI 120, Lake Geneva. This state park offers camping, hiking, and of course, the beach. State park vehicle sticker required.

✳ Lodging

✍ ♿ **The Cove of Lake Geneva** (262-249-9460; cove-lake-geneva.com), 111 Center Street, Lake Geneva. You couldn't ask for a better location. Right downtown, on the lake, you can walk to just about everything from this large property, including shops, the cruise line, dining, and the Lake Shore Path (see Green Space). It's great for anyone who wants convenience, but the spacious rooms, swimming pool, kids' activities, and onsite movies make it perfect for families. Even so, the rooms are quiet. Rent a poolside cabana and enjoy a little privacy. Rooms and suites $159–399.

❦ **Golden Oaks Mansion** (262-248-9711; goldenoaksmansion.com), 421 Baker Street, Lake Geneva. Tucked away, but close to the lake and shopping, this historic, 1856 bed & breakfast offers a romantic setting that's not too frilly. The Sunset Suite offers lots of space, furniture from the same era as the house, and a fireplace. A five-course breakfast is included, and served in the onsite Nicoise Restaurant, which also serves dinner. Rooms $175–275.

♿ **Lazy Cloud Lodge** (262-275-3322; lazycloud.com), W4033 Highway 50, Lake Geneva. Specializing in romantic getaways, this charming property includes a variety of suites, but all rooms include extras for sweethearts such as champagne, chocolates, bubble bath, and more. Given its romantic bent, the decor is, too, but tasteful nonetheless. Choose between the B&B and the inn (no breakfast). Rooms $140–230.

♿ **The Geneva Inn** (262-248-5680; genevainn.com), N2009 South Lake Shore Drive, Lake Geneva. A beautiful luxury hotel on the shores of Geneva Lake, the building is not, like many others, historic, but it occupies the footprint of a previous estate that stood here for 105 years. Warmly decorated with plenty of room to relax, you get continental breakfast in the Grandview Restaurant. Speaking of grand views—you'll pay extra for it, but be sure to get a lakeside room. $175–390.

& **Mill Creek Hotel** (262-248-6647; millcreekhotel.com), 123 Center Street, Lake Geneva. Within walking distance of downtown, this hotel offers plain but pleasant rooms. The pool is in an enclosed atrium, allowing you to enjoy water recreation even when the weather doesn't cooperate. Rooms $119–179.

& ✍ **The Abbey Resort** (800-709-1323; theabbeyresort.com), 269 Fontana Boulevard, Fontana. Renovated in 2008, this 334-room resort offers a quiet escape, but it's great for families with kids, too. Right on the lake,

you'll find plenty to do without leaving the property. With five dining options ranging from a coffee shop to upscale waterfront seating, swimming pools, and a spa, this is the place to relax. Rooms $249–299.

✳ Where to Eat

Your dining options are somewhat, but not completely, limited; Lake Geneva is a town full of fine dining and supper clubs, perhaps more than anywhere else in the state, save for the remotest towns in the Northwoods. Folks who enjoy four-star steakhouse dining and have money to burn will be in heaven, but the more casual diner, or those with special dietary needs, will have a slightly harder time. I've rounded up

✍ & GRAND GENEVA RESORT

Consisting of three properties, this is the, well, grandest property in Lake Geneva. The **Grand Geneva** (262-248-8811; grandgeneva.com), 7036 Grand Geneva Way, is Lake Geneva's most storied hotel. Originally the Playboy Club and Resort, opened by Hugh Hefner in 1968, it's now owned by Wisconsin's Marcus Corporation (it also owns the Pfister Hotel in Milwaukee), and it serves as the area's luxury resort. Golf the resort's two award-winning courses, ski in winter, or pamper yourself in the Well Spa. For all its well-heeled polish, the **Grand Geneva** is surprisingly kid-friendly, with daily activities and in-room child care. (Perhaps that's actually parent-friendly.) Six dining options, from coffee to upscale, mean you won't be going hungry. Rooms $229–439. If you want to treat the kids to even more, take them to the Grand Geneva's little sibling, the Timber Ridge Lodge and Waterpark (262-248-8811: timberridgeresort.com), 7020 Grand Geneva Way. It's a Wisconsin Dells-worthy resort, with a 30,000-square-foot waterpark, game rooms, and kid-friendly dining. $189–259. Orange Lake at Lake Geneva (866-915-4224; orangelake.com/lakegeneva), 7036 Grand Geneva Way. Offering one- and two-bedroom villas, complete with fireplaces and whirlpools, this one's for those who like a little more room. Villas $279–405. All properties share resort amenities, so no matter which one you stay at, you can use the golf course, ski, play in the water park, enjoy the spa, go horseback riding, play tennis, shop, whatever you'd like. If you're jetting in from somewhere, there's a private airport here, as well.

some of the best options for every traveler, including those looking for a decent to outstanding breakfast, a pizza, or just need a change of pace. I've listed summer hours here; be aware that winter hours vary.

DINING OUT There are loads of fine restaurants in the area, this being a resort town and all. I've chosen a few that stand out. I've listed summer hours here; be aware that winter hours vary.

Y & **Gilbert's** (262-248-6680; www .gilbertsrestaurant.com), 327 Wrigley Drive, Lake Geneva. Open for dinner Tuesday through Saturday. A refreshing change of pace from the seemingly limitless number of steakhouses and supper clubs in the area, Gilbert's offers a modern twist on fine dining. The menu changes daily, and focuses on local and organic ingredients. Housed in an old mansion with a storied history, if you aren't lucky enough to dine on the enclosed patio, you'll still be treated to beautiful surroundings. The original rooms of the mansion remain, which means yours is only one of a handful of tables you'll see. Come ready for new tasting experiences. Gilbert's offers a vegetarian dish nightly. Entrees $25–50.

Y & **Grandview Restaurant at the Geneva Inn** (800-441-5881; geneva inn.com), N2009 South Lakeshore Drive, Lake Geneva. Open for lunch Monday through Friday, dinner daily, brunch Saturday and Sunday. Classy and elegant, the Grandview offers eclectic contemporary dishes with something for everyone, ranging from pan-seared walleye to steaks and even a creative vegetarian dish. The view is, indeed, grand. Entrees $24–36.

Y & **Medusa** (262-249-8644; medusa grillandbistro.com), 501 Broad Street. Open for dinner Tuesday through Sat-

urday. Wildly popular, this unstuffy but sophisticated restaurant features upscale Mediterranean and American dishes on a menu that changes nightly. $16.50–34.50.

Y & **Geneva ChopHouse** (800-558-3417; chophouse411.com/geneva), 7036 Grand Geneva Way. Open for dinner daily. Located in the Grand Geneva Resort, it's elegant, to be sure, but the prices aren't out of proportion. Considered by many to be the best choice for fine dining, the menu focus squarely on steak and seafood. Creative extras seal the deal. Dishes $20–50.

Y & **Kirsch's** (262-245-5756; www .kirschs.com), W4190 West End Road. Open daily for dinner. French-inspired cuisine, and views of Lake Como. Dishes $24–50.

EATING OUT & **Daddy Maxwell's Diner & Cafe** (262-245-5757; daddy maxwells.com), 150 Elkhorn Road, Williams Bay. Open daily for breakfast and lunch, dinner Saturday. Here's a 1940s diner with pink walls and junk all over the place, and it's a great option for breakfast or casual lunch. But you'll have to beat the crowds. Dishes $6–15.

& **Grandma Vickie's Cafe** (262-249-0301), 522 Broad Street, Lake Geneva. Open for breakfast and lunch daily. Another little diner off the beaten path, where you can get your basic eggs and toast breakfast for a reasonable price. By off the beaten path, of course, I don't mean it's particularly far from the hustle and bustle of the main drag, in fact it's merely blocks, but those few blocks mean most tourists don't make it here. Dishes $5–10.

Y & **Chuck's Lakeshore Inn** (262-275-3222; chuckslakeshoreinn.com), 352 Lake Street, Fontana. Kitchen open 11–9 daily. Casual pub-and-grub bar atmosphere with one of the least expensive menus in the area. Popular for burgers and deep-fried sides (including sweet potato fries and cheese curds), Chuck's has Friday fish fry and even a veggie burger. Sandwiches $3–7.

🍴 ♿ **Millie's Restaurant and Shopping Village** (262-728-2434; millieswi .com), N2484 County Road O, Delavan. Open 8–4 daily July and August, weekends only January and February, Tuesday through Sunday the rest of the time. With a Victorian Room, Wicker Room, and Colonial Room to choose from, you'll feel pretty certain your dear Aunt Millie did, indeed, decorate this place. Breakfast offers all manner of tempting options, from huge German pancakes to the delicate Swedish variety, as well as eggs, potato pancakes, and so much more. Lunch options are more limited and run the typical gamut of sandwiches and meats, but the range is sufficient. Breakfast $4–9, sandwiches $9, dinners $13–16.

🍴 ♿ **Gino's East Pizza** (262-248-2525), 300 Wrigley Drive, Lake Geneva. Open 11–11 daily. It wouldn't be a Chicagoan's getaway without authentic Chicago style pizza, and Wisconsinites should delight in knowing they've got the real thing right here. Yes, Gino's serves a large variety of Italian dishes, but a big gooey hunk of deep-dish pizza is what you really want. Sandwiches $7, pasta dinners $10, large deep-dish cheese pizza $24.

🍷 🍴 ♿ **Next Door Pizza** (262-248-9551; nextdoorpub.com), 411 Interchange North, Lake Geneva. Open daily for lunch and dinner. The huge, low-priced menu offers all manner of Italian cuisine, along with sandwiches, burgers, and good pizza. It's a bar, but there's a kid's menu, and it's clean. The restaurant has karaoke on Wednesday nights. Dishes $6–12, pizza $10–20.

🍴 ♿ **Scuttlebutts Restaurant** (262-248-1111), 831 Wrigley Drive, Lake Geneva. Open for all three meals daily,

SCUTTLEBUTT'S RESTAURANT

winter hours vary. Swedish pancakes! In my book, that alone is a reason to go anywhere, but the lakeside location and big windows don't hurt. The clientele skews older, probably because the food is good and the prices are right. The time to come here is breakfast, when you can get those Swedish pancakes and any egg dish you can imagine, but an upscale dinner is served at night.

Y & **Houlihan's** (262-248-7047; houlihans.com), 111 Center Street, Lake Geneva. Open daily for lunch and dinner. It's a chain, yes, but it's popular with Lake Geneva tourists weary of all the fine dining and supper clubs, but wanting more than a diner. Sometimes you just want to put your elbows on the table, and a gimmicky chain restaurant is just the place to do it. Connected to the Cove of Lake Geneva, the menu has options to please everyone, and you can get dinner delivered. The menu offers sandwiches, seafood, burgers, and a ton of appetizers. Lunch $10–15, dinner $15–20.

Y ✿ & **Popeye's on Lake Geneva** (262-248-4381; popeyesonlakegeneva.com), 811 Wrigley Drive, Lake Geneva. Open for lunch and dinner daily. It's not the fast-food fried chicken chain. This Popeye's offers a fun sailor theme with traditional American dishes. Make sure to try the broccoli cheddar soup. Sandwiches, $10–15; dinners $15.99–49.99; Friday fish fry goes for $11.99.

✿ & **Egg Harbor Cafe** (262-248-1207), 827 Main Street, Lake Geneva. Open daily for breakfast and lunch. A charming, country-style cafe, this one's got a huge array of egg dishes made with eggs from cage-free chickens. You can also get Swedish pancakes, crepes, and Belgian waffles, so bring the kids! Dishes $6–10.

✿ & **Fiddlesticks Cafe** (262-743-2233; fiddlestickscafe.com), 101 Ever-

KILWIN'S CHOCOLATES & ICE CREAM

green Parkway, Elkhorn. Open 7–3 Saturday through Thursday, 7–9 Friday. Fiddlesticks offers a huge and tempting breakfast menu in this country cafe, but make sure you try a Door County pecan roll, which comes topped with cherries. Dinner focuses on comfort foods, such as chicken and dumplings and messy sandwiches. You can also get burgers, and veggie burgers, here. Dishes $7–10.

COFFEE AND SWEETS ✿ & **Kilwin's Ice Cream & Chocolate** (262-248-440; kilwins.com), 772 Main Street. Kilwin's is a national chain, but you'd never guess it from stopping into Wisconsin's only store in Lake Geneva. In true chocolatier fashion, Kilwin's interior is full of dark wood and counter after counter of freshly made candies. Inside, it smells like a chocolate-covered dream, as the aroma of taffy, fudge, caramels, and nuts blend to make you swoon.

& **The Malt Bar & Dessert Lounge** (262-248-8484), 221 Broad Street, Lake Geneva. Open 10–7 daily. A grown-ups' ice-cream shop, there are gelato, espresso, and truffles here. Treats $5–10.

✐ **Pedal and Cup** (262-249-1111; pedalandcup.com), 1722 WI 120, Springfield. Open 10–6 daily Memorial Day through Labor Day. Housed in a historic train depot, complete with the original ticket counter, Pedal and Cup is a spot where you can grab coffee and ice cream, or even lunch, then rent a bike and hit the White River State Trail, which runs between Elkhorn and Burlington. There's also a gift shop and local artwork; and the owners are very friendly. Sandwiches $5–10.

✳ Selective Shopping

The main shopping district in Lake Geneva lies on three streets right near the lake—Broad Street, Center Street, and Main Street. There are countless boutiques and unique shops to wander in and out of all day long. What you find will depend on your taste—there's something for everyone here.

Allison Wonderland (262-248-6500), 720 West Main Street, Lake Geneva. Open daily. A great toy store selling creative toys that don't rely on electronics to catch a kid's attention, you'll find more than you planned to buy here. Whether that's a good thing is up to you.

Bread Loaf Book Shop (262-248-9446), 835 Wrigley Drive, Lake Geneva. Open daily. Among the cutest bookshops around, and a breath of fresh air in an era when independents are going under, this one stocks all manner of literary reads, along with a great many local titles and books for kids. No need to worry if you forgot to bring a book to spend some time relaxing; Bread Loaf's got you covered.

Clear Water Outdoor (262-348-2420; clearwateroutdoor.com), 744 West Main Street, Lake Geneva. Open daily. A fantastic outdoor shop and kayak rental spot, Clear Water features many eco-friendly brands of clothing and gear to help you get out and explore.

E Street Denim (262-249-0922; estreetdenim.com), 741 West Main Street, Lake Geneva. Open daily. This boutique has an outstanding selection of trendy, designer clothes for juniors and women. You'll be fighting people at the racks here, but it's civilized.

SHOPPING IN LAKE GENEVA

Geneva Art Pottery (262-248-9078; geneva-art-pottery.com), W3403 County Highway BB, Lake Geneva. Open daily Wednesday through Monday. The working studio and retail outlet of artists Claire Berger and Jesse Healy, this tiny, roadside shop offers unique pieces you won't find just anywhere.

Beadology (262-248-1895; www .beadology-lakegeneva.com), 270 Broad Street, Lake Geneva. A charming and well-organized bead shop right along the main shopping strip, you'll find beads plus already-made jewelry here.

Lola's (262-248-6621), 736 West Main Street, Lake Geneva. Open daily. Hard to believe, but one of the most affordable, trendy boutiques I've found is right on Main Street in Lake Geneva. Packed with stylish clothing for juniors and women, it's a good place to check out.

Global Hands (262-248-6920; global handsfairtrade.com), 252 Center Street, Lake Geneva. Open daily. Most of the time, an import shop reeks of incense and sells gifts of questionable origin. You're never really sure if you're getting the real thing. This shop, housed awkwardly in what appears to be an old funeral home, is not like that. The objects for sale here are Fair Trade objects, carefully chosen for sale.

Scents and Sensibilities (262-248-5276), 725 West Main Street, Lake Geneva. Open daily. This soap shop is huge, and the wonderful scents hit you the instant you walk in. There are soaps in every imaginable shape and flavor—some look like cupcakes, some just smell that way. More refined scents like lavender oatmeal and green tea are more popular, but the novelty soaps are fun.

Delaney Street Mercantile (262-248-8008; delaneystreet.com), 905 West Main Street, Lake Geneva. Open daily. Specializing in a wide array of home goods and gift items gathered from around the U.S., as well as Italy and France, if you need a gift in any price range, and for anybody, this is the first place you should head. It's absolutely impossible not to think of someone you know at every turn in this wonderfully full, eclectic, two-story shop.

✳ Special Events

February: **National Snow Sculpting Competition**, Riviera Park, Lake Geneva. Each year, 15 snow-sculpting teams from around the country come here to compete for the national prize. The event draws more than 30,000 spectators.

June: **Native American Festival** (lakegeneva-powwow.org), Dunn Field, Lake Geneva. Held every year on Father's Day, the festival includes a traditional powwow.

Paint-In, downtown Lake Geneva. At this plein-air painting event held on

DELANEY STREET MERCANTILE

the streets of downtown, invited artists spend the day practicing their craft and chatting with onlookers.

July and August: **Concerts at the Lakefront**, Flat Iron Park, Lake Geneva. Free music on Thursdays for two months.

August: **Art in the Park**, Library Park, Lake Geneva. An annual art fair on the shores of Geneva Lake.

Venetian Festival, Flat Iron Park, Lake Geneva. This craft fair on the lake draws visitors from all around.

September: **Lake Geneva Wine Festival**, Grand Geneva Resort, Lake Geneva. Sample wines at this classy fest, and learn from sommeliers and winemakers.

October: **Oktoberfest**, Lake Geneva. Not exactly the German fest you might be thinking of, this one does feature polka and brats, but a lot of it seems more like a fall festival, with caramel apples, hayrides, and pumpkins. Nothing wrong with that!

December: **Festival of Lights**, downtown Lake Geneva. This holiday festival includes a tree-lighting ceremony and Santa.

Great Electric Children's Christmas Parade, downtown Lake Geneva. This holiday parade features floats, clowns, Santa, and more.

WALWORTH COUNTY FAIR
Organizers bill fair (at the **Walworth County Fairgrounds**, WI 11, Elkhorn. 262-723-3228; walworthcountyfair.com) as the best county fair in the nation, and I'm inclined to agree. Each summer, for one week, the population of Elkhorn, a tiny town of 9,000, swells to 150,000 people as fairgoers pack the area. The fair started in 1850, and today it often features the most exhibits of any in Wisconsin. More than this, though, it's a completely authentic agricultural fair. Grab something to eat on a stick, and mosey the day away.

South Central Wisconsin

LAZY JANE'S

Closed

MADISON AND SUBURBS

WISCONSIN DELLS AND BARABOO

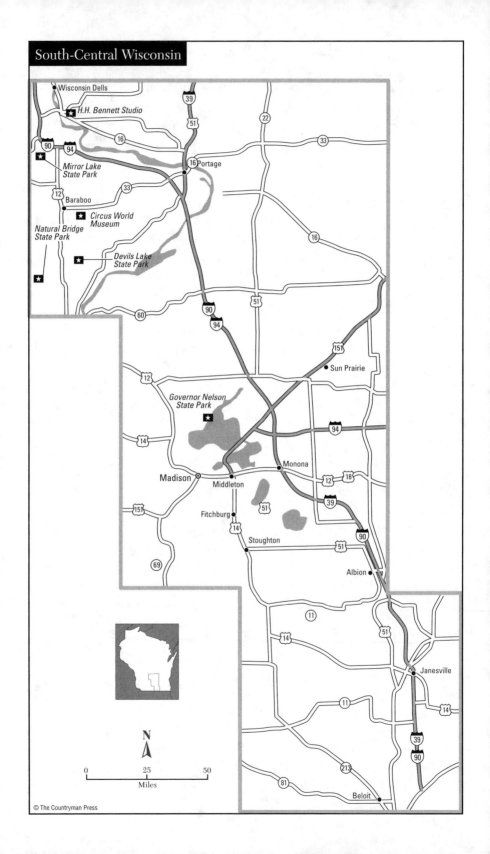

South-Central Wisconsin

Wisconsin Dells

H.H. Bennett Studio

39

51

22

16

33

90
94

Mirror Lake
State Park

16 Portage

12 Baraboo

33

Circus World
Museum

16

Natural Bridge
State Park

Devils Lake
State Park

60

90
94

51

151

Sun Prairie

12

Governor Nelson
State Park

94

14

Monona

Madison

Middleton

12 18

39

Fitchburg

51

151

14

90

Stoughton

51

69

Albion

11

14

51

Janesville

11

14

N

213

39

0   25   50
Miles

81

90

Beloit

© The Countryman Press

INTRODUCTION

S outh Central Wisconsin, part of the unglaciated region of the state, is home to beautiful and stunning land formations. Part of it also *was* touched by glaciers, which left sparkling lakes behind. It's one of the prettiest areas of Wisconsin. Among chimneys of sandstone, rushing rivers, thick forests, and deep gorges, there are miles of farmland, providing the perfect picture of the state's agricultural roots. In fact, probably no part of the state is prouder of that dairy claim to fame than Madison, home to the nation's first agricultural school, which continues to produce its own cheese and ice cream. Madison, of course, is not just about dairy (although there are cows at the capitol once a year during Cows on the Concourse); it's a bustling college town/state capital that's full of tempting restaurants and off-beat shops.

North of Madison is that wonderful tourist hotspot known officially as "America's Waterpark Capital of the World," with exciting, modern attractions and old-school, kitschy charm. Beyond all the flashing lights and fudge shops, though, is another of Wisconsin's natural wonders—the dells and sandstone formations lining this portion of the Wisconsin River, formed some 15,000 years ago. You wouldn't know it driving down the main drag in Wisconsin Dells, but this beautiful scenery is what first brought tourists here.

Before the tourists, though, this area (along with regions north into the Fox Valley and Green Bay, and over to the Mississippi River) was home to the Ho-Chunk. Although the U.S. government moved the tribe on numerous occasions, members continued to return to Wisconsin, longing for the lush and fertile land, and their home. The tribe was removed 11 times, and each time members returned. Today, the Ho-Chunk Nation does not have a reservation, but instead has managed to secure a scattered 2,000 acres of land. Among these is where the Ho-Chunk Casino is located.

Convenient to each other as well as other parts of the state and Wisconsin's neighbors, the main hubs of this region feature more than enough activity to fill up a lengthy vacation. Whether you're looking for performing arts or outrageous performance, tempting ethnic dishes or scrumptious saltwater taffy, there's a waterfront spot with your name on it. Just don't forget to take in the scenery.

MADISON AND SUBURBS

As home to both the state's largest university and its largest population of politicians, Madison has a long-standing reputation for being a liberal haunt, full of hippies and activists and tree-hugging intellectuals. Truth is, there is absolutely a laid-back vibe to this diverse college town, and it's one that visitors will find pleasant and refreshing. The people here are downright friendly and helpful, and not in nearly the hurry you'll notice in Milwaukee (that's a positive, but also a warning; lunch might take longer than you expect). Madison is so great because it has big-city features, like outstanding dining and cultural opportunities, with a friendly, small-town charm.

Madison's list of "best" ratings is long and backs up its reputation—most livable, most walkable, smartest, best education, best teeth. The magazine *Men's Health* ranked the teeth in Madison number one in the country. Maybe that's why the people here smile a lot. Or maybe they're smiling because they know they've got it all. Madison is the perfect spot for the state capital; the geography is a sampling of all Wisconsin has to offer. The capitol building itself sits on an isthmus between Lake Monona and Lake Mendota, the city is surrounded by dairy farmland (though less so as development continues), and it lies on a geographical line that separates the portion of the state that was left untouched by glaciers from the portion that was carved and molded during the Ice Age. This results in a huge range of landscape and recreational opportunities within minutes of the city.

There are five lakes here; three in addition to the two glacial lakes that form the isthmus, which means the sun bathing and sailing is outstanding. Unlike some other great recreational spots in Wisconsin, though, you get the bonus of being able to switch between an urban environment and a pleasant, tree-filled escape within minutes. Nearby, in the metro area, Middleton was rated *Money Magazine's* best place to live in the United States in 2008.

GUIDANCE **Greater Madison Convention & Visitors Bureau** (608-255-2537; visitmadison.com), 21 North Park Street. Open 9–4:30 weekdays; 11–2 Saturday. This address is for the welcome center, which is run collaboratively by the CVB and the university. All manner of guides, maps, and parking information are available here, along with students who man the reception area ready to answer questions. You can walk in, or there's a drive-through window if you just can't stop. UW-Madison also runs a Campus Information Center at the Red Gym, 716 Langdon Street, primarily geared to students and campus visitors. *The Isthmus* has a

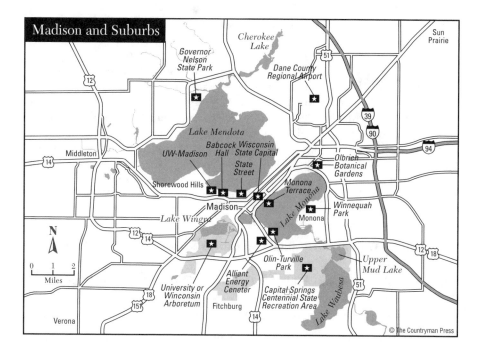

wealth of dining and entertainment information, as does the local A&E section of *The Onion (which started here)*. Find that at Madison.Decider.com. Downtown Ambassadors man kiosks and offer advice.

GETTING THERE *By Car:* Madison is served by several interstates and state highways. From Milwaukee, take Interstate 94 west to WI 30; from Beloit, take I-90 north to the Beltline; from the Fox Valley, take WI 151 all the way to Madison; from Dodgeville, take WI 18 to WI 151; from Wausau or La Crosse take I-90/94 to WI 151 going southeast.

By Bus: Both **Badger Coaches** (608-255-6771; badgerbus.com) and Greyhound (800-231-2222; greyhound.com) serve Madison from spots in Wisconsin. The Badger buses run solely between Milwaukee and Madison and are a great value; Greyhound buses come from all around the country. **Van Galder** (608-752-5407; coachusa.com) brings travelers from Minneapolis and Chicago.

By Air: **Dane County Regional Airport** (608-246-3380; msnairport.com) is served by eight commercial airlines. It's a little far from downtown, but nicer hotels offer free shuttles. Other options from the airport include taxis, the Madison Metro Transit bus, and onsite car rental agencies.

GETTING AROUND **Metro Transit** (608-266-4466; www.cityofmadison.com/metro). This is an extensive bus system that serves the area from downtown to the suburban communities. Fixed route buses have bike racks that can accommodate two bikes. Fare is $1.50.

The one complaint visitors almost always have is the swirling vortex of one-way streets around the capitol. To non-locals, it can be confusing as you drive in circles trying to reach your downtown destination, shouting, "Hey look—there's the capitol. Oh, no. There it goes . . ." I just park and walk as soon as the capitol building looks near. Renting a bike's not a bad idea, either, and Madison is Wisconsin's most bike-friendly city. Another tricky part about getting around is the directional descriptions people use here. The capitol building is the reference point for all directions, but it's not that simple. Because the building is on the isthmus, and the isthmus is at an angle relative to north and south, the term "east" here actually means northeast, and "west" means west and southwest. If you follow a compass headed east, for example, you'll end up in Lake Monona. Natives of Milwaukee and Chicago, who have been trained by proximity to Lake Michigan that a large body of water equals east, will find their internal compass is out of whack with all these lakes everywhere. Something else to keep in mind is that Williamson Street is called "Willy" by locals.

MEDICAL EMERGENCY Call 911.

University of Wisconsin Hospital and Clinics (608-263-6400), 600 Highland Avenue.

University of Wisconsin Children's Hospital (608-263-7337), 600 Highland Avenue.

Meriter Hospital (608-267-6000), 202 South Park Street.

St. Mary's Hospital (608-251-6100), 707 South Mills Street.

✳ To See and Do

&. ⊤ ❀ **Chazen Museum of Art** (608-263-2246; chazen.wisc.edu), 800 University Avenue. Open 9–5 Tuesday through Friday, 11–5 Saturday and Sunday. Part of UW-Madison, this museum features around 18,000 works in all media from ancient Egypt to the present day. A 75,000-square-foot expansion that will double the gallery space and add an auditorium and classroom is expected to wrap up in 2011. Temporary exhibits rotate throughout the year. Free.

&. ⊤ ❀ **Madison Museum of Contemporary Art** (608-257-0158; mmoca.org), 227 State Street. Open daily. Part of the Overture Center for the Arts, the MMOCA is a small but high-quality contemporary art gallery housed in an appropriately modern glass building. There's a sculpture garden and a restaurant, **Fresco** (see Eating Out), on the roof, where diners can enjoy a view of the city from a window seat, or, or better yet, out in the garden. Admission to the museum is free.

✎ &. ❀ **Henry Vilas Zoo** (608-266-4733; vilaszoo.org); 702 South Randall Avenue. Open 9:30–5 daily. Maybe it's not the biggest zoo around, but it's free, and you can't beat that. Well-loved and supported by the Madison community, this zoo is perfect for a trip with little ones, with a nice park and beach nearby. Concessions are available as well as a gift shop. Free.

✎ &. **Monona Terrace** (608-261-4015; mononaterrace.com), 1 John Nolan Drive. The building's architect, Frank Lloyd Wright, called it "the long-awaited marriage between the city and beautiful Lake Monona." While most convention centers tend to be behemoth structures awkwardly placed in downtown areas, sitting empty and unused between conventions, Monona Terrace is, in true Wright style, perfectly suited to its location on the lake and a popular public space. Features for the casual visitor include a bike path, a rooftop garden, and a cafe, along with the stunning view of Lake Monona. Free.

WISCONSIN STATE CAPITOL BUILDING

♿ ⬆ 💲 **Wisconsin State Capitol Building**, 2 East Main Street. The building is open to the public Monday through Friday from 8–6, 8–4 on Saturday and Sunday. Situated between Lake Monona and Lake Mendota on the Madison Isthmus, Wisconsin's capitol building is a majestic beacon guiding visitors toward downtown. The sight of this stunning neo-classical building really is breathtaking, and the grounds are equally beautiful and well maintained. But it isn't just the sight of it that makes the capitol building such a treat. On a hill smack in the middle of downtown, Capitol Square actually serves as a meeting grounds for UW-Madison students and politicos alike as they travel from point to point in the city. Capitol Square is, in fact, the intersection for downtown Madison's four major streets, and each of the building's four wings faces one. On Wednesdays and Saturdays, the **Dane County Farmers Market** is held here and families lounge about on the capitol lawn munching breakfast or lunch, then head into the building for a tour. Entry to the capitol is always free, and guided tours are conducted six times a day Monday through Saturday, and three times on Sunday. Free.

STATE CAPITOL BUILDING

THAI PAVILION AT THE OLBRICH BOTANICAL GARDENS

&. ❧ **Olbrich Botanical Gardens** (608-246-4550; olbrich.org), 3330 Atwood Avenue. Open Monday through Saturday 10–4 and Sunday 10–5. See listing under Green Space.

&. ⛧ **Wisconsin Historical Museum** (608-264-6555; wisconsinhistory.org/museum/), 30 North Carroll Street. Open 9 4 Tuesday through Saturday. Explore the history of this land we now call Wisconsin via exhibits that go back to prehistoric times in this fantastic museum on Capitol Square. Permanent collections contain 110,000 historical objects and around 400,000 archeological pieces. There are a few changing displays each year focusing on important events and personalities in Wisconsin's history. A gift shop features Wisconsin trinkets, Frank Lloyd Wright items, and more. Donation suggested: adults $4; kids, $3; families, $10.

♂ &. ⛧ ❧ **Geology Museum** (608-262-2399; www.geology.wisc.edu/~museum/), 1215 West Dayton Street. Open 8:30–4:30 Monday through Friday, 9–1 Saturday. Located in Weeks Hall on the UW campus, its displays include huge rock and mineral collections, fossils, and reconstructed dinosaurs, plus a model cave. Free.

❧ **The Governor's Mansion** (officially called the Executive Residence) (608-246-5501), 99 Cambridge Road. Tours offered 1–3 Thursdays from April through August, with special times during the holiday season. Free.

♂ &. ⛧ **Madison Children's Museum** (608-256-6445; madisonchildrensmuseum .org), 100 State Street. Moving to 100 North Hamilton in 2010. Open daily. This interactive museum suits kids up to age 12. Exhibits are perfectly matched to Madison, and include the "Milking Parlor," which explores the dairy industry; "Let's Grow," which teaches kids about nutrition through a play juice bar, community farm, and farmers market; and the "Polling Place," where kids can learn about the democratic process. Admission $5.

♿ **Unitarian Meeting House** (608-233-9774; fusmadison.com), 900 University Bay Drive. Designed by Frank Lloyd Wright in his later years, this church features dramatic lines and a repeating triangle theme throughout. A member of the First Unitarian Society, Wright helped raise the funds to build the meeting house.

♿ ♻ **Capital Brewery** (608-836-7100; capital-brewery.com), 7734 Terrace Avenue, Middleton. Open 9–5 Monday through Friday, 1–5 Saturday. Tours offered at 3:30 Friday, 1:30 and 3:30 Saturday. Producing up to 16 beers yearly, Capital Brewery is a craft brewer focused on traditional beers such as pilsners, ales, and lagers. The brewery's Island Wheat uses the grain grown on Door County's Washington Island.

✷ Outdoor Activities

University of Wisconsin-Madison Arboretum (608-263-7888; uwarboretum .org), 1207 Seminole Highway. Open 7 AM–10 PM daily, visitor center open 9:30–4 Monday through Friday and 12:30–4 Saturday and Sunday. Foresight, cheap Depression-era land, and similarly cheap Civilian Conservation Corps labor resulted in the University of Wisconsin's Arboretum, an undeniable trailblazer in ecological restoration. Established in the '30s, the arboretum boasts more than 1,200 acres of preserved land on Lake Wingra. The visitor's center offers maps for self-guided tours as well as guided ones, a bookstore, and classes.

BICYCLING With its reputation as one of the best cities in the Midwest for biking (Madison has more bikes than cars), if you're so inclined, you should bring your bike. Numerous trails and well-marked bike lanes make pedal-power so much more fun in Madison.

BIKE RENTALS **Budget Bicycle Center** (608-251-1663; budgetbicyclecenter .net/), 930 Regent Street. Open daily. In addition to normal rentals, this location also handles the Red Bikes Project, which allows riders to check out a bike for a returnable $40 deposit. When the project first started, you could simply hop on any spray-painted red bike you saw and ride it to your destination, without locking it up, but around 80 percent of the bikes were lost to theft and vandalism. These days, you sign out the bike and a lock (for an additional deposit) and you can use it for as long as you'd like. It works great for college students, but the casual visitor can use the bikes as well. Budget Bicycle Center has other locations, but this is the one with the most used bikes and rentals. Regular rentals run $10/day; $30/week.

Machinery Row Bicycles (608-442-9574; machineryrowbicycles.com), 601 Williamson Street. Open daily. Part of Budget Bicycle Center, Machinery Row has a good number of rentals and will perform service without charge if you're riding one of the free red bikes.

Williamson Bikes and Fitness (608-255-5292; willybikes.com), 640 West Washington Avenue. Open daily. Located in an old train depot, Willy Bikes has rentals starting at $15 a day or $70 a week. You can rent new bikes, child trailers, tandems, and more for varying rates. There's another location on East Washington, but it doesn't do rentals.

Yellow Jersey (608-257-4737; yellowjersey.org), 419 State Street. Open daily. This bike shop has a cool history; Yellow Jersey, which specializes in high-end European bikes, has been around since 1971, starting out as a co-op. It briefly ran a precursor to the Red Bike Project, painting beat-up old bikes white and leaving them around town for people to ride. As with the red bikes, most of these disappeared, but the little co-op grew. These folks are serious about bikes. While it's not its focus, Yellow Jersey rents mountain bikes starting at $9.50, with weekend and weekly rates as well. Reservations are not accepted.

BIKE TRAILS **Capital City State Trail**, like many trails, is still being expanded and offers a fantastic way to see the city and surrounding countryside; start downtown on this paved trail near the capitol building and hit Monona Terrace, Olbrich Gardens, the UW Arboretum, and more. It's actually the result of connecting multiple bike paths together, and you can ride the loops individually or go for a longer jaunt. The Lake Monona Loop takes you through the wonderfully restaurant-heavy Atwood neighborhood, past Olbrich Botanical Gardens and Monona Terrace, and through serene countryside. This shared-use path is extremely popular with bikers and hooks up with state trails which require a fee, but if you stay on the city path, it's free. The **UW Lakeshore Path** runs along Lake Mendota, and ends up at Picnic Point, part of the Lakeshore Nature Preserve.

✳ Green Space

The **City of Madison Parks Department** (608-266-4711; cityofmadison.com /parks) operates numerous parks throughout the county, but some stand out for their beauty and frequent activity. Likewise, there are four public golf courses run by the parks department—check online for details. Here are a few of the most popular spots to relax and enjoy the scenery.

& ❀ **Olbrich Botanical Gardens** (608-246-4550; olbrich.org), 3330 Atwood Avenue. Open Monday through Saturday 10–4 and Sunday 10–5. Voted a "Wonder of Wisconsin" by locals, the Olbrich Botanical Gardens features 16 acres of display

STATE CAPITOL FROM MONONA TERRACE

gardens across from Lake Monona, near the Isthmus Bike Path. It's exceptionally serene; the winding paths leading from garden to garden make for a perfect stroll. Don't miss the Thai Pavilion. Given to the University of Wisconsin-Madison in 2002 by the Thai government and the Wisconsin Alumni Association's Thai Chapter, the pavilion highlights the strong relationship between the University and Thailand. UW-Madison has long had one of the largest populations of Thai students in the United States, and this rare gift (there are only four such structures outside of Thailand) is certainly special. Walk through the Bolz Conservatory, which features 750 tropical plants and a few critters as well. Admission to the outdoor display gardens, including the Thai Pavilion, is free (donations are welcome), but the Bolz Conservatory costs $1.

Lakeshore Nature Preserve (lakeshorepreserve.wisc.edu), along the southern portion of Lake Mendota. Part of UW-Madison, this 300-acre preserve features woods, marshes, prairie land, an observatory, sand beaches, and the Lakeshore Path, which travels throughout the preserve. Picnic Point—a popular spot for, well, a picnic (and more)—is located on a mile-long peninsula forming University Bay.

Olin Park and Turville Point Conservation Park, 1156 Olin-Turville Court. Open daily 4 AM–10 PM. Together, these adjacent parks total more than 100 acres, and include prairie land, a beach, a playground, game courts, hiking, trails, and more.

Edna Taylor Conservation Park, 802 Femrite Drive. Wetland restoration is ongoing here, but you can still walk more than a mile of trail through this marshy park. There are boardwalks, Native American burial mounds, and lots of native plants.

Winnequah Park (608-222-2525), 5303 Healy Lane, Monona. This park has a little—a lot—of everything: six baseball diamonds, three soccer pitches, tennis courts, an arboretum, a skate park, senior center, pool with a water slide, ice skating in winter, and more. For the little ones, this is also the location of the **Monona Youth Dream Park**, a huge kiddie playground that looks like a castle. It's a great place to let the kids burn off a little car ride energy.

Aldo Leopold Nature Center (608-221-0404; naturenet.com/alnc/), 300 Femrite Drive, Monona. Open 9–4 Monday through Friday. Trails open daylight hours when classes aren't in session. Drop-in programs include the Leopold Interpretive Trail, where you'll learn about Wisconsin habitats, and the Family Trailside Backpack Program sends you out to the trails with a backpack full of exploration goodies.

✳ Lodging

Capitol/Downtown

✑ ♿ **Sheraton** (608-251-2300; sheratonmadison.com), 700 John Nolan Drive. It's a couple of miles from State Street, but this location has its conveniences: It's near the Alliant Energy Center, Olin-Turville Park, Monona Terrace, and WI 18. There's a bike path out front that runs along Lake Monona and straight to the action. Inside, the updated hotel offers some of the most comfortable beds around, a friendly staff, a sun-drenched atrium pool, and more. If you've got extra cash, spring for the upgraded Club features, which include breakfast, afternoon snacks, and more. Rooms $119–169.

MONONA YOUTH DREAM PARK

&. **Hilton Madison Monona Terrace** (608-255-5100; hilton.com), 9 East Wilson Street. With great views of the capitol building and Lake Monona, it's hard to find a better place to take in the city. The Hilton has luxury rooms available as well as comfortable, attractive guest rooms. The location is perfect, connected to Monona Terrace. Rooms $162–379.

&. **The Madison Concourse Hotel** (608-257-6000; concoursehotel.com), 1 West Dayton Street. More great views of the capitol in an older hotel near the Square. The Concourse likely has the best amenities, but it, like the others, is a little spendy due to its location. $164–179.

&. **Best Western Inn on the Park** (608-285-8000; innonthepark.net), 22 South Carroll Street. The main draw here is the location, right across from the capitol building. Aside from that, this Best Western is pretty average.

The rooms look like standard hotel rooms, and you won't get the frills of the other downtown spots, but for the site it's a decent value. Rooms $129–179.

&. **The Dahlmann Campus Inn** (608-257-4391; thecampusinn.com), 601 Langdon Street. Charming and beautifully decorated, this hotel almost has the feeling of a bed & breakfast. Guest rooms are spacious and cozy, while still offering business amenities such as WiFi and nice workspaces. Rates include cocktails in the evening and continental breakfast. Suites include larger sitting areas; the Presidential Suite and the Governor's Suite come with a wet bar, two bathrooms, and stunning views. Unlike a lot of other hotels near campus, this one has free parking. Rooms $140–175.

East Side
✂ &. **La Quinta Inns and Suites at the American Center** (608-245-1243;

lq.com), 5217 East Terrace Drive. This hotel is a great bet for singles and families alike; there's a play area near the pool for young kids and the free breakfast includes waffles. Rooms are all suites, and are clean and modern, but it's pretty standard hotel decor. The location is a little odd, essentially in an office park, but it's not really more than about 10 miles from anything you might want to do in Madison. Pets are welcome. Rooms $92–139.

&. **Hampton Inn East** (608-244-9400; hamptoninn.com), 4820 Hayes Road. With warmly decorated rooms with contemporary furnishings, free hot breakfast, a pool, and more, this Hampton is a good choice for families and business travelers alike. Rooms $99–129.

&. **Holiday Inn at the American Center** (608-249-4220; holidayinn .com), 5109 West Terrace Drive. Newer among the chain hotels, this one has a contemporary atmosphere, with neutral tones and flat-screen televisions. Rooms $99–129.

Suburbs/Elsewhere

♪ &. **Courtyard by Marriott** (608-203-0100; marriott.com), 2266 Deming Way, Middleton. Clean, spacious rooms in a newer hotel with contemporary decor. The pool room is large and features a separate kiddie pool, with water toys and slides. Breakfast is not free, but is made onsite in the hotel's cafe. Rooms $99–199.

&. **Arbor House** (608-238-2981; arborhouse.com), 3402 Monroe Street. Offers eight rooms with a focus on the environment; the rooms have organic mattresses and bedding, sustainable woods, and energy-efficient lighting in a contemporary setting. The inn also offers bikes and canoes for outdoor adventures, and breakfast includes organic and local foods. Travel Green Wisconsin certified. Rooms $150–230.

&. **The Speckled Hen Inn** (608-244-9368; speckledheninn.com), 5525 Portage Road. Decor in the four rooms here ranges from country to Asian-inspired, but it's the out-of-the-way feeling that's a real treat. Only minutes from the hubbub downtown, the inn is located on a tranquil 50-acre plot of land, complete with llamas, apple orchards, gardens, and trails. Breakfast features items grown on site, along with other local and organic ingredients. Travel Green Wisconsin certified. Rooms $125–210.

✳ Where to Eat

Madison is home to a remarkable number of excellent restaurants, and an equally remarkable variety of cuisines. In this city of fewer than 250,000 people, your dining choices, to name a few, include Afghan, Nepalese, Ethiopian, and Mediterranean, plus more typical offerings. You can thank a diverse university population for the outstanding dining options, and you'll find a lot of the ethnic eateries near campus. But while the State Street area is a natural destination for hungry locals and travelers alike, with restaurants featuring a multitude of cuisines and ranging from very casual to the finest around, there are wonderful dining places all around Madison, so don't be afraid to venture away from the capital. There are options for vegetarians on every block, but plenty of steakhouses, too. Many of Madison's favorite restaurants heavily feature local foods, and the quality in Madison eateries is generally high, so don't judge the menu by the facade. I'll put it this way: If I lived in Madison, I wouldn't need a kitchen in my home. Following is but a handful of the diverse dining options in town.

DINING OUT ⅄ ⅃ **L'Etoile Restaurant** (608-251-0500; letoile-restaurant .com), 25 North Pinckney Street. Open for dinner Tuesday through Saturday. Every city has at least one restaurant that is so highly esteemed its name is considered synonymous with "mouthwatering," and L'Etoile is Madison's. The seasonal menu boasts many organic ingredients from local farms, and the farms are named on the menu. The dishes, like the name, nod to the French, but the focus on Wisconsin ingredients and farm-to-table sourcing keeps the upscale offerings familiar. Entrees $29–36.

⅄ ⅃ **Harvest** (608-255-6075; harvest -restaurant.com), 21 North Pinckney Street. Open for dinner Monday through Saturday, and one Sunday a month. Highly regarded and well-loved by locals and visitors alike, Harvest has been hailed by *Gourmet Magazine* and many others for its top-notch fare. With a seasonal menu focused on locally sourced, organic foods, Harvest's founder is heavily involved in the Slow Food movement. Dishes are contemporary American, but draw on various European cuisines. Entrees $16–42.

⅄ ⅃ **Restaurant Magnus** (608-258-8787; restaurantmagnus.com), 120 East Wilson Street. Open for dinner daily. This contemporary, upscale restaurant features unpretentious fine dining with a menu aimed at small-plate and traditional dining. Local, seasonal ingredients make up the Scandinavian-inspired menu. Entrees $20–34, tapas $7–15.

⅄ ⅃ **Fresco** (608-663-7374; foodfight inc.com/fresco.htm), 227 State Street. Open for dinner Tuesday through Sunday. Housed atop the Madison Museum of Contemporary Art, Fresco offers a stunning view of downtown Madison. Dine alfresco on the patio, or stay inside—the walls are glass, so you still get the view. Local ingredients go into the contemporary menu, which includes dishes such as beef tenderloin, seared duck breast, and ricotta cheese gnocchi. Dishes $17–29.

⅄ ⅃ **Blue Marlin** (608-255-2255; the bluemarlin.net), 101 North Hamilton Street. Open daily for dinner. Blue Marlin, as you might guess, is primarily a seafood restaurant—although you *can* get steak, veggie lasagna, or even a burger here. Cool blue stained-glass windows provide the appropriate watery atmosphere. Entrees $9–12, dinner $18–46.

⅄ ⅃ **Tornado Steak House** (608-256-3570; tornadosteakhouse.com), 116 South Hamilton. Open daily for dinner. Here's Madison's supper club, complete with every kind of steak imaginable, iceberg lettuce salads, hash brown sides, and Friday fish fry. In true Madison style, however, the beef is organic and grass-fed. There's a simpler, less expensive late-night menu, as well. Dishes $19–35.

⅄ ⅃ **Sardine** (608-441-1600; sardine madison.com), 617 Williamson Street. Open daily for dinner, Saturday and Sunday for brunch. Sardine is a funny name for a bistro with such an open, airy dining room, but then, Sardine is just kind of a funny name. No matter; the French/Belgian menu and lakeside location are delightful. Dishes such as potato, gruyere, and leek croquettes, seared duck breast with Belgian endive and steak frites, plus mussels and Belgian waffles, tempt the taste buds. Dishes $15–24.

EATING OUT

Capitol/Downtown

⅄ ⅃ **The Old Fashioned** (608-310-4545: theoldfashioned.com), 23 North Pinckney Street. Open for lunch and dinner daily, brunch Saturday and Sunday. Late-night dining Wednesday through Saturday. Paying homage to Wisconsin's culinary traditions, there's all manner of fresh, local foods on the menu, from brats and cheese curds to fish fry and more. Some of the options might be less obvious to a non-Wisconsinite, such as mac and cheese with a side of ring sausage or Saturday night prime rib (a supper club standby), but everything on the menu, and even the kid's menu, has its roots in Wisconsin. The walls feature framed photos of typical Wisconsin scenes without being kitschy. Wash it all down with a Wisconsin beer—there are 150 to choose from. $9.95–$18.95.

♂ ᕀ **Marigold Kitchen** (608-661-5559; marigoldkitchen.com), 118 South Pinckney Street. Open 7–3 Monday through Friday, 7–2 Saturday. A great, friendly cafe that's popular for breakfast, the simple, fresh fare hits the spot. Organic eggs, folded into creative omelets with roasted peppers, zucchini, goat cheese, and parmesan, or pancakes with pure maple syrup are great eye-openers (especially with a shot of espresso). Lunch offerings include sandwiches ranging from grilled cheese to grilled talapia. Kid's menu available. Breakfast $4.50–6.99, lunch $7.99–11.99.

ᕀ **Cafe Soleil** (608-251-0500; letoile -restaurant.com), 25 North Pinckney Street. Open 7:30–2:30 Monday Saturday. The little sister and downstairs neighbor of L'Etoile, this cafe offers a huge array of handmade croissants, scones, and other pastries, plus sandwiches, soups, and pizza. Like L'Etoile, the ingredients are locally sourced and the dishes seasonal; unlike L'Etoile, the prices are affordable. Dishes $4.50–9.50.

Sunroom Cafe (608-255-1555; sun roomcafe.com), 638 State Street. Open for all three meals daily. The first impression as you climb the stairs to this second floor cafe isn't great, but once you're up there, the sunny dining room and seemingly endless menu will put your mind at ease. There's a little

STATE STREET

An entry for State Street could fit under almost heading, because it stands out as Madison's primary destination for dining, shopping, and entertainment—it's the vibrant center of the city. There are boutiques and chain stores, fast-food restaurants and ethnic eateries, buskers and drum circles, and other colorful characters. It's all tightly packed into an eight-block pedestrian mall between the state capitol and the university. During the school year, UW students line the street, but you'll see more than a few families with tots here, too; everybody is welcome.

Home to more than 60 restaurants, State Street's variety might pose one problem: indecision. Try something new—maybe Nepalese cuisine, if you've never had it—or stick with pizza, whatever you'd like. Some of the eateries and boutiques have been here since the '70s, when State Street first became a pedestrian mall, and even the cheapest restaurants are well-loved standbys. Sprinkled throughout the Where To Eat section, you'll find many State Street dining options. There are many more not listed—take a stroll down the street and see what looks interesting.

bit of everything here—omelets, French toast, a bevy of sandwiches both hot and cold, pizza, pasta, grilled salmon, and on and on. Without question, there's something here to suit every taste. Sandwiches $4–12.

& **Himal Chuli Restaurant** (608-251-9225), 318 State Street. Open for lunch and dinner daily. A haven for vegetarians, the bulk of the menu at this Nepalese restaurant is meatless, but there are a few options for carnivores. Best to stick with the veggie choices, though, because that's what this place does best. Like Indian cuisine, Nepalese dishes feature wonderful spices and chutneys. Himal Chuli is small and cramped, but that just adds to the charm. Dishes $10–15.

& **Chautara** (608-251-3626), 334 State Street. This Nepalese eatery has a *lot* more space than its sister restaurant, Himal Chuli (see below). Meatless dishes such as creamy tofu korma will keep vegetarians satisfied, but there are plenty of lamb and beef options, as well. Well-loved by locals, Chautara offers to shrink portions (and prices) for kids. $13–32.

& **Husnu's** (608-256-0900; husnus .com), 547 State Street. Open for lunch and dinner daily. This State Street standby offers a contemporary take on traditional Middle Eastern and Mediterranean cuisine. A huge menu of kabobs, stews, and Middle Eastern favorites share space with fettuccini Alfredo and chicken parmesan. The atmosphere is pleasant and welcoming, with brightly colored tapestries offset by white walls. Dishes $7–14.

& **Ian's Pizza** (608-442-3535; ians pizza.com), 115 State Street. Open for lunch and dinner daily. Grab a slice of pizza at this small State Street joint, then take it outside for some people-watching. You can get a slice of plain ol' cheese here, or jazz it up with crazy toppings such as French fries, macaroni, or pesto. Truly creative slices of pie for adventurous palates. Slices $2.50–3.50, pies $6.50–24.

& Ɏ **Gino's** (608-257-9022; ginos madison.com), 540 State Street. Open for lunch and dinner daily. Well-loved among college students and returning grads for its garlicky pasta, lasagna, and deep-dish pizza, Gino's offers a full Italian menu. Inside, it's a little less casual than many State Street eateries, but not so much that you should worry about how you're dressed. Big wooden booths complete a warm atmosphere. Dishes $12.95–17.95.

Ɏ & **Kabul** (608-256-6322), 541 State Street. Open daily for lunch and dinner. Kabul serves up Afghan and Mediterranean stews and plates like burani with eggplant and yogurt sauce, and qabuli murgh, which features sautéed carrots, chicken, and raisins. Kabobs are on the menu, along with pitas, which should satisfy almost anyone. Like most State Street restaurants, the dining room here isn't big, but it does the trick. Lunch $6.75–8, dinner $9–13.

& **Mediterranean Café** (608-251-8510), 625 State Street. Open for lunch Monday through Saturday. A colorful, casual atmosphere and low prices on good food make this lunch-only eatery a hit with the locals. Many cuisines are represented, but the hummus and falafel get tons of raves. Dishes $5–7.

& **Parthenon Gyros** (608-251-6311; parthenongyros.com), 316 State Street. Open for lunch, dinner, and late night dining daily. Parthenon served curious Wisconsinites their first gyros back in 1972, and today it remains a go-to spot for Greek fast food. Gyros, spinach pie, and pizzas made on pita bread (called "pitzas" here) rule the menu. Dishes less than $10.

East/Near East

✐ & **Ella's Deli** (608-241-5291; ellas-deli.com), 2902 East Washington Avenue. Open Sunday–Thursday 10–10; Friday and Saturday 10–11. This place is completely insane. That's a compliment, of course. If you're interested in food, you should know Ella's is consistently voted Madison's best deli by folks who vote in those things, and offers a 20-page menu with everything from matzo-ball soup to vegetarian kugel, all manner of hot dogs, salads, breakfast (including blintzes), and pretty much every sandwich anyone has ever thought of. The kid's menu is larger than a lot of restaurants' complete offerings, and it even includes a special plate just for babies, with "a very little of each" of 10 items. It's not surprising the kid's menu is so big, because Ella's is all about kids. You'll figure that out when you see the merry-go-round out front.

Inside, the dining room is packed with fun stuff, including animated displays that whir overhead and glass-topped tables with more displays inside. There's also a 12-page dessert menu if you're in the mood for something sweet. Dishes $5–$12; desserts $3–5 (except for the one with 32 scoops of ice cream).

✐ **Lazy Jane's Cafe and Bakery** (608-257-5263), 1358 Williamson Street. Open 7–3 Monday through Friday, 8–2 Saturday and Sunday. Breakfast offerings include egg dishes and waffles, with veggie specialties like seitan hash, plus the freshly baked pastries and locally famous scones—a perfect pairing with an espresso drink. For lunch, burgers and veggie melts hit the spot. Upstairs, there's a comfy-chair section with toys for the kids. Dishes $6–8.

ELLA'S DELI

✒ ♿ **Monty's Blue Plate Diner** (608-244-8505; foodfightinc.com/montys .htm), 2089 Atwood Avenue. Open for all three meals. Located not far from Olbrich Botanical Gardens in an eclectic neighborhood, Monty's is a clean take on the greasy spoon, with shiny blue booths, lots of chrome, and friendly employees. Traditional diner foods are served up as is or vegetarian-style. Kids are more than welcome, but according to a sign, they're given a shot of espresso and a puppy if left unattended. Dishes $5–10.

✒ ♿ **Willy Street Co-Op** (608-251-6776; willystreet.coop), 1221 Williamson Street. Open daily 7:30 AM–9:30 PM. This natural foods grocery store's deli offers made-to-order sandwiches, a healthy hot case, and cold deli options. Grab something, then sit out front on the patio. Take-out less than $10.

� ♿ **Weary Traveler** (608-442-6207), 1201 Williamson Street. Open daily for lunch and dinner. This cozy corner restaurant has a laid-back neighborhood pub feel to it, but the food is what brings people back. A great menu lists everything from vegan chili and Hungarian goulash to Bob's Bad Breath Burger, which involves a lot of onion and garlic. Dishes $4.25–11.75.

♆ ✒ ♿ **Roman Candle Pizzeria** (608-258-2000), 1054 Williamson Street. Open for lunch and dinner daily. Using local, organic ingredients, Roman Candle whips up some interesting pies, which feature both typical toppings and wilder additions, such as arugula, walnuts, and pesto. There's a pasta here, too, and salads, and the littlest diners— if pizza doesn't suit your kids for some reason—can order special items like fruit salad or carrot sticks. There's Chocolate Shoppe ice cream for dessert. Fourteen-inch pies $14–20, dishes $6–10, slices start at $2.75.

♆ ♿ **Bandung Indonesian Cuisine** (608-255-6910; bandungrestaurant .com), 600 Williamson Street. Open for lunch and dinner Monday through Friday; dinner only Saturday and Sunday. This is the only Indonesian restaurant around, and therefore a must for adventurous nibblers. Dishes such as sambel goreng papaya and gado gado share space with pad Thai and red curry squash. Dishes $7–15.

♆ ♿ **Bunky's** (608-204-7004; bunkys cafe.net), 2827 Atwood Avenue. Open for lunch and dinner Tuesday through Saturday. The interior is as fun and eclectic as the neighborhood. The prices are a little high compared to other restaurants around, but the service is friendly and the menu offers vegetarian, vegan, and gluten-free options. The menu is split between Italian and Middle Eastern—you can get veggie lasagna, spaghetti and meatballs, falafel, baba ghanouge, and pizza here, to list a small portion of the offerings. Pre-dinner options are Italian salad or lentil soup. Lunch $7.95–13.95, dinner $10.95–20.95.

♿ ♆ **Bon Appetit Café** (608-283-4266; bonappetitmadison.com), 2425 Atwood Avenue. Open for lunch and dinner Tuesday through Saturday. The menu here is an eclectic mix of dishes from around the world with its feet planted firmly in Mediterranean cuisine. Ingredients are local and the offerings change daily. Dishes $7–14.

♆ ♿ **Cafe Costa Rica** (608-256-9830), 141 South Butler Street. Open for all three meals daily. This small, colorful cafe was born from a State Street food cart. The menu features tacos, quesadillas, and Costa Rican specialties, including meat and vegetarian dishes. Plantains, mangoes, and cilantro are all over the menu, and breakfast ranges from traditional Costa Rican to traditional American. You can sip a mojito here, too, if you'd like. Breakfast and lunch, $4–10; dinner $12–23.

El Dorado Grill (608-280-9378; foodfightinc.com/eldorado.htm), 744 Williamson Street. Open for dinner daily, lunch Thursday, brunch Sunday. The menu in this spiffy eatery specializes in Southwestern and Mexican cuisine, but you'll find all kinds of American and other dishes among the eclectic offerings. Dishes $9–15.

Lao Laan-Xang (608-819-0140), 2098 Atwood Avenue. Open for lunch and dinner. There are two locations for this restaurant; this one is just bigger. Both offer Laotian dishes and other Asian cuisine, and both get rave reviews. Dishes $7–15.

West/Suburbs

Blue Moon Bar and Grill (608-233-0441; bluemoonbar.com), 2535 University Avenue. Open for lunch and dinner daily. The shiny retro atmosphere is perfect for a burger, which is Blue Moon's signature offering. There's also a Friday fish fry. Dishes $6–8.

Sushi Box (608-232-1432; sushiboxmadison.com), 2433 University Avenue. Open 11–8:30 Monday through Saturday. This casual option for Japanese fare has a huge menu with all kinds of sushi and maki rolls, plus tempura and noodle dishes and vegetarian choices. Rolls $4–7, dishes $10–15.

Sushi Muramoto (608-441-1090; muramoto.biz), 546 North Midvale Boulevard. Open 11–10 daily. Not just sushi, this upscale Japanese restaurant offers dishes such as rib eye, fried tofu, and seared organic Irish salmon. This location is near the Hilldale Shopping Center, but there are two other similar and related restaurants downtown. Dishes $10–25.

Roman Candle Pizzeria (608-831-7777), 1920 Parmenter Street, Middleton. See entry above.

Doug's Soul Food Cafe (608-819-8900), 1325 Greenway Cross, Fitchburg. A Fitchburg strip mall is a strange place for soul food, but rest assured, the owner does indeed hail from the South. Doug's is a good option for take-out. Fried chicken, catfish, hush puppies, mac and cheese, and collard greens are just some of the comfort-food options here. Dishes less than $10.

Great Dane Pub and Brewing Company (608-284-0000; greatdanepub.com), 123 East Doty Street; (608-661-9400) 357 Price Place; (608-442-9000) 2980 Cahill Main, Fitchburg. With three locations, this is a popular spot for craft beer and a decent meal, and the number of its area sites is increasing. The dinner menu is huge and offers everything from a Greek vegetable platter to the lagered sausage platter, and there's a kid's menu, too. Dishes $10–15.

COFFEE AND SWEETS **Mother Fool's Coffeehouse** (608-259-1301; motherfools.com), 1101 Williamson Street. Open 6:30 AM–11 PM Monday through Friday, 8 AM–11 PM. This is a coffeehouse's coffeehouse, with mix-and-match furniture and local art on the walls. Mother Fool's boasts vegan baked goods from Milwaukee's popular East Side Ovens and coffee from Milwaukee's Alterra Coffee Roasters, but the laid-back vibe and social consciousness is pure Madison.

Lazy Jane's Cafe and Bakery (608-257-5263), 1358 Williamson Street. Open 7–3 Monday through Friday, 8–2 Saturday and Sunday. Lazy Jane's has a delightfully ramshackle coffeehouse atmosphere to it, with thrift-store furnishings and eclectic decorations, but the sizable breakfast and sandwich menu qualify it as a restaurant.

&. **Bradbury's** (608-204-0474; bradburyscoffee.com), 127 North Hamilton. Open daily. This sunny spot on the Capitol Loop offers espresso and more, and specializes in crepes with either sweet or savory fillings. The focus is on fresh, local ingredients (the Nutella and banana crepe wouldn't qualify, but it certainly is tempting) that change seasonally.

&. **Dobra Tea Room** (608-258-0488; dobratea.com), 449 State Street. Open 11–11 daily. Dobra's richly decorated interior, with natural woods, dark fabrics, and beaded curtains, provides the perfect surrounding for stopping to enjoy a cup of tea, which is exactly what this place is for. Black, white, and green teas from around the globe share space on the detailed menu, and if you're hungry, there are some snacks and light dishes.

&. **Ancora Cafe** (608-255-0285; ancoracoffee.com), 112 King Street. Open 6:30–5:30 Monday through Friday, 7–2 Saturday. Ancora has seven locations in the Madison area, but this one is the first (and nearest the capitol building). Ancora roasts its own beans, and keeps its focus on a great shot of espresso.

&. **Chocolate Shoppe Ice Cream** (608-255-5454; chocolateshoppeicecream.com), 468 State Street. Open daily. Locally made and widely distributed, the State Street shop stocks 50 flavors and has frozen yogurt, soy, and gelato. But the rich, creamy, Wisconsin-made ice cream is what really brings people here. There are two other locations in town.

&. **Babcock Hall Dairy Store** (608-262-3045; foodsci.wisc.edu/store), 1605 Linden Drive. Open 7:30–5:30 Monday through Friday, 11–4 Saturday. Part of the Department of Food Science at UW-Madison, the dairy store sells cheeses and other products made at the Babcock Hall Dairy Plant, a dairy research center. Most people come here for the ice cream, which comes in a handful of yummy flavors.

&. **People's Bakery and Lebanese Cuisine** (608-245-0404), 2810 East Washington Avenue. Open 6–6. It kind of looks like a Starbucks from outside, but this is a doughnut shop that also sells falafel, which should resolve any sweet-versus-savory conflicts in the car.

&. &. **Washington Hotel Coffee Room** (608-257-2999; lakesidefibers.com), 402 West Lakeside Street. Open 7 AM –8 PM Monday through Saturday, 7–5 Sunday. Housed in a yarn shop with views of Monona Bay, this coffee shop features local, organic products and breads from the Washington Hotel on Door County's Washington Island. The warm, airy interior reflects the natural thread that runs through everything the Washington Hotel touches. The menu features hot espresso drinks and cold smoothies, plus treats for noshing.

✳ Entertainment

✧ &. **Memorial Union Terrace** (608-265-3000; union.wisc.edu/terrace/), 800 Langdon Street. This is popular spot for UW-Madison students to hang out on a sunny day, but folks from the local community enjoy it as well. You can get a brat, a scoop of Babcock ice cream, pizza, beer, and other favorites of college students (and Wisconsinites in general) here. Grab a seat in one of the colorful sunburst chairs and enjoy the view of Lake Mendota. More than 1,000 events are held here each year, ranging from music and family friendly performances to movies and more.

✧ &. **Overture Center** (608-258-4177; overturecenter.com), 201 State Street. Home to nine performing arts companies, including the Madison Ballet, the Madison Symphony Orchestra, the Madison Opera, and others which perform in the center's seven venues, the center also houses the **Madison Museum of Contemporary Art**, plus community galleries and more. Basically, it's a one-stop arts shop in a shiny building that welcomes local and touring acts.

Y & **Orpheum Theater** (608-255-8755; orpheumtheatre.net), 216 State Street. This historic theater retains much of its original architecture from its creation as a movie palace, even if it's a little bit shabby. The Orpheum shows independent and mainstream films, plus live music from a diverse range of touring bands. There's a bar and restaurant in the lobby, and there are plenty of options for dining nearby.

Y & **Sundance Cinemas** (608-316-6900; orpheumtheatre.net), 430 North Midvale Boulevard. Opened in 2007, this was the first of Robert Redford's high-end art house cineplexes. There are six screens with stadium seating, plus bars, a coffee shop, and a restaurant (you don't need a movie ticket to dine.) Ticket prices are standard, but there's an "amenities fee" of a couple of bucks or so, depending on what time and day you're going.

& **Wisconsin Union Theater** (608-262-2202; uniontheater.wisc.edu), 800 Langdon Street. The Union Theater hosts touring musicians and a travel-film series, which includes a related buffet dinner. Opened in 1939, the theater seats more than 1300 people.

& **Stoughton Opera House** (608-877-4400; stoughtonoperahouse.com), 381 East Main Street, Stoughton. A historic venue opened in 1901, this theater hosts local and touring acts.

& **Bartell Community Theatre** (608-294-0740; madstage.com/bartell/), 113 East Mifflin Street. Home to several community theater companies, this active playhouse features two intimate rooms and an opportunity to see local productions on the cheap.

MADISON MUSEUM OF CONTEMPORARY ART

& Y **High Noon Saloon** (608-268–1122; high-noon.com), 701 East Washington Avenue. This is a popular spot to check out local and touring rock, indie, and other bands with a beer in your hand.

& Y **Majestic Theater** (608-255-0901; majesticmadison.com), 115 King Street. The Majestic is a mid-sized venue that began in 1906 as a vaudeville theater. Today, it brings in a range of musicians and bands. Seating is general admission and shows are all-ages.

Y & **Ale Asylum** (608-663-3926; ale asylum.com), 3698 Kinsman Boulevard. Open 11 AM–midnight Monday through Wednesday, 11 AM–bar time Thursday through Saturday, 2 PM– midnight Sunday. Ale Asylum brews up an IPA, a number of Belgian ales, and others, and offers them up in this fun brew pub. There's pizza and a sandwich menu, too.

✹ Selective Shopping

Anthology (608-204-2644; anthology .typepad.com), 218 State Street. Open 11–7 Monday through Saturday, Sunday noon–4. This boutique sells handmade goods from local artists as well as the owners' own works, plus items culled from the nation's DIY crafters. Cute hairclips, sock monsters, handmade jewelry, and even handmade Madison souvenirs almost guarantee you won't leave empty-handed.

Pop Deluxe (608-256-1966; pop deluxe.net), 310 State Street. Open 10–7 Monday through Saturday, noon-5 Sunday. All kinds of hip and interesting home decor, stationery, purses, knick-knacks, and doohickeys. Need an Eiffel Tower bread stamp, a modern birdhouse, or a screenprinted dog pillow? This is your place.

THE DANE COUNTY FARMERS' MARKET

On Saturdays from mid-April through mid-November, Capitol Square becomes a festive celebration of local foods, as vendors line up around the capitol building to peddle produce such as yellow beans, maple syrup, rhubarb, and squash. Welcome to the Dane County Farmers' Market, the country's largest market that only allows local agricultural producers to sell. Across the street, folks who don't fit the bill for the official market—crafters, concession vendors, and street musicians—get in the game, and on the capitol lawn folks hawk ideas, like political messages and public information. It's like a very cramped, colorful microcosm of Madison attitude, and it's lots of fun.

The experience feels festive and ritualistic at the same time; people cram the sidewalk surrounding the capitol building and walk, slowly, counterclockwise around the square, stopping at their favorite stands and filling up reusable shopping bags and even Radio Flyer wagons. Local businesses, such as **L'Etoile** (see Dining Out), **Marigold Kitchen**, and the **Willy Street Co-Op** (see Eating Out), use products from the market, in keeping with their commitment to using local foods.

During winter and on Wednesdays in summer, the Dane County Farmers' Market runs at other locations, but if you can make it to a summer Saturday market, you should.

Happy Bambino (608-204-6147; happybambino.com), 2045 Atwood Avenue. Open Monday through Saturday. Everything the hip mama could want for herself and her little baby, this boutique offers all kinds of trendy breastfeeding supplies, eco-friendly baby goods like diapers and cute covers, maternity clothes, slings, and more. The store also functions as a neighborhood meeting ground and education center for new parents.

Satara (608-251-4905; satara-inc.com), 5621 Odana Road. Open 10–6 Monday through Friday, 10–4 Saturday. Satara sells all kinds of organic and natural home and baby goods, including non-toxic wood toys, bamboo baby clothes, and millet hull pillows.

Little Luxuries (608-255-7372; little luxuriesmadison.com), 230 State Street. Open daily. This gift shop offers a little bit of everything—unique purses, sunglasses, lunch bags, baby shoes, scarves, and more.

Capitol Kids (608-280-0744; capitol kids.com), 8 South Carroll Street. Open daily. This children's boutique and toy store offers the hippest name brands and safest toys, under one roof. The stuff's not cheap, but it's the cream of the crop.

Serrv (608-233-4438; serrv.org), 2701 Monroe Street. Open 10–6 Monday through Saturday, noon-3 Sunday. Serrv is a non-profit network of shops that sell ethically sourced, Fair Trade crafts and gifts. Find guilt-free dishware, baby items, purses, and more.

Orange Tree Imports (608-255-8211; orangetreeimports.com), 1721 Monroe Street. Open 10–8 Monday through Thursday, 10–5:30 Friday and Saturday, noon-4 Sunday. In the same spot since the '70s, this shop sells everything from the gourmet kitchen gadgets it's known for to jewelry, stationery, toys, and more.

Shangri-La Collections (608-259-9395; shangrilacollections.com), 125 State Street. Open 10–7 Monday through Saturday, 11–6 Sunday. This shop sells all manner of arts, crafts, jewelry, and more from the Himalayan region.

The Soap Opera (608-251-4051; the soapopera.com), 319 State Street. Open 10–8 Monday through Friday, 10–6 Saturday, 11–5 Sunday. A State Street staple since 1972, this place puts chain body-care shops to shame. All the usual name-brand natural lines are represented, such as Burt's Bees, Aura Cacia, Dr. Bronner's, and Kiss My Face, plus a whole bunch of brands you've never heard of. Pick up essential oils, sea sponges, and soap-making kits here as well.

A Stone's Throw (608-255-1925) 1925 Monroe Street. Open 10–7 Monday through Friday, 11–5 Sunday. This earth-friendly shop sells fashionable outdoor clothing brands such as Patagonia and Horny Toad, with discounted and used clothing upstairs.

Absolutely Art (608-249-9100; absolutelyartllc.com), 2322 Atwood Avenue. Open Tuesday through Sunday. Featuring the works of more than 200 area artists, this space is jam-packed with handmade goods and both functional and non-functional art in all media. This store's heart is in Door County, as the sculpture garden surely attests.

Fromagination (608-255-2430), 12 South Carroll Street. Open 9:30–6 Monday through Thursday, 9:30–6:30 Friday, 8–4:30 Saturday. Finally, a cheese shop that isn't cheesy. Offering artisan cheeses from Wisconsin—many from dairies not more than an hour away—plus locally sourced gourmet snacks and more, a visit to Fromagination is a great way to wrap your head around Wisconsin's love of cheese.

The Project Lodge (608-442-5339; theprojectlodge.com), 817 East Johnson Street. Open 11–5 Monday through Friday. A contemporary art space with regular local shows and other arts activities, run as a co-op.

A Room of One's Own Feminist Bookstore (608-257-7888; roomof onesown.com), 307 West Johnson Street. Open daily. Focused on women's literature as well as LGBT books, books on gender studies, children's books, and general fiction, the state's only feminist bookstore has been a State Street area institution since 1975.

Avol's Books at Canterbury (608-255-4730; madisoncanterbury.com), 315 West Gorham Street. Open 9–9 Monday through Saturday, 11–6 Sunday. Stocks more than 100,000 rare and out-of-print books.

University Book Store (608-257-3784; uwbookstore.com), 711 State Street. Open 9–7 Monday through Thursday, 9–5:30 Friday and Saturday, noon–5 Sunday. Yes, this is where the college students drop a ton of money at the beginning of every semester, but the second floor has a huge selection of UW clothing and gift items, plus general books and more, as well.

Hilldale Shopping Center (608-238-6640; hilldale.com), 702 North Midvale Boulevard. Open 10–9 Monday through Saturday, 10–6 Sunday. Anchored by Macy's, this upscale shopping mall on Madison's west side boasts hipper chains such as Anthropologie as well as locally owned shops. A few popular Madison restaurants have an additional location here, so instead of Applebee's, you get **Great Dane Pub and Brewery** and **Sushi Muramoto**. Sundance Cinemas is also here.

Ehlenbach's Cheese Chalet (608-846-4791; ehlenbachscheese.com), 4879 County Road V, DeForest. Open daily. Just north of Madison off I-90/94, this Swiss chalet peddles Wisconsin cheeses, sausage, and souvenirs. You won't miss it, and will likely be drawn to it because there's a larger-than-life-sized cow statue out front named Sissy.

EHLENBACH'S CHEESE CHALET

☀ Special Events

February: **International Festival**, Overture Center. This free, one-day event celebrates global cultures through food, music, performance, and crafts.

April: **Wisconsin Film Festival**, throughout Madison. Four days of independent and world films shown throughout the city, with nearly 200 screenings.

May: **Mifflin Street Block Party**, Mifflin Street. This wild party is held every year by students and residents of Mifflin Street. Originally begun as a Vietnam war protest, today it features bands and house parties—lots of them.

Audubon Art Fair, Warner Park Community Center, 1625 Northport Drive. This three-day annual art fair, formerly held at Olbrich Botanical Gardens, boasts more than 130 artists, kid's activities, and more. Proceeds benefit the Madison Audubon Society.

Fitchburg Days, McKee Farms Park, 2930 Chapel Valley Road, Fitchburg. This three-day festival celebrates the area's ethnic heritage with food, music, fireworks, and more.

Syttende Mai: Norwegian Constitution Day, Stoughton. Three days of Norwegian culture, music, art, and more. Food ranges from brats and burgers to lefse and other traditional Norwegian foods.

World's Largest Brat Fest, Alliant Energy Center. Held every year over Memorial Day weekend, this festival has entertainment, but it's really about the Johnsonville Brats. In 2008, the fest served up 191,712 brats to the willing public. All proceeds are donated to various charities.

June: **Cows on the Concourse**, Capitol Square. This annual celebration of all things dairy actually brings cows into the city.

Isthmus Jazz Festival, Memorial Union Terrace. This four-day festival boasts all kinds of jazz, from Dixieland to Latin.

Taste of the Arts Fair and Georgia O'Keeffe Celebration, Sun Prairie. This is actually two festivals in one—a regional arts and crafts fair, and an event celebrating artist Georgia O'Keeffe, who was born here.

July: **Art Fair on the Square**, Capitol Square. This huge art fair boasts more than 400 artists, plus music, food, and kid's activities all around the capitol building.

Dane County Fair, Alliant Energy Center. The Dane County Fair features rides, music, exhibits, and more over five days.

August: **Great Taste of the Midwest**, Olin-Turville Park. Try regional and home brews at this annual beer-tasting event, attended by more than 100 microbreweries from around the Midwest.

Sun Prairie Sweet Corn Festival, Sun Prairie. Music, a parade, crafts, plus hungry folks eating 70 tons of sweet corn make this one memorable.

Taste of Madison, Capitol Square. More than 60 of Madison's fabulous restaurants line up to fill bellies with affordable festival fare. There's also live music and other activities. Proceeds are donated to charity.

September: **Willy Street Fair**, Williamson Street. This neighborhood festival features eclectic music, lots of food, local crafts, and family fun the third weekend in September.

October: **Wisconsin Book Festival**, multiple locations. This book festival brings in around 15,000 attendees and notable authors from Wisconsin and beyond for this five-day event.

WISCONSIN DELLS AND BARABOO

A drive to the Dells from any direction takes you through miles of rolling farmland, lake after lake, and some of the state's most picturesque rural towns. When you get there, it's like a kiddie version of Las Vegas; the main strip, Wisconsin Dells Parkway, is an eyeful, to be sure. Lights, billboards, strange buildings, and amusement-park rides all compete for your attention—and your dollars. Welcome to the Waterpark Capital of the World. You'll be having fun, because that's what this place is all about.

The Wisconsin Dells is in the driftless region of the state, an area untouched by Ice Age glaciers. It was, however, touched by glacial melting; when an ice dam melted on Glacial Lake Wisconsin some 15,000 years ago, catastrophic flooding created the amazing rock formations, gorges, and bluffs that now define the region. It is this beautiful geography that first drew visitors to the area, and while it is a bit overshadowed by the hubbub on the Parkway, there are still plenty of opportunities to view the dells. Hop a boat tour or rent a kayak for a look at the stunning land. It's breathtaking.

Yes, the beauty is disarming, but now to the reason most people come here. A

DELLS OF THE WISCONSIN RIVER.

THE WISCONSIN DEER PARK

charming blend of old and new, some of the Dells' attractions remain largely the same as they were 30 years ago or more, while new ones pop up each season. Then again, some leave; the foam '70s "Home of the Future," called Xanadu, bit the dust in the early '90s, while the gravity-defying tourist trap Wonder Spot met its demise in 2007 after nearly 60 years (much to my chagrin). But Noah's Ark, billed as "America's Largest Waterpark," is still there, along with the Ducks tours, the Tommy Bartlett Show, and Storybook Gardens, plus countless kitschy hotels and restaurants. Some of the older, classic attractions are showing their age as they face stiff competition from newer kids on the block, but they're still delightful and even a little refreshing after a day with their flashy competitors.

All this pizzazz and touristy glitz means Wisconsin Dells is the ultimate staycation for state residents and neighbors—the area attracts more than 3 million visitors each year because of its fun and unique charm. A natural choice for families, adults enjoy themselves here, too. Sure, you can try some kid-free lodging and attractions, but most people want to jump right in the water with the little ones. There are slower-paced activities, such as Storybook Gardens and the Wisconsin Deer Park, that are well-suited to toddlers, and wilder rides for older kids and adults. There's entertainment of every sort, from music to comedy to the Tommy Bartlett Show, and loads of outdoor fun.

In nearby Baraboo, things are a little calmer, but no less worthy of a visit. State parks, Circus World Museum, the International Crane Foundation, and a darling downtown mean a side trip is in order, no matter what else you've got on your agenda.

GUIDANCE The friendly folks at the **Wisconsin Dells Visitor and Convention Bureau** (608-254-463; wisdells.com), 701 Superior Street, Wisconsin Dells, know their stuff, and they've got everything covered. I doubt there's a question about the

ANTIQUE TRAIN CAR AT CIRCUS WORLD MUSEUM IN BARABOO.

area they can't answer, and the visitor's guide, as well as Web site, has tons of information.

GETTING THERE *By Car:* The Dells sits at the convergence of Wisconsin Highways 13, 16, and 23, not far off I-90/94. From Milwaukee, take I-94 to Madison, head north on I-90, and hop off at WI 13. From Green Bay, take US 41 south to US 151, then west to I-90, and then WI 13. US 12/WI 23 runs between Baraboo and Wisconsin Dells.

By Bus: Few people come by bus, but if you choose, you can do so via Greyhound.

By Train: Again, it's not a common way to get here, but Amtrak does make a stop in the Dells.

GETTING AROUND A car is important, although if you're staying at a big resort, or downtown within walking distance of the attractions, you could still manage a lot of fun without one.

MEDICAL EMERGENCY Call 911.

St. Clare Hospital (608-356-1455), 707 Fourteenth Street, Baraboo.

St. Clare Urgent Care (608-254-5959), 530 Wisconsin Dells Parkway, Lake Delton.

St. Clare Urgent Care (608-253-8070), 1310 Broadway, Wisconsin Dells.

DEALS There are a number of coupon books and passes you can buy to lighten the stress on your wallet, but you'll want to be sure that the attractions are actually ones you want to visit—a deal for one person may not be a deal for another, so do

Bureau (608-254-463; wisdells.com), 701 Superior Street, rounds up current bargains on its Web site. Beyond that, the Wisconsin Dells City Pass is a great deal, offering admission to 12 attractions, such as the Wisconsin Deer Park, Mount Olympus, boat tours, and more, for about $100 a person. The Wisconsin Dells Coupon Book offers discounts on dining and attractions, including a lot of two-for-one deals, as does the Wisconsin Dells Fun Card. Dells Downtown Discovery Pass provides a three-fer on Wizard Quest, the Ripley's Believe it or Not Museum, and the 4D theater. Keep an eye out for coupons and deals on literature racks around town, too, because there are tons. Another way to save a few bucks is to get a package deal through your hotel—many offer free tickets to attractions with your room. And finally, consider coming in the off-season. In many cases, hotels halve their summer rate, and you can still enjoy those indoor waterparks. Many attractions are closed in winter, but there's still fun to be had.

✳ To See and Do

WATERPARKS AND AMUSEMENT PARKS When most people think of the Wisconsin Dells, they think of the waterparks and rides. What started as a unique attraction has become the Dells' defining characteristic. Here are the bigger amusement parks, but keep in mind that many of the resorts, such as **Great Wolf Lodge**, have their own impressive water parks, and you don't need to spend the night. For more information on those, see the listings under Lodging.

✍ ♿ **Noah's Ark Waterpark** (608-254-6351; noahsarkwaterpark.com), 1410 Wisconsin Dells Parkway. Open late May through early September. Opened in1979, Noah's Ark is the granddaddy of Wisconsin Dells water parks, and it's still a favorite among vacationers looking to soak in the sun. Boasting 49 water slides, plus water coasters, mini-golf, tot areas, and more, this park maintains its legendary status. Newer here is the 4D theater, featuring "Wet FX," which splashes you with water while you watch the flick. Admission $34.99; children younger than 2 free. Season pass $99.99.

✍ ♿ **Mount Olympus** (608-254-2490; mtolympuspark.com), 1881 Wisconsin Dells Parkway. 10:30–10 daily from the end of May through early September; off-season hours vary. This huge amusement park has just about everything—indoor and outdoor roller coasters and waterparks, go-carts, wave pools, plus a tot area and rides for the little ones. Dining options at this park range from burgers to Greek—get a gyro, or try a pie at My Big Fat Greek Pizza Joint. There are also lodging options at the park. Admission $39.99.

Timber Falls Adventure Park (608-254-8414; timberfallspark.com), 1000 Stand Rock Road, Wisconsin Dells. Open 10–6 daily. This popular park features four tree-lined mini-golf courses plus a roller coaster called the Avalanche and other amusement-park rides. Full admission $19.99–29.99; children younger than 5 free for mini-golf.

Riverview Park and Waterworld (608-254-2608; riverviewpark.com), WI 12, Wisconsin Dells. Open daily late May through early September. Other waterparks have bigger, wilder slides and more rides, but Riverview has traditional carnival rides such as the Tilt-a-Whirl and Scrambler, go-carts, a kiddie play area, and more, for about half the price. . Full admission $19; ages 4–5 $8.50; children younger than 4 $3.

✔ �& **Knuckelhead's Bowling & Indoor Amusement Park** (608-254-7332; dellsknuckleheads.com), 150 Gasser Road, Lake Delton. Open daily at 11. Located near the **Tanger Outlet Center** (see listing under Selective Shopping), this indoor park has cosmic bowling, rides, go-carts, an arcade, and pizza. There's a soft area for the littlest visitors, too. Rides $3–7, passes $13.95–$28.95.

MUSEUMS AND EXHIBITS

✔ ↑ **Tommy Bartlett Exploratory** (608-254-2525; tommybartlett.com), 560 Wisconsin Dells Parkway. Open 9–9 daily in summer, 10–4 daily fall through spring. It hasn't changed much since the '80s, so the technology might seem a little funny, but the kids still love it. That's because the hands-on science exhibits involving things like static electricity and holograms are still relevant and interesting. The original MIR space station is on display here, as well, which will wow kids and kids at heart. Adults $16–23; ages 6–11, $9–16.

✔ �& **Mid-Continent Railway Museum** (800-930-1385; midcontinent.org), E8948 Diamond Hill Road, North Freedom. Operates train rides at 11, 1, and 3 daily from the end of May through the beginning of September, weekends early May and late September, plus special events year-round. Take a seven-mile trip on a restored steel train; you leave from an 1800s depot and travel part of the former Chicago & Northwestern Railway. Train enthusiasts will be thrilled. Adults $13–15; ages 3–12 $7–8; children younger than 3 free.

CIRCUS WORLD MUSEUM

✔ �& **Circus World Museum** (866-693-1500; circusworld.wisconsinhistory .org), 550 WI 113, Baraboo. Open 9–6 daily mid-May through August (performance season), 10–4 daily mid-April through mid-May, 10–4 Saturday and Sunday January 1 through mid-April. The original winter home of the Ringling Bros. Circus, there are now more than 200 antique circus train cars on display here. The vibrant, intricate designs and sculptural flourishes on these restored wagons mark a bygone era and are amazing to see in person, but they aren't the only things to see.

Tours begin in a traditional museum, complete with dioramas and gallery space. The gallery has salvaged carvings from ruined wagons, photographs, and a collection of old circus posters and advertisements. Outside on the grounds, there are tents with circus acts performing throughout the day, concessions, an old merry-go-round you can ride, and a few train cars to check out. Cross back across the Baraboo River, and find Ringlingville— the historic collection of original buildings that made up the circus's winter quarters, with many structures built between 1897 and 1918. This is where the circus lived when it wasn't on the road. In all, there are 30 buildings on this 64-acre property, so plan on some time here. Adults $14.95, ages 5–11 $7.95, children younger than 5 free.

RUSSIAN MIR SPACE STATION AT TOMMY BARTLETT EXPLORATORY.

☂ **Ripley's Believe It or Not! Museum** (608-253-7556; www.ripleysbelieveit
ornotdells.com), 105 Broadway Street. Open daily May through October, Friday
through Monday November through April. One of 50 Ripley's attractions, this is
right at home in the Dells. Promising strange artifacts and odd legends, this museum has eight galleries, enough to satisfy fans of the bizarre. Little ones might be
freaked out by some of the displays, so choose carefully.

&. ☂ **H.H. Bennett Studio** (608-253-3523; hhbennettstudio.wisconsinhistory
.org/), 215 Broadway, Wisconsin Dells. Open 10–5 daily May 1 through October
31, 10–4 weekends November 1 through December 20 and March 1 through April
30. Not just for photography buffs, a visit to the Dells' oldest continually operating
business has historical appeal, too, and it's an official Wisconsin Historic Site. Bennett, a landscape photographer, is called "the man who made Wisconsin Dells
famous" because his pictures of the Dells' beauty created interest and tourism.
Taking it a step further, he set up shop to sell souvenir copies of his photos to all
these new visitors, and later added gifts and other items. Tour his studio and shop,
and pick up a postcard, just like they did in 1875. Adults $7; ages 5–17 $3.50; children younger than 5 free.

✴ Outdoor Activities

ANIMAL PARKS ✐ &. **Wisconsin Deer Park** (608-253-2041; wisdeerpark.com),
583 Wisconsin Dells Parkway. Open 9–7 daily Memorial Day through Labor Day.
This is a petting zoo with a variety of animals, but the real draw is the roaming
deer, which run up to you sniffing for a cracker as soon as you walk in the gate.
You'd think it would get old, all these deer following you around, but it doesn't—
it's delightful to be in the company of these gentle creatures. Don't bring your own

crackers, because human saltines aren't good for the deer, and are therefore banned from the park. You can purchase crackers on your way in. My recommendation is to buy more than you think you'll need. Adults $10; ages 3–11, $8; children younger than 3 free.

✄ ♿ **Timbavati Wildlife Park/Storybook Gardens** (608-253-2391; storybook gardens.net), 1500 Wisconsin Dells Parkway. Open 9–7 daily from early May through mid-September. Another classic Dells attraction, Storybook Gardens has been here since the '50's, making it among the earliest man-made attractions in town. Large nursery rhyme characters dot the gardens and make for great photo opportunities, but older kids might find it boring. There's a petting zoo here, as well. Adults $11.95; ages 2–12 $9.95; children younger than 2 free.

✄ ♿ **International Crane Foundation** (608-356-9462; savingcranes.org), E11376 Shady Lane Road, Baraboo. Open 9–5 daily mid-April through October. This 225-acre park is home to prairie land and native plants, and is the only place in the world where visitors can spy all 15 species of cranes. Not simply a preserve in Baraboo, the foundation works globally to provide refuge and preserve habitat for the endangered birds. View art exhibits, stroll the trails, take guided tours, and of course, see the whooping cranes (the U.S. population is about 80) and other birds. Adults $9.50; ages 6–17, $5; children younger than 6 free.

Evermor Sculpture Park, S7703 US 12, North Freedom. Open Thursday through Monday. The park is located behind **Delaney's Surplus** on US 12, about seven miles south of Baraboo. This stunning folk art environment was created by Tom Every, who had a hand in the Organ Room and the Carousel Room at the **House on the Rock**. Every, or his science-fiction alter-ego, Dr. Evermor, created the scrap-metal sculptures that make up this park. They are huge, 20 feet high in some cases, and the centerpiece—Dr. Evermor's Forevertron—weighs 320 tons. Throughout the park are other metal sculptures—birds, bugs, more machines— which all play into the Victorian saga Every created here.

BOAT TOURS **Original Wisconsin Ducks** (608-254-8751; wisconsinducktours .com), 1890 Wisconsin Dells Parkway, Wisconsin Dells. Open 8–7 daily in summer, 9–5 spring and fall. A scenic ride on a duck—a vehicle originally used WWII and so-named for its amphibious nature—is both exciting and educational. The first part of the ride takes you through rugged, wooded land until you reach the Wisconsin River, and drive right in. On the water, you'll see the true beauty of the Dells region; sandstone cliffs and chimneys of rock line the riverbanks, and the woods beyond are lush and green. What a contrast to all the hubbub downtown! Throughout the hour-long trip, your tour guide will impart nuggets of Dells knowledge (and dells knowledge) and a stream of corny jokes. This duck tour has been thrilling civilians since 1946, and is the largest such operation in the U.S. Adults $23; ages 5–11 $11.50; children younger than 5 free.

Dells Glacial Park Tours (608-254-6080; dellsducks.com), 1550 Wisconsin Dells Parkway. Operates tours daily in summer. With three different types of boats to get on the river and see the dells, young families and thrill seekers alike will find an option. The **Dells Army Ducks** is the Original Wisconsin Ducks' competitor in the amphibious tour market, while **the Mark Twain Boat Tour** and **Wild Thing Boat Tour** offer different takes on the water. Note that kids must be at least five

ORIGINAL WISCONSIN DUCKS ON THE RIVER.

years old to board the Wild Thing because it's a little, well, wild. Adults $23; children younger 12 $13.

Dells Boat Tours (608-254-8555; dellsboats.com), 107 Broadway Street, Wisconsin Dells. Tours mid-March through October. Tour the upper or lower dells of the Wisconsin River, take a thrilling ride on a speedboat, or set out on a dinner cruise. This tour company can get you to the famous Stand Rock, where others can't. Regular tours: adults $13–42, ages 6–11 half price.

Lake Delton Watersports (608-254-8702; wisconsindellswatersports.com), 255 Wisconsin Dells Parkway, Lake Delton. Open daily in summer. This outfit rents everything from kayaks to pontoons so you can get out on the lake. It also offers parasailing, and if you're staying at one of the lakeside resorts, will even pick you up.

MINI-GOLF AND GO-CART ✔ **Pirates Cove** (608-254-7500; piratescovewis dells.com), 31 Broadway Street, Wisconsin Dells. Open Memorial Day through Labor Day, and seasonal hours. This pirate-themed combination mini-golf and playground features lots to do for kids of all ages. Five 18-hole mini-golf courses, tall slides, intricate sandbox areas, and more will keep everyone occupied. Adults $12.55; ages 6–12 $10.55; children younger than 6 $3.

✔ **Timber Falls Adventure Park** (608-254-8414; timberfallspark.com), 1000 Stand Rock Road, Wisconsin Dells. Open 10–6 daily. This popular park features four tree-lined mini-golf courses, plus a roller coaster called the Avalanche and other amusement-park rides. Full admission $19.99–29.99; children younger than 5 free for mini-golf.

✳ Even More to See and Do

Lost Canyon Tours (608-254-8757; lostcanyontour.com), 720 Canyon Road, Wisconsin Dells. Open mid-April through October. A slower-paced tour than most of what you'll find in the Dells, this one goes by horse-drawn wagon. The mile-long tour through the forests and canyons around Lake Delton is a great option for a change of pace. Adults $8.75; ages 4–12 $5; children younger than 4 free.

Extreme World (608-254-4111; extremeworld.com), 1800 Wisconsin Dells Parkway, Wisconsin Dells. Open daily Memorial Day to Labor Day. Here's your opportunity to do crazy stuff like bungee jump and try other pulse-pounding, free-falling stunts. If you prefer to stay on the ground, there are go-carts here, too. Rides $19.95–$34.95.

✍ ↑ **Wizard Quest** (608 254-2184; wizardquest.net), 105 Broadway Street, Wisconsin Dells. Open daily March through October; Friday through Monday November through February. Like a video game come to life, players travel through tunnels, hidden passages, and traps, and answer questions on computers to achieve the game's objective: find and release imprisoned wizards. Adults $12.99; ages 5–11 $10.99; children younger than 5 free with adult.

✍ ⅙ ↑ **Dells Mining Company** (608-253-7002; dellsminingco.com), 427 Broadway Street, Wisconsin Dells. Open daily. Kids love sifting through the soil here in hopes of finding a gem. You pay by the bucket, and keep whatever you find. You can have the stones you find set in jewelry here, too, or just purchase it without the work, but what fun is that? Buckets $15.

✳ Green Space

⅙ **Devil's Lake State Park** (608-356-8301; devilslakewisconsin.com), S5975 Park Road, Baraboo. Open 6 AM–11 PM daily. Part of the Ice Age National Scenic Trail, this park boasts nearly 10,000 acres of scenery and fun. Two sand beaches on Devil's Lake, plus hiking, biking, kayaking, and rock climbing make this among the state's most popular parks. State park vehicle pass required.

⅙ **Mirror Lake State Park** (608-254-2333), E10320 Fern Dell Road, Baraboo. Open daily. This smaller but lovely state park is home to a calm, wooded lake that's perfect for a leisurely kayak trip, plus lots of hiking, biking trails, and skiing trails. There are cabins and campsites here, plus a Frank Lloyd Wright-designed cottage that's available for rent. State Park vehicle pass required.

Natural Bridge State Park (608-356-8301), County Highway C, Leland. Travel 15 miles northwest of Sauk City. Open daylight hours mid-April through mid-October. This small park has one big draw—a natural sandstone bridge, the largest in the state. It is thought that people lived here as far back as 9000 B.C., making it the oldest such site in the Midwest. Today, you can hike the trails to get a look. State Park vehicle pass required.

✳ Lodging

There are many lodging options in the Dells, and your choice depends largely on what you plan to do here. You can get a bare-bones motel room to rest your head at the end of a long day filled with excitement and saltwater taffy, or a luxury spa suite; water park resorts are popular and great in off-season as well as summer, but keep in mind that, of course, that the more you pay, the more you get. The newer, larger resorts are outstanding—don't use them as a yardstick for measuring the smaller ones. They simply can't compare, but the small ones do offer a fun option on a budget, particularly for families with little ones, and often include admission to area attractions. Some are hotels and motels that stepped it up when the water-park craze took off, and some are simply the original water park resorts, now dwarfed by the big guys. A big advantage to the "lesser" motels is their proximity to all the attractions—because they've been here so long, they are located next door to and across the street from places such as **Noah's Ark** and **Mount Olympus**. The higher-end resorts—and they really are fantastic—sit in a group at the edge of the hubbub.

I've listed summer rates because that's when most folks come, but if you stay during the off-season, you'll likely pay less.

Y ⌀ ♿ **The Great Wolf Lodge** (608-253-2222; greatwolf.com), 1400 Great Wolf Drive. The Great Wolf is a perfect family resort. Rooms range from standard doubles all the way to condos, with options such as family suites boasting plenty of breathing space and privacy walls so you don't have to go to bed when the children do. The decor makes a nod to the rustic, but it's sparkling clean. The indoor water park features wave pools, a tot area, and water slides ranging from small and straight to the Howlin' Tornado—a six-story funnel slide that drops you in the water. Add Wiley's Woods four-story arcade and play area, spas for adults and kids, onsite restaurants including a decent breakfast buffet that's free for kids, and full-service dining for dinner, and you won't ever have to leave the resort if you don't want to. Check out the evening entertainment for kids, with story time and an animated show in the lobby. Throw on some PJs and gather 'round. Suites $199–299, condos $269–659.

Y ⌀ ♿ **Kalahari Resort Waterpark** (877-525-2427; kalahariresorts.com/

NOAH'S ARK WATERPARK

wi/parks), 1305 Kalahari Drive, Wisconsin Dells. Another theme-park resort, Kalahari offers lots of playtime, on-site dining, and a spa. Rooms are fun, with African themes that aren't

GREAT WOLF LODGE IN WISCONSIN DELLS.

overdone, and come in a variety of suite sizes. There's an arcade, indoor and outdoor water park, and more. Suites $199–299.

Y ♂ ♿ **Chula Vista** (608-254-8366; chulavistaresort.com), 4031 River Road, Wisconsin Dells. This resort has huge indoor and outdoor water parks, plus golfing, a day spa, and dining ranging from buffet style to the more upscale Kaminski Brothers Chop House. There are rooms for everyone here (some with room *for* everyone) that range from double queen standard rooms to condos complete with full kitchens. Rooms and suites $199–299.

Y ♂ ♿ **Wilderness Resort** (800-867-9453; wildernessresort.com), 511 East Adams Street. Another waterpark resort with indoor and outdoor slides, a kiddie area, and cabanas, this one also has indoor mini-golf, plus regular golf outside, a four-story arcade, on-site dining, and more. The theme for this one is a little rustic, but it's a very comfortable, modern take on rustic. Options range from standard hotel rooms to whole cabins for rent. The setting, while right near the action, feels more secluded than some other hotels, with lush trees and pretty landscaping. Rooms $199–299, condos $325–599.

♂ ♿ **Raintree Resort** (608-253-4368; dellsraintree.com), 1435 Wisconsin Dells Parkway, Wisconsin Dells. Good for little ones, Raintree's water park won't compare to the Great Wolf's, but at more than 20,000 square feet, it should keep the kids entertained. Right on the strip, it's a stone's throw from Noah's Ark and other attractions. Rooms $99–159.

♂ ♿ **Copa Cabana** (608-253-1511; copacabanaresort.com), 611 Wisconsin Dells Parkway, Wisconsin Dells. The decor is meant to be a tropical, Florida-ish theme; today's travelers will see

the pink-lacquer accents as very '80s. The main draw to this place is not the rooms—although options vary from standard doubles to larger suites—but the location and mini water park. You can walk to many attractions from here—the Tommy Bartlett Show is across the street—and the small water park is perfect for small kids (bigger kids will get bored, though). Rooms $69–199.

♂ ♿ **Polynesian Resort** (608-254-2883; dellspolynesian.com), 857 North Frontage Road, Wisconsin Dells. A Wisconsin Dells pioneer, this hotel set off the water-park craze here. These days, the on-site parks are more moderate than the newer crop, but it's still a good facility for younger kids. Rooms $129–299.

♿ **Rhapsody on Lake Delton** (866-403-3557; artistaresorts.com), 1010 Wisconsin Dells Parkway, Wisconsin Dells. Offering only suites and condos with private entrances and parking, you'll get away from the touristy madness at some other resorts here. The decor in most units is warm and contemporary, and theme suites such as Hog Alley (a nod to Harley-Davidson) and the London Bridge (complete with a red phone booth!) add a touch of fun. Need extra room? Try the four-bedroom penthouse suite. There are indoor and outdoor heated pools here, but the big draw is the sand beach and view of Lake Delton. Rates $205–480.

♂ ♿ **Blackhawk Motel** (608-254-7770; blackhawkmotel.com), 720 Race Street, Wisconsin Dells. This motel has clean, simple rooms that are perfect for people on a budget. Try a tiny room with one double bed for low-for-the-Dells rates, or larger suites with as many as four queen beds. The rooms are basic, but you still get indoor and outdoor pools. Rooms $55–$230.

✍ ♿ **Carousel Inn & Suites** (608-254-6554; carousel-inn.com), 1011 Wisconsin Dells Parkway, Wisconsin Dells. Perfect for a classic Wisconsin Dells experience, this whimsical motel is old, but it offers a good value and perfect kitsch factor, plus it's right where the action is. There are standard guest rooms and larger suites, some with whirlpools. The small waterpark suits small children, although older kids might be bored. Rooms $129–299.

✍ ♿ **Dell Creek Motel** (608-253-7301; dellcreek.com), 501 Wisconsin Dells Parkway, Wisconsin Dells. Opened in 1955, this motel features updated, charming rooms, pretty landscaping, a playground, and a pool. Room options are standard doubles, queens, and kings. $64–94.

♿ **Sundara Inn and Spa** (608-253-9200; sundaraspa.com), 920 Canyon Road, Wisconsin Dells. This adults-only spa resort features luxury suites and villas off the beaten path—but not far—for a little peace. Rooms have king featherbeds, fireplaces, and Kohler fixtures in the bathrooms. Take advantage of the spa services and complimentary breakfast, then head out to the golf course. The setting is stunning, and takes advantage of the Dells' beauty. Travel Green Wisconsin certified. Suites and villas $279–454.

♿ ✍ **Yogi Bear's Camp Resort** (800-462-9644; dellsjellystone.com), S1915 Ishnala Road, Lake Delton. Pitch a tent, haul a camper, or rent a lodge for a different and inexpensive way to take a Dells vacation. Aside from camping, there are swimming and water slides, mini-golf, go-carts, special events and entertainment, and other activities. Campsites $29–89, cabins and lodges $119–299.

✍ ♿ **Baraboo Hills Campground** (800-226-7242; baraboohillscamp ground.com), E10545 Terrytown Road, Baraboo. Open mid-April through mid-October. Featuring wooded campsites plus basic and deluxe cabins complete with kitchenettes, there are options at this Baraboo park to suit all kinds of groups. There's a snack shop with food and camping supplies in case you forgot anything, activities ranging from volleyball to mini-golf, and a new skate park. $38–130.

🍸 ✍ ♿ **Ho-Chunk Hotel & Casino** (608-356-6210; ho-chunk.com/lodging .htm), S3214 WI 12, Baraboo. Even if you're not here to gamble, the hotel offers a good value for adults traveling here with or without kids. The rooms are warmly decorated, rustic-inspired standard doubles and suites with typical modern amenities and balconies. No water park here, but there is a kid's play area, arcade, and hourly child care, in case you want to sneak off to the casino for a bit. There are also five restaurants on site ranging from family-friendly fare to the Copper Oaks Steakhouse's fine dining. Rooms $89–159.

✳ Where to Eat

Dining in the Dells means a lot of touristy, kid-friendly places. If that sounds like a nightmare, don't worry. The restaurants have huge dining rooms to accommodate all those hungry vacationers and the food, happily, is above average in most places. A lot of the eateries you might dismiss as tourist traps actually have a comfortable atmosphere, tasty dishes, and extensive menus that will please kids and adults alike.

DINING OUT There just isn't a lot of four-star, fancy-pants dining in the Dells, because kids don't usually get into that, period. Nonetheless, there are a few options, so if you're here taking advantage of the waterslides yourself, holed up at the no-kids-allowed

Sundara (see resorts under *Lodging*), or have well-behaved children, check these out (some do offer a children's menu and are more kid-friendly than others).

Ⓨ & **The Del-Bar** (866-888-1861; del -bar.com), 800 Wisconsin Dells Parkway. It's a Dells classic, for sure, having been around since the '30s, with traditional Wisconsin supper club ambiance but a slightly updated menu. Not just a steakhouse, Del-Bar's got everything from pasta primavera to wiener schnitzel, as well as Friday fish fry. Kid's menu available. Entrees $20–39, Friday fish fry $12.95.

Ⓨ & **House of Embers** (608-253-6411; houseofembers.com), 935 Wisconsin Dells Parkway, Lake Delton. Opened in a different building in 1959, this supper club has been a Dells favorite all along. Themed dining rooms range from Victorian decor to classic Northwoods to a little bit kitschy—all appropriate for the area. Dishes range from burgers, pizza, and pasta to shrimp de jongue and Austrian veal, but the house specialty is ribs. There's a kid's menu, too. Burgers, pizza, and pasta $7.99–14.99, dinner entrees $19.99–33.99.

Ⓨ & **Field's at the Wilderness** (608-253-1400; fieldsatthewilderness.com), 511 East Adams Street, Wisconsin Dells. Open daily for dinner. Located inside the Wilderness Resort, this is among the most celebrated new fine-dining options in the Dells. Steak options such as prime rib and champignon brie filet rule the menu here, but there are a couple of chicken and pasta options for lighter appetites. $19.99–$32.99.

EATING OUT ✐ & **Cheese Factory Restaurant** (608-253-6065; cooking vegetarian.com), 521 Wisconsin Dells Parkway, Wisconsin Dells. Open daily except Tuesday for all three meals. Don't let the name fool you—although you *can* get cheese here, what stands out at this charming eatery are the vegan and vegetarian dishes. This is your chance to eat a healthy meal in the Dells; it's also a distinctly un-touristy restaurant. There's pizza, salad, and sandwiches, plus specialties such as Malaysian coconut noodles, Hungarian goulash, and chèvre crêpes, but as you read this, I'm probably still thinking about that chimichanga. To sweeten the deal, there's also a soda fountain here, complete with phosphates and ice cream. Dishes $8.95–14.95.

✐ & **Mr. Pancake** (608-253-3663; mrpancake.com), 1011 Wisconsin Dells Parkway, Wisconsin Dells. Open 7–1:30 daily. Housed across from Noah's Ark in a building that looks like a riverboat, the specialty here is, yes, pancakes. If that puts you in mind of something like IHOP, you're in for a treat. Opened in 1962, this family-owned eatery has flapjack offerings like buttermilk pancakes in short and tall stacks, peanut butter crepes, Swedish pancakes, and Belgian waffles with a selection of 10 different toppings. There are traditional egg breakfasts here, too, and even sandwiches for lunch, but how anyone could pass over the pancakes is beyond me. Dishes $5–15.

Ⓨ ✐ & **Moosejaw Restaurant** (608-254-1122; dellsmoosejaw.com), 110 Wisconsin Dells Parkway, Wisconsin Dells. Open daily for lunch and dinner, bar open until midnight. With its woodsy, rustic decor, arcade, and big moose statue out front, it's no secret this place is family friendly, but what's surprising is that it's also a microbrewery, whipping up batches of its own pilsners, lagers, bocks, and ales—it even makes an IPA. The dining menu has tasty offerings of everything from sandwiches and burgers to pasta and pizza and even steak, so there won't be a quarrel over tastes. The kid's menu offers favorites such as chicken nuggets and grilled cheese. Dishes $7.99–14.99, steak entrees $15.99–28.99, 14-inch pizza $20.99.

Y & ↑ **Marley's** (608-254-1800; marleysclub.com), 1470 Wisconsin Dells Parkway, Wisconsin Dells. Open for lunch and dinner daily. This Caribbean-themed restaurant is a fun place for something a little different, but not *too* different. The menu is all over the board, with options like jerk chicken or shrimp, veggie pasta, stir fry, and more. $9.99–15.99.

✂ & **Paul Bunyan's Famous Cook Shanty** (608-254-8717; paulbunyans .com), 411 WI 13, Wisconsin Dells. Open for all three meals daily from late May through early September; off-season hours vary. Promising "lumberjack style" dining, you get all-you-can-eat meals served family-style in a rustic, cafeteria-like atmosphere. Diners share space at big picnic tables and eat from tin dishes, like, I suppose, a legendary lumberjack would. Breakfast starts with a plateful of warm sugar doughnuts, and continues with endless servings of eggs, sausage, pancakes, potatoes, and—if you request—biscuits and gravy. It's all good, but good luck saying no to another doughnut; they're delicious. In keeping with touristy tradition, there's a gift shop here as well. $10–15, kids pay based on age.

Y ✂ & **Pedro's Mexican Restaurante** (608-253-7233; pedrosmexicanres taurant.com), 951 Stand Rock Road, Wisconsin Dells. Open daily for lunch and dinner. The menu, like the atmosphere, is typical Americanized Mexican food at this large restaurant, but the

food is good and the portions are large. It's in the middle of the action, just off the main drag, which makes it an easy stop after a day in the amusement parks. The menu offers a host of enchiladas, burritos, fajitas, and more. Dishes $10–15.

Y ✂ & **Carvelli's** (608-254-6156; carvellispizzaandpastahouse.com), 505 Broadway Street, Wisconsin Dells. Open daily for lunch and dinner. Located downtown near all the shopping, Carvelli's offers Italian dishes in an open, two-level space. The pasta is homemade, which means whatever you choose from the extensive menu is going to have a leg up on most Italian restaurants. Pizzas come with traditional toppings or wilder ones—try the Nova pizza, with salmon and capers, or the Tropical, with kiwi, pineapple, and mango. There's tiramisu, cannoli, and gelato for dessert. Kid's menu available. Lunch $6.99, dinner $9.99–18.95, 18-inch pizza $16.99–23.99.

Y ✂ & **Ginza of Tokyo** (608-254-8883; ginzaoftokyo.net), 481 Wisconsin Dells Parkway, Wisconsin Dells. Open daily for dinner. Here's a clean break from all the pizza parlors and steak-houses here. Ginza of Tokyo has three locations in Madison as well as this one in the Dells and is well-loved by visitors. Don't expect sushi, but you'll find tempura, udon, and teriyaki, plus a lot more. Kid's menu available. Dishes $9.95–15.95.

Y ✂ & **Pizza Pub** (608-254-7877; pizzapub.com), 1455 Wisconsin Dells Parkway. Open daily for lunch and dinner. Although it's popular, Pizza Pub doesn't sell only pizza, but also burgers, pasta and ribs. There's a salad bar, too, and a kid's menu, so everyone should be happy. Dishes $9.99–16.99, 14-inch pizza $12.99–20.64.

'SKI, SKY, AND STAGE'

&. ⌀ **Tommy Bartlett Show** (608-254-2525; tommybartlett.com), 560 Wisconsin Dells Parkway. Shows at 4:30 PM and 8:30 PM daily from late May through early September. After waterparks, the most enduring emblem of the Wisconsin Dells' over-the-top tourist attractions has to be the Tommy Bartlett Show. H. H. Bennett may be "the man who made Wisconsin Dells famous," but Tommy Bartlett certainly took things up a notch. Setting roots in the Dells in 1952, the 90-minute show featuring acts on "ski, sky, and stage" retains its wholesome charm after all these years. The meat of the show—daring acrobatics, family-oriented magicians, jugglers, and comedians, and of course, that dazzling and daring water ski presentation—has changed little over the decades, and this timeless charm makes it a quintessential Wisconsin Dells experience. When the Nerveless Nocks stunt team climbs onto that spinning, 65-foot-tall wheel, it's still breathtaking. No amount of time can change that.

After the devastating floods of June 2008 emptied out Lake Delton—the Tommy Bartlett Show's water playground—a remarkable display of fortitude and endurance followed. The show went on, despite pitfalls and thin audiences. Some resorts gave out free show tickets with rooms, and the public saw a side of the Dells they'd never seen; the businesses, each dependent on tourism dollars and thrilling attractions, banded together to get through a rough season. At the center of this effort to simply keep going was the Tommy Bartlett Show. Today, Lake Delton is back and so are the water skiers, like nothing ever happened. They said the show must go on, and it did. That's fortunate, because even with all the new parks and other attractions, the Dells just wouldn't be the same without Tommy Bartlett's thrilling show. Adults $16–23; ages 6–11 $9–16; children younger than 5 free.

THE TOMMY BARTLETT EXPLORATOR

✳ Entertainment

⚓ **Big Sky Twin Drive-In Theater** (608-254-8025; bigskydrivein.com), N9199 Winnebago Road, Wisconsin Dells. Open nightly Memorial Day through Labor Day, weekends in May and September. There isn't a more appropriate place for the nostalgia and charm of an outdoor big-screen than the Wisconsin Dells. Offering double features on first-run films, free popcorn and candy, and an unusually low admission price, this is a deal. Admission $8 adults; children younger than 11 $5.

⚓ ♿ ↑ **Rick Wilcox Magic Theater** (608-254-5511; rickwilcox.com), 1670 Wisconsin Dells Parkway, Wisconsin Dells. The 90-minute Grand Illusion Show consistently gets rave reviews from kids and adults alike. Rick and Suzan Wilcox—a husband-and-wife magician team—opened the theater in 1999, making it a relative newcomer in Wisconsin Dells terms. Today, it's among the most popular shows here, thanks to flashy theatrics and well-executed tricks. Tickets $26–39.

⚓ ♿ ↑ **Desert Star Cinema** (608-253-7827; www.starcinema.com), 1301 Wisconsin Dells Parkway, Lake Delton. Boasting 15 curved screens with stadium seating, this theater plays first-run movies in style. It's located right on the main drag, which means popping in for a change of pace is no problem.

⚓ ♿ ↑ **Broadway Dinner Theatre** (608-253-2006; broadwayinthedells .com), 564 South Wisconsin Dells Parkway. This popular dinner theater puts on family friendly musicals throughout the year. Admission includes dinner. Productions change regularly, but there's always an all-song-and-dance show, the *American Musical Celebration*. Adults $15–42, children younger than 12 $10–17.

⚓ ♿ ↑ **Wisconsin Opry** (608-254-7951; wisconsinopry.com), E10964 Moon Road, Baraboo. Open late May through late September. There's a little bit of country everything here—down-home meals, hay rides, an antique and flea market, plus nightly shows featuring bluegrass, country music, and comedy. $18 show only, $30.50 dinner and show.

🍸 ♿ ↑ **Ho-Chunk Casino** (608-356-6210; ho-chunk.com), S3214 WI 12, Baraboo. Open 24 hours daily. Among Wisconsin's most popular casinos, Ho-Chunk is the fifth-largest Native American casino in the U.S. With on-site dining and lodging, anyone who wants to toss a few coins in the slots or get in on a game of blackjack or bingo should be all set here. The Casino also periodically hosts touring acts.

🍸 **Showboat Saloon** (608-253-2628; showboatsaloon.com), 24 Broadway Street, Wisconsin Dells. Open daily. With exception of the Prohibition years, this place has been a bar since it opened in 1907. It's a bit of a local hide-out, but on weekends, no business is safe from the tourists. The saloon features live music, karaoke, and regular specials.

♿ **Al Ringling Theatre** (608-356-8864; alringling.com), 136 Fourth Avenue, Baraboo. Opened in 1915 by circus legend Al Ringling, this impressive space was modeled after French opera houses of the time and has played everything from vaudeville shows to movies. Today, the theatre is host to community performing arts groups and retains its original architecture.

The Village Booksmith (608-355-1001), 526 Oak Street, Baraboo. Open Monday through Saturday. This charming bookstore and coffee shop in Baraboo's downtown sells new and used titles and a selection of gifts, but it's known for its community events, which range from author appearances and poetry slams to storytelling events and live music. The store even hosts a community reading of James Joyce's *Ulysses* on Bloomsday, beginning at 8 AM and wrapping up when the readers have completed the tome.

✳ Selective Shopping

♂ ♿ ↑ **Tanger Outlet Center** (608-253-5380; tangeroutlet.com), 210 Gasser Road, Wisconsin Dells. Open 9–9 Monday through Saturday, 10–7 Sunday from early March through December; 10–6 Monday through Thursday, 10–9 Friday and Saturday, 10–7 Sunday from January through early March. Unlike a lot of outlet malls, which tend to have off-brand stores and other shops you've never heard of, this one has popular chains with great deals packed inside. The Gap Outlet and Stride Rite will keep parents happy, but there's Banana Republic, Ralph Lauren, and more here, too. A mall has to be exceptional to pass muster as an attraction, and this one does.

♿ **Book World** (608-254-2425; bookworldstores.com), 317 Broadway Street, Wisconsin Dells. Open daily 9 AM–10 PM in summer, 9–8 Monday through Friday and 9–5 Saturday and Sunday in winter. This regional, independent chain of bookstores offers a broad selection of titles for kids and adults, in addition to lots of local titles plus magazines and newspapers. This outlet is downtown in a Swiss-looking building, and there are others in the nearby communities of Baraboo (608-356-5155; 135 Third Street) and Portage (608-742-1989; 120 West Cook Street).

Original Wisconsin Dells Fudge (608-253-3373; wisdellsfudge.com), 108 Broadway Street, Wisconsin Dells. Open 8 AM–11 PM daily in summer,

shorter hours in winter. was the first fudge shop in the area, opened in 1962, and they still use the same recipes and method to make fresh fudge daily. The shop also sells saltwater taffy, nut brittles, and addicting Bavarian frosted nuts. You can try to walk by when you're shopping downtown, but it'll be hard.

Goody Goody Gum Drops Candy Kitchen (608-253-7983; goodygumdrop.com), 401 Broadway Street. Open 9–5 daily. This corner candy store is a decadent one-stop shop for fudge, ice cream, saltwater taffy, caramel apples, and other things to make your teeth rot but your taste buds happy. This one's downtown, but there's another, summer-only location at Riverview Park.

Dandelion Boutique (608-253-7197; shopdandelion.com), 232 Broadway Street, Wisconsin Dells. Open daily. Here's a refreshing, unique store amid all those tee-shirt and souvenir shops. Pop in and check out the eclectic array of goods from pottery to stationery before you hit another touristy store.

The Grapevine (608-253-5311; dellsgrapevine.com), 312 Washington Avenue, Wisconsin Dells. Open daily in summer, Friday through Monday in winter. Located near downtown, this shop has all sorts of craftsy home goods such as twig wreaths, yard art, scented candles, and other accessories. Maybe not what you thought you'd find in the Dells, but then again—why not?

Carr Valley Cheese Company Store (608-254-7200; carrvalleycheese.com), 420 Broadway Street, Wisconsin Dells. Open daily. This is a retail outlet for the local cheese producer, located right downtown. Pop in for some squeaky cheese curds, aged cheddar, other dairy goodness, and cocoa and sausage.

An Siopa Eire (608-356-5578; ansiopaeire.com), 112 Third Street, Baraboo. Open 10–5 Monday through Friday, 9–4 Saturday. Here's a delightful shop devoted to Irish gifts in downtown Baraboo. Get Claddagh rings, Beleek china, knit sweaters, kilts, and more.

The Village Booksmith (608-355-1001), 526 Oak Street, Baraboo. Open Monday through Saturday. Best known for hosting events (see Entertainment), this bookstore also carries new and used titles as well as gifts.

Gem City Candy (608-356-4922; gemcity-baraboo.com), 102 Fourth Avenue, Baraboo. Open 10–5 Monday through Friday, 9–4 Saturday. Oh, boy. There's ice cream, espresso drinks, homemade Ringlingville chocolates, cheese, fudge, saltwater taffy, and a candy counter filled with treats from around the world. Stop here for a sweet break before you head to Circus World.

Wollersheim Winery (800-847-9463; wollersheim.com), 7876 WI 188, Prairie du Sac. Open 10–5 daily. The land where Wollersheim Winery sits, near the Wisconsin River, has a long history as a wine producer. All the way back in the 1800s, a man named Agoston Haraszthy tried growing grapes here. Haraszthy gave up quickly and headed west, where he is credited with pioneering the California wine industry.

✳ Special Events

May: **Automotion**, downtown Wisconsin Dells. This classic car meet features more than 1,000 vehicles, plus live music, activities for kids, and more.

Faire on the Square, downtown Baraboo. This annual arts fair brings in more than 100 artists, plus live music and games.

June: **Taste of Wisconsin Dells**, downtown Wisconsin Dells. It's small-ish for this sort of thing, with around 20 restaurants participating, but that, plus live music, a craft show, and a microbrewery beer tent, should be enough.

June/July: **The Great Circus Parade Festival**, Circus World, Baraboo. This event begins with the week-long **Wagon Roll-Out Days** as the antique circus wagons are readied for the big parade in Milwaukee.

Buffalo Bill's Wild West Show, Circus World, Baraboo. Just what it sounds like—sharpshooters, trick-ridin' cowboys, roping, and more wild west antics on the Circus World grounds. Yeehaw!

September: **Polish Fest**, Mount Olympus, Wisconsin Dells. This annual festival serves up Polish foods and entertainment for three days.

Wo-Zha-Wa Days, downtown Wisconsin Dells. This three-day, family friendly street festival has lots of free activities plus a parade.

October: **Autumn Harvest Fest**, downtown Wisconsin Dells. Two days of fall festival fun, including hayrides, music, and pumpkin decorating.

Southwestern Wisconsin

THE UPLANDS AND COULEE REGION

LACROSSE AND ONALASKA

GREAT RIVER ROAD AREA— NORTH OF LA CROSSE

INTRODUCTION

If you've never visited Southwestern Wisconsin or traveled the Great River Road, you might mistakenly believe it is nothing more than endless farmland. To be sure, traveling between the towns *does* take you past a great number of Wisconsin's farms, many of them dairy, some of them corn and other veggies and livestock. But unlike the flat farmlands to the north, these are set on hilly terrain, the verdant hills providing a beautiful backdrop to your travels. Along the Mississippi River, imposing but lovely bluffs offer amazing views from up top and alongside. This is the Driftless Area, untouched by glaciers, and it's the prettiest part of the state, if you ask me. The hills and valleys, ridges and coulees, bluffs and chimneys of rock, plus plenty of forest, prairie, rivers, and lakes, make a simple drive a thrill. This area is also home to another surprise: a desert, complete with cacti and reptiles. Really. Beyond the land, though, the towns here are the best small towns around—and a number of them have the awards to prove it. Rich with culture, arts, excellent dining, and heavy-hitting tourist attractions, there's enough here to keep you busy for longer than your vacation allows. There's no hustle and bustle, but it's not isolated, either—unless, of course, you pitch a tent at one of the many state parks in the area and spend your time riding the bike trails. Whatever you want from a vacation, the stunning and rich Driftless Area probably has it.

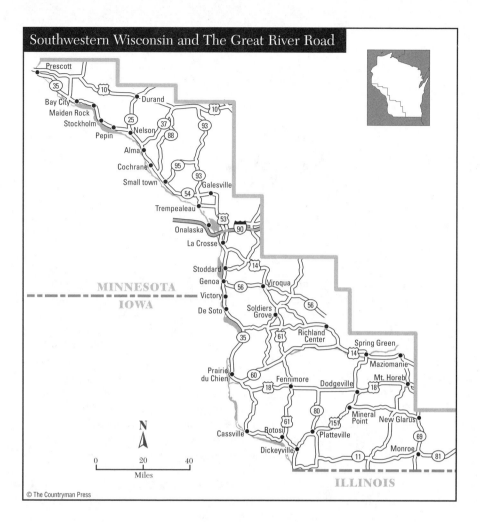

Southwestern Wisconsin and The Great River Road

Prescott
35
10
Bay City
Maiden Rock
Stockholm
Pepin
25
Durand
37
10
Nelson
88
93
Alma
Cochrane
95
93
Small town
Galesville
54
Trempealeau
53
Onalaska
90
La Crosse
Stoddard
14
Genoa
56
Viroqua
Victory
De Soto
56
Soldiers Grove
35
61
Richland Center
Spring Green
14
Maziomanie
Prairie du Chien
60
Fennimore
Dodgeville
Mt. Horeb
18
18
80
Mineral Point
151
New Glarus
Cassville
61
Potosi
Platteville
69
Dickeyville
Monroe
81
11

MINNESOTA
IOWA
ILLINOIS

N

0   20   40
Miles

© The Countryman Press

THE UPLANDS AND
COULEE REGION

The uplands area of Southwest Wisconsin is a beautiful, green, hilly region punctuated by some of the most intriguing small towns around. Once a mining region, attracting European settlers for its "gray gold," or lead, Wisconsin got its nickname, "The Badger State," from these early miners who carved caves into the hillside for shelter while they worked. Apparently only the Wisconsin miners did this, and when they carried the custom to Illinois, their co-workers called the impromptu abodes "badger dens," and the Wisconsin miners "badgers." (And so began a long history of Illinois-rooted nicknames; "Cheesehead" was only a matter of time. That's okay—in every case, Wisconsin has taken ownership of the insult!)

Beyond giving the state its nickname, the uplands settlers brought with them ethnic customs and pride which are still very prominent in many of the towns. Mineral Point, settled by miners from Cornwall, is the best place around for Cornish pasties and other delights, and the many 1800s stone buildings here comprise a direct inheritance. Monroe and New Glarus not only hold an abundance of Swiss festivals, but many buildings feature Swiss-style architecture, the charming brown buildings crossed with white. Monroe is home to the Chalet Cheese Co-op, the only maker of Limburger cheese in the United States. You'll have an opportunity to eat a Limburger-and-onion sandwich while here.

It's not just this heritage that makes the uplands special. There's a creative edge to the area, with more galleries packed into some of these towns than many bigger cities have. This is where Frank Lloyd Wright was born, and lived much of his life. But it's not only the serious, well-schooled artists who drive the creativity; this region is home to wondrous folk art, such as the Dickeyville Grotto, and the even more eccentric, like the House on the Rock and its amazing, obsessive collections. The food is good in Southwestern Wisconsin, and many restaurants keep it local by getting much of their ingredients from nearby farms.

Keep this all in mind as you travel through rolling hills and pastoral farmland from one town to the next. As stunningly beautiful as this region is, there's even more going on here than you realize.

GUIDANCE The most useful guide to the uplands region is produced by a non-profit group called **Uplands, Inc.** (800-279-9472; uplands.ws), but **Green County Tourism** (888-222-9111; greencounty.org), N3150 B, WI 81, Monroe, has a good

WORLD'S LARGEST CAROUSEL AT THE HOUSE ON THE ROCK

guide that includes Monroe and New Glarus, along with the areas many intriguing towns. Contact also the **Spring Green Chamber of Commerce** (608-588-2054; springgreen.com), and the **Mineral Point Chamber of Commerce** (888-764-6894; mineralpoint.com). In New Glarus, visitors can stop by the old depot at Sugar River State Trail head to visit the **New Glarus Chamber of Commerce** (800-527-6838; swisstown.com), where trail passes are sold and information given freely.

GETTING THERE *By Car:* The southern portion of WI 35, or the Great River Road, travels the westernmost edge of this area, from Prairie du Chien to Dickeyville. From Dickeyville or Madison, WI 151 travels through Platteville, Mineral Point, Dodgeville, and Mount Horeb. WI 69 travels to New Glarus, as does WI 39. WI 69 also goes to Monroe. WI 11 travels west from Monroe to Janesville. In short, you'll need a car and a map to travel the uplands and coulee region. The State of Wisconsin publishes and distributes widely a state map; the visitors guides you pick up along the way include maps, too, as does this book.

GETTING AROUND Most of us need a vehicle, but this area is perfect for biking, with connected state trails running through most of the counties.

MEDICAL EMERGENCY **Call 911**

Southwest Health Center (608-348-2331), 1400 East Side Road, Platteville.

Monroe Clinic (608-324-2000), 515 22nd Avenue, Monroe.

Uplands Hills Health (608-930-8000), 800 Compassion Way, Dodgeville.

JAIL ALLEY IN MINERAL POINT.

Prairie du Chien Memorial Hospital (608-357-2000), 705 East Taylor Street, Prairie du Chien.

✳ To See and Do

Spring Green Preserve, Angelo Lane, off Jones Road, just past a house with Fire Number E5196A, Spring Green. (nature.org/wherewework/northamerica/states/wisconsin/preserves/art32.html) See Green Space.

Cedar Grove Cheese (608-546-5284; cedargrovecheese.com), Mill Road, Plain. Open 8–4:30 Monday through Saturday and 9–1 Sunday from April through December, 10–3 Monday through Saturday January through April. Tours available daily. See cheesemaking in action and pick up some cheese and curds to take with you, including organic and hormone-free varieties.

Pendarvis State Historical Site (608-987-2122), 114 Shake Rag Street, Mineral Point. Open 10–5 daily mid-May through October. Explore the limestone buildings of an 1830s Cornish settlement, preserved in the late 1930s, and learn about the lives of the lead miners who developed the area. Adults $9; ages 5–17 $4.50; children younger than 5 free.

✐ **Cave of the Mounds** (608-437-3038; caveofthemounds.com/) 2975 Cave of the Mounds Road, Blue Mounds. Open 10–7 daily from Memorial Day through Labor Day; 9–5 Monday through Friday and 9–6 Saturday and Sunday in spring and fall; 9–5 Saturday and Sunday in winter. Considered the most important cave in the Midwest for its beauty and complexity, visitors enjoy the colorful formations and satellite caves that branch off the main path. Back up on ground, there's prairie land to explore, a gift shop stocking lots of rocks, picnic areas, and more. The cave is a constant 50 degrees Fahrenheit, which can be a nice break on a hot August day. Adults $14; ages 4–12 $7; children younger than 4 free.

Little Norway (608-437-8211; littlenorway.com), 3576 County Road JG North, Blue Mounds. Open 9–7 daily July and August, 9–5 daily September through June. Who said you have to go to Door County to see goats on a roof? This outdoor museum features examples of old Norwegian architecture and includes a large collection of artifacts. Its history dates back to the 1800s, when an immigrant named Osten Olson Haugen settled here and began farming the land. In 1927, a Chicagoan named Isak Dahle purchased the property, added buildings, and by 1937 he opened it as a tourist attraction. Today, the museum is owned by Dahle's great-nephew, who lives on the site with his family. Costumed guides lead tours of the replica stavkirke (Norwegian church), a sod-roofed cabin (with goats), and much more. Adults $12; ages 5–12 $5; children younger than 5 free.

Nick Engelbert's Grandview (608-967-2322; nicksgrandview.com), 7351 WI 39, Hollandale. Open 10–4 Tuesday through Sunday from Memorial Day to Labor Day. Grounds are open daylight hours year-round. Beginning in the late 1930s, Nick Englebert decorated his farmhouse and fashioned concrete sculptures with found objects. By the 1950s, there were 40 sculptures on the property. After years of wear, many of the sculptures have been restored. Tour the house and grounds for a peek. Free, donations suggested.

Mount Horeb Mustard Museum (608-437-3986; mustardmuseum.com), 100 West Main Street, Mount Horeb. Open 10–5 daily. Who would have thought there were 4,800 different mustards in the world? Well, there are, and they are all on display at the Mustard Museum. Other exhibits include antique items such as mustard tins and advertisements, and the gift shop sells 500 varieties of the spread to take home. Free.

Swiss Historical Village (608-527-2317; swisshistoricalvillage.org), 612 7th Avenue, New Glarus. Open 10–4 daily from May through October. This living museum features original and replica buildings for a glimpse into the lives of the area's early Swiss immigrants and the founding of New Glarus. Adults $9, children $3.

New Glarus Brewing Company (608-527-5850; newglarusbrewing .com), 119 WI 69, New Glarus. Open 10–4 daily for tours and tastings. Makers of local favorites Spotted Cow and Wisconsin Belgian Red, this award-winning craft brewery sells its beer only in Wisconsin. Beermaster Daniel Carey is always brewing up something new, so a trip to the tasting room is in order. Tours, free; tasting $3.50.

MOUNT HOREB MUSTARD MUSEUM.

THE HOUSE ON THE ROCK

'The House on the Rock (800-334-5275; houseontherock.com), 5754 WI 23, Spring Green. Open 9–5 daily April through September, Friday through Monday January through March. Some call it an over-the-top tourist trap, but I say it's a must-stop. I *love* the House on the Rock. It's beautiful and strange, and although it *is* showing its age a little, this attraction remains as intriguing as ever.

THE INFINITY ROOM AT THE HOUSE ON THE ROCK

The story of the House on the Rock begins in the 1940s, when the somewhat eccentric (and surprisingly reclusive) Alex Jordan built a Japanese-style house atop a 60-foot chimney of rock, called Deer Shelter Rock. It's said that Jordan was actually giving Frank Lloyd Wright the architectural finger with this house, that it was designed in a way to mock Wright. That's entirely possible, considering its proximity to Taliesin. The story goes that Wright once told Jordan's father, a student at Taliesin, "I wouldn't hire you to design a cheese crate or a chicken coop." Official word is that Jordan never intended the house to be an attraction, but people kept knocking on the door to get a look. Eventually he began charging admission, and expanding both the collections here and the buildings that house them.

It's true that the collections are part snake oil, part authentic; but this is not a historical museum, it's a bizarre and obsessive collection of all manner of strange and wonderful objects. And the tour is *long*—a visit here can be an all-day event, after which you will want to sit down and rest your feet. The tour begins with the house, a dark, low-ceilinged wonder filled with natural accents and lots of carpet. The final room of the house is the Infinity Room, a long, narrow walkout above the valley below, with more than 3,000 windows from which to enjoy the view. Those with a stomach for heights are in for a treat. You can tour just a portion of the attraction, and if you choose only the first tour, it ends here.

Tours two and three get into the stuff the House on the Rock is known for—the collections. Huge—*huge*—displays of dolls, dollhouses, guns, crowns, old advertisements, model airplanes, and other objects are contained in the winding exhibits, but the best parts are coming up. The Music of Yester-day exhibit features enormous automated music machines playing instruments, loudly, and while there may be higher-tech ways of accomplishing this today, these remain fascinating. Be sure to bring cash to buy tokens so you can operate these machines (although you can always loiter until someone else comes along and does it), because these larger-than-life, animated music boxes bang out tunes and are a treat. In the Carousel Room, you'll find the world's largest merry-go-round. It's bittersweet—each of its 269 animals is stunning, and the thousands of lights draw you in. But you can't ride it, and that's a heartbreaker.

There's more. I haven't even mentioned all the displays, and there's more. The Circus Room is my favorite of the windowed displays, featuring many circus scenes in miniature, behind glass. Then there's the mesmerizing Doll Carousel Room—yes, it contains dolls riding two different carousels—and the Organ Room, quite possibly the coolest room here, with its three large organs, bridges, and walkways making this feel like an adventure or Tim Burton set.

Don't forget to peek outside at the gardens, which are more recent additions. Along the way, there are cafes offering food and drink, and more importantly, a place to sit down. Portions of the tour, particularly the house itself, are not wheelchair- or stroller-accessible. Full tour: Adults $22–28.50; ages 5–17 $11.50–15.50; children younger than 5 free.

TALIESIN

FRANK LLOYD WRIGHT

A native of this area, Frank Lloyd Wright's legacy is all over the uplands region. Born in Richland Center, he attended college at UW-Madison, and eventually made his home in Spring Green, where he'd spent many summers as a child with his uncle. The most important stop for the architect's fans is **Taliesin**—Wright's home for many years—and its accompanying buildings, but there are other sites worth visiting around the area, as well.

&. **The National Historic Cheesemaking Center** (608-325-4636; nationalhistoriccheesemakingcenter.org), 2108 6th Avenue, Monroe. Open 9–4 daily April through October. Exploring the history of cheesemaking, in particular as it relates to the area, this museum offers exhibits and photographs of cheesemaking days gone by. This building is also the location for the Green County Welcome Center, where you can pick up tons of area brochures, trail passes, and other information, plus the Milk House Gift Shop, which peddles Monroe souvenirs.

&. ↑ **Chalet Cheese Cooperative** (608-325-4343;wisconsincheese-mart.info/Chalet.html), N4858 County Road N, Monroe. Open 7–3:30 Monday through Friday, 8 AM–10 AM Saturday. Tours by appointment. This is the only factory in the U.S. that produces the notoriously stinky Limburger cheese. Operating

Taliesin (608-588-7900; taliesinpreservation.org), 5607 County Road C, Spring Green. Open for tours May through October. Operated by the nonprofit Taliesin Preservation, Inc., this is the biggest attraction for any fan of Frank Lloyd Wright. Visitors can be guided through portions of the estate, or dive right in and take the full four-hour tour. Located in the rolling hills of Spring Green, along the Wisconsin River, tours of Wright's home and studio for many years promise education and a peek at his life. The full tour includes **Unity Chapel** (built for his mother's family, and where Wright was first buried), Hillside (a school built for his aunts), the Romeo and Juliet Windmill Tower, Tan-y-deri (a home for his sister), and the outside and inside of Taliesin, his home. Three other, shorter tours are available. Entry to the visitors' center, bookstore, and **Riverview Terrace Cafe** are free. Tours $16–80, children free, but they are not allowed on all tours.

Lloyd-Jones Family Cemetery and Unity Chapel, County Road T, Spring Green. The Wright-designed Unity Chapel is part of the official Taliesin tour, but you can swing by for a look at the gravesite of Wright and his family. That is, the *original* gravesite. After 30 years here, Wright's body was moved in 1985 to meet the dying wish of his third wife, Olgivanna. Today, a marker remains, and members of his family are buried here.

A. D. German Warehouse (608-647-2808), 300 South Church Street, Richland Center. Call ahead for tours. Built in 1915, this is a unique example of Wright's architecture, and it's highly ornamental. It's worth a visit to Wright's birthplace to see this unusual example of his work.

Aldebaran Farm (773-334-4924; aldebaranfarm.us), Spring Green. Not designed by Frank Lloyd Wright, but for anyone interested in Wright's life, this is where he spent childhood summers, and probably first fell in love with the area. You can see Taliesin from here. (See Lodging.)

since 1885, the co-operative also makes and sells various types of Swiss and brick cheeses.

Minhas Craft Brewery (608-325-3191; minhasbrewery.com), 1208 14th Avenue, Monroe. Tours given at 1 on Fridays, 1 and 3 on Saturdays. While most craft breweries these days focus on high-end brews and hoppy ales, Minhas delivers quality, cheap beers such as Rhinelander and Huber. Tours get you tastings and a 7-pack of bottles to take home. $10 ages 13 and up.

✂ **Toy Train Barn** (608-966-1464; whrc-wi.org/trainbarn), 9141 WI 81, Argyle. Open 10–5 daily. Here's a Wisconsin experience you might not expect: An old dairy barn now houses an astonishing collection of toy trains laid out throughout the space for visitors to enjoy. Adults $5; ages 4–10 $2.50.

Milton House Museum (608-868-7772; miltonhouse.org), 18 South Janesville Street, Janesville. Open 10–5 daily in summer, weekends in winter. This museum has many claims to fame: It was a stop on the Underground Railroad, and has tunnels that were used to hide slaves. It was the first grout building in the U.S. It's a hexagonal inn built in the 1840s by pioneer Joseph Goodrich, who ran it and provided refuge for slaves. Adults $6; ages 5–12, $3; children younger than 5 free.

Rotary Botanical Gardens (608-752-3885; rotarygardens.org), 1455 Palmer Drive, Janesville. Open daily. This 20-acre garden has formal displays focused on international themes, plus fern gardens, and more. Adults $5; ages 6–15 $3; children younger than 6 free.

& **Potosi Brewery** (608-763-4002; potosibrewery.com), 209 South Main Street, Potosi. Undergoing restoration, the brewery was built in the 1800s, but declined after the Potosi company shut down in 1970. Today, in addition to once again brewing beer, the property is the location of the National Brewery Museum, the Great River Road Interpretive Center, and the Transportation Museum.

National Brewery Museum (608-763-4002; nationalbrewerymuseum.org), 209 South Main Street, Potosi. Open 10–6 daily. Housed in the Potosi Brewery, tours offer a look at 1800s brewing equipment along with advertising and packaging exhibits on loan from members of the American Breweriana Association. Adults $7; ages 7–17 $4; children younger than 7 free.

The Mining Museum (608-348-3301; mining.jamison.museum), 405 East Main Street, Platteville. Open 9–5 daily May through October. Get a look at the history of mining, so important to this area, through exhibits and an underground tour of a lead mine to see how it was done in the early 1900s. Fee includes entry to the Rollo Jameson Museum next door, which includes collections of artifacts from everyday life at the turn of the 1900s. Adults $8; ages 5–15, $4; children younger than 5 free.

St. John Mine (608-763-2121), 129 South Main Street (WI 33), Potosi. A naturally occurring cave, in the 1800s this became a mine worked by both French settlers and Native Americans for a time, and it was the area's most productive mine during the Lead Rush. After it was worked out in 1870, the cave remained untouched until it was opened in 1969 as a show cave, and today visitors can tour it. Unique for both its natural features and historical significance, you'll almost certainly something.

Stonefield (608-725-5210), 12195 County Road VV, Cassville. Open 10–4 daily late May through mid-October. Across the street from **Nelson Dewey State Park**, this historic site offers a peek into the life of Nelson Dewey, Wisconsin's first governor, plus early 1900s farm life. The **State Agricultural Museum**, with its large collection of farm tools and artifacts, is here, as well as re-creations of a 1901 farmstead and a rural farming village. Adults $8; ages 5–17 $4; children younger than 5 free.

& **Dickeyville Grotto** (608-568-3119; dickeyvillegrotto.com), 305 West Main Street, Dickeyville. Open for guided tours 11–4 daily from June through August, 11–4 Saturday and Sunday September and October. Gift shop open daily April through October, weekends November to mid-December. Many folk-art grottos were built throughout the Midwest during the 1930s; this one is impressive and unique for its inclusion of political themes as well as functioning as a religious shrine. Father Matthias Wernerus, a Catholic priest, constructed the grotto on the grounds of Holy Ghost Parish over five years, from 1925 to 1930, using stone materials, concrete, and found objects, some of them donated by parishioners. The gift shop sells souvenirs and religious items. Free, donations encouraged.

Villa Louis Historic Site (608-326-2721; villalouis.wisconsinhistory.org), 521 Villa Louis Road, Prairie du Chien. Open 10–5 daily May through November. An official Wisconsin Historical Site, this 1800s Italian villa was home to members of the area's wealthy Dousman family. Tours include the mansion, decorated in period furnishings, as well as its outbuildings and gardens on St. Feriole Island. Adults $9; ages 5–17 $4.50; children younger than 5 free.

St. Feriole Island. Enter from Blackhawk Avenue or Washington Street. The original center of Prairie du Chien, many historical buildings remain here, including the Villa Louis Historic Site. This was the location of the Battle of Prairie du Chien during the War of 1812; appropriately, numerous historical reenactments and festivals are held here. There's also the Mississippi River Sculpture Park, a beach, and a popular park.

DICKEYVILLE GROTTO

✳ Outdoor Activities

Cheese Country Recreation Trail (608-574-2911; tricountytrails.com), Old Darlington Road, Mineral Point. This multi-use trail travels from Mineral Point to Monroe through forest, prairie, and farmland. A trail sticker is required for vehicles.

Tyrol Basin Ski & Snowboard Area (608-437-4135; tyrolbasin.com), 3487 Bohn Road, Mount Horeb. Open late November through March. With 16 trails and challenging jumps, plus a half-pipe, this ski hill is popular with snowboarders and suitable for families.

Sugar River State Trail (608-527-2334), 418 Railroad Street, New Glarus. Stop at the charming railroad depot to rent a bike or pick up a trail pass (plus plenty of visitor information), then hit the road. This trail is perfect for biking and walking, and passes through prairie, farmland, and forest on its 23-mile journey.

VILLA LOUIS IN PRAIRIE DU CHIEN

Badger State Trail. Traveling from Madison to the Wisconsin-Illinois border, this trail connects to 13 communities, many other trails, parks, and more.

Military Ridge Trail. This 40-mile trail runs from **Governor Dodge State Park** and **Blue Mound State Park**, and connects Dodgeville with Madison.

Argue-ment Golf Course (608-527-6366; arguementgolf.com), N9603 Argue Road, New Glarus. Despite its foreboding name, this nine-hole golf course is made with affordability in mind, but promises to challenge experienced golfers while still suiting families. Rates $4.75-24.

✳ Green Space

🐾 **Spring Green Preserve**, Angelo Lane, off Jones Road, just past a house with Fire Number E5196A, Spring Green. At the Wisconsin desert, visitors will be shocked to find black widow spiders, lizards, and prickly pear cacti, right here in Wisconsin. This sand prairie was once part of the Wisconsin River. The preserve is owned by The Nature Conservancy, and low-impact recreation is the limit, in order to preserve this very unique Wisconsin space. Free.

Tower Hill State Park (608-588-2116), County Road C, Spring Green. With a great view of the Wisconsin River and bluffs for hiking, this park takes advantage of the uplands terrain. There's camping here, but an off-beat attraction (for a state park) is the reconstructed shot tower and buildings featuring mining exhibits.

Governor Dodge State Park (608-935-2315), WI 23, Dodgeville. With more than 5,000 acres, this is among the state's largest. There are 269 campsites, plenty of hiking trails, two lakes with swimming beaches, a waterfall, chimneys of rock for the adventurous to climb, and more.

Blue Mound State Park (608-437-5711), 4350 Mounds Park Road, Blue Mounds. Set atop the highest point in the southern part of the state, this park features camping, hiking, swimming, and more, and connects with the Military Ridge State Trail.

New Glarus Woods State Park (608-527-2335), WI 69, New Glarus. It connects to the Sugar River State Trail, but even if you're not biking the trails, this small park (comparatively, at 411 acres) offers plenty to do. Prairie restoration is underway here, as well.

Grant River Recreation Area, Park Lane, Potosi. This is the only Class A Mississippi River Project Recreation Area in Wisconsin. Operated by the U.S. Army Corps of Engineers, this park is used primarily for camping and fishing; it's a popular place for anglers in search of Mississippi River catfish.

Wyalusing State Park (608 996-2261), 13081 State Park Lane, Bagley. This park sits atop a bluff where the Mississippi River and the Wisconsin River meet. Good for canoeing, the park also features 23 miles of trail, including portions that are wheelchair accessible.

Nelson Dewey State Park (608-725-5374), 12190 County Road VV, Cassville. A popular camping park, this provides a great view of the Mississippi River. It sits across the street from Stonefield, a Wisconsin Historical Site.

La Riviere Park (608-326-2718), 62036 Vineyard Coulee Road, Prairie du Chien. This large city park features trails, backpack camping, horse riding, and more. Natural prairie and great bird watching are draws here.

TRAIN TRACKS, THE MISSISSIPPI, AND THE BLUFFS IN MINNESOTA.

✳ Lodging

Y ✿ ♿ The House on the Rock Resort (608-588-7000; thehouseonthe rock.com), 400 Springs Drive, Spring Green. One of three lodging options associated with the House on the Rock, this one is an upscale golf resort located right near **Taliesin** (see To See and Do). Onsite dining, tennis courts, hiking trails, and a highly rated golf course complement the roomy suites. Rooms $205.

Aldebaran Farm (773-334-4924; aldebaranfarm.us), Spring Green. True Frank Lloyd Wright fans traveling in packs might want to consider staying here. Aldebaran Farm was the home of Wright's uncle James Lloyd-Jones, and it was where the architect spent his summers as a child. With five updated sleeping rooms and a loft, the house sleeps 12. $1200/week.

Y ✿ ♿ The House on the Rock Inn (888-935-3960; thehouseontherock .com), 3591 WI 23, Dodgeville. Just down the road from the attraction is this hotel, which has a facade that matches the **House on the Rock** (see To See and do). Rooms are standard but comfortable and clean; get a suite for the extra legroom. There's a great pool and waterpark here suitable for little ones (though older kids might not find it as exciting). In the bar, listen for patrons to pound out something on the piano. Continental breakfast is typical but broad enough to suit all tastes. Rooms $155–195.

Y Brewery Creek Inn (608-987-3298; brewerycreek.com), 23 Commerce Street, Mineral Point. Here's a perfect way to really take in the 1800s atmosphere of Mineral Point, right in the center of it all. Lodging options include sleeping rooms above the brewpub, plus two limestone cottages. The Miner's Cottage and the Springside Cottage, which is divided into two suites, include a full kitchen, one bedroom, and a living room on each side. Rooms $149–169; cottages $169.

✿ Cothren House (608-987-1522; cothrenhouse.com), 320 Tower Street, Mineral Point. Romantic yet child-friendly, the lodging here consists of an 1850s stone cottage with two bedrooms and an 1835 log cabin. Either option is steeped in history, although the decor and amenities—including WiFi and cable television—maintain modern conveniences you're probably a little itchy without. It's a short walk to the main drag in Mineral Point. Cabin, $139; cottage $159.

The Coach House at Shake Rag Alley (608-987-3292; mineralpoint lodging.com), 18 Shake Rag Street, Mineral Point. Choose from three rooms in this converted 1800s coach house. Rooms one and three feature queen beds, while the sun-drenched room two offers a full-sized brass bed. All rooms have private bathrooms, and guests can enjoy the grounds at Shake Rag Alley. Rooms $99.

♿ The Mousehole at Shake Rag Alley (608-987-3292; mineralpoint lodging.com), 14 Shake Rag Street, Mineral Point. Rent a side of this 1800s townhouse for longer stays or extra travelers. The apartments have two bedrooms (one queen bed, two twin beds) and a full, thoroughly modern kitchen. The decor is contemporary, with appropriate nods to the historic surroundings. Apartment $159.

♿ Walking Iron Bed & Breakfast (1-877-572-9877; walkingiron.com), 21 State Street, Mazomanie. This restored Victorian mansion boasts five beautiful rooms outfitted in period furnishings and other touches meant to evoke thoughts of the home's original occupants. Rooms have private bathrooms, and other treats include spa services,

WiFi, and full breakfast in the dining room. $140–160.

Earth Rider Hotel (608-897-8300; earthridercycling.com/hotel), 929 West Exchange Street, Brodhead. Adjacent to a bicycle boutique, this eco-conscious hotel offers warmly decorated rooms with modern furnishings, and bike rentals for hitting the nearby trails. The five rooms are named after Tour de France winners; the Bernard Hinault room is the only one with two beds, but each room has special features. There's a four-poster bed in the Lance Armstrong room. Both child-friendly and pet-friendly, this little hotel is also Travel Green Wisconsin certified. Rooms $99.

&. Y **Chalet Landhaus Inn** (608-527-5234; chaletlandhaus.com), 801 WI 69, New Glarus. An impressive hotel with Swiss-style architecture, you won't be able to miss it from the highway. Although the room decor is not as charming as the exterior, the wood-beamed ceiling adds ambiance, and the dining room is as Swiss as you'd expect. Take a dip in the pool or relax in the sauna. Full breakfast buffet is included. $120–225.

Swiss Aire Motel (608-527-2138; swissaire.com), 1200 WI 69, New Glarus. This typical 1960s roadside motel offers the basics in recently updated rooms. Sometimes all you need is a clean place to rest your head, and this is it. $69–89.

✳ Where to Eat

DINING OUT Y &. **Grandview Restaurant** (608-935-3639; thehouse ontherock.com), 400 Springs Drive, Spring Green. Open for all three meals daily. A great option for finer dining, the menu and atmosphere is more traditional, with options such as sweet-pepper shrimp and Texas rib eye. Located in the verdant, rolling hills of Spring Green, the views are truly grand. Dishes $18–29.

Y &. **The Bank Restaurant and Wine Bar** (608-588-7600; thebank restaurantandwinebar.com), 134 West Jefferson Street, Spring Green. Open for dinner Tuesday through Sunday and lunch on weekends in summer; dinner Saturday and Sunday in spring and fall. This restaurant gets its name from the building's original purpose, and many of the bank's interior details, such as the vault and teller cages, remain. The menu veers contemporary, with small plates and cheese boards, and entrees include popular meat and fish dishes with an emphasis on local ingredients. Entrees $18–30.

Y &. **Arthur's Supper Club** (608-588-2521), 4885 WI 14, Spring Green. Open for dinner Tuesday through Sunday, brunch on Sunday. Arthur's has all the markings of a proper Wisconsin supper club—a seafood and steak-focused menu, salad bar, old-school drinks, and entrees with a wide range of potato choices. Still, you can get a selection of pastas here and local craft brews, so it's not quite time-warp city. Dishes $9.99–33.99.

Y &. **Bistro 101** (608-437-9463; hoff bistro101.com), 101 East Main Street, Mount Horeb. Open for dinner Tuesday through Saturday. This upscale, contemporary bistro offers tapas, sandwiches such as the roast beef and dill havarti panini, and dinners that range from vegetable Wellington to filet mignon, plus bold daily specials. Save room for dessert, which includes coffee chocolate cake and apple cider sorbet. Dishes $8.50–20.

Y &. **New Glarus Hotel Restaurant** (608-527-5244; newglarushotel.com), 100 Sixth Avenue, New Glarus. Open for lunch and dinner daily in summer, Friday through Monday and lunch only on Wednesday and Thursday in winter.

The menu is heavy on Swiss dishes, such as Kaesechuechli (a cheese pie) and vegetarian roesti, plus a couple of fondue options. If you'd rather stick to ordinary meat and fish entrees, you can do that, too. But why? The big wooden booths with carved details, the lace curtains, and the architecture of this building—built in 1853 by Swiss immigrants—almost ensure you'll be ordering a specialty. Housed here, too, is the unlikely **Ticino Pizzeria Restaurant**. Lunch, $7–17.50, dinner $9–23.

Y & **Chalet Landhaus Inn** (608-527-5234; chaletlandhaus.com), 801 WI 69, New Glarus. Open for dinner Tuesday through Saturday. Offering Swiss and American specialties, this hotel's restaurant has a menu where dishes like rahmschnitzel and grilled chicken breast occupy equal space. $9–23.

Y & **Deininger's Restaurant** (608-527-2012), 119 5th Ave, New Glarus. Open for lunch and dinner daily. Housed in a Victorian mansion, the menu includes Swiss, German, and French dishes. In summer, dine on the porch. Dishes $15–30.

Y & **The Dining Room** (608-938-2200; 209main.com), 209 Main Street, Monticello. This upscale storefront restaurant has a bistro feel, with wood chairs, white tablecloths, and a changing art display. Dishes are adventurous and tempting, with entrees such as tortilla and pecan encrusted mahi-mahi, sweet potato and parmesan ravioli, and cornmeal and habenero-crusted pork cutlets. For dessert, try a traditional crème brulee or the sticky toffee pudding. Dishes $20–30.

EATING OUT & **Spring Green General Store Cafe** (608-588-7070; springgreengeneralstore.com), 137 South Albany Street, Spring Green. Open daily for breakfast and lunch. Breakfast ranges from oatmeal to waffles, but what you really ought to try is a cheese curd scramble—because I don't know where else you'll find eggs and cheese curds served up on a plate. If dairy's not your thing, the cafe offers tofu scrambles, too, and more. Lunch includes a good selection of sandwiches, many of them vegetarian, plus quiche, a burrito, hummus, and more.

& **Riverview Terrace Cafe** (608-588-7900; taliesinpreservation.org), 5607 County Road C, Spring Green. Open 9–4 daily May through October, lunch served 10:30–2:30. Frank Lloyd Wright fans who want their vacation to be all Wright, all the time, will be happy to know that it's possible. The only stand-alone restaurant the architect ever designed, this cafe is mainly used by folks taking tours, but anyone is free to come have lunch, and there *is* a kid's menu. Enjoy the view while you nibble on a sandwich. Dishes $8–9.

& **The Old Feed Mill** (608-795-4909; oldfeedmill.com), 114 Cramer Street, Mazomanie. Open for lunch and dinner Tuesday through Saturday, brunch and dinner Sunday. As you might suspect, this restaurant is housed in an old feed mill, and the decor is suitably rustic. Focusing on what the restaurant calls "American Country" cuisine, dishes include tempting items such as haystack onion rings, meatloaf, and chicken pot pie. Locally sourced vegetable wheat pasta and a mushroom strudel mean vegetarians are right at home here, too. Lunch $5.95–8.95, dinner $8.95–19.95.

& **Whistle Stop Cafe** (608-795-2414; oldfeedmill.com/whistlestop), 18 Brodhead Street, Mazonanie. Open for breakfast and lunch daily. I couldn't find fried green tomatoes on the menu at this storefront cafe, but I did find inexpensive breakfast items from eggs to Belgian waffles, a ton of sandwiches, and Chocolate Shoppe ice cream, plus espresso drinks to get you going. Dishes $4–9.

Y & Brewery Creek Brewpub (608-987-3298; brewerycreek.com/brewpub .php), 23 Commerce Street, Mineral Point. Open for lunch and dinner daily in summer, Thursday through Sunday in winter. The 1800s limestone building and simply decorated interior make a perfect setting in which to knock back one of the house brews, but the food is what brings people in. Locally sourced and made from scratch, the menu tends toward upscale comfort foods, such as bourbon steak, salmon, and vegetarian pastas in freshly prepared sauces. Lunch brings burgers and sandwiches, like the Brewery Burger, loaded with caramelized onions, Colby cheese, and more, and the walnut burger. Lunch $8–10, dinner $9.50–17.25.

Red Rooster Café (608-987-9936), 158 High Street, Mineral Point. Open daily for all three meals. This homey cafe really belongs to the locals, but the pasties draw visitors in all the time. The café may be known for its Cornish meals, but it also has traditional American café dishes like sandwiches and straightforward breakfast. Dishes less than $10.

Gundry and Gray (608-987-4444; historicgundryandgray.com), 215 High Street, Mineral Point. Open 10–5 Monday through Saturday, 11–4 Sunday. Closed Tuesday. This shop's cafe offers sandwiches, soups, tacos, and a kid's menus. Stop for lunch or coffee. Dishes $7.95.

Y & Cafe Four (608.987-2030; four cafe.com), 20 Commerce Street, Mineral Point. Open for lunch and dinner Wednesday through Sunday. Perfect for a casual but nice dinner out, Cafe Four veers from the down-home and traditional offerings of the area to serve up contemporary Italian dishes. The menu features wood-fired pizza, both Italian

---

PASTIES AND FIGGYHOBBIN IN MINERAL POINT

As though the abundance of restored stone buildings and **Pendarvis State Historical Site** (see *To See and Do*) weren't enough to make picturesque Mineral Point seem like you'd crossed the ocean in a floating time machine, the traditional local foods here sound straight out of a Dickens novel. Figgyhobbin? Who can resist?

Pasties developed out of necessity; the Cornish miners needed a sturdy, portable food to get them through their workdays, so their wives whipped up what might be considered the great-granddaddy of the Hot Pocket. A pasty is an enclosed, dense crust filled with meats, potatoes, onions, and butter, and some say they're too dry and bland, but not always. What do you want from an old English miner's lunch? Many people love them; you'll have to find out for yourself.

A treat no one will argue with is figgyhobbin—a sweet, raisin-and-nut-filled pastry topped with caramel. If that sounds like too much, you won't have trouble finding bread pudding in Mineral Point—and you can always switch that pasty for a Cornish hen if you must. The **Red Rooster Cafe** (see *Eating Out*) offers all this and more on its menu.

and French, calzone, panini, and pasta dishes, made with local and organic ingredients. Dishes $7–14.

🍸 ♿ **The Grumpy Troll Brewery, Restaurant and Pizzeria** (608-437-2739; thegrumpytroll.com), 105 South Second Street, Mount Horeb. Open for lunch and dinner daily. A step up from simple bar fare, the Grumpy Troll offers everything from walleye sandwiches and burgers to quesadillas, and at night it serves up steaks, pastas, and more. There's even a huge selection of pizzas and a kid's menu. Be sure to wash down dinner with one of the pub's award-winning craft brews. Lunch $6.25–9.95, dinner $12.95–18.95.

♿ **Maple Leaf Cheese and Chocolate Haus** (608-527-2000; mapleleafcheeseandchocolatehaus.com), 554 First Street, New Glarus. Open 10–5 daily May through October. A great place to pick up treats (see Selective Shopping), but you can satisfy your sweet tooth on the premises, too.

♿ 🏵 **Baumgartner's Cheese Store and Tavern** (608-325-6157; baumgartnercheese.com), 1023 Sixteenth Avenue, Monroe. Open daily. It's a little surprising that there aren't combination tavern/cheese shops all over Wisconsin, really, but at least it's here in cheese country. Offering locally brewed beers and a menu full of cheese sandwiches in a colorful bar atmosphere, it's a compulsory stop. The adventurous, and fans of stinky cheese, must try a Limburger and onion sandwich (the not-so-adventurous can wimp out with cheddar). At the counter you can find a wide variety of cheeses to take with you.

✱ Entertainment

American Players Theatre (608-588-7401; playinthewoods.org), 5950 Golf Course Road, Spring Green. Open summers. There's nothing like seeing a Shakespeare play in a beautiful, natural amphitheater. Set on a wooded hill, the grounds feature concessions and picnic areas to enjoy prior to the show. Productions tend largely toward Shakespeare, but other classical plays are performed as well.

Mineral Point Opera House (608-987-3201; mpoh.org), 225 High Street, Mineral Point. This theater is home to the Shake Rag Players, a community theater company, but it also brings in touring acts and screening independent and world cinema. Built in 1914, the theater seats 400.

Alley Stage (608-987-3292; alleystage.com), 18 Shake Rag Street, Mineral Point. This small, outdoor theater stages local productions throughout the summer. Part of the Shake Rag Alley arts center, it puts local talent on the stage all summer long.

✱ Selective Shopping

🌂 **Taliesin Bookstore** (608-588-7900; taliesinpreservation.org) Spring Green. Open daily. You don't need to take the tour to stop by the bookstore and browse the books and Frank Lloyd Wright gift items available. Browse the large selection here to learn a little more about Wisconsin's favorite architect.

43/90 North Earth (608-588-3313; northearth.com), 130 South Albany Street, Spring Green. Open daily in summer, Thursday through Sunday in winter. Stocking a huge selection of new age, spiritual, and healing titles, this shop also sells its own line of clothing, called Celtic God and Goddess Apparel.

Spring Green General Store (608-588-7070; springgreengeneralstore.com), 137 South Albany Street, Spring Green. Open daily. Like any good general store, this one offers a little bit of everything, with a focus on natural and organic items like groceries and cosmetics, plus all manner of other goods, including toys, stationery, and clothing. Next door, you'll find a delightful cafe for breakfast or lunch.

Gundry and Gray (608-987-4444; historicgundryandgray.com), 215 High Street, Mineral Point. Open 10–5 Monday through Saturday, 11–4 Sunday. Closed Tuesday. This charming shop is packed full of antiques and new gift items, plus offerings from local artists. There's everything here from home decor to gourmet foods. The zinc dog statue out front has promoted business in Mineral Point since the 1800s.

The Foundry Books (608-987-4363; foundrybooks.com), 105 Commerce Street, Mineral Point. Open 11–4:30 Thursday through Sunday from April to December. Specializing in out-of-print and antiquarian books, with a focus on Wisconsin history and children's literature, this store also carries maps and the works of Wisconsin poets and authors. Housed in an old foundry, the shop is suited to its surroundings.

Set in Stone (608-987-1123; setinstonebooks.com), 210 Commerce Street, Mineral Point. Open daily. Offering a wide, general selection of new books, plus Wisconsin culinary gifts, needle arts supplies, stationery, and other odds and ends, this is a great place to browse. When you find something you like, they've got espresso drinks and seating for relaxing.

The Spotted Dog Gallery (608-987-2855; spotteddoggallery.com), 148 High Street, Mineral Point. Open 9–5 daily. More like a boutique selling the works of more than 50 artists from near and far, this shop has pottery, paintings, jewelry, and works in many media in this 1900s storefront building.

Prairie Oak Artisans (608-987-3757; prairieoakartisans.com), 207 Commerce Street, Mineral Point. Open 11–5 Friday through Sunday from June through October. The works of owner Karma Grotelueschen and some 30 other area artists are featured in the gallery, all with a focus on nature. The building, since its construction in 1836, has always been intended as a combination commercial and living space. Grotelueschen and her sons live upstairs, and promise to open up the shop outside normal hours if they're home—just give a knock.

✿ **Leaping Lizards** (608-987-4528), 9 Fountain Street, Mineral Point. Open daily. A delightful toy shop, featuring specialty playthings and books for kids of all ages.

☂ **The Barn Shops** (608-987-2779; thebarnshops.net), 100 Merry Christmas Lane, Mineral Point. Open 9:30–5 daily. This old limestone horse barn serves as a mall of sorts; there are 10 shops here selling everything from pottery and gourmet foods to baby items and home décor, and much, much more.

Prairie Bookshop (608-437-4118), 117 East Main Street, Mount Horeb. Open 10–5:30 Monday through Friday, Saturday 10–5, Sunday 11–5. Located on Mount Horeb's main drag, this indie bookstore sells a little bit of everything, including fiction and kids' books, but the focus is on regional interest, Norway, and Wisconsin. Author appearances are scheduled throughout the year.

Artisan Woods (608-437-1811; artisanwoodsgallery.com), 109 East Main Street, Mount Horeb. Open daily. This shop sells handcrafted wood items including everything from salad bowls to cribbage boards and kaleidoscopes. All that wood makes the store right at home on the Trollway.

The Bramble Patch (608-527-4878; http://www.thebramblepatch.biz/index .html) 526 First Street, New Glarus. Open daily. You can pick up Polish pottery here, plus the shop's own maple syrup, jewelry, and more. Worth a look.

Maple Leaf Cheese and Chocolate Haus (608-527-2000), 554 First Street, New Glarus. Open 10–5 daily May through October. It doesn't take a Swiss genius to figure out that this is a brilliant concept for a store. Chocolate and cheese? Yes, please! Tucked away in New Glarus' downtown, the cow in front of the store might beckon you, and the goodies inside will make you glad. The store doesn't just have fudge and cheese (although really, that would be plenty), but ice cream in waffle cones, espresso, and other Swiss foods.

Baumgartner's Cheese Store and Tavern (608-325-6157; baumgartner cheese.com), 1023 Sixteenth Avenue, Monroe. Open daily. A great place to have a sandwich or a brew (see Eating Out), you can also get a wide variety of cheeses to go here.

New Glarus Bakery (866-805-5536; newglarusbakery.com), 534 First Street, New Glarus. Open 7–5 daily. A Swiss bakery worth the stop, you'll find beer bread, Gipfel, nut horns, and many American pastries as well.

✳ Special Events

March: **St. Patrick's Day Parade**, Prairie du Chien. An annual parade celebrating the Irish holiday.

May: **Spring Festival**, Gays Mills. This festival features folk music and dance, including clogging, a May Pole dance, and more. Tour the apple orchards while you're here.

June: **Spring Green Arts & Crafts Fair**, Jefferson Street, Spring Green.

This two-day art fair features more than 200 artists from around the country.

Spring Art Tour, Mazomanie and Mineral Point. Artists around the area open up their studios and invite the public in.

Roger Bright Memorial Polkafest, New Glarus. This festival honors a late local musician with free music and dancing all weekend.

Heidi Festival and Taste of New Glarus, New Glarus. Combined, these two events promise family activities, music, crafts, and plenty of food all weekend long.

Prairie Villa Rendezvous, Prairie du Chien. This annual festival recreates 1840s life here, and features music, food, and crafts.

July: **Fourth of July Celebration**, Mineral Point.

Fourth of July Celebration, Mazomanie.

August: **National Mustard Day**, Mount Horeb. This annual festival features games, music, kid's activities, and the Poupon U Accordion Band. Unusual for a festival: The hot dogs are free, although only if you take them with mustard.

Swiss Volkfest, Tell Shooting Park, New Glarus. The annual celebration of Swiss Independence Day features music, yodeling, alphorn playing, flag throwing, and accordion music.

Wilhelm Tell Festival, New Glarus. Held late August or early September. This annual three-day festival features kid's activities, art, ethnic foods, a yodeling contest, the Wilhelm Tell drama in both German and English, and more.

Prairie Dog Blues Festival, Prairie du Chien. Two-day music festival on the banks of the Mississippi River.

Iowa County Fair, Mineral Point. This traditional county fair spans five days and features agricultural exhibits, music, food, and more.

September: **Spring Green Literary Festival**, Taliesin, Spring Green. This three-day event celebrates the literary arts, brings in authors for talks, and offers workshops.

Thirsty Troll Brew Fest, Mount Horeb. Breweries from around the area and beyond come together for fun, with trolls.

Cornish Festival, Mineral Point. This three-day festival celebrates the food and culture of the area's original settlers.

Taste of Mineral Point, Mineral Point. Features foods from the area's restaurants.

Green County Cheese Days, Monroe. Held the third weekend in September in even-numbered years, this festival features cheese and other foods, plus celebrations of Swiss culture, including a yodeling contest, arts, and music. The festival even has its own song, "Come to Cheese Days in Monroe."

Festival of the Mounds, Mounds View Park, Blue Mounds. The annual two-day festival offers polka, games, and a chicken wing cook-off.

Gays Mills Apple Festival, Gays Mills. Three days of apple fun include a carnival, parade, games, and more.

October: **Fall Art Tour**, Spring Green, Mineral Point, Dodgeville, Baraboo. Artists throughout the area open up their studios for this annual event.

Fall Heritage Festival, Mount Horeb. Celebrates the town's Norwegian heritage with arts, food, buggy rides, and more.

LA CROSSE AND ONALASKA

LA CROSSE, ONALASKA, WEST SALEM, HOLMEN, WESTBY, AND VIROCQUA

With more than 51,000 residents, La Crosse is the largest city in Southwestern Wisconsin, and it boasts a vibrant arts and entertainment scene. Home to many art galleries and museums, plus a rich performing arts scene, La Crosse is culturally very active. Combine that with its college-town feel—and its associated bar district—plus an environmentally friendly culture, and you've got the makings of

BIG FISH OUTSIDE ONALASKA, NEW LA CROSSE

a small city with big-city benefits. What's more, the beautiful Mississippi River provides endless water recreation, and the pedestrian-friendly Riverside Park is great for a relaxing stroll.

Like all of Wisconsin, La Crosse was first home to Native Americans. The name is said to come from explorer Zebulon Pike, who traveled up the Mississippi on an expedition. Upon arriving here, he saw members of the Ho-Chunk tribe playing a game, and called this location *Prairie La Crosse.* Fur trade helped develop the area through the mid-19th century, and the Industrial Revolution took over from there. A railroad from Milwaukee was constructed, and industry took advantage of the Mississippi River's power. Today, La Crosse continues to grow and change.

East from La Crosse, into the coulee region as you edge toward the uplands, there are interesting towns. Soldier's Grove is known as America's First Solar Village; after repeated flooding, the town was moved to higher ground in 1978 with the help of the U.S. government. That help, however, was conditional on all new construction using some solar power. In Vernon County, Virocqua is the hub of the state's largest organic farming area, and its historic downtown hosts a weekly farmers' market in summer. Round barns, beautiful scenery, and community spirit make this a worthy side trip.

GUIDANCE **La Crosse Area Convention and Visitors Bureau** (608-782-2366; explorelacrosse.com), 410 Veterans Memorial Drive. Right downtown along the river, next to the Friendship Gardens at Riverside Park, Veterans Memorial Drive. You'd probably want to stop here anyway. The CVB stocks area menus for browsing as well as information about the entire area. La Crosse is also home to one of Wisconsin's official welcome centers, on an island in the Mississippi.

Onalaska Tourism Commission (608-781-9570; discoveronalaska.com), 1101 Main Street, Onalaska.

GETTING THERE *By Car:* Head west on I-90 from most parts of Wisconsin, or travel the Great River Road from Minnesota or Iowa.

MEDICAL EMERGENCY Call 911.

✳ To See and Do

ART GALLERIES **Pump House Regional Arts Center** (608-785-1434; the pumphouse.org/), 119 King Street. Open noon–5 Tuesday through Friday, noon–4 Saturday. Admission to the gallery is free, donation recommended. Originally a pump house providing La Crosse with water to fight fires, the building is on the State and National Historic Registers. Today, the Pump House serves the area with visual and performing arts programming, along with classes.

Two other places to check out art are the colleges; both feature national artists as well as work by university students and faculty. **UW-La Crosse Art Gallery** (608-785-8230; www.uwlax.edu/art/gallery), corner of 16th and Vine Streets, is open noon–8 Monday through Thursday, noon–5 Friday and Saturday. The Viterbo University Art Gallery is located in the **Viterbo University Fine Arts Center** (608-796-3737; www.viterbo.edu/finearts1.aspx), 929 Jackson Street.

City Brewery Tours (608-785-4820; citybrewery.com), 1111 South Third Street. Tours noon, 1, and 2, Monday through Saturday in summer, Friday and Saturday

October through May. Bargain brewery tours include samples and a free glass, plus a look at the "World's Largest Six-Pack" and some interesting history. This was home to the G. Heileman Brewing Company from 1858 until 1996, and the six-pack used to boast the Old Style name (these days it's La Crosse Lager). City Brewing Company is actually the original name Heileman gave the brewery, a nice nod to its origins. After years of struggling, the company is now owned locally and functions primarily as a contract brewer and bottler for other beverages, but it continues to produce craft beers available regionally. Tours $5.

♼ **Riverside Museum** (608-782-2366; lchsweb.org/riverside.html), 410 Veterans Memorial Drive. Open 10:30–4:30 Monday through Saturday, 10:30–4 Sunday. Located in Riverside Park, it's a natural location in which to browse the history of the Mississippi in the area. Adults $2, children $1.

♼ **Hixon House** (608-782-1980; lchsweb.org/hixon.html), North Seventh and Badger Streets. Open 10–5 Tuesday through Sunday during summer, weekends and special hours in fall and winter. This National Historic Landmark has something a lot of historical houses do not: almost all of its original furnishings remain. Recent restorations inside this Italianate home, such as repairs to rugs, have kept the house and its contents intact. Adults $8.50, children $4.50.

♼ **Swarthout Museum** (608-782-1980; lchsweb.org/swarthout.html),112 South Ninth Street. Open 10–5 Tuesday through Friday, 1–5 Saturday and Sunday. Where the Riverside Museum concentrates on the Mississippi River, the Swarthout is focused on La Crosse history. It's not big, but there's a lot of information, along with a kid's room, where little ones can don period garb. The La Crosse County Historical Society maintains a gift and bookshop here. $1 donation.

♈ ♪ ♼ **Children's Museum of La Crosse** (608-784-2652; childmuseumlax.org), 207 Fifth Avenue South. Open 10–5 Tuesday through Saturday, noon–5 Sunday. This three-floor, hands-on museum features a Mississippi River exhibit where kids can control the flow of water, along with old favorites such as a fire truck and huge Brio train set. $5.

Shrine of Our Lady of Guadalupe (608-782-5440; guadalupeshrine.org), 5250 Justin Road. Open daily 9–4. A new (2008) Marian shrine at the south end of La Crosse, the setting is beautiful and perfect for some inner reflection. The Pilgrim Center greets Catholic and casual visitors alike with a reception area, a cafe called "Culina Mariana" (which translates as "Mary's Kitchen"), and a shop with all manner of Catholic gifts, including books, jewelry, rosaries, and more. The grounds include the Votive Candle Chapel, with the largest candle rack in the U.S., a rosary walk, devotional areas, and the Shrine Church. Free, donations welcome.

BOAT EXCURSIONS The best way to experience the Mississippi is to hop on a boat. Scenic cruises offer unbeatable views, and the grand riverboats provide nostalgia and excitement—some cruises lock through Lock and Dam Number 7.

The Julia Belle Swain (608-784-4882; juliabelle.com), 227 Main Street. Runs May through October; schedule varies. An authentic steam-powered boat, and as pretty as her name, this steamer is propelled by an engine first installed in the ferry *City of Baton Rouge* in 1915, which adds to her charm, as does the steam calliope on board. You can choose from all manner of cruises, from breakfast to cocktails to longer, overnight trips. Rates vary.

LACROSSE RIVERBOAT

La Crosse Queen Cruises (608-784-2893; lacrossequeen.com), 405 Veterans Memorial Drive, at the north end of Riverside Park. Runs May through October; schedule varies. *The La Crosse Queen* is a reproduction of a late-19th century river boat, but is actually propelled by its paddlewheel, which is rare. You've got many cruise choices here, as well, from brunch to moonlight and everything in between. Rates range from $13.95 for a scenic cruise to $38.95 for weekend dinner.

Island Girl Cruises (608-791-3548; islandgirlcruises.com), 127 Marina Drive. Runs June through October; schedule varies. If you're into climate control and modern amenities, this is probably the one for you. The *Island Girl* is actually replaced every spring with a brand-new, million dollar yacht as part of a product improvement program, so the features are always state-of-the-art. It's perfect for weddings and business occasions, but commoners can cruise daily, too, from breakfast to moonlight, plus special themed cruises. Rates range from $14.95 for a scenic cruise to $38.95 for weekend dinner.

Mississippi River Eco-Tours (877-647-7397; mississippiexplorer.com), loads at the Best Western Midway Hotel (877-688-9260; midwayhotels.com), 1835 Rose Street. Offering a rare opportunity to check out the Upper Mississippi River National Wildlife & Fish Refuge on a boat that can handle the shallow backwaters, these tours are educational and entertaining. Rates include a voucher for a meal at the hotel's restaurant. Adults $29.99, children $19.99.

✳ Green Space

Grandad Bluff (800-658-9424), east of the city. Follow Main Street east to Bliss Road, follow Bliss Road up the bluff. At about 600 feet, the park at Grandad Bluff offers stunning views of the Mississippi River and three states. Given to the city of La Crosse in 1912 by the locally prominent Hixon family to keep the land from becoming a quarry, Grandad Bluff continues to serve as a wonderful city park.

Myrick Hixon EcoPark, 2100 La Crosse Street. Renovated and expanded in 2008 to include the former Hixon Nature Center, the city-owned EcoPark is a one-stop shop for outdoor family fun. The grounds contain a zoo, the educational nature center, the huge Kids Coulee playground, bike trails, concessions, a wading pool, and more. Historically, admission has been free; as of this writing it's undetermined whether there will be a fee.

Friendship Gardens (608-791-4769; riversidegardens.org), 410 Veterans Memorial Drive. Open daily. A unique and beautiful tribute to La Crosse's sister cities, this work-in-progress is already a fantastic place to look and relax. Located near Riverside Park, where the La Crosse, Black, and Mississippi rivers meet, the Friendship Gardens reflect the styles of the sister cities, and prove a great spot to picnic or read through the literature you gathered next door. Free.

Riverside Park (608-789-7557), Veterans Memorial Drive. As the name suggests, this park is along the Mississippi River, and it's a lovely spot from which to enjoy the water. Actually, it's where three rivers meet—the Mississippi, the La Crosse, and the Black. A 25-foot statue called Hiawatha, or sometimes "The Big Indian," stands watch over the park. The statue has seen plenty of controversy; some feel it is an insulting caricature of Native Americans, while others view it as a La Crosse icon. Plenty of open space to relax on a summer day.

✳ Outdoor Activities

Upper Mississippi River National Fish and Wildlife Refuge (608-783-8405; www.fws.gov/Midwest/uppermississippiRiver). The refuge runs 260 miles along the Mississippi River, providing habitat for fish and wildlife. An excellent spot for bird watching, if you're here at the right time, you might even see eagles.

The La Crosse River State Trail and the **Great River State Trail** connect in Onalaska; from there you can pick up the Elroy-Sparta State Trail in Sparta. All three are rail-trails, meander past fabulous scenery, and require Wisconsin trail passes ($4 per day or $15 per year).

Goose Island County Park (608-788-7018), W6488 County Road GI, Stoddard. Just south of the city on WI 35. Stay for the day or camp out as long as you want. On an island in the Mississippi River, you can canoe guided paths in the backwaters, fish, bird watch, laze on the beach, or stay overnight at one of more than 400 campsites available for a small fee.

Van Loon Wildlife Area. At the north end of La Crosse County you'll find almost 4000 acres of wetlands, woods, and other wildlife habitat, plus restored historic bridges along the trails.

ON THE MISSISSIPPI RIVER
If the romantic notion of taking on the Old Miss yourself is stuck in your head, you're in luck. It's almost impossible to leave here without a river trip. Whether you plan to canoe, rent a houseboat, or take a leisurely tour on one of the beautiful steamboats, there are plenty of activities available.

500 Holmen Drive, Holmen.

Blue Heron Bicycle Works (608-783-7433; blueheronbikes.com), 213 Main Street, Onalaska.

CANOE AND KAYAK RENTALS **UW-La Crosse Outdoor Connection** (608-785-8860; www.uwlax.edu/recsports/), 1601 Badger Street, in the Recreational Eagle Center on the UW-La Crosse campus. Open 11–6 Monday through Friday; 10–4 Saturday; noon–4 Sunday. Don't be shy; the rentals and clinics here aren't just for students. The general public simply pays a couple of bucks more on reasonable rates for everything from canoes and kayaks to bikes, camping equipment, and more. The Outdoor Connection also holds clinics and classes available open to the general public, as well.

Three Rivers Outdoors (608-793-1470; threeriversoutdoors.com), 400 Main Street. Open at 10 Monday through Saturday, 11–4 Sunday. Offers all manner of outdoor gear for sale, as well as kayaks and canoes to rent starting at $20.

✳ Lodging

Bentley-Wheeler Bed & Breakfast (608-784-9360; bentley-wheeler.com), 938 and 950 Cass Street. The two properties restored and maintained by the owners have won several historic preservation awards. Options include the third-floor Ballroom Suite, with loads of space and views; a smaller but charming Guest Suite, or the entire Guest House at 938 Cass Street. The main house is more ornate, but both properties are tastefully decorated with period pieces. Breakfast is a basket of baked goods delivered to your door— nice if you are hungry but don't want to schlep down to a dining room. Modern amenities include free W-Fi and air conditioning. $135–175.

Wilson Schoolhouse Inn (608-787-1982; wilsonschoolhouseinn.com), W5720 WI 14/61. On the outskirts of town, you get an entire schoolhouse for your stay. There's lots of dancing room, for sure; the open layout of the original 1917 schoolhouse is evident here. The inn can accommodate up to six adults with an extra fee, but kids are also welcome, and a crib or futon is available. A minimum two-night stay is required. $120–150.

Rainbow Ridge Farms Bed & Breakfast (608-783-8181; rainbow ridgefarms.com), N5732 Hauser Road, Onalaska. Four country guest rooms on a small hobby farm, the charm here is the animals. Help the owners feed the animals, and enjoy a full breakfast— weekends have farm-fresh eggs. Travel Green Wisconsin certified. $79–160.

Westby House Victorian Inn (608-634-4112; westbyhouse.com), 200 West State Street, Westby. Westby House is a well-loved B&B in the area, about 25 miles east of La Crosse. Nine rooms, seven of which are open year-round, feature charming furnishings appropriate to the Victorian architecture without overdoing it. All rooms have private baths and options range from whirlpool suites and kitchenettes to simpler, cozier rooms. The tag line here is "Return to a simpler time," but that doesn't mean you'll be cut off from the world—there's free WiFi, cable, and DVD players in all the rooms. Travel Green Wisconsin certified. $75–205.

Huck's Houseboat Vacations (920-625-3142; hucks.com), 691 Park Plaza Drive. This is lodging and recreation;

bring a tent and drop anchor at a sandbar for free—all you need to add is a grocery bag. Huck's boats sleep 10–12 people and are equipped with central air and heat; some have hot tubs and more. A complete training cruise is included. Summer rates $2,000–4,000 for a three-day weekend, up to $8,199 for a week on their largest boat.

Stoney Creek Inn (608-781-3060; stoneycreekinn.com), 3060 Kinney Coulee Road South, Onalaska. This is a growing Midwestern chain of Northwoods-themed hotels with a variety of room options, ranging from simple double rooms to suites with full kitchens and family suites with bunk beds. Rates start at $125.

Grandstay Suites (608-796-1615; grandstaylacrosse.com), 525 Front Street North. For a little more space, Grandstay's all-suite property is a good option, and its location right by Riverside Park is perfect. There's a pool, free WiFi, continental breakfast, and a full kitchen in each suite. Perfect for longer stays, or trips with kids. Rates start at $119.

Courtyard by Marriott on the River (608-782-1000; marriott.com), 500 Front Street South. Right on the river, this is one of the nicer hotel options in La Crosse. Great views, free WiFi, and comfortable rooms, plus onsite breakfast and the popular Piggy's Restaurant across the street. Rates start at $159.

CAMPGROUNDS **Veterans Memorial Campground** (608-786-4011), N4668 County Road VP, West Salem. The campground features120 large campsites, a fishing pond, access to the La Crosse River State Bike Trail, and more. Campsites start at $16.

Goose Island County Park (608-788-7018), W6488 County Road GI, Stoddard. Just south of the city on WI 35. On an island in the Mississippi River, you can canoe guided paths in the backwaters, fish, bird watch, laze on the beach, or stay overnight at one of more than 400 campsites. Sites with electric and water are available. Campsites start at $16.

✷ Where to Eat

DINING OUT 🍸 ☂ **Piggy's Restaurant** (608-784-4877; piggys.com), 501 Front Street South. Open for dinner daily. Piggy's is housed in a former metal works foundry that once made parts for the old paddlewheelers cruising the Mississippi. These days, it's an upscale dinner spot overlooking the river with a reputation of being the best in the state for prime rib and pork chops. Desserts are creative and sinful, and the wine list is extensive and award-winning. Entrees $14.95–29.95.

🍸 ♿ **Freight House Restaurant** (608-784-6211; freighthouserestaurant.com), 107 Vine Street. Open for dinner daily. Located along the Mississippi River in a restored train depot, this steak and seafood favorite is a great alternative to stuffier fine dining. With loads of train memorabilia on the walls and a National Historic Site designation, the Freight House has true-to-its-past ambience and very happy customers. Entrees $15–35.

🍸 ♿ **The Waterfront** (608-782-5400; thewaterfrontlacrosse.com), 328 Front Street South, Suite 100. Open for lunch Monday through Friday, dinner Monday through Saturday. Steaks and seafood with fantastic river views. Entrees $17–$27.

EATING OUT ♿ **Hackberry's Bistro** (608-794-5798; pfc.coop), 315 Fifth Avenue South, above the People's Food Co-op. Open daily for lunch and dinner, brunch served on weekends. Charming and casual, Hackberry's has creative and delicious healthier fare. Lots of local and organic foods are on the menu, and although vegetarians and vegans will feel right at home here, meat eaters have plenty of options, too; there's everything from tenderloin steak to lentil loaf. Lunches offer all manner of burgers, and the kids menu is outstanding. Sandwiches $7–9, entrees $12–20.

Kate's on State (608-784-3354), 1810 State Street. Open for dinner daily. Charming and homey, Kate's serves up huge portions of mouthwatering, creative northern Italian fare at reasonable prices. This place is small, so you might want to consider reservations. And be forewarned, Kate's is friendly, but the menu does include two rules: "No crybabies or cell phones." Fair enough. Dishes $10–15.

Y & **Edwardo's Pizza Wagon** (608-783-8282), 1930 Rose Street. Open daily for dinner. Edwardo's offers pasta and burgers, but you're really here for the wood-fired pizza. Dishes $7–15.

Y **Bodega Brew Pub** (608-782-0677), 122 Fourth Street South. Open daily. This popular bar is a smoke-free brew pub with more than 400 beers to choose from in the historic downtown. It's got a great night scene, but it also offers lunch. Grab a sandwich and a hard-to-find beer. Lunch $5–7.

Rudy's Drive-In (608-782-2200; rudysdrivein.com), 1004 La Crosse Street. Open March through October, 10–10 daily. Don't miss this one—it's the genuine article. Run by a family that's been in the drive-in root beer stand business since 1933, Rudy's has real, live, roller-skating car hops. If you want to keep your car clean, you can sit inside, as well. Rudy's has standard burger-joint fare as well as the unexpected, such as local meatless favorite The Historic Trempealeau Hotel Walnut Burger®. Kids younger than five

are offered free root beer. Burgers $1.60–4.25.

Buzzard Billy's (608-796-2277; buzzardbillys.com), 222 Pearl Street. Open daily for lunch and dinner. Located in a restored historic downtown hotel, this popular spot for Cajun food offers loads of atmosphere and options, including everything from Gator Fingers to Voodoo Tuna. Vegetarians will be pleasantly surprised— unlike most Cajun-themed restaurants, this one's got more than a couple of meatless options. Upstairs, the Starlite Lounge is a retro '50s place to chill. Burgers and po' boys $7, entrees $10–15.

Y & **The Wine Guyz** (608-782-9463; wineguyz.com), 122 King Street. Open 11–8 Monday, 11–10 Tuesday through Thursday, 11–11 Friday and Saturday. It's a store where you can eat, or shop while sipping wine. Lunch hour's a great deal, with reasonably priced cheese plates and downright cheap sandwiches, which gives you more room to spend sampling the tasty wine. Then grab a bottle and some specialty foods as you head out the door. Sandwiches $4–6, cheese plates $8.50, nine-inch pizza $7–8.

COFFEE SHOPS AND ICE CREAM PARLORS & ᵀ **Jules' Coffee House** (608-796-1200), 327 Pearl Street. Open daily. Big wooden booths create a cozy atmosphere. Jules' has specialty coffees, soups, and desserts, which should satisfy any midday need.

Grounded Specialty Coffee (608-784-5282; groundedspecialtycoffee .com), 308 Main Street. Open 6–6 Monday through Saturday, 8–3 Sunday. Grounded offers standard coffee shop fare plus smoothies, bakery, and a few sandwiches. $5.

& ᵀ **The Pearl** (608-782-6655; pearlst west.com), 207 Pearl Street. Open daily. Holy cow, what more could you want? Homemade ice cream and old-fashioned confections, espresso drinks, and a soda fountain, all under one roof! No reason to ever leave, really. Authentic '30s decor seals the deal, and octogenarian soda jerk Oscar Peterslie keeps people coming back. $5.

✷ Entertainment

La Crosse Community Theatre (608-784-9292;), 118 Fifth Avenue North. This community theatre puts on seven shows a year, including comedies, musicals, and drama, as well as two productions for kids. The theater is looking for new digs as of this writing; be sure to call or check the Web site on that address.

La Crosse Symphony Orchestra (608-783-2121; lacrossesymphony.org). Performances held at the Viterbo University Fine Arts Center, 929 Jackson Street. More than a century old, the orchestra runs about six programs a year.

⇡ Rivoli Theatre & Pizzeria (608-785-2058; rivoli.net), 117 North Fourth Street. $4 adults. Dinner and a movie all wrapped up in one, for a quick date. The Rivoli shows second-run movies in a historic venue at bargain prices, and you can have pizza and beer during the screening.

✷ Selective Shopping

Pearl Street Books (608-782-3424), 323 Pearl Street. Open daily. Pearl Street is a good, well-rounded independent bookstore in La Crosse's historic downtown, stocking more than 20,000 new and used titles. Grab a book, then hop on over to Jules' Coffee House, right next door.

Simply Living (608-788-1192; simply livingonline.com), 410 Main Street.

Open Monday through Saturday. Simply Living has all sorts of earth friendly products, from organic cotton blankets and fair trade soaps to jewelry made from recycled materials and much more.

Satori Arts Gallery (608-785-2779), 201 Pearl Street. Open Monday through Saturday. Stocking unique arts gifts and artifacts, you'll find Mississippi River pearls and hand-made jewelry in this shop in the heart of historic downtown.

Cheddarheads (608-784-8899; cheddarheads.com), 215 Pearl Street. Open daily. This is your spot to get cheesy Wisconsin souvenirs. All manner of foam cheese headgear is available here, as well as Cheddarheads tee-shirts, cow themed-items, and all the actual cheese you can eat. A great Wisconsin shop.

Pleasoning Outlet Store (608-787-1030; pleasoning.com), 2418 South Avenue. Open 8:30–5 Monday through Friday. Tour, browse, and try out spices at this family owned spice shop. I'm sure one of the 31 gourmet seasonings—

CHICKENCUE

Baffled by the banner advertising "chickencue"? It's not exactly a chicken barbeque, and it's got nothing to do with a pool game. Chickencue is a simple chicken dinner often sold as a fund raiser, and sometimes at festivals, in the La Crosse area. Usually it's served in a Styrofoam container, and usually it's sold in a parking lot. Locals go crazy for it, so you might want to find a church that's raising money, and experience chickencue firsthand.

maybe Caution!—will suit your palate.

UnWine'd (608-781-2626; unwinedwi
.com), 1125 Main Street, Suite 160,
Onalaska. Open daily. No, it's not in a
charming historic building, but
UnWine'd has a great selection of
wines and craft beers, as well as specialty food items to take back to your
hotel room or put together a gift basket. It also hosts monthly wine tastings.

Valley View Mall (608-781-4700;
myvalleyview.com), 3800 WI 16. Open
10–9 Monday through Saturday, 11–6
Sunday. If you're looking for a mall in
the area, this is it. Valley View has a
Macy's, a Barnes and Noble, and all
the usual suspects among its 71 stores.

✳ Special Events

April: **Beer, Wine, and Cheese Festival**, Fest Grounds, La Crosse. Sample these culinary delights, listen to
live music, and enter the home brew
contest.

July: **Riverfest**, Riverside Park, La
Crosse. This five-day festival features
live music along the river, games, five
stages with live music, area food vendors, and more.

Art Fair on the Green, UW-La
Crosse, La Crosse. This two-day art
fair draws artists from around the
nation.

August: **Irish Fest**, Fest Grounds, La
Crosse. A celebration of Irish culture
with traditional dance, music, an Irish
baking contest, a harp competition,
and lots more.

Great River Folk Festival, UW-La
Crosse, La Crosse. Ethnic crafts,
music, foods and more.

September: **Oktoberfest**, Fest
Grounds, La Crosse. This is the area's
most popular festival, and considered
one of the best Oktoberfests in the
U.S. Check out traditional German
beer, foods, music, and more.

GREAT RIVER ROAD AREA—
NORTH OF LA CROSSE

North of La Crosse along the Mississippi River you'll find what might be Wisconsin's most stunningly beautiful scenery. Many of the small towns dotted along WI 35, or the Great River Road, are home to cute coffee shops, art galleries, and hip boutiques. The dining is diverse, and the opportunities for outdoor recreation are endless. Really, a surprising thing about the sleepy towns is that there's something along the river for every type of traveler.

The Great River Road is often overlooked by Wisconsin travelers, many of whom are unaware of the remarkable beauty in this part of the state. It's a shame, on the one hand; on the other, it makes savvier travelers feel as though they've really discovered something. The geography of this region, with its green bluffs, peaks and valleys, and the Mississippi River banks, makes it visually distinct from most of the rest of Wisconsin. Even the nearby Hidden Valleys region, replete with rolling hills, doesn't feel as unique as the area north of La Crosse. In a way, it feels like you've left Wisconsin—or reminds you that this state is way more complex than you realized.

This area isn't entirely secret—motorcycle riders who enjoy long, lazy highway rides have long known about the beauty here, and without question, the towns along WI 35 depend on a steady tourist business. What's more, the folks across the river have enjoyed these towns for years. Sharing some of the features of bigger tourism areas such as Door County and the Northwoods, the Great River Road region is perfect for a relaxed vacation that doesn't feel like you're in the middle of nowhere.

And then there's that river. Narrow this far north, and tamed somewhat by the imposing lock and dams, the Mississippi still maintains its majestic hold on visitors, and it gets stuck in your mind. By all means, if you've got a canoe handy, check out the backwaters—there are many, many opportunities. But just gazing at the river, or watching the sun set beyond it, is a pleasure.

The Great River Road in Wisconsin runs mostly along WI 35, and the way is marked by its logo, a green ship's helm on a white background. If you stay on this road and head north from La Crosse, you will be treated to some of the most charming towns and gorgeous landscapes in the state. The mighty Mississippi River is to the west, and towering bluffs are to the east. If it's your first time here, you might get a sore neck trying to take it all in—but lucky you; we all only get to discover it once. Once you've gotten used to the natural beauty here, you might consider a couple of scenic drives as side trips. Navigate away from WI 35 just outside of Trempealeau and head north on WI 93 to the town of Arcadia. The road climbs bluffs and offers astounding views of the valleys below. There are a handful of scenic overlooks where you can pull over and snap a picture. Travel WI 95 south from Arcadia for even more remarkable scenery; it's like driving up a mountain as you follow the narrow, winding road clinging to rocky bluffs. There isn't a safe place to pull over and hop out, so I can't recommend it, although you'll be tempted.

Back on the Great River Road, Trempealeau has an easy, small-town charm, historical and quaint yet still progressive, like much of this region. The name translates from French as "soaked in water," from the longer phrase, "La montagne qui trempe a l'eau," or "mountain soaked in water," but locals frequently shorten it to "Tremplo," a more phonetic version that's easier for visitors who aren't francophones to handle. Perrot State Park, right on the river, and right near Trempealeau's center, is home to the town's namesake. The adventurous can take a canoe out to the mountain for a closer look. On land, this town is friendly and offers good food, relaxation, and community events. Trains pass on both sides of the river, and there's a well-landscaped pedestrian walkway with benches to watch them thunder by. Here, too, is Lock and Dam Number 6, which has an observation deck, or you can just watch ships lock through from Trempealeau's benches.

Fountain City's picturesque downtown is set beneath towering bluffs—and sometimes that's a bad thing, like when boulders fall from above. Don't worry, it's a rare enough occurrence that a tourist trap has been fashioned out of a fallen boulder (see **Rock in the House** under To See and Do). This town is lovely, if quirky, and a perfect stop along the river. You'll find folk art, a toy museum, good food, and more here, plus beautiful scenery and bird watching.

North from Fountain City, the towns are just as cute. Alma has a charming commercial district, with lots of art galleries and boutiques in a pedestrian-friendly

TREMPEALEAU MOUNTAIN

VIEW OF THE MISSISSIPPI RIVER FROM BUENA VISTA PARK IN ALMA

city center. Take the steep drive up the bluffs to Buena Vista Park, and catch one of the best views on the river. Pepin is best known for its association with Laura Ingalls Wilder. The author was born here, in a little house in what once was big woods. These days, it's mostly farmland, but that doesn't make a visit to the Little House Wayside any less appealing. Pepin is also home to a number of cute boutiques and restaurants, and Lake Pepin, a pool on the Mississippi River, is considered the birthplace of water skiing. In Stockholm you'll find loads of art galleries and dining; it's a bit more touristy than the other towns (though not much).

There are more than 30 towns along the Great River Road in Wisconsin, both north and south of La Crosse; I've only highlighted a handful here. This drive is made for exploring, and vacationing any way you wish.

GUIDANCE The **Trempealeau Chamber of Commerce** (608-534-6780; door county.com), 24455 Third Street, Trempealeau, is probably the most active and helpful town chamber included in this chapter, effortlessly guiding you to the area's treasures. Pick up a brochure highlighting Trempealeau's history, or information on the region's many wildlife areas. Check, too, the Pepin Area Community Club (800-442-3011; pepinwisconsin.com), which publishes a brochure you'll find at businesses around the area. The **Prescott Chamber of Commerce** (715-262-3284; pressenter.com), 233 Broad Street North, operates the Welcome and Heritage Center, where Minnesotans can stop to pick up some information as they prepare to head south down the Great River Road. There's a very handy map put out by Wisconsin Great River Road (wigreatriverroad.org) that highlights the unique features of each town. You can pick it up just about everywhere along the river here.

along the Mississippi River, so there are many, many entry points.

GETTING AROUND A vehicle is a must for this area, but many people like to bike it.

MEDICAL EMERGENCY Call 911.

There are clinics in the towns along the river, otherwise, many medical emergencies will be handled across the river in Minnesota. I've included some of those hospitals here. It's important to note that depending on your location, cell phone function can be spotty.

Community Memorial Hospital, (507-454-3650), 855 Mankato Avenue, Winona, Minnesota.

Franciscan Skemp Arcadia Campus, (608-323-3373), 464 South St. Joseph Avenue, Arcadia.

Lake City Medical Center (651-345-3321), 500 West Grant Street, Lake City, Minnesota. Operates a clinic in Alma.

Fairview Red Wing Medical Center (651-267-5000), 701 Fairview Boulevard, Red Wing, Minnesota.

✳ To See and Do

Elmer's Auto and Toy Museum (608-687-7221; elmersautoandtoymuseum.com), W903 Elmers Road, Fountain City. Open 9–5 varying weekends, call ahead. Located on a bluff overlooking the Mississippi River, this huge museum is housed in six buildings, and features a huge selection of antique cars, bikes, and toys. Thousands of playthings, including hundreds of antique dolls from around the world, are a sight to behold; consider this a prelude to your stop at the **House on the Rock**. Bring a picnic for lunch outside. Adults $7, seniors $6, ages 6–11 $3.

Rock in the House, 440 North Shore Drive, Fountain City. Open daily 10–6. Here's an honest-to-goodness tourist trap, awaiting your amazement and scorn, not to be confused with the **House on the Rock**. *This* a house where a big boulder tumbled down a bluff and smashed into the master bedroom. And . . . that's it. Strange, and especially cool that it's run on the honor system. Leave your buck in a box and check out the disaster up close. $1.

Prairie Moon Sculpture Garden (608-687-8250), S2727 Prairie Moon Road, Cochrane. One of a handful of Wisconsin sculpture parks and other outdoor art spaces preserved by the Kohler Foundation, this is a great side-trip or destination for fans of folk art. Self-taught artist Herman Rusch began the project in 1959 at age 74, creating 40 concrete, rock, and found-object sculptures over the next 16 years. The site now also includes the works of another folk artist, Fred Schlosstein.

✂ ♿ **Nelson Cheese Factory** (715-673-4725; nelsoncheese.com/contact.htm), WI 35, Nelson. Open daily. This is a great stop for all your dairy needs, particularly ice cream. Around since 1850, this fun shop offers all kinds of cheese shopping, plus a couple of cozy spots inside and out to grab soup and a sandwich.

Ellsworth Co-op Creamery (715-273-4311; ellsworthcheesecurds.com), 232 North Wallace Street, Ellsworth. Open 8–5 Monday through Friday, 8–2 Saturday.

Declared the "Cheese Curd Capital of the World" in the '80s by former governor Tony Earl, I'd be remiss if I skipped this one. Before you buy them, my own status as a cheesehead requires I inform you that the proper way to eat a cheese curd is at room temperature, which brings out all the squeaky goodness. While purists might settle for nothing less than a simple cheddar curd, this creamery offers up all kinds of wild flavors, such as taco and Cajun. The creamery also stocks a large variety of cheeses, sans curd, and gifts.

✒ ♿ **Wings Over Alma** (608-685-3303; wingsoveralma.org), 118 North Main Street, Alma. Open 10–5 daily. This nonprofit center offers education about the area's wildlife, rotating local art and history exhibits, and viewing platforms for bird watching. It's even got binoculars to help you spot a bald eagle.

♿ **Lake Pepin Art and Design Center** (715-442-4442; pepinartdesign.org), 406 Second Street, Pepin. Hours vary. Hosts gallery exhibits, workshops, and special events. Frequently screening independent films and bringing in performers, this space is a one-stop arts venue.

♿ **Maiden Rock Winery and Cidery** (715-448-3502; maidenrockwinerycidery .com), W12266 King Lane, Stockholm. Tour this winery, where hard cider and apple wines are made from the fruits of its own orchard containing some 25 varieties of apples (you can also visit the orchard). Stop in the tasting room to sample the goods, and check out the gift shop for all kinds of apple treats.

Rush River Produce (715-594-3648; rushriverproduce.com), W4098 200th Avenue, Maiden Rock. Open 8–2 Thursday through Sunday in July and August, depending on the supply—call first. The farm sells a variety of produce, but the main draw here is the blueberry crop. A full nine acres of fresh, sustainably farmed blueberries for you to pick and enjoy.

✳ Green Space and Outdoor Activities

While canoeing the backwaters and general water recreation on the Mississippi is a no-brainer along the Great River Road, the area offers more than kayaks and camping, which you can fine, really, almost anywhere in Wisconsin. Trempealeau, for example, is perfect for bike riders. Seven trails converge here, and numerous special events devoting to biking happen throughout the year. Bird watching along the river is a treat; as part of the Mississippi River Flyway, birds stop at habitats along the way en masse, and much of the land along the river has been converted to state parks or national refuges; there's outdoor recreation here for even the least athletic traveler! And if you're so inclined, there's a spot to drop a line and hope for catfish here with your name on it.

In Trempealeau

Trempealeau National Wildlife Refuge (608-539-2311), W28488 Refuge Road. Along the Mississippi River, this 6,200-acre refuge is a day-use park featuring wetlands, bottomland forests, prairie, trails, and more. As this backwater land provides habitat for numerous birds and is part of the Mississippi flyway, the bird watching is grand here. If you just want to take a gander, the Prairie's Edge Wildlife Drive offers sightseeing opportunities from within your car (but you can hop out at designated stops along the way). A two-sided leaflet is available from the refuge.

Perrot State Park (608-534-6409), W26247 Sullivan Road. A beautiful state park with a lot of history, this is where you'll get a peek at Trempealeau's namesake "mountain soaked in water." Trempealeau Mountain is not really a mountain, but it's one of only three rock islands in the Mississippi River. The mountain itself is worth a visit—although you'll need a canoe to get there—but the park, too, with its many campsites, nature center, and bike trails is especially nice. The park's rich history begins with the Native American effigy mounds here, and travels through its use as a French post and Civilian Conservation Corps camp during the Great Depression. Today, the park is perfectly suited to its location in Trempealeau, where the residents take pride in and make good use of the beauty. The Great River State Bike Trail travels through here, as well. State park sticker required.

In Fountain City

Eagle Bluff. Thought by many to be the highest point on the upper Mississippi, the bluff is just north of **Merrick State Park** and offers a breathtaking view of the area.

Merrick State Park (608-687-4936), S2965 WI 35. This 330-acre park offers camping, fishing, hiking, and more, and is a great spot to spy migrating birds. Located along the Mississippi River, the backwaters offer a unique state park setting. State park sticker required.

In Alma

Buena Vista Park, County Road E, just off WI 35. Offering one of the most stunning views along the Great River Road, you can watch barges lock through Lock and Dam Number 4, or just take in the Old Miss from a height of 500 feet. The river is narrow here, so you can see clear across to Minnesota. There's a picnic shelter on the bluff, as well as toilets, so it's a beautiful, relaxing spot at which to spend a sunny day.

Rieck's Lake Park (608-685-3330). There's hiking here, plus backpack camping, picnic shelters, and a playground, but the real reason people come is to catch a glimpse of the migrating tundra swans. Although the peak population has dwindled dramatically, you can still see the swans en masse each fall. Restoration of the habitat is underway, which means the numbers should swell again.

In Nelson

Tiffany Bottoms Wildlife Area (608-685-6222), WI 35 and WI 25. Home to flood plane forest trees and habitat for numerous animals, there are key birding opportunities here—see if you can spot a red-shouldered hawk or great blue heron. There are eight miles of hiking trails in this 13,000-acre natural area, but you can also hop an open-air train to get a peek. There are numerous public boat launches here as well.

GREAT NORTHERN FLYWAY

More than 300 species of migrating birds travel roughly along the Mississippi River each fall and spring, using the north-south route that's free of mountains as a perfect path. This means great opportunities exist for bird watching all along the Upper Mississippi River, so pack the binoculars and vest. The National Audubon Society has a wealth of information on the entire flyway, and offers maps. Catch a glimpse of swans, eagles, herons, raptors, and many, many more.

LITTLE HOUSE WAYSIDE IN PEPIN

In Pepin

Little House, Wayside County Road CC. This wayside is a little out of the way, but it's worth the trek through seemingly endless farmland if you have even the slightest soft spot in your heart for Laura Ingalls Wilder. For fans, of course, it's a must. The wayside includes a replica of Wilder's childhood home, on the plot of land where the author was born. Marvel at how a family lived in such a small home. Ah, but for simpler times.

Laura Ingalls Wilder Museum (715-442-2142), 306 3rd Street. Open 10–5 daily May 15 through October 15. Right on WI 35, this museum is small, but it's a charmer, and who could skip a Laura Ingalls Wilder education while visiting her birthplace? Devoted to artifacts from pioneer days as well as Wilder's life, it's worth a wander.

Pepin Depot Museum (715-442-6501), 806 3rd Street. Open 10–5 daily May 15 through October 15. Located right near the Laura Ingalls Wilder Museum, this one completes a two-fer in small-town museum perusal glory. Yes, yes—train museums are a dime a dozen, but they're also loads of fun.

In Maiden Rock

Freedom Park (715-262-0104; freedomparkwi.org), 200 Monroe Street, Prescott. Perched on a bluff where the Mississippi River and St. Croix meet, Freedom Park is home to the Great River Road Visitor and Learning Center. Aside from a great view, bird-watching, and educational programs, art fairs are held here in summer, as well as the weekly farmers market on Thursdays.

In Stockholm

Maiden Rock Bluff Natural Area Long Lane. Home to nesting peregrine falcons, the bird watching and scenic views here are phenomenal. At 400 feet high, this bluff extends for about a mile. Ongoing prairie restoration here means there are many native plants to view, as well. Walk or take a peek, just remember to stay on the trails.

✳ Lodging

In Trempealeau

♿ **Pleasant Knoll** (608-534-6615), 11451 Main Street. The Pleasant Knoll is really a motel, but it offers a pleasantly "green" experience. From its healthy continental breakfast to biodegradable serve-ware, the owners run an environmentally tight ship. Rooms range from standard doubles to large suites where the kids can stretch their legs. Not the highest tech or most modern, but it's a great budget choice that suits its name.

♿ **Inn on the River** (608-534-7784; innontheriverwisconsin.com), 11321 Main Street. You don't get closer to the river—or the train tracks—than this. Twelve standard rooms all offer balconies with spectacular views of the Mississippi, and the pretty landscaping will make you feel right at home. Rooms $79.95.

In Fountain City

♿ **Hawk's View Cottages and Lodge** (866-293-0803), 17 North Street. Nestled in the wooded bluffs high above Fountain City, this grouping of cottages offers rustic appeal with modern conveniences, and loads of room. Check in at the Seven Hawks Vineyard, then make the steep climb up the bluff to your cottage. Large decks, Jacuzzis, and potbelly stoves,

---

TREMPEALEAU HOTEL

Among a handful of buildings to survive a fire in 1888, the **Trempealeau Hotel** (608-534-6898; trempealeauhotel.com, 150 Main Street, Trempealeau) is alluring and special, with a surprising sophistication that's hard to pin down. Maybe it's that so many *newer* places try to capture what the Trempealeau Hotel already has: history, charm, and authenticity. The building was moved to its present location by a team of horses following the town's devastating fire, and has functioned just as it does now—as a combination restaurant and bar with sleeping rooms upstairs—since the 1930s. Somehow, that history is evident the moment you walk in; every inch of the place is steeped in character.

Lodging options range from European-style rooms above the restaurant to traditional motel rooms and roomy cabins with spa tubs. Train fanatics will *love* staying here, right on the Mississippi River and its parallel train tracks. Light sleepers should take note—trains thunder by at a regular clip all day and night, but I wasn't bothered. It just adds another bit of excitement to your stay.

Known to vegetarians around the state for its outstanding walnut burger, the restaurant here is a must stop; the food is *good*. At night, the bar is lively and welcoming, but be warned: You might start to think of packing up and moving here after a few.

Serving somewhat as the town center, there are basketball courts, volleyball courts, and bike rentals here, plus special events and a live music series held on the grounds. If you want to mix with the locals—and you should—this is where you need to be.

plus full kitchens and tons of windows for the stunning view, separate Hawk's View from other options. Most of the cottages require a significant stair climb, but the Marshhawk is wheelchair accessible. Cottages $170–195, lodges $220–280.

In Alma
Hotel De Ville (612-423-3653; hoteldevillealma.googlepages.com), 305 North Main Street. Oh, what a charming hotel, and what charming proprietors. The owners modeled the hotel, and the experience they provide, after the atmosphere they fell in love with in southern France. Four lavish suites housed in a historic building offer period charm and furnishings blended smartly with modern features such as flat-screen televisions and pillow-top mattresses, and all overlook the river. The Eagle Suite has two bedrooms and two stories with an open staircase, and includes a full kitchen for longer stays. The Swan Suite is smaller but also features a full kitchen. The grounds boast a carefully tended formal garden, which is really the icing on the European-feel cake. Suites $95–140.

In Pepin
Harbor Hill Inn (715-442-2324; harborhillinn.net), 310 Second Street. The three rooms in this Victorian mansion are each named after an English harbor town and boast eclectic furnishings. The best view comes with the Portsmouth Room, but if you're looking to soak in a Jacuzzi tub, try the Plymouth room. Locally sourced English breakfast fills you up in the morning and gets you on your way. Rooms $120–140.

A Summer Place (877-442-2132; summerplace.net), 106 Main Street. Open March through November. The three sunny rooms in this hilltop home all offer quiet luxury for travelers.

Romantic without being frilly, the wicker furniture and sun-drenched windows justify the hotel's name, but it's the abundance of flowers outside that really does the trick. Rooms $160.

In Stockholm
River Road Inn (612-306-2100; river roadinn.com), W12360 Great River Road. Modern decor and a great river view are obvious draws to this newly constructed inn. The atmosphere of the rooms ranges from the Jade Room's Asian-inspired furnishings and walk-in tile shower to the more nautical Stockholm Suite. A separate carriage house, offering more privacy, is also available. $200–245.

&. **Great River Amish Inn** (715-442-5400; greatriveramishinn.com), 311 Third Street, Pepin. Eight simple, attractive rooms outfitted with Amish furnishings and quilts make this a great, wallet-friendly choice. Options are limited to one queen or two double beds, but if you're looking for a clean, above-average landing pad that won't break the bank, this is it. Rooms $65–$75.

In Prescott
&. **Arbor Inn Bed & Breakfast** (715-262-2222; thearborinn.com), 434 North Court Street. If you'd like a room with a view and onsite spa services to boot, the Arbor Inn ought to be your place. The decor veers toward country charm without being overdone. Three rooms offer whirlpool tubs, but the Silhouette Room has its own hot tub on an enclosed patio. Rooms $159–199.

✴ Where to Eat
&. ⓨ **The Historic Trempealeau Hotel** (608-534-6898; trempealeau hotel.com), 150 Main Street, Trempealeau. Open for lunch and dinner. Located along the Mississippi River,

this hotel offers a perfect historic atmosphere with sumptuous, sophisticated cuisine. A must stop for vegetarians, the walnut burger is a nutty patty that puts other veggie burgers to shame, but there are plenty of meat and fish options, too. $10–20.

Y & **Sullivan's** (608-534-7775; sulli vanssupperclub.com), W25709 Sullivan Road. Open for dinner daily, closed Wednesday. An old-school supper club on the banks of the Mississippi, the menu is heavy on meat and seafood. Try locally caught catfish, and cap off dinner with an ice-cream drink, such as a Grasshopper or Pink Squirrel—it's that kind of place. Dinners come with a trip to the salad bar, which is proper for a supper club. "Lighter" entrees here are not different, just smaller. Dishes $13.99–32.99.

Y & **The Monarch Public House** (608-687-423119; monarchtavern .com), North Main Street, Fountain City. Open daily for dinner. Some businesses prompt love at first sight; this is one of them. Surprisingly family friendly and wholly relaxed, the Monarch Tavern skillfully blends a number of the elements that make a great bar: an Irish atmosphere, historical fidelity, onsite brewery, and good food. Make that outstanding food, and with a menu that ranges from sandwiches and salads to pizza and Irish cuisine, even a group with the most divergent tastes will be satisfied. Whatever you do, be sure to try the potato soup; it's the thickest, creamiest soup I've ever had. In the event you can't settle on something from among the many options here, there's the Potato Famine Pizza, loaded with Irish champ (buttery mashed potatoes), cheese, and more butter. Wash it all down with a Fountain Brew, and start making plans to return next year. Dishes, $5–8, 16-inch pizza, $11–17.

The Stone Barn (715-673-4478; nelsonstonebarn.com), S685 County Road KK, Nelson. Open for dinner Friday through Sunday, closed in winter. Wood-fired pizza, and nothing else, but all from the freshest ingredients. The building is the result of creative preservation; the foundation is the remains of an old Norwegian stone barn. Pizza starts at $16.

& **Kate and Gracie's** (608-685-4505; kateandgracies.com), 215 North Main Street, Alma. Open for lunch and dinner daily except Tuesday, breakfast on Saturday and Sunday. There's something for everyone in this simple, airy cafe. Housed in the oldest building in Alma, built in 1861, the menu features everything from pastas to rib eye, including a large selection of sandwiches and a well-rounded appetizer selection. The owners grow their own herbs outside near the lovely patio. Dishes $9–25.

& **Harbor View Cafe** (715-442-3893; harborviewpepin.com), 314 First Street, Pepin. Open mid-March through mid-November for lunch and dinner Thursday through Monday. This place is loved for miles around for its changing contemporary menu (written on a chalkboard) and relaxed atmosphere. It's charming inside, with books lining the walls and wood tables and booths. Entrees $20–30.

& **The Pickle Factory Pub and Grill** (715-442-4400; pepinpicklefac tory.com), 250 First Street, Pepin. Open daily for lunch and dinner. Housed in—what else? An old pickle factory! Casual and bright, you'll find a range of burgers, sandwiches, seafood, and steaks, plus loads of fried appetizers, including deep-fried pickles. There's also a dock for your boat. Sandwiches $7–9, dinners $13–18.

& **Third Street Deli & Juice Bar** (715-442-3354; pepinbrands.com),

1015 Third Street, Pepin. Open for breakfast and lunch daily except Tuesday and Friday. To suit healthier cravings, this modern little deli offers organic egg omelets and build-your-own sandwiches, although a burger is not out of the question. Desserts range from freshly baked cookies and pies to fruity smoothies, or just throw caution to the wind and get a scoop of handmade ice cream. Dishes $5–10.

Bogus Creek Cafe and Bakery (715-442-5017), North 2049 Spring Street, Stockholm. Open daily for breakfast and lunch. You get to have Swedish pancakes with lingonberries in Stockholm, what more could you want? Breakfast is served all day, but try not to overlook the sandwiches and pastas available later. A small selection of wines and beers is available, along with espresso drinks, in this casual cafe. Vegetarians have lots of options, and a kid's menu is available. Dishes $8–13.

A to Z Bakery—The Pizza Farm (715-448-4802), N2956 Anker Lane, Stockholm. Open Tuesday evenings, 4:30 or so. On a warm Tuesday night, head to this farm tucked away in the countryside for freshly made brick-oven pizza. This isn't a restaurant, it's a farm, complete with animals. As such, you should bring your own chairs, picnic blanket, plates, wine, and whatever else you think you'll need; the only thing the owners provide is a pizza made to order and packed with farm-fresh toppings. Waits can be long, so get there early, then pop a squat on the lawn and enjoy. Pizzas start around $22.

The Boxcar Restaurant (715-262-2026), 211 North Broad Street, Prescott. Open for dinner Tuesday through Sunday, brunch on Sunday. Offering an upscale twist on Southern grub, the dining room is loaded with

area history, well suited to the restaurant's downtown location. Familiar dishes are livened up, such as smoked cheese curds, fried baby dill pickles, pulled pork marinated in Guinness, and macaroni and cheese with bratwurst (welcome to Wisconsin!). Dishes $6–22.

Muddy Waters Bar and Grill (715-262-5999; muddywatersbarandgrill.com), 231 North Broad Street, Prescott. Open daily for lunch and dinner. The menu at this riverfront eatery is all over the board, from Southern to Greek with pizza, steak, and seafood in between. Different decks and sections of the restaurant offer atmospheres from casual to a little more upscale. Lunch $6–8, dinner $10–20.

COFFEE AND SWEETS **The Coffee Attic** (608-534-5282), 24010 Third Street, Trempealeau. Open daily. A cozy stop for espresso and a snack, this little coffeehouse greets you as you drive into downtown. It doesn't look like much from the outside, but inside the atmosphere is friendly and relaxed, if a little craftsy. It's a great stop for that essential latte, but they've also got a decent menu of panini sandwiches and wraps. $5–10.

Jackie O's (608-582-2669), 6846 South Davis Street, Galesville. Open daily for breakfast and lunch. This cute coffee shop is housed in a historic building in charming downtown Galesville. Wood floors, big booths, and a veritable Jackie Kennedy shrine make it a standout among small-town coffeehouses, but the best part is that they serve Intelligentsia Coffee, and the owner knows her stuff. Fresh baked goods every morning and friendly service make this one a no-brainer.

Fire and Ice (612-423-3653), 305 North Main Street, Alma. Open daily.

This is the kind of place, and owner Jeffrey Shilts the kind of welcoming soul, that fills me with romantic notions of picking up and moving to a town after only five minutes. Doubtless, if I lived in Alma, I'd spend all my time here, loitering. And why not? Fire and Ice offers excellent coffee and Chocolate Shoppe ice cream in an atmosphere that's darling without being precious. From the eagle-topped Italian espresso machine to the proper ice cream-parlor chairs and the gorgeous garden out back, this place is in every way perfect.

♧ **Great River Coffee Roasters Cafe** (715-442-4100; www.greatriver coffee.com), 415 3rd Street, Pepin. Open daily for breakfast and lunch. This cheery cafe is the retail outlet for the coffee roaster, where servers try out new roasts on the willing public. Grab a sandwich or muffin, and head outside to the large patio, where a growing perennial garden provides eye candy.

The Stockholm Pie Company (715-442-5505; thestockholmpiecompany .com), N2030 Spring Street, Stockholm. Open daily in summer, weekends in winter. If the sweet aroma of fresh-baked pie doesn't knock your socks off the second you walk in the door, there's something wrong with your sniffer. This smart little shop offers up delicious pies and out-of-this-world handmade ice cream. Grab a stool and enjoy.

♧ **Flat Pennies Ice Cream** (715-594-3555; flatpennies.com), W6442 WI 35, Bay City. Open daily. This little ice-cream shop will satisfy your sweet tooth and provide cool respite on a warm summer day. It's a little log cabin, paying homage to all things train, and there's even an old Soo Line caboose parked outside. As if ice cream wasn't enough to thrill the kids!

They love dogs here, too, and there is plenty of space outside for your pooch.

❂ **Selective Shopping**

Art and Soul Gallery (612-423-3653), 305 North Main Street, Alma. Open daily. Adjacent to **Fire and Ice**, this charming little boutique offers gifts and imports of all kinds. Packed full, it'll take longer than you'd think to dig through all the wares. Luckily, if you're worn out at the end, you can just pop next door for ice cream and coffee.

Mississippi River Pearl Jewelry Co. (651-301-1204; nadineleo.com), 125 North Main Street, Alma. Open 10–5 Thursday through Sunday, April through November. This shop, located in Alma's commercial district, specializes in designer jewelry featuring natural Mississippi River pearls. Prices range from highly affordable to, well, high.

BNOX Gold and Iron (715-442-2201; bnoxgold.com), 404 First Street, Pepin. Open afternoons and evenings Thursday through Monday in summer. Featuring the works of artists in all kinds of media, the cornerstone of this gallery and shop is the one-of-a-kind jewelry designed by owner Rebecca Johnson. Plan on spending some time here.

Green Gables (715-442-2113), N2037 Spring Street, Stockholm. Open 10–5 daily in summer, weekends in winter. Closed January and February. The green and white building, completed in 1867, was once a hotel, but today its 10 rooms are crammed full of goodies ranging from home furnishings and decor to stationary and even tea.

Adobe Gallery (715-442-2266; abode gallery.com), N2030 #3 Spring Street, Stockholm. Open 10–5 daily in summer, weekends in winter. Featuring unique, handcrafted items from around the world, this gallery stocks everything from organic body-care products to its own line of home furnishings.

Up a Creek (715-442-2900, N2020 Spring Street, Stockholm. Hours vary, call ahead. This little red wood building is home to girlie gifts and repurposed furnishings, colorful linens and more.

The Good Apple (715-442-9077; the -goodapple.com), N2030 Spring Street, Stockholm. Open 10–5 daily in summer, weekends in winter. You can load up on yummy apple butter here, but there's far more to find. Wisconsin wines and craft beers, cheeses, jams, and more mean you'll be spending more than a few minutes browsing this culinary gem.

Stockholm Pottery and Mercantile (715-442-9012; stockholmpottery.com), N2020 Spring Street, Stockholm. Open weekends in summer. Owner and potter Diane Millner sells her functional, hand-thrown pottery here, along with the works of several other area artists.

Out of the Blue (715-442-2583), W12117 WI 35, Stockholm. Open daily. Offering a wide range of gifts and handcrafted items, art prints, candles, and more. This is one of those shops you can't help but spend far too much time—or money—in.

✳ Special Events

May: **Annual Hip Breaker Bike Tour**, Trempealeau. Take the full 43-mile trek that heads up Hip Breaker Hill if you think you can do it, or stick with the lighter 10-mile trek. Meets at the Trempealeau Hotel.

Reggae Fest, The Trempealeau Hotel, Trempealeau. This one-day music fest brings in well-known reggae acts, plus food and crafts, for a fun-filled evening on the river.

Fresh Art Tour, Pepin. Tour 11 artists' studios during this three-day event.

Great River Birding and Nature Festival, Tiffany Bottoms Wildlife Area, Alma. A chance to dip your feet into the world of birding, this guided tour takes you on the mini-train through Tiffany Bottoms to spy some feathered friends. Proceeds benefit Wings Over Alma.

June: **Stockholm Art Fair**, Stockholm Park, Stockholm. This juried art fair brings in more than 100 exhibitors each year.

July: **Catfish Days**, Trempealeau. This three-day festival combines a fishing festival with an annual bike tour for the area's major summer event. There's lots for both kids and adults, including carnival rides, live music, a kiddie parade, and the crowning of Miss Trempealeau.

September: **Laura Ingalls Wilder Days**, Pepin. Pepin's annual celebration of the author's life includes two days of period-appropriate activities, such as a fiddle contest, hand-spinning demonstrations, and pioneer games for the kids, plus a parade, food, and more.

Music and Art Festival, Alma Beach, Alma. A one-day festival held on Labor Day Weekend, it has music, food, kids activities, and artists exhibiting their wares.

Prescott Daze, Prescott. This annual event features music, art, a fishing contest, car show, and geocaching.

North-Central Wisconsin and West-Central Wisconsin

505

JANKE'S
BOOKS
MAGAZINES
MAPS

JANKE'S
CARDS
ART & OFFICE
SUPPLIES

WAUSAU, STEVENS POINT, AND
MARSHFIELD

CRANBERRY COUNTRY: WISCONSIN
RAPIDS TO TOMAH

CHIPPEWA FALLS AND EAU CLAIRE

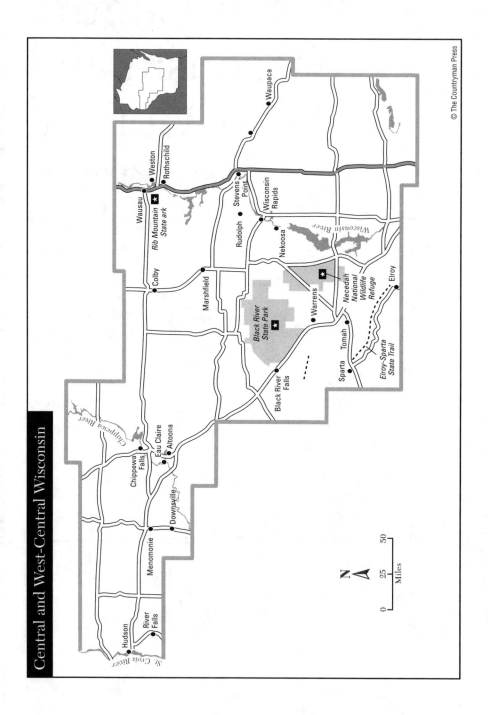

Central and West-Central Wisconsin

© The Countryman Press

WAUSAU, STEVENS POINT, AND MARSHFIELD

I t's easy for travelers to overlook Wausau. Right on WI 51, most people drive by as they head north for fishing weekends or summer-long cottage stays. That's too bad, because it's worth a stop. Surrounded by woods, home to an impressive stretch of the rushing Wisconsin River (and its championship kayak course here), and graced by Rib Mountain, there's plenty to satisfy anyone who itches to get outdoors. Wausau's downtown, however has enough charming shops, cafes, and cultural activities to meet a visitor's city needs, too. The visitor's bureau insists that Wausau is "as up north as you need to be"—I like that, because it really rings true, at least for people who just want to dabble in "up north" vacationing. The city's name, after all, comes from the Ojibwa language, and means "a faraway place." You can enjoy a peaceful, outdoorsy getaway without much threat of, say, bears, then slip away to a spa or cafe. And a lot of people will probably admit it: That's as up north as they need to be.

The same could be said of Stevens Point, where the University of Wisconsin's environmental program is a natural fit for the lovely surroundings, but the downtown offers specialty shopping and cafes.

GUIDANCE **Wausau/Central Wisconsin Convention and Visitors Bureau** (715-355-8788; visitwausau.com), 10204 Park Plaza, Rothschild.

Stevens Point Convention and Visitors Bureau (715-344-2556; spacvb.com), 340 Division Street North, Stevens Point.

Marshfield Convention and Visitors Bureau (715-384-4314; visitmarshfieldwi .com), 700 South Central Avenue, Marshfield.

The *Wausau Daily Herald* (wausaudailyherald.com), *Stevens Point Journal* (stevenspointjournal.com), and *Marshfield News-Herald* (marshfieldnewsherald .com) are the dailies here, but I especially like the *City Pages* (715-845-5171; thecitypages.com) in Wausau. This free, well-rounded arts and entertainment paper manages to get along, while many larger cities don't even have an alt-weekly. I'd check here first for the latest scoop on what to do and where to go.

GETTING THERE *By Car:* Stevens Point and Wausau are both on WI/US 51, which bisects the state, traveling from Beloit to Hurley.

By Air: The Central Wisconsin Airport (715-693-2147; fly-cwa.org) in Mosinee connects with Minneapolis, Chicago, Detroit, and Milwaukee, and is served by Northwest Airlines (800-225-2525), Midwest Airlines (800-452-2022), and United (800-241-6522).

GETTING AROUND You'll want a car to travel the area, but while in Wausau, the **Metro Ride** (715-842-9287), 420 Plumer Street, offers seven routes Monday through Friday in summer, and Monday through Saturday in winter. It stops running by 6:30 PM during the week and 5:30 PM on Saturday, so keep an eye on the time. The bus system in Stevens Point is pretty much the same.

MEDICAL EMERGENCY Call 911.

Aspirus (715-847-2160), 333 Pine Ridge Boulevard, Wausau.

St. Clare's Hospital (715-393-2950), 3400 Ministry Parkway, Weston.

St. Michael's Hospital (715-346-5000), 900 Illinois Avenue, Stevens Point.

St. Joseph's Hospital (715-387-1713), 611 Saint Joseph Avenue, Marshfield.

Marshield Clinic (715-387-5511), 1000 North Oak Avenue, Marshfield.

✳ To See and Do

In Wausau
✍ ♿ ♟ **Leigh Yawkey Woodson Art Museum** (715-845-7010; lywam.org), 700 North 12th Street. Open 9–4 Tuesday through Friday, noon–5 Saturday and Sunday. This small art museum houses a permanent collection of more than 2,000 works and features rotating exhibits as well. Best known for its annual juried show *Birds in Art,* which attracts artists from around the globe, the museum's permanent collection is also largely focused birds. Outside, the sculpture garden and serene setting highlight the Woodson's focus on the intersection between art and nature. There's a kids' center here called Art Park, where tykes can play games, paint, and try on bird costumes. Free.

♿ **Grand Theater on ARTSblock** (715-842-0988; onartsblock.org), 401 North Fourth Street. The centerpiece of Wausau's downtown ARTSblock, this space began in 1927 as a vaudeville theater. Today, it's home to many resident companies, including the Wausau Dance Theatre, Wausau Community Theatre, and Wausau Symphony and Band. The theater also hosts Broadway productions and other touring acts.

♿ ♟ **Center for the Visual Arts** (715-842-4545; cvawausau.org), 427 North Fourth Street. Open 10–5 Tuesday through Friday, noon–4 Saturday and Sunday. Right near the Grand Theater, the contemporary art gallery shows seven to nine exhibits each year, and the center offers classes and workshops for all ages. There's a nifty gift shop here representing more than 200 artists.

In Stevens Point
♿ ♟ **Stevens Point Brewery** (800-369-4911; pointbeer.com), 2617 Water Street. Open for tours Monday through Saturday. Opened in 1857, the Stevens Point Brewery is among the oldest continuously operating breweries in the nation. It has seen the Civil War and the Great Depression, and managed to carry on through Prohibition. Until 1990, Point's products were only available in Wisconsin, depriv-

ing the rest of the nation its award-winning Pale Ale and Special Lager. These days, the brews are available in 15 states. Tours get you more history plus a look at modern production and a few samples to boot. Non-beer drinkers get soda, such as root beer or orange cream. Adults $3; ages 5–11 $1; children younger than 5 free.

♿ ☂ **Central Waters Brewing Company** (715-824-2739; centralwaters.com), 351 Allen Street, Amherst. Tap room open 4–9 Friday, 3–9 Saturday. This is a tiny brewery with a huge line of beers, including favorites such as Ouisconsing Red Ale, Bourbon Barrel Cherry Stout, and the hilariously named Kosmyk Charlie's Y2K Catastrophe Ale. In 2009, the brewery went full-on green, with solar panels powering the beer production, a grain silo to reduce packaging, and other sustainable practices. It's only available in this part of the state, so drink up.

ReNew the Earth Institute (715-592-6595; the-mrea.org), 7558 Deer Road, Custer. Open 10–4 Monday through Friday. Take a tour and learn about alternative energies and construction technologies at this demonstration site. The institute shows solar energy in use, plus less common green technology, like a composting toilet. Donation.

♿ ☂ **Wisconsin Conservation Hall of Fame at the Schmeeckle Reserve** (715-346-4992; wchf.org), 2419 North Point Drive, at UW-Stevens Point. Open daily 8–5. Wisconsin has long been home to environmentalists, including John Muir, who founded the Sierra Club; Gaylord Nelson, who started Earth Day; and Aldo Leopold, who is said to be the father of modern environmentalism. But the concern for nature in Wisconsin goes further back, probably due to the abundance of natural beauty here. Tour the history of conservation in Wisconsin, and learn about the people who've made a difference. Free.

♿ ☂ **Riverfront Arts Center** (715-343-6251; uwsp.edu/cofac/rac), 1200 Crosby Avenue. Open 11–5 Tuesday through Friday, 11–3 Saturday and Sunday. Established in 1999 by the city of Stevens Point, this small gallery features around seven exhibits a year and is run almost entirely by volunteers. Free.

🖍 ♿ ☂ **Central Wisconsin Children's Museum** (715-344-2003; cwchildrens museum.org), 1201 Third Court. Open Wednesday through Sunday. This hands-on children's museum features exhibits such as Life on a Log, which walks kids through forest life cycles, and a farm-to-foods exhibit that explores how our food ends up on the table, plus arts areas and more. $3.

In Marshfield

♿ ☂ **New Visions Gallery** (715-387-5562; newvisionsgallery.org), 1000 North Oak Avenue. Open 9–5:30 Monday through Friday, 11–3 Saturday. Located in the lobby at **Marshfield Clinic**, this gallery shows six or so exhibits each year, including regional works, touring exhibits, and pieces on loan from private collections.

☂ **Upham Mansion** (715-387-3322; uphammansion.com), 212 West Third Street. This Victorian house, built in 1880, was once the home of Wisconsin governor William Henry Upham, who served from 1895–1897, and many of the furnishings on display are original. Outside, the Heritage Rose Garden features more than 30 historical plants.

World's Largest Round Barn, 513 East 17th Street. It's a big, round barn, all right. Located at the Central Wisconsin State Fairgrounds, this barn, built in 1916, has room to seat 1,000 people. Originally, though, it was housing for purebred animals.

✳ Outdoor Activities

In Wausau

Granite Peak Ski Area at Rib Mountain State Park (715-845-2846; skigranite peak.com), 3605 North Mountain Road. Open mid-November through March, depending on the weather. The state's largest ski area boasts a high-speed chairlift and runs ranging from beginner to double-black diamond. Granite Peak also has rentals, a shop, lounge, and restaurants, making it a prime destination for skiers around the Midwest.

Mountain-Bay State Trail. This trail runs from Wausau to Green Bay, through Shawano. The 18-mile section in Marathon County features interpretive signs describing the history of the area. The path is good for hiking and biking, plus snowmobiling in winter. Fees vary by county.

Wausau Whitewater (715-574-5263; wausauwhitewater.org), 200 River Drive. The Wisconsin River and its rapids here make this one of the top spots for kayaking in the nation. The controlled course has been used by the U.S. Kayak and Canoe team, but beginners shouldn't shy away. Contact Wausau Whitewater (Wausau Kayak/Canoe Corporation) for information on lessons and events.

In Stevens Point

Green Circle Trail (715-346-1433; greencircletrail.org). Traveling along the Wisconsin River and nearby Plover River, this 30-mile trail is good for biking, hiking, and skiing. Not far from the city at any point, the trail winds past wetlands, towering pines, and the rivers. The trail also connects with a number of area parks.

Sentry World Sports (715-345-1600; sentryworld.com), 601 North Michigan Avenue One of the top golf courses in the state, the 7,000 yards are punctuated by lovely flowerbeds, including the distinctive Flower Hole. There's tennis here as well, plus a snack bar and an upscale restaurant.

QUEEN'S CHAIR AT RIB MOUNTAIN

VIEW FROM RIB MOUNTAIN

&. ↑ **Kids Are Special Here Playground** (715-346-1531; kashplayground.org), at West Clark Street and West Whitney Street. This large playground was designed to accommodate kids of all ages and abilities, and includes a tunnel large enough to fit a wheelchair, adult-size swings, ramps to upper levels, and more. The equipment is safe, and the playground features a soft rubber surface.

✳ Green Space

&. **Rib Mountain State Park** (715-842-2522), 4200 Park Road. Just southwest of Wausau off WI 51, this is a great park for hiking or just taking in nature, and the view from atop the tower can't be beat. Not actually a mountain, Rib Mountain is a monadnock, or quartz formation that resisted erosion. So rather than rising up from the earth, the land around it wore away. It's one of the oldest geologic formations on the planet, dating back around 2 billion years. The park features 30 campsites, 15 miles of trails good for hiking and snowshoeing, and Granite Peak Ski Area. State park vehicle sticker required.

&. **Dells of the Eau Claire Park** (715-261-1566), County Road Y. Just 15 miles east of town, this lovely county park has 27 campsites, but it's great for day use. There are hiking trails, a swimming beach, plus waterfalls and gorges.

Nine Mile County Trails (715-261-1550), 8704 Red Bud Road. Open daily until 9 PM. Actually, it's 18 miles, but who's counting? The groomed snowshoe and ski trails here offer something for beginners and advanced skiers alike. Lighted trails are open past dusk, and there's a chalet offering rentals, restrooms, and a warming area. A trail pass is required (available at the chalet).

Mountain Loop (715-261-1550) Among the Wausau area's 800 miles of snowmobile trails, the Mountain Loop is well-maintained and winds around the county.

In Stevens Point

& ♈ **Wisconsin Conservation Hall of Fame at the Schmeeckle Reserve** (715-346-4992; wchf.org), 2419 North Point Drive, at UW-Stevens Point. Open daily 8–5. The abundance of natural beauty makes Wisconsin a logical home for environmentalists. This is the place to learn about the history of conservation in the state, and the figures who made a difference. Free.

& **Schmeeckle Reserve** (715-346-4992; uwsp.edu/cnr/Schmeeckle), 2419 North Point Drive. This 275-acre reserve functions as a field station for UW-Stevens Point environmental programs, and makes up a large chunk of the campus. There are around five miles of trails to bike and hike, and the reserve connects up with the Green Circle Trail, which travels throughout Stevens Point. The reserve also boasts a small man-made lake that's good for fishing and kayaking.

& **George W. Mead Wildlife Area** (715-457-6771; meadwildlife.org), S2148 County Highway S, Milladore. Open 6–4:30 Monday through Thursday, 10–2 Saturday in summer, 8–4:30 Monday through Friday in winter. Smack between Wausau, Stevens Point, Marshfield, and Wisconsin Rapids, the Mead sits in three counties. Hike and bike more than 70 miles of trails on more than 33,000 acres of land. Pick up a bird checklist and see if you can spy some of the 267 species of birds here, or kayak the Little Eau Pleine River. There's a visitor's center with history and more. Free.

& **Hartman Creek State Park** (715-258-2372), N2480 Hartman Creek Road, Waupaca. About 20 miles east of Stevens Point, on the line between Waupaca County and Portage, this 1,400-acre park has about 100 campsites, nature programs, and lots of hiking, but the real reason people come here is to get on the water. The park sits along the peaceful, spring-fed Chain O' Lakes—22 in all, and all connected. It's perfect for kayaking and anything else you want to do on water, but the biking is good here, too.

In Marshfield

JuRustic Park (715-387-1653; jurustic.com), M222 Sugarbush Lane. Open 10–4:30 daily, but call to be sure. This whimsical garden has iron dragons, frogs, and other animals created by the retired nurse and attorney who own the place. They also sell sculptures, jewelry, and more—and it would appear they have a good time doing it.

Foxfire Botanical Garden (715-387-3050; foxfiregardens.com), M222 Sugarbush Lane. Open 10–4:30 May to October. You've never seen so many hostas. An official display garden for the American Hosta Society, you can enjoy a stroll and get some ideas to take home to your own garden.

& **Wildwood Park & Zoo** (715-486-2056; ci.marshfield.wi.us/pr/zoo/), 608 West 18th Street. Open 7:30–7:30 daily. This 60-acre zoo is home to a number of North American animals. Its history stretches back to the early 1900s, when the city's mayor served as the zookeeper. Today, the zoo has an actual keeper on staff, and also boasts a garden area. Free.

& **McMillan Marsh Wildlife Area** (715-457-6771), County Road C. Just a mile north of Marshfield, this 6,000-acre area offers hiking trails, bike trails (during summer), and good bird watching.

✴ Lodging

In Wausau

Y ♿ **Lodge at Cedar Creek** (715-241-6300; lodgeatcedarcreek.com), 805 Creske Avenue, Rothschild. This family resort has a rustic logging theme, in keeping with the area's historical industry. There's a huge water park with slides, a treehouse, toddler area and more, plus arcades, a fitness area, and dining at the **Sawmill Grill**. Suites layouts include a double queen, a two-bedroom with breakfast bar, and a deluxe three-bedroom, among others. Suites $99–399.

Y ♿ **Jefferson Street Inn** (866-855-6500; jeffersonstreetinn.com), 201 Jefferson Street. Right downtown, this is a great spot to stay if you plan on taking in the arts and shopping Wausau has to offer (and it's not too far from Rib Mountain, either). This contemporary, upscale hotel offers room options from double queens to luxury suites with full kitchens and whirlpool tubs. Continental breakfast is included; in the evening, try dinner in the popular onsite **City Grill Bistro**. Travel Green Wisconsin certified. Rooms $109–279.

♿ 🐾 **Stewart Inn** (715-849-5858; stewartinn.com), 521 Grant Street. Although this Arts and Crafts mansion was renovated in 2002, it still contains a great deal of its original touches, such as the light fixtures, woodwork, and curved glass windows. Guest rooms are homey and inviting, with natural woods and simple decor. Three of the five bedrooms have fireplaces, and all have private bathrooms. Rooms $150–215.

♿ **Rib Mountain Inn** (715-848-2802; ribmtninn.com), 2900 Rib Mountain Way. Perfect for a ski getaway, this inn has standard hotel rooms in the main lodge, plus townhomes and condos for more space. Rooms $129–339; villas 219–419; townhomes $484–499.

♿ **Stoney Creek Inn** (715-355-6858; stoneycreekinn.com), 1100 Imperial Avenue, Rothschild. This is a big hotel that works hard to maintain a small, Northwoods lodge atmosphere. A nice pool area and included hot breakfast round it out. Rooms $89–180.

In Stevens Point

♿ **The Inn on Main Street** (715-343-0373; innonmainstreet.com), 2141 Main Street. Once home to the president of UW-Stevens Point (at the time called the Normal School), this 1920s Colonial revival home now features three guest rooms boasting a romantic, 19th-century theme. It's just a quick walk to campus. Travel Green Wisconsin certified. Rooms $65–85.

♿ **Dreams of Yesteryear Bed & Breakfast** (715-341-4525; dreamsofyesteryear.com), 1100 Brawley Street. This carefully restored Queen Anne has a half-dozen rooms, all decorated in an appropriately Victorian theme. All but Gerald's Room and the Maid's Quarters have private baths. Breakfast offerings include scrumptious delights like a German apple pancake and strawberry-stuffed French toast. Travel Green Wisconsin certified. Rooms $85–160.

✴ Where to Eat

DINING OUT

In Wausau

Y ♿ **The Wright Place** (715-848-2345; wrightplaceon6th.com), 901 North Sixth Street. Open for dinner Monday through Saturday. This Italianate mansion and historic landmark was once the home of a prominent businessman. Today, it's a popular restaurant serving upscale, contemporary American cuisine. Inside, it's elegant but comfortable, with touches of the original interior's character. Entrees $17.99–34.99.

Mino's Cucina Italiana (715-675-5939; minoscucina.com), 900 Golf Club Road. Open for dinner Monday through Saturday. Mino's is an upscale but inviting restaurant serving up traditional Italian dishes. It's a little spendy for Italian food, but by all accounts, owner Mino Spada knows his business, and the fresh ingredients and homemade sauces prove it. Entrees $17.95–33.95.

Wagon Wheel Supper Club (715-675-2263), 3901 North Sixth Street. Open 5–9 Monday through Saturday. Fans of traditional supper clubs will be happy with the darkened interior, dining room fireplaces, and steak-

TELEPHONE BOOTH IN DOWNTOWN WAUSAU

and-seafood cuisine. A little pricey, but its supporters swear by the wild-rice soup and ribs. Entrees $20–40.

In Stevens Point

Silver Coach Restaurant (715-341-6588), 38 Park Ridge Drive. Open for dinner Monday through Saturday. Usually, train car dining is the domain of greasy spoons, but here a 19th-century Barney & Smith sleeper car does service as an upscale restaurant. Dishes lean heavily toward the steak and seafood, with Cajun specialties. Entrees $17.95–33.95.

Bernard's Country Inn (715-344-3365; bernardscountryinn.com), 701 Second Street North. Open for dinner Tuesday through Sunday. That's a strange name for a German restaurant, but one look at the menu and decor, and you'll know you're in the right place. You'll find sauerbraten, schnitzel, and stroganoff on the menu, plus the unique Bavarian pizza, made with a rye crust and topped with German sausage. Dishes $15–25.

EATING OUT **Back When Cafe** (715-848-5668; backwhencafe .com), 608 Third Street. Open 11 AM–3 PM and 5 PM–10 PM Tuesday through Saturday. This charming spot has multiple interiors, owing to its 2003 expansion from casual eatery to more upscale dining. The old room is rich with dark woods and historic photos, while the new room has a more modern appeal, with exposed brick and checkered tablecloths, and a screened-in patio and outdoor seating make a perfect spot on a sunny day. The menu boasts organic and local ingredients, with more than a few vegetarian options and a nod to the Slow Food movement. Lunch offers lots of burgers, sandwiches, and salads, and dinner items include pastas, steaks, seafood, and more. Lunch $7–12, dinner $12–28.

BACK WHEN CAFÉ IN WAUSAU

The Mint Cafe (715-845-5879), 422 Third Street. Open for all three meals Monday through Friday, 7–3 Saturday. This is a charming, old-school diner serving up classic diner fare, and then some. Popular for its traditional and filling breakfasts, the Mint offers burgers, cheese curds, and hot beef sandwiches as well. Dishes less than $10.

Downtown Grocery (715-848-9800; downtowngrocery.com), 607 Third Street. Open 8–8 Monday through Saturday, 11–5 Sunday. This little natural-foods store serves the grocery needs of the health conscious and those on special diets, but it also has a rotating menu of soups and entrees in its deli. Dishes less than $10.

Red Eye Brewing Company (715-843-7334; redeyebrewing.com), 612 Washington Street. Open for lunch and dinner daily. First, the beer. Red Eye brews up Belgian dubbels and a handful of IPAs in small batches for thirsty Wausau beer drinkers. Stop in if only to see what's on tap. If you're hungry, the menu goes a step beyond

pub grub, with a focus on local and organic ingredients plus hummus, tomato basil sandwiches, and gourmet pizzas. Unlike most brew pubs, the atmosphere here is bright, colorful, and contemporary. Dishes less than $10.

Y & **Wausau Mine Company** (715-845-7304; wausaumine.com), 3904 West Stewart Avenue. Open for lunch and dinner daily. First things first: The interior is made to look like a mine; it's a themed bar and restaurant that will almost certainly please the kids, but that doesn't mean adult fans of over-the-top kitsch won't be thrilled as well. The menu has a little bit of everything, including pizza, burgers, pasta, seafood, sandwiches, and more. Burgers and sandwiches, $5.99–7.99, entrees $8.99–12.99, 14-inch pizza $14.99–23.99.

Y & **Yao's Grand Dragon** (715-842-5627; yaosgranddragon.com), 412 Third Street. Open for lunch Monday through Friday, dinner daily. This downtown restaurant offers Asian fusion, with dishes ranging from sushi and hibachi-cooked entrees to Chinese. The decor is almost over-the-top, with red carpets and statues at every turn, and the vibe is upscale but still comfortable. Dishes $9–13.

In Stevens Point

& **Matsu Ya** (715-341-8893; matsuya sushi.net), 5725 Windy Drive. Open for lunch and dinner Monday through Saturday. With its sushi bar and typical sleek décor, this sushi bar and Japanese grill has a strong following. Dishes $6–15.

Polito's Pizza (715-341-9980; politos pizza.com), 960 Main Street. Open for lunch and dinner Monday through Saturday. This wood-floored, casual pizzeria is popular with UW-Stevens Point students for its affordable prices and specialty pizzas, such as the Nacho Pizza and the BBQ Steak and Fries pie. If you've got a group that can agree, try the Monster Pizza—at 28 inches, it should feed a crowd. A 14-inch pie starts at $11.

& **Emy J's** (715-345-0471), 1009 First Street. Open daily. This cute, colorful coffee shop serves up strong, fair trade espresso drinks, Chocolate Shoppe ice cream, smoothies, and a handful of tempting breakfast and lunch items. Dishes less than $10.

& **The Wooden Chair** (715-341-1133), 1059 Main Street. Open 7–2 daily. This cozy downtown spot features antique wooden chairs (hence the name) and an overall warm, old-fashioned feeling. The cafe serves up wholesome omelets, bakery, and sandwiches. Grab some exclusive Fudge Utopia treats here, too. Dishes less than $10.

In Marshfield

♈ & **Blue Heron Brew Pub** (715-389-1868; blueheronbrewpub.com), 108 West Ninth Street. Open for lunch and dinner Monday through Saturday. The building was once an ice-cream processing plant; today, it's a microbrewery and pub. Nothing too wild, but a good selection of craft pilsners, stouts, and ales are on tap in this modern, airy pub. Dishes include pastas, pizza, and sandwiches, and there's a kid's menu available. Dishes $10–15.

✳ Entertainment

In Wausau

& **Grand Theater on ARTSblock** (715-842-0988; onartsblock.org), 401 North Fourth Street. The centerpiece of Wausau's downtown ARTSblock, this space began in 1927 as a vaudeville theater. Today, it's home to many resident companies, including the **Wausau Symphony and Band** (715-845-2144; wsandb.org), 401 North Fourth Street. The history of the Wausau Symphony stretches back to 1898, making it one of the oldest such groups in the state. These days, it performs around eight concerts a season, including one in summer at Rib Mountain State Park. Other groups performing here are **Wausau Dance Theatre** (715-843-5444; wausaudancetheatre .com), **Allegro Regional Dance Theater** (715-842-0988; allegro dance.org), **Wausau Community Theatre** (715-359-3972; wausau communitytheatre.org), **Central Wisconsin Children's Theatre** (715-842-4416), and the **Wausau Lyric Choir** (715-847-1155; wausaulyricchoir.com). The theater also hosts Broadway productions and other touring acts.

The **Wausau Concert Band** Performs free concerts at Marathon Park all summer long.

In Marshfield

& **LuCille Tack Center for the Arts** (715-659-4499; lucilletackcenter.com), 300 School Street, Spencer. Housed at the Spencer Middle School, this performing arts center hosts community groups as well as touring acts throughout the year. The theater also runs a travel film series, as well as other special events.

✳ Selective Shopping

& **Janke Book Store** (715-845-9648; jankebookstore.com), 505 Third Street. Open 9–7 Monday through Friday, 9–5 Saturday, noon–4 Sunday. A holdout in an age when indie bookshops are giving way to online commerce, this independent bookstore has been going strong since 1874. It's a treasure, with a broad selection of titles, community involvement, and a long-term (one more than five decades!) and passionate staff.

& **Book World** (715-344-5311; bookworldstores.com), 1136 Main Street. Open 8–8 Monday through Thursday, 8–9 Friday, 8–5 Saturday and Sunday. This independent Midwestern chain carries a broad selection of titles, including children's books and bestsellers, but it has a focus on regional and nature books. The store also carries a large number of newspapers and magazines. There are locations in Marshfield (715-387-6667), at 414 South Central Avenue, and in Waupaca (715-256-9393), at 121 North Main Street.

& **Sweets on Third** (715-842-7171; sweetson3rd.com), 615 North 3rd Street. Open daily. This little downtown shop has all kinds of yummy treats, including irresistible chocolates and candies. Don't miss the Babcock Hall dairy products, like cheese and ice cream from the University of Wisconsin-Madison.

& **Water Street Arts, Coffee, and Deli** (715-355-6868; waterstreetarts .com), 10209 Market Street, Rothschild. Open 8–3 Tuesday through Saturday, Friday 5–8. This place covers a lot of bases, promising an art gallery with your espresso. Weekends have live entertainment.

& **Wausau Center Mall** (715-842-0475; ShopWausauCenter.com), 101 Washington Street. This is a smallish but complete mall with some 65 stores. What makes it worth a look is its downtown location; while the best

---

WISCONSIN GINSENG

When you think of Wisconsin's chief agricultural exports, most likely dairy comes to mind. And it's true that dairy is still the state's leading commodity, but the rich land produces so much more, such as cherries in Door County, cranberries in Wisconsin Rapids, soybeans, corn, and American ginseng. Wisconsin is the leading producer of ginseng in the U.S., growing a full 95 percent of the nation's crop, and it happens to be the most sought-after ginseng in the world. It's said to be more potent and pure than other varieties, whether it's helping fight cancer, lowering blood sugar, or heading off a cold. It costs a bit more, too, and for that reason has been subject to pirating—unscrupulous ginseng peddlers pass off Chinese ginseng as the Wisconsin variety. When shopping in the Wausau area, though, you can be sure you're getting the real thing, because most of the state's crop is grown right here in Marathon County, also known as the Ginseng Capital of the World.

shopping is in the boutiques outside the mall, it's convenient to pop in here for the Gap or Younkers, if you need to.

In Stevens Point

& **Mullins Cheese** (715-693-3205; mullinscheese.net), 598 Seagull Drive, Mosinee. Open 8–5 Monday through Saturday, 9–5 Sunday. No tours here, but you'll find a sizeable selection of cheeses and the requisite cheese curds, plus Wisconsin souvenirs and other goodies.

& **Bookfinders** (715-341-8300), 1001 Brilowski Road. Open daily. Offers a broad selection of titles, plus magazines and more.

& **Kindred Spirit Books** (715-342-4891), 1028 Main Street. Open daily. This downtown indie bookshop focuses

DOWNTOWN WAUSAU

on kid's books, nature, and politics, plus it carries a selection of gifts and music.

& **Gepetto's Workshop** (715-341-8640; gepettosworkshop.com), 1121 Main Street. Open daily. This is a great toy shop, stocking all sorts of unique and quality toys for kids of all ages. Find Brio train sets, tin toys, and other fun stuff.

& **Sugar3 Confections and Gifts** (715-341-5556), 1336 Strongs Avenue. Open 10–6 Monday through Friday, 10–4 Saturday. This downtown shop is a cute place to stop for goodies, but there's a lot more than candy here. Pick up yummy chocolates and truffles, gluten-free bars, and cotton candy, or browse the gourmet non-candy snacks.

& **Dala's Import Oasis** (715-341-4433), 925 Main Street. Open 10–6 Monday through Friday, 10–5 Saturday. This imported gifts and clothing shop has been around for decades. Find flowing skirts and unusual knick-knacks, plus lots more.

✳ Special Events

January and February: **Badger State Winter Games**, various locations around Wausau. Like the Olympics in both philosophy and scope, these competitive games are open to amateur Wisconsin athletes of all ages and abilities. With 17 events, including skating, skiing, and hockey, there's plenty to watch.

May: **Exhibitour**, Downtown Wausau. This twice-yearly art walk—it's held in July and September—hits around 30 spots downtown, and doesn't skimp on the wine and crackers.

June: **Summer Kick-Off Celebration**, City Square, Wausau. Head downtown to the square for this festival, featuring live music by day, and an outdoor film at night.

Concerts on the Square, City Square, Wausau. Free outdoor concerts are held Wednesday evenings throughout summer and include a diverse mix of genres.

July: **Screen on the Green**, City Square, Wausau. This is a family-friendly, outdoor movie night held downtown in July and August.

Balloon Rally & Glow, Wausau Airport (downtown). This free event has a little bit of everything—live music, food, rides, fireworks, and hot air balloons.

Chalkfest, City Square, Wausau. This colorful two-day event features artists of all ages and abilities creating art on the sidewalks around City Square.

September: **Riverfront Jazz Festival**, Pfiffner Pioneer Park, Stevens Point.

This free, two-day jazz festival is the largest in the area, and draws musicians from around the Midwest and beyond.

Dozynki Harvest Festival, downtown Stevens Point. It's a little bit fall fest, with pumpkins and a pie-eating contest, and a little bit Polish fest, with traditional costumes and crafts.

Art in the Park, Pfiffner Pioneer Park, Stevens Point. Artists from around Wisconsin sell their work at this annual event. It also has also kids' activities, food, and more.

December: **Holiday Parade**, Stewart Avenue, Wausau. Held in the evening, this parade features all the usual suspects: Santa, Rudolph, hot chocolate, and floats.

CRANBERRY COUNTRY: WISCONSIN RAPIDS TO TOMAH

J ust south and west of Stevens Point is Wisconsin Rapids, named for the forceful Wisconsin River running through the city. Like much of the region, this area has an industrial foot in papermaking. Coated paper was invented here, and the industry still provides an economic boost. But the area stretching from Wisconsin Rapids in Wood County south and west to Tomah in Monroe County is known instead for its cranberries. More cranberries—300 million pounds!—are grown in Wisconsin than anywhere else in the U.S., and most of those are grown in the area stretching from Wisconsin Rapids to Tomah. What's more, the state's cranberry crop is expanding. In 2008, Wisconsin produced more than half the nation's cranberries, bringing in around $350 million, and more marshes are being planted to meet growing demand. Hands down, the time to come is late September through October, when the cranberries are plump and ready for harvest. It's a feast for the eyes and, of course, the tummy.

GUIDANCE **Wisconsin Rapids Convention and Visitors Bureau** (800-554-4484; visitwisrapids.com), 841 Goodnow Avenue, Wisconsin Rapids. Aside from providing great information on the area, this CVB provides a self-guided tour called the Cranberry Highway.

Greater Tomah Area Chamber of Commerce and Convention & Visitors Bureau (608-372-2166; tomahwisconsin.com), 901 Kilbourn Avenue, Tomah.

GETTING THERE *By Car:* Wisconsin Rapids lies on WI 13, east of I-39/US 51 and south of US 10. WI 54 from the east and WI 73 from the west will get you there, as well. There are numerous ways to get here; here are a couple: From Milwaukee, take I-94 through Madison and the Wisconsin Dells, then exit to I-39/US 51 north, continuing until Plover, where you'll pick up WI 54. From Minneapolis, take I-94 east to US 10, where you'll hit WI 13 just outside of Marshfield. Follow 13 to Wisconsin Rapids.

Tomah and Sparta are just off I-90, and Warrens is north of Tomah on I-94 west.

By Air: The **Central Wisconsin Airport** (715-693-2147; fly-cwa.org) in Mosinee connects with Minneapolis, Chicago, Detroit, and Milwaukee, and is served by

SPARTA

Northwest Airlines (800-225-2525), **Midwest Airlines** (800-452-2022), and **United** (800-241-6522).

GETTING AROUND No way around it; most visitors will need an auto in this area, but plenty of people who visit Sparta—the "Bicycling Capital of America"—and Tomah will be pedaling on the popular **Elroy-Sparta State Trail**, Sparta, which links up with the La Crosse River State Trail, stretching all the way to Onalaska on the Mississippi River. The **La Crosse River State Trail**, in turn, connects with **the Great River State Trail**, which heads north through scenic bluffs and wetlands to Trempealeau. (There are even more trails to hit there.) Heading the other way from Sparta, the **400 State Trail** connects with the Elroy-Sparta trail and travels all the way to Reedsburg, not terribly far from Baraboo.

MEDICAL EMERGENCY Call 911.

Riverview Hospital Association (715-423-6060), 410 Dewey Street, Wisconsin Rapids.

Tomah Memorial Hospital (608-372-2181), 321 Butts Avenue, Tomah.

Franciscan Skemp Sparta Campus (608-269-2132), 310 West Main Street, Sparta.

✳ To See and Do

In Wisconsin Rapids
🔗 ♿ ⛪ **Wisconsin River Papermaking Museum** (715-424-3037), 730 First Avenue South. Open 1–4 Tuesday and Thursday. Explores the history of papermaking and brings in touring exhibits on the subject. Free.

✂ ఉ ⚲ **Alexander House** (715-887-3442; alexanderhouseonline.org), 1131 Wisconsin River Drive, Port Edwards. Open 1–4 Tuesday, Thursday, and Sunday. This Colonial home functions as an art gallery and history museum, with a papermaking display from the collections of the Nekoosa-Edwards Paper Company. Free.

In Tomah, Warrens, and Sparta

Rudolph Grotto and Wonder Cave (715-435-3120), 6957 Grotto Avenue, Rudolph. Open daily May through October. Just north of Wisconsin Rapids is the small town of Rudolph, home to the Rudolph Grotto. Like most Midwestern devotional grottos, this one was built by a Catholic priest beginning in 1928 on a sprawling 12-acre site. In some ways, it's more modest than others; religious sculptures are framed by a locally found red rock with plants woven among some of them, and the decorations include less broken glass and found art. In this respect, they're simpler than, say, the Dickeyville Grotto—but no less astounding. Follow paths through the gardens to see the Lourdes Shrines, a wishing well, a small stone church, and much more. Father Phillip J. Wagner, the architect of the grotto, also built the Wonder Cave here, and it's the site's most unusual feature. Anyone who's

CRANBERRY HIGHWAY

The red-dotted bogs in central Wisconsin offset by fall's yellow and orange trees make this a popular spot when September rolls around. Wisconsin is the nation's top producer of cranberries, with more than 18,000 acres of cranberry farms, and central Wisconsin pulls most of that weight. There are marshes in northern Wisconsin, too—everywhere from Manitowish Waters to Superior—but the area stretching from Wisconsin Rapids all the way west to Tomah is the prime cranberry region. Visit this area in the fall for a peek at the stunning cranberry harvest.

Cranberries have been harvested in Wisconsin since the mid-1800s, but the fruit is native to the area, which means it's been around much longer. It surprises many people to learn that cranberries actually grow on a vine in sandy marshes; the marshes are intentionally flooded in the fall to make the harvest easier, as the berries float right to the top. But it's no secret that cranberries are good for you. Full of antioxidants and natural antibiotics, the tart berry has a place beyond the Thanksgiving table. In Wisconsin, that place is as the state's largest fruit crop.

Glacial Lake Cranberry Tours (715-887-2095), 2480 County Road D, Wisconsin Rapids. Tours offered Monday through Saturday during harvest season, usually late September through October. Call ahead.

Splash of Red Cranberry Tours (715-884-6412), 5407 First Avenue, Pittsville. Meets at Pittsville High School. 9:30–noon Wednesday and Friday. This tour is run by Pittsville High School student members of the Future Farmers of

not claustrophobic should go on into this man-made hill, as there is more artwork inside. The grotto is adjacent to St. Philip's Church, which was renamed in 1961 to honor Father Wagner. The grottos are free, but there's a small fee to enter the cave.

Deke Slayton Memorial Space and Bike Museum (608-269-0033), 200 West Main Street, Sparta. Open 10–4:30 Monday through Saturday, 1–4 Sunday in summer, 10–4 Monday through Friday in winter. Part bike museum, part tribute to hometown hero Donald "Deke" Slayton, who was among the first U.S. astronauts, this strange and interesting museum is worth a stop.

✳ Outdoor Activities

In Wisconsin Rapids

Lake Arrowhead (715-325-2929; lakearrowhead-golf.com), 1195 Apache Lane, Rome. Just 15 minutes south of Wisconsin Rapids, this club offers public golfing and access to its restaurants. Two award-winning, 18-hole courses here, The Pines Course and The Lakes Course, are suitable for golfers of all abilities.

America, who are enrolled in the nation's only Cranberry Science Class. Tours visit several area marshes and take in various steps in the production. A box lunch, complete with cranberry goodies, is provided.

Cranberry Highway and Cranberry Bike Trail. The Cranberry Highway follows a 50-mile path between Wisconsin Rapids and Warrens, past marshes and farms, and hits many of the area's major attractions. On the bike trail, the 29-mile route takes you right through the marshes and hits important sites, as well. Contact the **Wisconsin Rapids Area Visitor and Convention Bureau** (715-422-4650; visitwisrapids.com), 841 Goodnow Avenue, Wisconsin Rapids, for a map of these self-guided tours.

Wisconsin Cranberry Discovery Center (608-378-4878; discovercranberries.com), 204 Main Street, Tomah. Open 9–5 Monday through Saturday from June through October. Learn all about the cranberry's history and how the tart fruit is grown at this museum. There's a taste test kitchen, with all kinds of tempting delights such as cranberry scones, pie, and cookies, plus an old-fashioned ice cream parlor with more than 50 flavors, including Cranberry Cheesecake. Be sure to stop at the gift shop. Adults $4; students grades K–12 $3.

Be sure to watch for cranberry festivals and special events in this part of the state, including the **Wisconsin Rapids Cranberry Blossom Festival** in June, **Warrens Cranfest** in September, and **Wetherby Cranberry Harvest Day** in October. Check with the **Wisconsin State Cranberry Growers Association** (715-423-2070; wiscran.org) for more information on the crop.

In Sparta

Elroy-Sparta State Trail (608-463-7109; www.elroy-sparta-trail.com). Hop on at the **Sparta Depot** (608-269-4123), 111 Milwaukee Street, or various points along the trail. This is considered the first and among the most popular rails-to-trails bike paths in the nation. The 32-mile trail travels through five towns and features three darkened rock tunnels (bring a flashlight), plus astonishing views of western Wisconsin's varied geography. Sparta—the "Bicycling Capital of America"—is a great place to start an extended bike ride around this part of the state. The Elroy-Sparta trail links up with the **La Crosse River State Trail**, stretching all the way to Onalaska on the Mississippi River. The La Crosse River State Trail, in turn, connects with the **Great River State Trail**, which heads north through scenic bluffs and wetlands to Trempealeau. (There are even more trails to hit there.) Heading the other way from Sparta, the **400 State Trail** connects with the Elroy-Sparta trail and travels all the way to Reedsburg, not terribly far from Baraboo.

✳ Green Space

Along with great state and national parks, there are numerous lakes in central Wisconsin. Wood County—where Wisconsin Rapids is the county seat—is home to some 42 lakes, plus the impressive Wisconsin River, and of course, its rapids. It won't be hard to get out on the water here.

In Wisconsin Rapids

Sandhill Wildlife Area (715-884-2437), 1715 County Highway X, Babcock. At more than 9,000 acres, this serene space shared by seven counties is marked by sandy ridges, marshes, and wooded areas. Owls, cranes, bison, and deer all make their home here. Walk the unmarked trails or drive the 14-mile Trumpeter Trail, with interpretive stops and access to the park's three observation towers. There's a shooting range here, as well.

In Tomah, Warrens, and Sparta

Necedah National Wildlife Refuge (608-565-2551; midwest.fws.gov/Necedah), W7996 20th Street West, Necedah. Open dawn until dusk. Home to wolves, endangered Karner blue butterflies, cranes, trumpeter swans, and more, this 43,000-acre park boasts numerous hiking trails and a driving tour. The bog land is the result of retreating glacial lakes; after European settlers drained the marshes and tried unsuccessfully to farm the land, it took the Depression-era Civilian Conservation Corps to restore it.

&. **Buckhorn State Park** (608-565-2789), W8450 Buckhorn Park Avenue, Necedah. This 5,900-acre park sits on a peninsula in the Castle Rock Flowage, between the Wisconsin River and the Yellow River, making it perfect for water recreation. There's a sand beach here (but no lifeguard) and great fishing. The park's 60 campsites and cabins have won it accolades as among the best family camping.

✳ Lodging

In Tomah, Warrens, and Sparta

Caboose Cabins (608-269-0444; caboosecabins.com), 1102 South Water Street, Sparta. Among the most unique lodging a family can find, this rehabbed Soo Line caboose is outfitted with nice amenities such as a microwave and fridge, air conditioning, and satellite

TV, but still has original features. The caboose has one queen bed, one twin bed, and a toddler bed. There's a deck attached to the caboose, with a grill for cooking, and you can see trains rushing by. The Elroy-Sparta Trail is a quick block from the property, so bring your bikes, or plan to rent them. $125–145.

Justin Trails Resort (608-269-4522; justintrails.com), 7452 Kathryn Avenue, Sparta. This is actually a bed & breakfast, plus a collection of cabins ranging from a modern log cabin to a 1920s granary. In all cases, the decor is a charming country style. The property offers lots of hiking, biking, disc golf, and more, along with winter activities such as skiing, sledding, and skijoring (where a person on skis gets pulled by a dog). Kids are welcome, and there's even a playground just for them. Travel Green Wisconsin certified. Rooms $135–325. Weekly rates available.

& **Franklin Victorian Bed & Breakfast** (608-366-1427; franklinvictorianbb .com), 220 East Franklin Street, Sparta. This impressive red Victorian mansion

has four romantic guest rooms to choose from. Private baths all feature high-end showers and tubs. Breakfast might feature crème brulée, French toast, or wild rice quiche. Rooms $109–129.

& **Cranberry Country Lodge** (608-374-2801; cranberrycountrylodge .com), 319 Wittig Road, Tomah. Perfect for families, room layouts range from simple but roomy queen suites to larger two-room setups, all with a clean, rustic style. In winter, pick a room with a fireplace. Suites $174–254.

✳ Where to Eat

Y & **Ed Thompson's Tee Pee Supper Club** (608-372-0888; teepee supperclub.com), 812 Superior Avenue, Tomah. Open for lunch and dinner daily. An old-school supper club housed in an old theater, this restaurant features classic American fare such as steaks, pastas, sandwiches, and seafood. Get your fish fry here. Owner Ed Thompson is the brother of former Wisconsin governor Tommy Thompson, and Ed was elected to a second—though nonconsecutive—term as

CABOOSE CABINS IN SPARTA

Tomah's mayor in 2008. Ed Thompson also ran as the Libertarian candidate for governor in 2002, but his brother supported the Republican candidate. (Democrat Jim Doyle won, anyway.) Dishes $15–25.

& **Jamaican Kitchens** (715-421-3930; jamaicankitchens.com), 161 Second Street North, Wisconsin Rapids. Open for lunch and dinner Monday through Saturday. Serving up authentic Jamaican dishes in a casual downtown eatery, this is perfect for something a little different in these parts. There's jerk all over the menu, plus even a few vegetarian options. Dishes $6–13.

& **Gina's Pies Are Square** (608-435-6541), 400 Main Street, Wilton. Open daily. Just off the Elroy-Sparta State Trail, this charming cafe looks like an antique store and features sandwiches including roast beef and a veggie burger, veggie chili, beer, and of course, square pies. Dishes less than $10.

& **Ginny's Cupboard** (608-269-6669), 127 North Water Street, Sparta. Open 7 AM–8 PM Monday through Saturday, 9–2 Sunday. Ginny's has an antique soda fountain, traditional ice cream parlor chairs, a tin ceiling, and loads of charm. There are a few sandwiches and salads on the menu, but what you come here for is espresso, ice cream, and your pick of 40 soda flavors. Dishes less than $10.

✳ Entertainment

In Wisconsin Rapids
Arts Council of South Wood County (715-421-4552; savorthearts.com), 240 Johnson Street, Wisconsin Rapids. This organization brings in touring performers from around the state and around the globe. Performances are held at the **Performing Arts Center of Wisconsin Rapids**,1801 Sixteenth Street South, at Lincoln High School.

Rainbow Casino (800-782-4560; rbcwin.com), 949 County Road G, Nekoosa. Among the states smaller casinos, this one is owned by the Ho-Chunk Nation—original residents here, particularly along the Fox, Wisconsin, and Mississippi Rivers. Today, the Ho-Chunk own scattered plots of land throughout Wisconsin.

✳ Selective Shopping

& **Book World** (715-421-2570; book worldstores.com), 253 West Grand Avenue, Wisconsin Rapids. Open 9–8 Monday through Thursday, 9–9 Friday, 9–5 Saturday and Sunday. This independent Midwestern chain carries a broad selection of titles, including children's books and bestsellers, but it has a focus on regional and nature books. The store also carries a large number of newspapers and magazines.

In Wisconsin Rapids
& **Dairy State Cheese** (715-435-3144), WI 34, Rudolph. Open 8-5:15 Monday through Friday, 8-5 Saturday, 9-noon Sunday. Pick up 100 different types of Wisconsin-made cheese here, including super-fresh cheese curds, and watch the cheese being made through observation windows.

Beaver's Dime Store (715- 886-4371), 410 Market Street, Nekoosa. Open Monday through Saturday. This old-school dime store has a little bit of everything, as it should, including a candy counter.

& **Knitwise Yarns and Fiber Arts Gallery** (715-886-1030), 421 County Road G, Nekoosa. Open 1–6 Thursday and Friday, 10–3 Saturday. Sells an array of knitting needs, offers classes, and displays fiber crafts made locally.

& **Back to the Country Store** (715-435-3492), 7220 Third Avenue, Rudolph. Open Wednesday through

AMISH SHOPS

West-central Wisconsin is home to the state's largest population of Amish, and you'll see horse-and-buggy signs along rural roads here. There are tours and shops sprinkled throughout the area.

Amish Country Corner (608-372-3222), 1101 Superior Avenue, Tomah. Open 10–5:30 Monday through Friday, 10–4 Saturday. Sells furniture, crafts, and more.

Burnstad's European Village (608-372-5355; artbyjon.com/burnstads.html), 701 East Clifton Street, Tomah. Open daily. Burnstad's sells not just European gifts, but a wide selection of Amish crafts and foods, plus Wisconsin treats.

Berry Amish (608-378-3409), 205 Main Street, Warrens. Open 10–5:30 Monday through Saturday, 11–3 Sunday in summer, 10–4 Thursday through Saturday in winter. This shop combines the area's cranberry bounty with Amish handicrafts. Look for home decor, furniture, gifts, and more.

Down a Country Road (608-654-5318; downacountryroad.com), 12651 WI 33, Cashton. Gift shops open 10–5 Thursday through Saturday from May through October. Tours require advance reservation. There are four gift shops, supplied with the handicrafts of 45 area Amish families, plus an ice cream shop.

Sunday. This store sells a little bit of everything good to eat. Not quite a natural foods store, you'll find organic coffees, specialty pastas, gourmet candies, soups, and jams, plus natural body-care products and special Wisconsin treats.

✳ Special Events

June: **Cranberry Blossom Festival**, various locations, Wisconsin Rapids. Usually the plump berries are celebrated, but here the blossoms before the fruit rule the day. They really pull out all the stops for this five-day event. There are plenty of kid's activities, plus

WARRENS CRANBERRY FESTIVAL

Held in the "Cranberry Capital of the World," this festival is, by many accounts, among the best festivals anywhere, period. It's been voted a favorite by folks in Wisconsin as well as awarded national "best of" distinctions. Why all the fuss? Well, where else do you get to tour a cranberry bog, or eat cranberry-cream puffs? That's what makes it unique, but here's what make it outstanding: more than 850 artists and crafters, more than 350 antique dealers and flea-market vendors, and more than 100 farm market vendors. Bring some cash, because you'll want to spend it. On Sunday, there's a huge parade to wrap things up. It's a shame it's only three days!

art shows and walks, live music, a pow-wow, and full meals every day. And that's just some of it.

July: **Monroe County Fair**, Recreation Park, Tomah. This classic, five-day county fair has all the animals, live music, and yummy fair foods you'd want.

August: **Rapids Balloon Rally & Music Fest**, Alexander Field, Wisconsin Rapids. This three-day, free balloon rally features music, rides, food, fireworks, and, of course, balloons.

September

Lake Arrowhead Craft Show, Lake Arrowhead Club House, Rome. More than 100 crafters from around the Midwest show up to sell their works.

WEST-CENTRAL WISCONSIN: CHIPPEWA VALLEY
Including Chippewa Falls and Eau Claire

E au Claire's lovely name means "clear water" in French; it sits at the confluence of two rivers, the Chippewa and the Eau Claire. The commercial heart of the Chippewa Valley, Eau Claire is home to about 61,000 people and a state university, but the population of the entire metro area is more than 100,000. While not exactly a metropolis, Eau Claire is home to great restaurants and shopping, but it's also home to innumerable outdoor activities. The biking is great here—hop on 70 miles of interconnected trails—as is the water fun. Nearby Chippewa Falls, best known for its beer export, Leinenkugel's, has 449 lakes. Some are just puddles, not good for fishing, but head out in a canoe, and you'll be fine.

GUIDANCE **Visit Eau Claire** (715-831-2345; visiteauclaire.com), 4319 Jeffers Road, Eau Claire.

Pick up the *Eau Claire Leader-Telegram* (715-833-9200; leadertelegram.com), 701 South Farwell Street, Eau Claire, for daily news and tips for what's going on. *Volume One* (715-552-0457; volumeone.org), 17 South Barstow Street, Eau Claire, is a free arts and entertainment magazine published twice a month, and a good source of local info.

GETTING THERE *By Car:* Eau Claire and Chippewa falls—just 20 minutes apart—are a short hop off I-94. WI 29 travels here from Wausau, and US 53 heads to the cities from Superior.

By Bus: **Greyhound** (715-874-6966; greyhound.com), 6251 Truax Lane, Eau Claire, makes a stop here, and the bus station is located inside a McDonald's, in case you're hungry.

By Plane: **Chippewa Valley Regional Airport** (715-839-4900; chippewavalley airport.com), 3800 Starr Avenue, Eau Claire.

GETTING AROUND A car is your best bet, but Eau Claire Transit operates 11 routes Monday through Saturday to help you get around town. Chippewa Falls has the **Shared Ride Taxi Service** (715- 726-2728), which costs significantly less than an ordinary taxi, but it doesn't run past 7 PM on weekdays or 4:30 PM on weekends and holidays.

MEDICAL EMERGENCY Call 911.

Sacred Heart Hospital (715-717-4121), 900 West Clairemont Avenue, Eau Claire.

Luther Hospital (715-838-3311), 1221 Whipple Street, Eau Claire.

St. Joseph's Hospital (715-726-3220), 2661 County Highway I, Chippewa Falls.

Black River Memorial Hospital (715-284-5361), 711 West Adams Street, Black River Falls.

✳ To See and Do

In Eau Claire

Carson Park. Located on a peninsula in Half Moon Lake, this park is home to a number of attractions. The **Chippewa Valley Museum** (715-834-7871; cvmuseum .com), 1204 Carson Park Drive, is a historical museum that traces the area's history from the Ojibwa, who lived here hundreds of years ago, through European settlement. The **Paul Bunyan Logging Camp Museum** (715-835-6200; paul bunyancamp.org) is a recreation of an 1800s logging camp, along with an interpretive center and exhibits exploring logging's history here.

& **Eau Claire Regional Arts Center** (715-832-2787; eauclairearts.com), 316 Eau Claire Street. See Entertainment.

& ✐ **Children's Museum of Eau Claire** (715-832-5437; www.cmec.cc), 220 South Barstow Street. Open Tuesday through Saturday in summer, Tuesday through Sunday in winter. This well-rounded kids' museum features exhibits such as the Itty Bitty City, complete with a play post office, market, and diner, plus other exhibits like a construction site, toddler park, and more. Admission $5.

Dells Mill and Museum (715-286-2714; dellsmill.com), E18855 County Road V, Augusta. Open 10–5 daily May through October. Built in 1864, this flour and feed mill still operates, although it mainly functions as a museum. This five-story historical landmark is picturesque and worth the side trip.

In Chippewa Falls

Ⓨ & **Leinenkugel's Brewery Tour and the Leinie Lodge** (715-723-5557; leinie .com), 124 East Elm Street. Open 9–5 Monday through Thursday and Saturday, 9–8 Friday, 11–4 Sunday. Tours given every half-hour. The brewery dates back to 1867, when Jacob Leinenkugel set up shop in Chippewa Falls, at the time largely a logging camp comprised of burley, thirsty lumberjacks. The Leinenkugel family, however, had been brewing beer in Germany for generations. In 1988, Leinenkugel's became part of Milwaukee's Miller Brewing Company (which merged with out-of-state Coors in 2008 to become MillerCoors). Maybe a bit large for a craft brewery, there are still folks named Leinenkugel involved, and the specialty beer is still good. Learn more about the company, tour the brewery, and sample the brews. Free.

& **Chippewa Falls Museum of Industry and Technology** (715-720-9206; cfmit.org), 21 East Grand Avenue. Open 11–4 Tuesday through Friday, 10–4 Saturday. This museum's exhibits explore the history of area industry, including the

Jacob Leinenkugel Brewing Company, Great Northern, and Presto. Adults $3; children younger than 18 $1.

The Cook-Rutledge Mansion (715-723-7181; cookrutledgemansion.com), 505 West Grand Avenue. Open for tours at 2 PM Thursday through Sunday. Tour the 1873 mansion of a Chippewa Falls lumber baron. Adults $5; children younger than 18 $1.

& **Rassbach Museum** (715-232-8685), 1820 Wakanda Street, Menomonie. Open 10–5 Wednesday through Sunday in summer, noon–4 Wednesday through Sunday in winter. This museum highlights Dunn County's history—everything from an interactive bank robbery exhibit to local names, such as the Stouts. Adults $5.

Mabel Tainter Theatre (715-235-0001; mabeltainter.com), 205 Main Street, Menomonie. Open for tours 10–5 Monday through Friday. See Entertainment.

Wilson Place Museum (715-235-2283), 101 Wilson Circle, Menomonie. Open by appointment. This building served as the home of lumber baron William Wilson, then his son-in-law James Huff Stout, and later Wilson's grandson, William LaPointe Jr. It was built as a Colonial, but the Stouts took it up a notch by turning it into a Queen Anne mansion, complete with 17 fireplaces and a ballroom. The LaPointes actually reduced the size of the home and turned it into its present Mediterranean-style villa incarnation. Admission $5.

In Black River Falls

Υ & **Sand Creek Brewing Company** (715-284-7553; sandcreekbrewing.com), 320 Pierce Street. Tours given at 3 on Fridays. It's been Sand Creek since 2004, but the building was a brewery even when it was built back in 1856. Swiss immigrant Ulrich Oderbolz opened one of the first breweries in the state here, and it functioned as such until Prohibition. Over the next 75 years, it was used to make near-bear, as a soda-bottling plant, and for poultry processing. In 2000, it became Pioneer Brewery, changed hands, and is now Sand Creek. The brewery makes 12 craft beers, including stouts, lagers, porters, ales, and an IPA.

✳ Outdoor Activities

In Eau Claire

& **Chippewa River Trail** (715-232-1242). This rails-to-trails, multi-use path runs between Eau Claire and Durand, with a handful of access points, including one at **Phoenix Park** in downtown Eau Claire. The trail follows the Chippewa River through lush forests, prairies, and wetlands. It connects to the **Red Cedar State Trail** (715-232-1242), which starts at an old depot and visitor's center in Menomonie, and passes through the **Dunnville State Wildlife Area**. Bike, hike, or rollerblade, and in winter, cross-country ski. State trail passes are required for some portions, and are available at the depot.

In Chippewa Falls

& **Irvine Park** (715-723-0051), Bridgewater Avenue. Open daily until dusk. See Green Space. Free.

Old Abe Trail. This 19-mile multi-use trail connects Lake Wissota State Park and Brunet Island State Park, and work is ongoing to link it up with the Chippewa river Trail and the Red Cedar State Trail. Hop on at the state parks. State trail pass required.

✳ Green Space

Lake Wissota State Park (715-382-4574), 18127 County Highway O, Chippewa Falls. Home to forests and prairies, this is a great spot for bird watching (pick up a checklist at the park office) as well as swimming at the 285-foot beach on man-made Lake Wissota. A state park vehicle sticker is required.

Irvine Park (715-723-0051), Bridgewater Avenue, Chippewa Falls. Open daily until dusk. This 318-acre park features a zoo, the **Glen Loch Dam**, hiking trails, and more. At the holidays, the park lights up more than 100,000 Christmas bulbs to the delight of, well, everyone. Free.

Brunet Island State Park (715-239-6888), 23125 255th Street, Cornell. Just northeast of Chippewa Falls, this 1,200-acre park lies at the confluence of the Chippewa and Fisher rivers. Popular for camping and all water recreation, the lagoons around the island are perfect for canoeing. A state park vehicle sticker is required.

Chippewa Moraine Ice Age State Recreation Area (715-967-2800), 13394 County Highway M, Chippewa Falls. This 3,000-acre park is part of the Ice Age National Scientific Reserve, and features the carved glacial landscape and numerous kettle lakes that make this part of the state so beautiful. There's an interpretive center here, and the Ice Age National Scenic Trail. A state park vehicle sticker is required.

Willow River State Park (715-386-9340), 1003 County Road A, Hudson. Home to waterfalls, camping, trails, and a ski festival in winter, this 3,000-acre state park is great for fishing the river and winter fun. A state park vehicle sticker is required.

Black River State Forest (715-284-4103), 910 WI 54 East, Black River, just off I-94. This 67,000-acre forest is prime deer-hunting land, but when that's not going on, it's good for hiking, mountain biking, fishing the rivers, wildlife viewing, camping, and more. State park vehicle sticker required.

✳ Lodging

&. **Fanny Hill Victorian Inn and Dinner Theater** (715-836-8184; fannyhill.com), 3919 Crescent Avenue, Eau Claire. Ten rooms all feature whirlpools and fireplaces, and all are decorated in an appropriately Victorian style, right down to the flowery wallpaper. Breakfast options include mango French toast or regular, hearty egg dishes. Rooms $169–199.

Y ✐ &. **Metropolis Hotel** (715-852-6000; metropolishotel.com), 5150 Fairview Drive, Eau Claire. This sleek, modern hotel has a huge variety of room options. There are family rooms with bunk beds, smaller (and that's relative) king studios, and a handful of deluxe suites themed after flashy cities. A bar and a coffee shop sit onsite, plus all the business amenities you could want, and a water park next door. Rooms $124–153, suites and apartments $239–278.

Y &. **Creamery Restaurant and Inn** (715-664-8354; thenewcreamery.com), E4620 County Road C, Downsville. The 10 sunny rooms in this renovated creamery all boast king beds fitted with Wisconsin-made organic cotton bedding and sheep's wool covers. Rent bikes here for the Red Cedar River Trail, or relax and enjoy the spa. Rooms $160–170.

✳ Where to Eat

DINING OUT ⊻ ♿ **Sweetwaters** (715-834-5777; sweetwatersec.com), 1104 West Clairemont Avenue, Eau Claire. Open for lunch and dinner Monday through Friday, dinner Saturday and Sunday. The cozy, romantic dining room is casual enough to feel unstuffy, which suits the area. Dishes are traditional but not tired; supper-club favorites get a modern treatment here, such as the almond-crusted salmon and Asian-style barbecued ribs. Dishes $15–26.

⊻ ♿ **Mona Lisa's Restaurant** (715-839-8969; monalisas.biz), 428 Water Street, Eau Claire. Open for dinner Tuesday through Saturday. With exposed brick, wood floors, and even a couple of couches, this place feels like an upscale, urban cafe. The menu changes weekly, but always offers Italian dishes and pizzas. Dishes $15–23.

⊻ ♿ **Fanny Hill Victorian Inn and Dinner Theater** (715-836-8184; fannyhill.com), 3919 Crescent Avenue, Eau Claire. Open for dinner Thursday through Saturday, brunch on Sunday. The menu is small, but should please almost anyone, with a vegetarian pasta dish, seafood, chicken, and steak. It's surprisingly affordable for all its accolades and awards. See also Entertainment. Entrees $14.99–26.99.

⊻ ♿ **High Shores Supper Club** (715-723-9854; highshores.com), 17985 County Road X, Chippewa Falls. Open for dinner daily, brunch on Sunday. Perched on the shores of Lake Wissota, the windowless facade on this log-cabin style building is a dead giveaway that you've found a traditional Wisconsin supper club. Lakeside, though, the building offers great views, inside and out. The menu features traditional steak favorites and chicken livers, plus a few vegetarian dishes (sure, it's stir-fry and pasta, but vegetarians are lucky to find anything aside from salad in many supper clubs). Dishes $15–25.

⊻ ♿ **Creamery Restaurant and Inn** (715-664-8354; thenewcreamery.com), E4620 County Road C, Downsville. Open for dinner Thursday through Sunday, brunch on Saturday and Sunday. Just south of Menomonie, the restaurant is heavily focused on local and organic foods, from visits to the farmer's market to the herb garden on the property. Because of this, the menu changes regularly, but might include something like miso-glazed halibut or beets with mustard greens. The building is actually an old brick creamery, and houses lodging and a cafe, as well. Dishes $15–26.

EATING OUT ♿ ⊻ **Stella Blues** (715-855-77771; stellablues.biz), 306 East Madison Street, Eau Claire. Open for dinner Monday through Saturday. Stella's offers a warm, casual, atmosphere with local art on the walls. The menu leans Cajun, with catfish and jambalaya, but there are vegetarian choices as well, like pastas with tofu and black bean burgers, plus lots of sandwiches. Dishes $10-20.

⊻ ♿ **Acoustic Cafe** (715-832-9090; theacoustic.com), 505 South Barstow, Eau Claire. Open for all three meals daily. This bright, airy coffee shop offers a host of sandwiches which come on homemade hoagie buns or pita, plus a handful of soups and munchies such as hummus or chips and guacamole. It's a great place to relax and knock back a latté. Dishes less than $10. There's live music in the evening Thursday through Friday.

♿ **Brickhouse Bakery and Cafe** (715-664-8354; thenewcreamery.com), E4620 County Road C, Downsville. Open 10–7 Thursday through Sunday. Located in the old creamery in Downsville, this cafe is the casual sibling of the Creamery Restaurant. Like the other, this cafe features homemade, locally sourced, and organic items when possible. Grab fresh pastries, soup, sandwiches, and more, then wash it down with a double espresso or a hot cup of tea. This contemporary space also features a rotating art exhibit and WiFi for checking your email. Dishes less than $10.

& **The Nucleus** (715-834-7777; racys nucleus.com), 405 Water Street, Eau Claire. Open for breakfast and lunch daily. This place is popular for breakfast, and it's no wonder: The menu offers all manner of creative omelets, crêpes, and pancakes for hungry morning types. Just a hop from the Red Cedar Bike Trail, if you stop here for lunch, the vegetarian Coup d'Etat or Thanksgiving On Bread—turkey, cheese, and cranberry-mango chutney—should hit the spot. Dishes less than $10.

& **The Goat Coffee House** (715-831-4491), 408 Water Street, Eau Claire. Open for all three meals daily. A good stop for a shot of espresso and a sandwich, including plenty of options for vegetarians, this coffee shop is right at home on Water Street. Hang out, use the WiFi, and relax a little.

& **Norske Nook** (715-597-3069; norskenook.com), 13804 Seventh Street, Osseo. There's another location in Eau Claire, Rice Lake, and Hayward. Open for all three meals daily. This Norwegian-themed restaurant serves up classic American fare mixed with traditional Norwegian favorites, resulting in things like the lefse wrap. Breakfast, which includes dishes such as eggs, potato pancakes, waffles, and more lefse wraps, is popular; even more popular are the pies. Dishes $6–15.

Y & **Black Bear Supper Club** (715-286-2687), S2001 WI 27, Augusta. Open for dinner Tuesday through Sunday. A traditional and popular Wisconsin supper club, featuring the increasingly rare relish tray, steak lovers rave about this place. The atmosphere is distinctly Northwoodsy, which pairs well with that relish tray. Dishes $10–20.

✳ Entertainment

Eau Claire Regional Arts Center (715-832-2787; eauclairearts.com), 316 Eau Claire Street, Eau Claire. Right downtown, the main attraction here is the rehabbed 1926 vaudeville theater, now hosting community and touring performers throughout the year. The 1,100-seat theater draws an audience from around the Chippewa Valley. The center is also home to an art gallery, which features regional artists in monthly shows.

Mabel Tainter Theatre (715-235-0001; mabeltainter.com), 205 Main Street, Menomonie. Open for tours 10–5 Monday through Friday. This remarkably lavish and carefully restored Victorian theater was built in 1889 by Captain and Mrs. Andrew Tainter as a memorial to their daughter, Mabel, who died at age 19. Intricate details are everywhere, from the carved pine archways and sandstone exterior to the Steere and Turner pipe organ (which was originally water-powered). In addition to the theater, which hosts movies, community, and touring productions, there's an art gallery here and a reading room.

Fanny Hill Victorian Inn and Dinner Theater (715-836-8184; fanny hill.com), 3919 Crescent Avenue, Eau Claire. This is a one-stop shop if you're looking for a quick getaway, but the restaurant, dinner theater, and lodging may be enjoyed separately if you wish. Popular for its year-round comedy, the dinner theater offers a meal and show for around $40 per ticket. Entrées range from veggie linguini to salmon and pork—it's rare to find such choices in a dinner theater.

Heyde Center for the Arts (715-726-9000; cvca.net), 3 High Street, Chippewa Falls. Hosts community and touring acts in a 330-seat auditorium.

Majestic Pines Casino (715-284-9098; mpcwin.com), W9010 WI 54 East, Black River Falls. Among the states smaller casinos, this one is owned by the Ho-Chunk Nation—original residents here, particularly along the Fox, Wisconsin, and Mississippi Rivers. Today, the Ho-Chunk own scattered plots of land throughout Wisconsin. This one has an attached hotel.

✳ Selective Shopping

& **Oakwood Mall** (715-839-7677; oakwoodmall.com), 4800 Golf Road, Eau Claire. Open 10–9 Monday through Saturday, 11–6 Sunday. Anchored by Macy's, Sears, and JC Penney, and boasting more than 120 stores, this is the largest mall in western Wisconsin.

& **The Woodshed** (715-286-5404), 105 West Lincoln Street (WI 12), Augusta. Open 10–5:30 Monday through Saturday. Sells Amish and Mennonite furniture and gifts. The Woodshed also offers Amish tours daily.

& **Crossroads Books** (715-831-9788; crossroadbookstore.com), 301 South Barstow Street, Eau Claire. Open Monday through Saturday. Towering but well-organized shelves of used and rare books make this a great place to round up a read for your downtime. Crossroads specializes in history, science, and regional books.

& **Cadeaux** (715-514-2236; cadeauxgifts.com), 312 South Barstow Street, Eau Claire. Open Monday through Saturday. This gift store has a little bit of everything, including wine, truffles, accessories for your dog, jewelry, gour-

met foods, and more. The staff will even whip up a gift basket for you.

& **Whippersnappers** (715-835-4022; whippersnappersboutique.com), 418 South Barstow Street, Eau Claire. Open 10–6 Tuesday through Friday, 10–3 Saturday. Good for a gift for your favorite little one, this shop is full of adorable, boutique-brand clothes for babies and toddlers, plus a few things for expectant moms, such as Bella Bands and some maternity clothes. Many of the kids' products are organic.

& **Eclectica on Grand** (715-834-7811; eclecticaongrand.com), 106 West Grand Avenue, Eau Claire. Open Tuesday through Saturday. As the name suggests, this homey store run by a father-daughter team offers a huge array of wonderful items. It's a little bit antique store, a little bit specialty imports shop, and you'll find everything from handmade jewelry and silk scarves to Eau Claire memorabilia.

& **Autumn Harvest Winery** (715-720-1663; autumnharvestwinery.com), 19947 County Road J, Chippewa Falls. Open 10–5 Wednesday through Saturday, 11–4 Sunday from May through October. The McIlquham family has been in the apple orchard business since 1924; these days, they also make an assortment of 12 fruit wines from their orchards and other regional crops. Northern Lights apple wine is a favorite, but don't overlook the raspberries and blackberries. The tasting room is fun for adults, but kids love the autumn pumpkin patch and corn maze.

& **Blakelee's Chocolates and Sweet Things** (715-514-0226), 416 Water Street, Eau Claire. Open daily. An old-fashioned candy shop with wood floors and overflowing barrels and bins of irresistible candies and trays of fudge, it'll be hard to make it out of here with your diet intact.

✳ Special Events

July: **Karner Blue Butterfly Festival**, Black River Falls. Held on a single day in July, this festival features music, food, games, craft vendors, and a look at the habitat of the endangered butterfly.

August: **Chippewa Valley Outdoor Games**, Eau Claire. Put on by the Eau Claire Rod and Gun Club, this one features events such as a lumberjack challenge and trapshooting contest.

Festival in the Pines, Carson Park, Eau Claire. There's food and live music, plus more than 250 arts and crafts vendors.

Northeastern Wisconsin

GREEN BAY

MANITOWOC

SHEBOYGAN

FOX VALLEY
Including Appleton, Neenah, Menasha,
and Oshkosh

GREEN BAY

Green Bay is Wisconsin's oldest city, and it once had the distinction of being its largest. These days, Green Bay's claim to fame, like it or not, is the Packers, and there's no question the town is fiercely loyal to its team. There are green and gold houses here, and cars, too. It's not *the* Packers, it's *our* Packers, and you come wearing another team's logo at your own peril. But if all that green and gold blinds you to the other things in town, take a second look. While it's no cultural metropolis, Green Bay has some surprising things going on—an art collective, a vegetarian coffeehouse, a specialty cheese shop, a performing arts center that draws people from around the state, and huge arts festivals. So if you think meat, potatoes, and Packers when you think of Green Bay—well, you're right. But it's not *all* that's here. You just have to know where to go.

Packers aside, Green Bay is, for one, a great destination for families with small children: Bay Beach Amusement Center offers carnival rides all summer long for a quarter or two, the National Railroad Museum is delightful to kids of all ages, and the NEW Zoo and wildlife sanctuary provide great outdoor recreation. Adult

TITLETOWN BREWING COMPANY

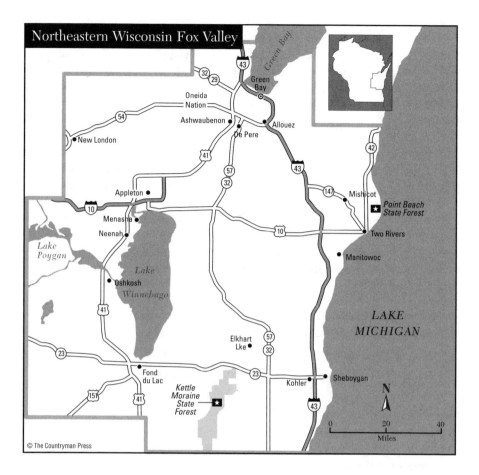

playtime happens at the Oneida Bingo Casino, among the state's most popular. The Oneida Nation isn't just about slot machines, though. Head over to visit the Oneida Museum, which explores Oneida and Iroquois history, to learn more. For another outing, Green Bay's neighbor, De Pere, is home to St. Norbert College—worth a visit to check out the beautiful campus alone. The small downtown is attractive, and makes for a nice stroll.

Whether you've come for the Packers or couldn't care less, you'll probably have a good time.

GUIDANCE The **Green Bay Visitor & Convention Bureau** (920-494-9507; greenbay.com), 1901 South Oneida Street, Green Bay.

Oneida Tourism (920-496-5020; oneidanation.org/tourism).

Check out the *Green Bay Press Gazette* (greenbaypressgazette.com) for local news and information.

GETTING THERE *By Car:* Green Bay is accessible via both I-43 and US 41, as it sits at the edge of the bay, where these two highways meet. From the west, WI 29/32 heads straight in. Take WI 57 to and from Door County.

By Air: **Austin Straubel International Airport** (920-498-4800; www.co.brown .wi.us/departments/?department=2f6d7cc8e7df), 2077 Airport Drive, Green Bay, is the state's third largest airport, served by Allegiant Air (702-505-8888; allegiantair .com), Delta (800-354-9822; delta.com), Midwest Airlines (800-452-2022; midwest airlines.com), Northwest Airlines (800-225-2525; nwa.com), United (800-241-6522; united.com), and American Eagle (800-433-7300; aa.com).

By Bus: **Greyhound Bus Lines** (920-432-4883; greyhound.com), 800 Cedar Street, serves Green Bay.

GETTING AROUND You need a car to quickly get around Green Bay. But there *is* a bus system: **Green Bay Metro** (920-448-450; www.ci.green-bay.wi.us/transit) operates 13 routes reaching all parts of the area, including the University of Wisconsin-Green Bay campus, Oneida, De Pere, and downtown, and buses are equipped with bike racks.

Car rentals are available at the airport through **Avis Rent-A-Car** (920-496-3840; aviswi.com), **Enterprise Rent-A-Car** (800-736-8222; enterprise.com), and **Hertz Rent-A-Car** (920-498-6400; hertz.com).

MEDICAL EMERGENCY Call 911.

Bellin Hospital (920 445-7373), 744 South Webster Avenue, Green Bay.

St. Vincent Hospital (920-433-0111), 835 South Van Buren Street, Green Bay.

Aurora BayCare Medical Center (920-288-8000), 2845 Greenbrier Road, Green Bay.

St Mary's Hospital (920-498-4200), 1726 Shawano Avenue, Green Bay.

✳ To See and Do

& **Heritage Hill State Park** (920-448-5150; heritagehillgb.org), 2640 South Webster Avenue. Open Tuesday through Sunday from May through August, Saturday and Sunday in September. This living history museum comes complete with costumed guides and explores the Green Bay area's industrial, agricultural, and ethnic history. The collection of 25 historic and replica buildings house include a print shop, cheese factory, and Belgian farm, plus period artifacts to really give you a feel for 1800s Green Bay. Adults $8; ages 5–17 $6; children younger than 5 free.

✐ & **National Railroad Museum** (920-437-7623; nationalrrmuseum.org), 2285 South Broadway Street. Open Monday through Saturday May through December, Tuesday through Saturday January through April. In addition to the more than 70 rail cars and locomotives on display, the museum has galleries, more than 5,000 rail artifacts, changing exhibits, and special events, with themes around *The Polar Express,* and *Thomas the Tank Engine.* You certainly don't have to be a kid to love this museum, but it's almost a sure bet if you are. Make sure to take the 25-minute ride on the vintage train, where the conductor dutifully yells "All aboard!" Adults $10; ages 3–12 $6.50; children younger than 3, free.

& ⇡ **Neville Public Museum** (920-448-4460; nevillepublicmuseum.org), 210 Museum Place, Green Bay. Open daily. Located right downtown, the Neville is a museum of history, science, and art. Its collections number over 100,000, and it

NATIONAL RAILROAD MUSEUM IN GREEN BAY

features rotating art exhibits as well as hosting national, traveling exhibits. Adults $4; ages 6–15 $2; children younger than 6, free.

&. **Oneida Nation Museum** (920-869-2768; museum.oneidanation.org), W892 County Road EE, Oneida. Call for directions. Open 9–5 Tuesday through Saturday from June through August, 9–5 Tuesday through Friday from September through May. Exhibits include examples of handicrafts like Iroquois beadwork and basketry and Oneida lace. There's a gift shop that sells books, corn-husk dolls, clothing, jewelry, and more made by contemporary Oneida and Iroquois artists. Adults $2; younger than 18 and older than 55 $1.

&. **Lawton Gallery** (920-465-2916; uwgb.edu/lawton/gallinfo.html), 2420 Nicolet Drive, room 230 in Theatre Hall at UW-Green Bay. Open 10–3 Tuesday through Saturday during the spring and fall semesters. Home to a permanent collection of more than 500 works of art, including gifted student and faculty works, art purchased by the UWGB student organization Art Agency, and a collection of works by Native American artists. At any given time, about two-thirds of the permanent collection is displayed. Changing exhibits include student and faculty shows, the Biennual Midwest Photography Invitational, and others. Free.

&. ☂ **Packers Hall of Fame** (920-569-7512; packershalloffame.org), 1265 Lombardi Avenue. Located at **Lambeau Field**, this is a compulsory stop for any Packers fan. Open 9–6 daily when there isn't a game; game-day hours vary. See a recreated version of Vince Lombardi's office, admire Super Bowl trophies, and let the kids throw on a uniform and run around like a Packer in the kid's area. Adults $10; ages 12–17 $8; ages 5–12 $5; children younger than 5, free.

&. **Lambeau Field Stadium Tours** (920-569-7513; lambeaufield.com), 1265 Lombardi Avenue, Green Bay. Tour times vary, check ahead. This is it—the

Frozen Tundra, home of the Lambeau Leap, hallowed ground to all Packer fans. The Pack has been playing here since 1957, and today it's considered the best stadium in the NFL. Guides walk you through the storied stadium and onto the field, offering history all the while. Tours $8–11.

Hazelwood Historic House (920-437-1840), 1008 South Monroe Avenue. Open for tours noon-4 Thursday through Sunday from June through August, noon-4 Saturday and Sunday in May. This 10-room, columned mansion is built in the Greek Revival style, and contains many of its original furnishings. Originally home to the Martins, a prominent political family in the area, the property was purchased by the Brown County Historical Society in 1989. It's located in the Astor Historic Neighborhood, so you'll get a chance to see (from the outside) many of this neighborhood's beautiful private homes. Tours $3.

✳ Outdoor Activities

✔ ♿ **Bay Beach Amusement Park** (920-448-3365; baybeach.org), 1313 Bay Beach Road. Open 10–9 daily late May through mid-August, 10–6 in spring and fall. Bay Beach's history dates back to 1892, and there remains an old-fashioned feel to this city-owned park. Maybe that's because rides cost 25–50 cents, or maybe it's the grand 1930s pavilion that houses concessions and plays host to weddings. There are five mild rides for the littlest visitors, plus more exciting carnival rides such as a Tilt-a-Whirl and Scrambler. Take a spin on the classic carousel or Ferris wheel, buy some cotton candy, and enjoy an inexpensive day. Admission is free. ♿ **Kastle Park** (920-465-6121; kastlepark.com), 2301 North Irwin Avenue. Open daily May through August, Saturday and Sunday in April and September. This private enterprise sits right next to **Bay Beach Amusement Park**, so it's an easy add-on to a day outside. Kastle park features a two-acre mini-golf course, go-carts, a climbing wall, bumper boats, and more. Game rates $4–6.50.

THE PAVILION AT BAY BEACH AMUSEMENT PARK

&. ✿ **Bay Beach Wildlife Sanctuary** (920-391-3671; baybeachwildlife.com), 1660 East Shore Drive, Green Bay. Open 8–7:30 daily mid-April through mid-September, 8–4:30 the rest of the year. See Green Space.

✿ &. **NEW Zoo** (920-434-7841; newzoo.org), 4378 Reforestation Road. Open 9–6 daily. Located on the Brown County Reforestation Camp, this zoo is home to native animals as well as Australian and African species such as wallabies and lions. Kids can take advantage of the petting zoo, or feed the giraffes at designated times. Adults $5; ages 3–15 $3; children younger than 3, free.

Ⓨ **Thornberry Creek at Oneida** (920-434-7501; thornberrycreekcc.net), 4470 North Pine Tree Road, Oneida. Billed as "everyone's country club," this golf course was acquired by the Oneida Nation in 2008. The 27-hole course was popular for its difficulty range and beauty before shutting down briefly in 2007. The sports bar in the clubhouse serves up traditional Wisconsin pub grub as well as wood-fired pizza, salads, tribal foods such as Oneida corn soup, and more.

&. **Green Bay Botanical Garden** (920-490-9457; gbbg.org), 2600 Larsen Road. Open daily May through October, Monday through Friday November through April. Forty-seven acres of formal gardens are on display throughout the year. The gardens play host to workshops and special events, as well. Adults $7; ages 5–12 $2; children younger than 5 free.

Resch Aquatic Center, 1058 Reed Street. Open daily June through August. A fun park for a little water entertainment, it has a wading pool, lap pool, tot area, whirl cove, and a couple of water slides. Green Bay summers can get hot, and this is a great place to cool off. Admission $3.25–4.75.

Foxy Lady Cruises (920-432-3699; foxyladycruises.com). Dinner cruises on the Fox River are a great way to get a different perspective on Green Bay. Foxy Lady has cocktail cruises, narrated sight-seeing tours, Italian dinner cruises, and more to choose from. $16–42.

✳ Green Space

Cofrin Memorial Arboretum, 2420 Nicolet Drive. Part of the UW-Green Bay campus, the arboretum features paved trails, a lookout tower, and more than 270 acres of preserved land. It's perfect for a quiet walk.

&. ✿ **Bay Beach Wildlife Sanctuary** (920-391-3671; baybeachwildlife.com), 1660 East Shore Drive, Green Bay. Open 8–7:30 daily mid-April through mid-September, 8–4:30 the rest of the year. This city park is impressive at more than 600 acres, and provides habitat for wolves, deer, ducks, and many other native animals. The nature center has hands-on exhibits, an art gallery, and gift shop, and an observation building houses even more animals. Buy a bag of corn for $1, and feed the ducks. Free.

✿ &. **Pamperin Park**, 2477 Shawano Avenue. With its attractive stone pavilions, this large park on Green Bay's west side is a popular spot for weddings, but visitors can take advantage of the serene wooded areas, Duck Creek, and a disc golf course. There's a great playground here, too, with wooden structures, slides, and sand.

Barkhausen Waterfowl Preserve Park (920-448-4466), 2024 Lakeview Drive, Suamico. Open daily. This nature preserve boasts nine miles of hiking and skiing

BAY BEACH WILDLIFE SANCTUARY

trails, marsh lands and forest, plus habitat for waterfowl. There's an interpretive center with exhibits and educational opportunities throughout the year.

🦆 ♿ **Ashwabomay Park** 2881 South Broadway, Ashwaubenon. Open 11–6 daily from June through mid-August. This 84-acre park features trails, game courts, a playground, and more, but it also features a rare-for-Green Bay sand beach. The small, man-made lake offers up sunbathing and swimming fun on those hot summer days. Lake admission $3–4.

✳ Lodging

It's important to note that unlike most areas, summer is not necessarily the time for high-season hotel rates here. You pay more when the Packers are playing in town, and if you haven't planned ahead, you'll be lucky to get a room. Packers games are sold out from now until Vince Lombardi rises from the grave, so you can count on this.

🍸 🦆 ♿ **Tundra Lodge Resort and Waterpark** (920-405-8700; tundra lodge.com), 865 Lombardi Avenue. It's right near Lambeau Field, and if you're here with kids (or just like waterslides), this is a fun hotel. The three-story indoor waterpark is the cure for the Frozen Tundra winter blues (or humid Green Bay summers),

and the rustic, Northwoodsy suites offer enough breathing room for everyone. Onsite restaurants include a kid-friendly buffet, and a parent-friendly bar and grill. Suites $149–349.

♿ 🍸 **Radisson Inn** (920-494-7300; radisson.com/greenbaywi), 2040 Airport Drive. Right near the airport and attached to **Oneida Bingo Casino**, this hotel is popular for its location and full-service amenities, not to mention the Sleep Number beds. The hotel has on-site dining options, or you can head over to the casino for more choices. $135-349.

♿ **Cambria Suites** (920-569-8500; cambriasuites.com), 1011 Tony

Canadeo Run. Within walking distance of **Lambeau Field**, this hotel has a contemporary, urban feel. Rooms are warmly decorated and boast flat-screen televisions and stylish furnishings. Dining options include a breakfast buffet and a bistro. It also has a nice pool and fitness area. Rooms $149–299.

& **Hilton Garden Inn** (920-405-0400; hiltongardeninn.com), 1015 Lombardi Avenue. This standard but pleasant Hilton is a short walk from **Lambeau Field**, making it a popular choice with Packers fans. Room options are simple double doubles, single kings, or king suites, and feature contemporary décor. Rooms $99–199.

& **Kress Inn** (920-403-5100; kressinn .com), 300 Grant Street, De Pere. Located on the campus of St. Norbert's college, this hotel is a short walk from De Pere's downtown restaurants. Warmly decorated, spacious rooms (some feature whirlpools and fireplaces) and a host of upscale amenities make this a popular place to stay. Rooms $99-499.

✳ Where to Eat

DINING OUT ♈ & **A Bravo Bistro and Wine Bar** (920-432-7286; abravo .net), 2069 Central Court. Open for all three meals Monday through Saturday, brunch on Sunday. A Bravo started as a catering business, but food this good deserves mass exposure. The changing menu is a perfect match to the contemporary bistro setting, and includes dishes such as pineapple skewered Asian shrimp and Mediterranean tortellini. Breakfast offers egg dishes as well as tempting treats like chocolate and raspberry French toast. The wine list is a carefully chosen selection of top-notch, but not too pricy, options. Breakfast $6–10, lunch $8–12, dinner $14–25.

& ♈ **Cheffetta's** (920-437-7107; chef fettas.com), 347 S Washington Street. Open for lunch Tuesday through Friday and dinner Thursday through Saturday. The airy dining room and climbing vines set you to thinking about a glass of wine almost immediately. This is a popular spot for a nice meal out, and the contemporary menu, while creative, doesn't stray too far from traditional favorites. Lunch $7.95–11.50, dinner $9.95–17.95.

♈ & **The Wellington** (920-499-2000; thewellingtongb.com), 1060 Hansen Road. Open for dinner Monday through Saturday. The dining room has a casual supper club feel, but the menu is way more innovative than you'd expect. Try a lobster martini (with avocado and potato salad) as a starter, and move on to a main dish like Door County cherry-marinated pork tenderloin or the Wellington's signature stuffed tenderloin, filled with garlic, brie, and pearl onions. Entrees $17.99–34.99.

♈ & **Prime Quarter Steakhouse** (920-498-8701; primequarter.com), 2610 South Oneida Street. Open for dinner daily. This is a popular, casual spot for steak—choose among five different cuts. Line up at the grill with other hungry diners and cook your own meat and Texas toast at the big grill. The fun comes from watching everybody else, but if you believe a dinner out should not involve preparing your own meal, a chef will do it for you for a couple of bucks more. Lighter eaters can order just the salad bar if they wish. A kid's menu is available. Grill-your-own, $19.95.

♈ & **Black and Tan Grille** (920-430-7700; greenbay.blackandtangrille.com), 130 East Walnut Avenue, Green Bay. Open for dinner daily. Housed in the historic Belling Building, the decor is upscale but casual, with lots of natural wood, and the menu features contemporary dishes such as Mediterranean chicken and vegetarian manicotti, although Black and Tan is more known for its steaks. It has a decent wine list and lengthy martini menu, plus a host of nightcaps for rounding the night out. Dishes $22–38.

EATING OUT ⛉ & **Kavarna** (920-430-3200; kavarna.com), 143 North Broadway Street. Open for all three meals daily. Opened in 1999, this vegetarian coffeehouse continues to survive in a city that heavily favors meat because the dishes are delicious and familiar. Favorites are the black-bean burger and the Southwestern wrap. The warm atmosphere, a creation of founder Linda Bengtson's artistry, is the perfect place to settle in for a cup of Alterra coffee or a shot of Intelligentsia, and a sweet treat, too. In 2009, Kavarna moved down the street and added an adjacent eatery, Parisi's Deli, which focuses on locally sourced and organic meats and artisan cheeses, as well as select imports. Dishes less than $10.

⛉ ✦ & **Kroll's West** (920-497-1111; krollswest.com), 1990 South Ridge Road. Open for lunch, dinner, and late night. This is one of two Kroll's restaurants in town—the other is the original on the east side (1658 Main Street)— but locals tend to prefer the west side location for its comfortable seating and large, retro dining room. The butter burgers and deep-fried cheese curds, if you ask me, are just as good at either place. You can get healthier options, like salad, too, but I don't know why you would do that. Kroll's West is right across from Lambeau Field, and the restaurant recently opened a location in Chicago, presumably for all those Bears fans who've raved about the place for years. Dishes less than $10.

⛉ & **Jake's Pizza** (920-432-8012; jakesgb.com), 1149 Main Street. Open for dinner daily. This unassuming bar on Green Bay's east side doesn't *look* like it would have phenomenal pizza, but then, that's often the case with great pizza places. The thin crust, perfect sauce, and loads of fresh garlic (if you choose) make Jake's one of the

KAVARNA VEGETARIAN COFFEE HOUSE

best pizza's around. Fourteen-inch pizza starts at $13.

Caffé Espresso (920-432-9733; cafesprso.com), 119 South Washington Street. Open 11 AM–midnight Monday through Saturday, 5 PM–10 PM Sunday. Caffé Espresso's cozy dining room feels at once casual and classy; space is tight, but not cramped, and the eclectic decorations are fun but not overdone. Although the name sounds like it's a coffee shop—and it *does* serve espresso—this is a restaurant with time-tested house specialties and a broad menu. You can get everything from a taco basket to veal marsala here, plus creative pasta dishes, Greek plates, and more. Plenty for vegetarians and meat-eaters alike. Whatever you do, order the chili con queso—I don't know what they do to it, but it's heavenly. Sandwiches, Mexican fare, etc., less than $10; house specialties and entrees $11.99–18.50.

Los Banditos (920-432-9462), 1258 Main Street. Open for dinner daily, lunch Monday through Saturday. Green Bay's favorite Mexican restaurant, the food here is consistently good. The atmosphere is intimate and warm, a stark change from many too- festive spots. The menu boasts Mexican cuisine standbys such as enchiladas, chimichangas, and fajitas, but also includes pasta and burgers. Like any good Mexican restaurant does, Los Banditos serves up addicting chips and salsa, and fried ice cream for dessert. Dishes $10–20.

Titletown Brewing Company (920-437-2337; titletownbrewing.com), 200 Dousman Street. Open 11–9 daily. Housed in an 1899 downtown train depot that once served the Chicago & Northwestern Railway, this microbrewery serves upscale bar food and an impressive array of craft ales, lagers,

bocks, and others. Out front stands the locally famous, giant, Green Bay Packers receiver statue, which watched over the Hall of Fame before the hall moved inside Lambeau Field. Dishes $7.99–17.99.

Hinterland (920-438-8050; hinterlandbeer.com), 313 Dousman Street. Open for dinner daily. Hinterland serves up creative American fare using locally sourced and seasonal foods. Dishes such as morel mushroom-dusted butter cod and small plates featuring local cheeses keep the dishes fun but familiar. Entrees $30–38.

Victoria's (920-468-8070), 2610 Bay Settlement Road. Victoria's is right near the UW-Green Bay campus, and it's been serving up huge, delicious portions of Italian dishes for years. The menu is the size of a small-town phone book, which means it has everyone's tastes covered from primavera to veal, and the large dining room can accommodate groups. Nice for a pleasant, but absolutely non-stuffy, night out. Dishes $10–20.

Curly's Pub (920-965-6970; lambeaufield.com/dining/curlys_pub), 1265 Lombardi Avenue. Open 11–10 daily. Replete with Packers memorabilia, servers trained in Packers history, and 138 televisions (yes, 138) so you don't miss a moment of an away game, you'd think the food was secondary here. The menu, however, is extensive and features Wisconsin favorites such as cheese curds and brats, but you can also get a fresh vegetable wrap if you've had enough of cheese. Something rewarding to try is the local specialty booyah, which is usually hard to find outside of church picnics. Dishes $9–16.

✳ Entertainment

Green Bay Symphony Orchestra (920-435-3465; greenbaysymphony .org). The Green Bay Symphony Orchestra is the state's third-largest professional orchestra, and dates back to 1914. The GBSO is well-loved in the community, and performs throughout the year at the Weidner Center for the Performing Arts on the UW-Green Bay campus.

Ⴏ & **Weidner Center for the Performing Arts** (920.465.2217; uwgb .edu/weidner), 2420 Nicolet Drive. Located on the UW-Green Bay campus, the Weidner Center functions as a cultural hub for Northeastern Wisconsin. Productions range from Green Bay Symphony Orchestra performances, touring Broadway shows, bands, and comedians to student productions and everything in between. The center's main theater, the Cofrin Family Hall, seats just more than 2,000.

& **Meyer Theatre** (920-433-3341; meyertheatre.org), 117 South Washington Street. Dating back to 1930, when it had a short life as a movie palace and vaudeville theater, the Meyer functioned for years as the triplex cinema. An extensive renovation and restoration took place in 2002, including the installation of a Wurlitzer organ, returning the theater to its opulent glory. Today, it hosts community performing arts groups, children's productions, and touring acts in a 1000-seat space.

Ⴏ & ↑ **Oneida Bingo and Casino** (920-494-4500; oneidabingoandcasino .net), 2100 Airport Drive. Open daily. The casino has bingo, slots, and blackjack, plus live entertainment, including well-known national acts, year-round in the lounge.

✳ Selective Shopping

Cooks Corner (920-964-0249; cooks corner.com), 969 Waube Lane, Green Bay. Open 9–8 Monday through Friday, 9–6 Saturday, 11–5 Sunday. Cooks Corner claims to be the nation's largest kitchen store, and since it carries 20,000 different products, I'm not inclined to doubt that. Even the most casual cook will be delighted here, but people who take it more seriously will be in heaven. When I visited this store

BOOYAH

If you've never been to Green Bay, the food term "booyah" probably sounds silly. This Belgian-American food is believed to have been developed in Green Bay by a fellow named Andrew Rentmeester. Basically, it's a Belgian soup made on a very large scale—intended to feed hundreds, or even thousands of people. Many cooks spend a day or two throwing various meats and vegetables into a huge kettle until the soup is ready to eat. It's most commonly seen at functions such as church picnics and family reunions, because you just can't make a little bit of booyah. Booyah, or sometimes booya, got its name, as the story goes, simply: Rentmeester, speaking to a reporter about his culinary creation, called it "bouillon," but his French accent sounded like "booyah" to the reporter, who wrote it down phonetically. Booyah!

at its old location in Manitowoc, I left with a pastry blender, a guitar-shaped cookie cutter, and a moka pot. Because all this thinking about cooking is likely to get you hungry, the store stocks specialty food items as well, and there's a cafe offering up espresso and baked goods.

Nala's Fromagerie (920-347-0334; nalascheese.com), 2633 Development Drive, Green Bay. Open daily. With more than 100 artisan and imported cheeses, plus an olive bar, specialty meats, oils, and more, this is a great stop to stock up on favorites or try something new.

Packers Pro Shop (920-569-7510; lambeaufield.com/pro_shop), 1265 Lombardi Avenue, Green Bay. Open daily. Located at Lambeau Field, you can pick up Packers apparel and merchandise you won't find anywhere else. More, there's a football chandelier and other bizarre homages to the game on display.

Seroogy's Chocolates (920-336-1383; seroogys.com), 144 North Wisconsin Street, De Pere. Open daily. Family run since 1899, Seroogy's makes hand-dipped chocolates in small batches to the delight of locals. The company also roasts its own coffee, and sells a variety of other yummy treats as well.

Beerntsen's (888-986-6937), 200 North Broadway Street, Green Bay. Open daily. This is a charming candy store with handmade chocolates and an ice-cream counter. It's a great stop if you're on Broadway checking out the shops. It's not as cool as the one in Manitowoc (and not related, either), but the candy is delicious, and that's where it counts.

Captain's Walk Winery (920-431-9255; captainswalkwinery.com), 345 South Adams Street, Green Bay. Open 11–7 Tuesday through Saturday, noon–4 Sunday. Housed in an 1857 Greek Revival mansion in downtown Green Bay, this winery doesn't offer cellar tours, but the tasting room features a viewing window so visitors can peer downstairs.

The Reader's Loft (920-406-0200; readersloft.com), 2069 Central Court, Green Bay. Open daily. Begun as a small shop in De Pere, this bookstore now has much bigger digs in Green

BEERNTSEN'S IN GREEN BAY.

Bay. Stocking more than 12,000 titles, this independent shop has a warm feel and a palpable love of literature you just won't find at a chain. The bookstore also plays host to author events and readings throughout the year.

✳ Special Events

January: **Winterfest on Broadway**, Broadway Street, Green Bay. A winter warm-up in Green Bay's downtown historic district, this festival features arts, ice sculpture, kids' activities, and a chili cook-off.

February: **Artigras**, Lambeau Field, Green Bay. This annual winter art festival showcases artists from around the Midwest plus entertainment and more.

June: **Bayfest**, Leicht Memorial Park, downtown Green Bay. The largest festival in the area, this one features four music stages, carnival rides, crafts, food, and more.

Oneida Family Carnival, Norbert Hill, Oneida. This free, two-day event includes live music, rides, games, fireworks and more.

July: **Oneida Nation Pow Wow**, Norbert Hill Center, Oneida. Held every year over the Fourth of July weekend.

Fire Over The Fox, downtown Green Bay. Green Bay's Fourth of July celebration starts around noon and ends with an impressive fireworks display along the Fox River.

August: **Artstreet**, downtown Green Bay. Always a good time, Green Bay celebrates visual and performing arts during this lively festival. More than 200 artists participate, and four stages feature music, theater, and dance. Roaming performers add to the mix.

Taste on Broadway, Broadway Street, Green Bay. Broadway's eateries offer a sampling of their fare during this annual event.

November: **Holiday Parade**, downtown Green Bay.

MANITOWOC

With a sizeable stretch of Lake Michigan shoreline, charming downtown shopping districts, and a rich maritime history, Manitowoc County makes a great getaway that's often overlooked. Recreational opportunities abound on the beautiful beaches and in lush parks, and the galleries, shops, and museums make it a perfect appetizer for a Door County weekend. Why not add a day or two and stay here? At very least, this is the route you should take if Door County is your destination—travel WI 42 through Mishicot and Algoma. It's prettier, and there are plenty of unique stops along the way.

Manitowoc grew up around the shipbuilding industry, and today it continues to be an important part of the economic landscape. For a visitor, this means opportunities to tour a submarine, see the state's maritime history, or simply head out on the lake. But that's not all. Head downtown for old-fashioned shopping: Beerntsen's Confectionary, opened in 1932, still serves up sundaes and chocolates in its original spot. Nearby, Warren's Restaurant is an authentically retro diner with a lunch counter, and in Two Rivers, Schroeder's Department store has been running strong since 1891. And there are more than a few traditional Wisconsin supper clubs in the area, too. But it's not just quaint, old-fashioned appeal. Manitowoc is home to many art galleries, museums, and performing-arts groups, and newer, hipper restaurants and boutiques are opening up all the time. The blend of old and new in well-used downtown spaces make Manitowoc particularly appealing.

GUIDANCE **Manitowoc Area Visitor & Convention Bureau** (800-627-4896; manitowoc.org), at I-43 and US 151.

Historic Washington House (920-793-2490). 1622 Jefferson Street, Two Rivers. Open 9-9 daily May through October, 9-5 daily November through April. This 1850s immigrant hotel houses the Two Rivers visitor's center, but what's special is the old-fashioned ice-cream parlor, a replica of the one where Ed Berners is said to have invented the ice cream sundae.

GETTING THERE *By Car:* Manitowoc County is just off I-43.

By Ferry: The **S.S. Badger Carferry** (800-841-4243; ssbadger.com), has been traveling between Manitowoc and Ludington, Michigan since 1952. Wine, dine, and shop aboard this four-hour cruise.

GETTING AROUND You'll need a car, without question, but in a pinch, the **Maritime Metro Transit** operates a small bus system, with six fixed routes traveling between the City of Manitowoc and Two Rivers. Important to note: The bus does not run on Sunday, and you have to actually hail the bus, even if you're standing at a bus stop, or it will just keep going. This is because, according to the transit's website, "people stand on corners for many reasons." You can also call Maritime Cab (920-686-1300), or rent a car through **Enterprise** (920-652-9994; enterprise.com).

MEDICAL EMERGENCY Call 911.

Holy Family Memorial Hospital (920-320-2011), 2300 Western Avenue, Manitowoc.

✳ To See and Do

The Bernard Schwartz House (612-840-7507; theschwartzhouse.com), 3425 Adams Street, Two Rivers. Open for tours the first Sunday of every other month. Call for schedule. You can stay overnight at this *Life Magazine* Dream House— a great example of Frank Lloyd Wright's Usonian spaces—or you can just take a tour.

↑ ⅄ **Rahr West Art Museum** (920-683-4501; rahrwestartmuseum.org), 610 North Eighth Street, Manitowoc. Open 11-4 daily, 11-8 Wednesday. This is a great little art museum focused on regional works. Housed in an expanded wing of a Victorian mansion, visitors get double the museum. The mansion features original furnishings plus unique historical collections, including ivory carvings and antique dolls. Make sure to head downstairs for a look at the replica Sputnik fragment. Free.

⅄ ↑ **Hamilton Museum of Wood Type** (920-794-6272; woodtype.org), 1619 Jefferson Street, Two Rivers. Open 9–5 Monday through Saturday, 1–5 Sunday from May through October, 1–5 daily November through April. This museum is dedicated to the preservation of wood type artifacts and antique printing technologies. In additional to hosting educational demonstrations, the museum sells things such as posters and circus broadsides. Free.

↑ **The Old School** (920-755-4560; theoldschoolgifts.com), 315 Elizabeth Street, Mishicot. Open 10–5 Monday through Saturday, 10–4 Sunday. Built in 1905, and today functioning as a gift shop and museum, the rooms here still display old desks, chalkboards, and other schooldays memorabilia. It was used as a school until 1976, and in 1980 it reopened as a gift shop.

Pine River Dairy (920-758-2233; pineriverdairy.com), 10115 English Lake Road, Manitowoc. Open daily except Tuesday and Sunday. Operated by a six-generation dairy-producing family, today the manufacturing operation is focused solely on butter, including an extra-fatty specialty, European-style butter. Watch the butter-making process through the observation window, then pick up samples at the farm's shop.

⅄ **Pinecrest Historical Village** (920-684-4445; mchistsoc.org), 1701 Michigan Avenue, Manitowoc. Open 9–4 daily May through October. This 60-acre living museum is home to 25 historical buildings and depicts 1800s rural life in Manitowoc. Adults $6; ages 6–17 $4; children younger than 6, free.

SPUTNIK SPACE JUNK

In 1961, a pair of Manitowoc police officers spotted something unusual indeed: a glowing chunk of Sputnik IV, embedded a few inches deep into Eighth Street. Today, there's a plaque in the sidewalk near the site of the incident, and a metal ring in the street where the debris landed. In the basement at the **Rahr West Museum**, a replica of the space junk rests behind glass, and in the fall, the city celebrates with a wacky festival called **Sputnikfest**.

The reason you only get to see a replica is that the original was given back to the Soviet Union—eventually, after the Russians finally admitted it was theirs and that Sputnik had indeed blown up on re-entry. Before returning it, though, NASA made two copies; the other is housed at the Manitowoc police department. To the best of anyone's knowledge, this 20-pound hunk of metal is all that survived.

REPLICA OF SPUTNIK FRAGMENT THAT LANDED IN MANITOWOC

♂ ᕱ ↑ **Point Beach Energy Center** (920-755-6400), 6400 Nuclear Road. Open 9:30–4 Tuesday through Saturday. It's not every day you get to visit a nuclear power plant. Well, the center is right next to the power plant, anyway, and offers hands-on exhibits and education about clean energy. Free.

ᕱ ↑ **Rahr-West Art Museum** (920-683-4501; rahrwestartmuseum.org), 610 North Eighth Street, Manitowoc. Open 11–4 daily, 11–8 Wednesday. This is a great little art museum focused on regional works. Housed in an expanded.wing of a Victorian mansion, visitors get double the museum. The mansion features original furnishings plus unique historical collections, including ivory carvings and antique dolls. Make sure to head downstairs for a look at the replica Sputnik fragment. Free.

✧ & ↑ **Wisconsin Maritime Museum** (920-684-0218; wisconsinmaritime.org), 75 Maritime Drive, Manitowoc. Open daily April 1 through October 31, Saturday through Monday in winter. This museum explores the maritime history of Wisconsin and the Great Lakes in general. See boats, engines, try the virtual fishing exhibit, or let the kids play in the Waterways Room. Outside, a moored WWII submarine, the *USS COBIA,* is open for tours. Adults $12; ages 6–15 $10; children younger than 6, free.

& **Rogers Street Fishing Village** (920-793-5905; rogersstreet.com), 2010 Rogers Street, Two Rivers. Open 10–4 daily May through October. Five historic buildings along the East Twin River house galleries exploring the commercial fishing history of the area, including a shipwreck exhibit. Check out the 1886 lighthouse—Two Rivers' first—and get a feel for the area's history. Adults $4; children younger than 16, $2.

☀ Outdoor Activities

Mariners Trail. This six-mile trail runs along Lake Michigan, and is perfect for a bike ride or a stroll. Pick up the trail in Manitowoc near the Wisconsin Maritime Museum.

Rawley Point Trail This limestone trail is six miles long, and connects Two Rivers with **Point Beach State Park**.

Hidden Valley Ski Area (920-863-1450; skihiddenvalley.us), 7711 Hidden Valley Road, Maribel. Open 10–4:30 Friday through Sunday, 4:30–9 Tuesday through Saturday in winter. Offers seven runs for skiers plus a snowboard park, rentals, and lessons. Rates $17–29; children younger than 6, free.

& ✧ **Lincoln Park Zoo** (920- 683-4685), 1215 North Eighth Street, Manitowoc. Open daily mid-April through October, Monday through Saturday November through March. This small, municipal zoo on wooded land features animals native to the area, like deer, wolves, and owls. There's also a farm animal exhibit and an education center. Free.

Shipwreck Adventures (920-482-0725; shipwreckadventures.com), 1611 Washington Street, Two Rivers. Open daily in summer. Offers snorkeling and extending diving trips and training, plus kayak rentals and more.

☀ Green Space

Point Beach State Forest (920-794-7480), 9400 County Highway O, Two Rivers. Open for day use 6 AM–11 PM. Great for camping and hiking, the beach here, with more than six miles of shoreline and surprisingly clear waters, is a gem. A word of warning—the waters get deep not far from shore, and Lake Michigan is especially cold here. Given the right day, though, that's a bonus. A state park vehicle sticker is required.

Neshotah Beach, 500 Zlatnik Drive, Two Rivers. This 50-acre park offers some of the best beach-bumming in the area. The white sands are beautiful, and the park includes picnic areas, concessions, and restrooms.

&. ♪ **Woodland Dunes Nature Center** (920-793-4007; woodlanddunes.com), 3000 Hawthorne Avenue, Two Rivers. This 1,200-acre preserve boasts a butterfly garden, interpretive center, and trails that explore the native plants, like the Cattail Trail and the Conifer Trail. Two of the trails feature wheelchair-accessible boardwalks.

West of the Lake Gardens (920-684-8506; westofthelake.org), 915 Memorial Drive, Manitowoc. Open 10–4 daily from Mother's Day through mid-October. This six-acre estate features rose gardens, formal gardens, a Japanese garden, and more. Free.

✳ Lodging

The Bernard Schwartz House (612-840-7507; theschwartzhouse.com), 3425 Adams Street, Two Rivers. Open for tours the first Sunday of every other month. Call for schedule. A realization of the 1939 *Life Magazine* Dream House built for Two Rivers businessman Bernard Schwartz, this house is an excellent example of Frank Lloyd Wright's Usonian spaces, meant to be well-designed, affordable homes for average Americans. Better than simply touring this lovely riverside home, you can stay overnight here. Rent the house for a night (with a two-night minimum) for $295–350 a night.

Y &. **Fox Hills Resort Golf Course** (920-755-2376; fox-hills.com), 250 West Church Street, Mishicot. Fox Hills boasts 500 acres of wooded land, 45 holes of golf, four swimming pools, a spa, bar, and restaurants. Room decor is a tad generic, but they're spacious and comfortable. Rooms $109–129.

&. **Lighthouse Inn** (888-228-6416; lhinn.com), 1515 Memorial Drive, Two Rivers. This family-owned property has an old-school charm, its lighthouse-shaped building a nod to a bygone era. Unlike a lot of quaint holdovers, this one features modern amenities such as WiFi and a fitness room. Room decor leans country, but common areas, including the pool and the restaurant, boast a nautical theme. Rooms $89–149.

✳ Where to Eat

DINING OUT Y &. **Courthouse Pub** (920-686-1166; courthousepub.com), 1001 South Eighth Street, Manitowoc. Open 11–9 Monday through Friday, 3:30–9:30 Saturday. It's not typical pub grub, that's for sure. Dishes such as pecan-encrusted duck breast with maple glaze and garden vegetable Wellington take brewpub fare into the fine dining category. Make sure to try one of Courthouse's brews. Dishes $15.95–39.95.

Y &. **Machut's Supper Club** (920-793-9432; machuts.com), 3911 Lincoln Avenue, Two Rivers. Open for dinner Wednesday through Sunday, lunch on Sunday. This is a pretty traditional supper club, inside and out. The low profile, '60s architecture, plus padded bar and glass-paned hanging lamps set the tone for a proper Wisconsin fine dining experience. Like it should, the menu focuses on meat and seafood, with sandwiches (including pizza burgers) and a liver-and-onions special. Dinners come with salad bar, and there's a kid's menu available. Sandwiches $3.95–5.95, dinner $14.95–22.95.

EATING OUT Y &. **Mishicot Pizzeria** (920-755-2134), 312 North Rockway Street, Mishicot. Open daily for dinner. Outside of Racine and Kenosha, it's hard to find a really good thin-crust pizza, but the Mishicot Pizzeria has it covered. The menu also boasts pasta dishes and other entrees, but the pizza here is where it's at. Pizza $10–20.

SUNDAE RIVALRY

Although it may be up for dispute with Ithaca, New York, Two Rivers claims to be the birthplace of the ice-cream sundae. The story is that a soda fountain owner by the name of Ed Berners started scooping up the creamy dessert back in 1881. As a Wisconsinite, I have every reason to believe it's true. After all, ice cream *is* a dairy product, and where dairy is concerned, this state is king. (Or queen.) The tussle with Ithaca is serious business: In 2006, the Two Rivers City Council drafted a hilarious resolution formally challenging Ithaca's claim as the sundae's birthplace, sent Ithaca residents coupons for free sundaes—with the disclaimer that use meant they acknowledged Two Rivers' rightful place in the ice-cream sundae timeline—and mailed postcards to Ithaca's mayor. In the city's downtown Central Park, there's a historical marker, erected in 1973, commemorating the 1881 creation of the sundae.

If you can't make it to the annual Ice Cream Sundae Thursday in Central Park, which features live music, kid's activities, and 25-cent sundaes once a year in June, head over to **Beerntsen's Confectionary** in Manitowoc (see listing under Eating Out) for an authentic, old fashioned ice-cream parlor experience.

&. **Culture Cafe** (920-682-6844; culture-cafe.com), 3949 Calumet Avenue, Manitowoc. Open daily. In an age when coffee shops so often are sleek and contemporary to the point of being sterile, it's good to know you can still find one with mix-and-matched furniture, live music, and outspoken politics. At Culture Cafe, you get all of this plus coffee roasted onsite, breakfast made with eggs from free-range hen, and a small but cheap sandwich and wraps menu. Dishes less than $10.

Y &. **Friar Tuck's** (920-682-5111), 3702 Calumet Avenue, Manitowoc. Open daily for lunch and dinner. Dark woods lend an old-world feel to Friar Tuck's, which serves up cocktails and sandwiches to hungry locals. Less than $10.

Y &. **Kurtz's** (920-793-1222), 1410 Washington Street, Two Rivers. Open daily for lunch and dinner. This German pub has a laid-back feel, a host of German beers, and popular sandwiches. You'll be packing in with lots of locals, too, so you know it's good. Dishes less than $10.

&. **Penguin Drive-In Restaurant** (920-682-4107), 3900 Calumet Avenue, Manitowoc. Open for all three meals daily. A lot of restaurants try to simulate the retro drive-in experience; the Penguin is the real thing. Dating back to 1946, the current building was constructed after a fire in 1961. These days there's more indoor seating, which fills up at dinner time with locals gobbling the burgers and fries. Less than $10.

COFFEE AND SWEETS &

Beerntsen's Confectionary (920-684-9616; beerntsens.com), 108 North Eighth Street, Manitowoc. Open 10–10 daily. You can pick up fancy chocolates to go, or have a seat in a big, wooden booth and grab a sandwich for lunch. Better yet, get an ice cream sundae.

Cedar Crest Ice Cream (920-682-5577; cedarcresticecream.com), 2000 South 10th Street, Manitowoc. Open daily April through November. This ice cream plant has a parlor, too, with 26 flavors ready for you to enjoy. If you're having trouble finding the place, just look for the big cow.

✳ Entertainment

& **Capitol Civic Centre** (920-683-2184; cccshows.org), 913 South 8th Street, Manitowoc. This restored vaudeville theater now hosts community productions, children's programming, touring productions, and more.

Manitowoc Symphony Orchestra (920-684-3492; manitowocsymphony-orchestra.org), 913 South 8th Street, Manitowoc. At around 34,000 people, Manitowoc is among the smallest cities in the U.S. to boast its own symphony orchestra. The orchestra performs at the **Capitol Civic Centre**, as well as a handful of other locations around town.

✳ Selective Shopping

The Old School (920-755-4560; www.theoldschoolgifts.com), 315 Elizabeth Street, Mishicot. Open 10–5 Monday through Saturday, 10–4 Sunday. This jam-packed gift shop serves equally as a museum. In addition to ornaments, quilts, baby items, and many other gifts, The Old School's many classrooms are home to the **Francis Hook Museum**, which displays and sells original works by the 1940s illustrator; the **Norman Rockwell Center**, home to hundreds of Rockwell's paintings; and a Fontanini gallery.

PENGUIN DRIVE-IN RESTAURANT

THE OLD SCHOOL IN MISHICOT

&. **Beerntsen's Confectionary** (920-684-9616; beerntsens.com), 108 North Eighth Street, Manitowoc. Open 10–10 daily. Walking into Beernsten's is like walking into a chocolate covered time warp. The booths, the candy counter, the dark walnut accents—it's all original and dates back to 1932.

Unique Flying Objects (920-793-9599; uniqueflyingobjects.com), 2022 Washington Street, Two Rivers. Open 10–5:30 Monday through Saturday, noon–4 Sunday. If it flies on a string, they probably have it here. The windy shores of Lake Michigan are perfect for kite-flying, and picking up a cool kite couldn't be easier than this. The store also sells other wind-dependent doo-dads, like windsocks, chimes, spinners, and flags.

Book World (920-682-9202; book worldstores.com), 907 South Eighth Street, Manitowoc. Open daily. This independent Midwestern bookstore offers an impressive selection of titles, plus magazines, newspapers, and gifts.

RiverEdge Galleries (920-755-4777; riveredgegalleries.com), 432 Main Street, Mishicot. Open daily May through December, Friday through Sunday from January through April. Originally built in the early 1900s as a meat market with upstairs living quarters, today it's a charming antiques and art gallery. The old meat market is home to the antiques, and it has its own vintage appeal, with the original tile and objects leftover from its market days. Upstairs is the art gallery, featuring changing exhibits including paintings and pottery. Be sure to take a walk outside to check out the sculpture garden along the banks of the East Twin River.

Pine River Dairy (920-758-2233; pineriverdairy.com), 10115 English Lake Road, Manitowoc. Open daily except Tuesday and Sunday. This family-owned dairy operation offers 250 varieties of cheese for sale in the retail store. Yes, it has cheese curds, plus everything from 10-year aged cheddar to chocolate cheese, chunk asiago, horseradish havarti, and more.

✱ Special Events

May: **Village-wide Rummage Sale**, Mishicot. The people of this town of about 1,400 come together to throw a fabulous yearly rummage sale. Come prepared to find a steal.

June: **River Rendez-Vous**, Wisconsin Maritime Museum, Manitowoc. Fur trade re-enactors, paddling demonstrations, and live music help you imagine you're an 18th-century French explorer.

Ice Cream Sundae Thursday, Central Park, Two Rivers. This annual event celebrating Two Rivers' rightful place as the birthplace of the ice cream sundae features live music, kids' activities, and 25-cent sundaes.

Thunder on the Lakeshore, Manitowoc. This exciting air show features two days of aviation stunts from military performers and groups such as Franklin's Flying Circus.

Cool City Classic Car Show, Two Rivers. Held downtown, this is the place to admire some classic cars, grab some food, and visit the downtown businesses.

July: **Mishicot Riverfest**, Mishicot Village Park, Mishicot. This festival spans four days and features a carnival, fireworks, fish boil, parade, live music, tractor pulls, and more.

September: **SputnikFest**, downtown Manitowoc. In 1962, a chunk of the Sputnik Space Station fell to earth and landed smack in the middle of Manitowoc's North Eighth Street. Today, it's a reason to party! Lighthearted and fun, the festival features an art show (because the debris landed in front of the Rahr-West Museum), food, music, and tinfoil hats.

October: **Pumpkinfest**, Manitowoc. This annual fall festival features music, kids' activities, and lots of yummy pumpkin treats.

November: **Christmas Parade**, Two Rivers. An evening holiday parade to get you in the spirit, held downtown.

SHEBOYGAN

About halfway between Milwaukee and Green Bay, Sheboygan makes a great day or weekend trip from a lot of spots in the state. This unique port town—part industrial, part resort destination—has a lot to offer, from sandy beaches to retail therapy. The village of Kohler was built up around the Kohler Company—the folks who make those fancy faucets and showers—and now functions as a seamless resort community. Here you'll find high-end hotels, boutique shopping, top-notch dining, and lots of golf. If you can break away from all the spa services and relaxation, be sure to check out the Kohler Arts Center and the Kohler Design Center. Back in Sheboygan proper, great pizza and lakefront fun are the rule.

GUIDANCE **Visit Sheboygan** (800-689-0290; visitsheboygan.com), 3347 Kohler Memorial Drive, Sheboygan.

Destination Kohler (800-344-2838; destinationkohler.com) is a one-stop shop for information on all the Kohler properties, including lodging, dining, museums, and shopping.

Sheboygan Falls Chamber (920-467-6206; sheboyganfalls.org), 504 Broadway Street, Sheboygan Falls.

Elkhart Lake Tourism (877-355-4278; elkhartlake.com).

GETTING THERE *By Car:* Sheboygan is located along I-43, about equidistant from Milwaukee and Green Bay. Kohler is just west of the interstate, follow the signs. Elkhart Lake is further west; take I-43 to WI 57, then WI 23 to WI 67. If coming from the Madison area, follow 151 to Fond du Lac, then WI 23 to WI 67.

GETTING AROUND You'll want a car to travel around Sheboygan, although **Sheboygan Transit** (920-459-3281; www.sheboygantransit .com)does operate a small bus system with seven routes.

MEDICAL EMERGENCY Call 911.

St. Nicholas Hospital (920-459-8300), 3100 Superior Avenue.

Aurora Sheboygan Memorial Medical Center (920-451-5553), 2629 North Seventh Street, Sheboygan.

⚲ ♿ ⛫ **John Michael Kohler Arts Center** (920-458-6144; jmkac.org), 608 New York Avenue, Sheboygan. Open daily. This broad-based arts center covers everything from visual to performing arts, but the galleries are especially unique in scope. With an emphasis on contemporary art, including folk art, crafts, and self-taught artists, particularly from Wisconsin, the Kohler Arts Center has been responsible for the preservation of a number of state treasures. For kids, there's an interactive gallery, and everyone should check out the bathrooms, which were created by artists using, of course, Kohler fixtures. Free.

♿ ⛫ **Kohler Design Center** (920-457-3699; us.kohler.com),101 Upper Road, Kohler. Open 8–5 Monday through Friday, 10–4 Saturday and Sunday. Factory tours at 8:30 AM Monday through Thursday. Not just for home owners and renovators, the three levels of the bath and kitchen manufacturer's history, displays of artistic design, and product showcases are astounding. If you get here early on a weekday, you can take the factory tour, and learn about all the engineering and

BUBBLERS

In the eastern part of the state, particularly Southeastern Wisconsin, that source of refreshment known in most of the U.S. as a drinking fountain or water fountain is called a bubbler. If you ask us where to find a water fountain, we'll point to the centerpiece of an '80s-designed shopping mall (see **Regency Mall** in Racine). If you ask us where to find a drinking fountain, we'll simply know you aren't from around here. It's a bubbler, and we're sticking to it.

While it seems at first to be a quaint Wisconsin linguistic quirk, there's actually a logical reason for the word's usage, and it all goes back to Sheboygan's Kohler Company. Back in 1888, the company—called Kohler Water Works at the time—introduced a type of, ahem, drinking fountain with the patented name, Bubbler. It's like any trademarked name that finds its way into common use, like Kleenex. But for some reason, it didn't stick in most other places. We're proud of our word, though, and if you want a great Wisconsin souvenir, pick up bubbler tee-shirt from the **Wisconsin Historical Society** (shop.wisconsinhistory.org).

Kohler's impact in Wisconsin is unmistakable; the company and its charitable foundations are responsible for the restoration and preservation of many folk-art sites around the state, actively fund local projects and university centers, and operate an outstanding arts center. Kohler is also the largest employer in Sheboygan County, and has developed its own eponymous village there. But does any of this eclipse the cultural effect of introducing a wonderful word to the Wisconsin vernacular? Today, Kohler still sells Bubblers—capital B—and this polished chrome beauty still quenches many a Southeastern Wisconsinite's thirst on a hot, muggy day.

work that goes into Kohler's products. Bonus: You get to joke that you're going to look at a toilet museum. Free.

&. **Henchel's Museum of Indian History** (920-876-3193), N8661 Holstein Road, Elkhart Lake. Open 1–4 Tuesday from June through August. This museum on an archeological dig site houses Native American arts and artifacts dating back to 8000 B.C. Admission $3–5.

♂ &. ♈ **Above and Beyond Children's Museum** (920-458-4263; abkids.org), 902 North Eighth Street, Sheboygan. Open 10–5 Tuesday through Saturday, noon–4 Sunday. This two-level museum features interactive exhibits for kids, perfect for playing doctor, teacher, or house. Admission $5.

✳ Outdoor Activities

Old Plank Road Trail (920-459-3060) This multi-use trail runs along the lake, parallel to WI 23. It's wide enough to accommodate all kinds of users, from horseback riders to joggers and skaters, and in winter functions as a ski and snowmobile trail. The trail hits Sheboygan, Kohler, Sheboygan Falls, Plymouth, and Greenbush, and links up with the **Ice Age National Scenic Trail** in **Kettle Moraine State Forest**.

Sheboygan Shoreline Cruises (920-451-0201; sheboyganshorelinecruises.com), 644 South Pier Drive, Sheboygan. Cruises run Memorial Day weekend through October. Runs three daily cruises, a dinner cruise, and an evening cocktail cruise. Daily cruise: Adults, $15, children $9.

Dumper Dan's Charter Fishing Fleet (920-457-2940; dumperdan.com), 4022 North Fifty-first Street, Sheboygan. This charter company runs the most fish trips in the state.

✳ Green Space

Kohler-Andrae State Park (920-451-4080), 1020 Beach Park Lane, Sheboygan. Open daylight hours for day use. This state park has a beautiful stretch of Lake Michigan shoreline, perfect for sunning and swimming. Campsite range from wheelchair accessible cabins to rustic plots. There are wooded trails, sand dunes, and an interpretive center with educational programs.

Deland Park 715 Broughton Drive, Sheboygan. This sand beach offers swimming, playgrounds, and access to the Lakefront Trail. No lifeguards, though.

General King Park 1601 South Seventh Street, Sheboygan. Another popular sand beach with children's play areas and restrooms.

✳ Lodging

Ⴒ &. **American Club** (800-344-2838; destinationkohler.com), 419 Highland Drive, Kohler. Boasting the status of the Midwest's only AAA-rated five-diamond resort, the American Club certainly is Wisconsin's premier luxury getaway. The decor is warm and tasteful, with Baker furnishings, and while standard king rooms aren't particularly small, the Presidential Suite features a fireplace in its 1,450 square feet. Of course, nice as the rooms are, you're going to want to spend your time getting pampered at the Kohler Waters Spa after you nibble on chocolate-dipped strawberries and fennel-scented salmon in the Carriage House lounge. Rooms $380–676, suites $830–1,281.

&. **Inn on Woodlake**, (800-344-2838; destinationkohler.com), 705 Woodlake Road, Kohler. Kohler's other hotel isn't a five-diamond resort, but it's no slouch, either. Sleek, modern rooms in five different layouts all feature 42-inch plasma televisions and other top-notch amenities in this hotel overlooking Wood Lake. The Shops of Wood Lake are right next door. Rooms $228-320.

Y & & **Blue Harbor Resort** (920-452-2900; blueharborresort.com), 725 Blue Harbor Drive, Sheboygan. Owned by Great Wolf Resorts, this one boasts a 54,000-square-foot indoor waterpark, spas for adults and kids, restaurants with shipwreck themes, and even a wine and tapas bar. It's basically like most every other contemporary waterpark resort in the state, but with a nautical theme. Rooms and suites $179–479.

Y & **Harborside Villas** (920-451-0200; harborsidevillas.com), 650 South Pier Drive, Sheboygan. With decks overlooking the water, spacious one-, two-, and three-bedroom suites decorated in a tasteful nautical theme, full kitchens, and fireplaces, this is a great place for families or anyone who needs a little more room. Below the villas are a restaurant, gift shop, and other retailers. Suites $109–549.

& Y **Victorian Village Resort** (920-876-3323; vicvill.com), 276 Victorian Village Drive, Elkhart Lake. This resort dates back to 1872, and it shows in the stunning Victorian architecture. Lakeside accommodations, upscale dining, and on-site entertainment make it a great little getaway. Room options range from standard hotel rooms to condos and private homes. Rooms $180-270, condos in the original hotel $175-595, private home $595.

✳ Where to Eat

DINING OUT Y & **Trattoria Stefano** (920-452-8455), 522 South Eighth Street, Sheboygan. Open for dinner Monday through Saturday. This is the older, fancier cousin of Il Ritrovo, and both are owned by self-taught chef Stefano Viglietti. The food is upscale, but the atmosphere is comfortable, and the food consistently garners rave reviews. There's everything from steak to pasta on the menu, with an emphasis on fresh and organic ingredients. Dishes $20–30.

& Y **The Immigrant Restaurant** (800-344-2838; destinationkohler.com), 419 Highland Drive, Kohler. Open for dinner Monday through Saturday June through October. One of several restaurants at the American Club, this is the one that gets all the raves. The European ethnic heritage of Wisconsin's early settlers is reflected in the inviting decor. You can get everything from a bento box to an artisan cheese flight here, plus $100-per-ounce caviar. My suggestion is to come hungry. Entrées $35-65.

& Y **The Wisconsin Room** (800-344-2838; destinationkohler.com), 419 Highland Drive, Kohler. Open daily for breakfast and dinner. The dining room was once used to feed the Kohler Company's immigrant workforce, and today it is a classy, traditional fine dining restaurant. The menu is focused on regional dishes done in style. Entrées $22-36.

Y & **Margeaux** (920-457-6565; dine margaux.com), 821 North Eighth Street, Sheboygan. Open for dinner Tuesday through Saturday. This upscale, modern restaurant along Sheboygan's main drag has fancy burgers made with veal and andouille sausage, as well as duck gumbo and stuffed crêpes. Small-plate offerings and a tasting menu are part of the seasonally changing menu, so it's always a new experience. Entrees $20–26.

Ⓨ & **Seabird Restaurant** (920-453-4000; weissgerbers.com), 229 South Pier Drive, Sheboygan. Open for dinner Tuesday through Sunday June through August, Tuesday through Saturday September through May. Seabird's beautiful location on the shores of Lake Michigan is a draw itself. Dishes such as pistachio-crusted walleye and tournedos and lobster make this popular for seafood lovers, but there are chicken and steak options, too. Dishes $19–46.

EATING OUT Ⓨ **Osteria Nonna Maria** (920-458-3412), 1402 South Eighth Street, Sheboygan. Open for dinner daily. This unassuming eatery looks like a neighborhood bar from the outside, but inside it looks a bit like a model train museum. A train museum, that is, with accordions and an organ, which get played on weekend nights. If you're not already in love with the place, the friendly family that runs it will win you over—and this is all before the wonderful pizza comes. Serving both traditional and creatively topped pies, such as the tomato, caper, and salsa pizza or the green cheese and ham, Nonna Maria uses fresh herbs and homemade Italian sausage and sauces. Fourteen-inch pizza $15.25–23.25, pasta dishes $14.99–18.99.

Ⓨ & **Il Ritrovo** (920-803-7516), 515 South Eighth Street, Sheboygan. Open for lunch and dinner Monday through Saturday. This downtown pizzeria boasts authentic Neapolitan-style pizza, including a perfect Margherita, in a trendy, casual setting. Adjacent to the restaurant is Field to Fork, a specialty foods shop focused on unique Italian and local products. Il Ritrovo gets packed on weekends, and the

space is small, so be prepared to wait. Pizza $15–22.

Ⓨ & **Craverie Chocolatier Cafe** (920-208-4933), 725 Woodlake Road, Kohler. Open 7–7 daily. At the prompting of Kohler Company president and CEO Herbert V. Kohler Jr., this indulgent cafe opened up at the **Shops at Woodlake** in 2007. Chocolates kept in jewelry cases, drinks including espresso, beer, and wine, and buttery pastry tempt even the strictest dieter. If you really do behave yourself, there is a selection of low-sodium sandwiches and salads boasting organic ingredients and clocking in under 200 calories, but I'd just use that as an excuse to eat more chocolates. Dishes $6–12.

Ⓨ & **Charcoal Inn** (920-458-6988), 1313 South Eighth Street, Sheboygan. Open Tuesday through Saturday for all three meals.This little diner serves up traditional Sheboygan brats and steak sandwiches, burgers, and other local diner fare. Buns come toasted and loaded with butter, so don't come planning to eat light. Dishes less than $10.

Ⓨ & **Mucky Duck Shanty** (920-457-5577; muckyduckshanty.com), 701 Riverfront Drive, Sheboygan. Open 11–9 Monday through Saturday, 11–8 Sunday. Housed in an old fish shanty along the boardwalk on the Sheboygan River, you probably won't find a more appropriate place to grab Friday fish fry. If that's not your thing, though, there are lots of other seafood, vegetarian pastas, and meat options as well. Kid's menu available. Dishes $9–16.

✳ Entertainment

Stephanie H. Weill Center for the Performing Arts (920-208-3243; weillcenter.com), 826 North Eighth Street, Sheboygan. This theater began its life in 1928 as a movie theater for Universal Pictures Corporation. Like many old theaters, it changed hands and went through unfortunate remodels before it ultimately closed in the '90s. Restored and reopened in 2001, the theater now hosts community and touring performing arts groups and screens classic film revivals periodically.

Sheboygan Symphony Orchestra (920-452-1985; sheboygansymphony .org), 921 North Eighth Street, Sheboygan. Sheboygan's orchestra has been putting on shows since 1918. Today, it includes a chorus and performs at the **Stephanie H. Weill Center for the Performing Arts**, putting on five shows each season, with other special events year round.

Sheboygan Theatre Company (920-459-3779; www.sheboygantheater company.com), 607 South Water Street, Sheboygan. This company performs at the Leslie W. Johnson Theatre

at **Horace Mann Middle School**, 2820 Union Avenue, Sheboygan.

Victorian Village Theatre (920-876-3323; vicvill.com), 279 Victorian Village Drive, Elkhart Lake. This 100-year-old theater hosts community performances and other shows year round.

Road America (920-892-4576; road america.com), N7390 Highway 67, Elkhart Lake. This speedway has been a racing fan's destination since 1955. The road course hosts races such as the Speed World Challenge Series, American Le Mans, Superbike, and others.

✳ Selective Shopping

In Sheboygan
The Shops at Woodlake (920-459-1713), 725 Woodlake Road, Kohler. Open 10–6 Monday through Friday,

---

BRATWURST

Wisconsin's German heritage, particularly in the southeastern part of the state, resulted in many culinary traditions, not the least of which is the bratwurst. This spicy sausage is compulsory fare at nearly every cookout and tailgate party, but Sheboygan lays claim to the title of "Bratwurst Capital of America." Both the Sheboygan Bratwurst Company and Johnsonville Foods are based here, so that boast might hold true. What is undeniable is that Sheboygan maintains its own standards for brats, separate from the rest of Wisconsin. For instance, in most parts of the state, sauerkraut is liberally piled onto a single brat, cradled in a softish bun. In Sheboygan, two brats share space on a hard Bavarian semmel roll, and you don't use sauerkraut as a topping. Brown mustard, pickles, onions—yes. That's a double with the works, and if you want to blend in at a Sheboygan festival, that's what you'll order. Moreover, while it's common for grill chefs in, say, Milwaukee, to soak and parboil their brats before throwing them on the grill, in Sheboygan this is bratwurst heresy. Instead, Sheboyganites slow-cook their brats entirely on the grill, and they insist that the patience pays off.

A perfect opportunity to grab a Sheboygan brat is **Bratwurst Day** in early August, but if you can't make it then, try a meal at **Charcoal Inn**, where grilling up brats is the specialty.

10–5 Saturday, noon–5 Sunday. This modern, upscale shopping center features some 25 specialty shops, boutiques, and restaurants. Finds include Craverie Chocolatier Cafe, With Child (a trendy maternity shop), and more.

Book World (920-694-0011; book worldstores.com), 537 South Taylor, Sheboygan. Open 9–8 Monday through Saturday, 11–5 Sunday. This independent Midwestern bookstore offers an impressive selection of titles, plus magazines, newspapers, and gifts.

Bahr Creek Llama and Fiber Studio (920-668-6417), N1021 Sauk Trail, Cedar Grove. Noon–6 Monday through Friday, 10–4 Sunday. This shop doesn't just sell yarn and needles, but looms, spinning wheels, and other fiber-arts goodies, it also raises llamas with silky wool and teaches knitting classes.

Riverfront Boardwalk and Fish Shanty Village (800-457-9497), Riverfront Drive, Sheboygan. Walk along the boardwalk to check out the original and replica fish shanties, which boast restaurants, galleries, and shopping.

Two Fish Gallery & Sculpture Garden (920-876-3192; twofishgallery .net), Elkhart Lake. Open Friday, Saturday, and Sunday. This house-turned-art gallery features unique, contemporary works in a variety of media, including pottery, paintings, book arts, and more.

✳ **Special Events**

Brat Days is held in late July and early August each year. This three-day festival features music all day long, a carnival, craft fair, kid's activities, and of course, brats.

FOX VALLEY
Including Appleton, Neenah, Menasha, and Oshkosh

Originally home to the Ho-Chunk Nation, the area we now call the Fox Valley ended up in the hands of French explorers, and ultimately the tribes were forced off the land. European settlers moved in, as they did all over the state, and industrialization soon defined the area. Here, it was a paper mill, opened in 1854. Over time, the region would become a major papermaking center. A boon to the economy, for sure, but detrimental to the Fox River, which remains heavily polluted with Polychlorinated biphenyls and other waste from the paper mills between Oshkosh and Green Bay. It's still a popular spot for fishing—the fishing is good here—but most people don't eat what they catch. Despite the pollution, the river is pretty, and provides miles of scenic land for boardwalks and riverside parks and dining in the valley. Ongoing efforts to get the river cleaned up seem to be picking up steam, and there are signs that the water quality is improving.

If you're not coming here to fish, you're probably coming to shop. Oshkosh's

SUNSET IN OSHKOSH

outlet mall, Appleton's large Fox River Mall, and downtown shopping districts (but mostly the malls) draw a large number of visitors from Northeastern Wisconsin and beyond. Appleton, a city of about 70,000, boasts the best shopping, dining, and entertainment in the region. Home to a top-notch performing arts center, art museum, historical venues and nature centers, there's a lot going on in Appleton, things you won't even find in larger Green Bay. Appleton's downtown is lively, with many attractions crammed onto a single street, book-ended by Lawrence University and the Fox River Mall. Park the car and walk around a bit—you'll find cafés, boutiques, upscale as well as inexpensive dining, museums, kid's activities, and more.

GUIDANCE The **Fox Cities Convention & Visitors Bureau** (920-734-3358; foxcities.org), 3433 West College Avenue, Appleton, publishes a guide annually with information on the region. Stop by the downtown office for the guide, plus state of Wisconsin maps, and more. The *Appleton Post-Crescent* (postcrescent .com), owned by Gannett, is the area's main daily newspaper.

GETTING THERE *By Car:* The Fox Cities are located along US 41, and this is the road most people will take, but WI 10, 45, and 76 link up as well.

By Air: The **Outagamie County Regional Airport** (atwairport.com), County CA, Appleton, is served by **Midwest Airlines** (800-452-2022; midwestairlines .com), **Delta** (800-354-9822; delta.com), **United** (800-241-6522; united.com), and **Northwest** (800-225-2525; nwa.com), with connections in Milwaukee, Minneapolis, Chicago, Detroit, and Cincinnati.

By Bus: Greyhound Bus Lines (800-231-2222; greyhound.com) makes a stop at the **Valley Transit Depot** (920-733-2318), 100 East Washington Street, in downtown Appleton.

GETTING AROUND To travel between the cities, you'll need a car. In Appleton, **Valley Transit** (920-832-8500; appleton.org/departments/transit), operates 16 routes which run from 6 A.M. to 10 P.M. daily. A few cab companies work in the area; call **Appleton-Neenah-Menasha Taxi** (920-733-4444), **Community Cab** (920-788-4645), and **Fox Valley Cab** (920-734-4546).

MEDICAL EMERGENCY Call 911

Appleton Medical Center (920-731-4101), 1818 North Meade Street, Appleton.

St. Elizabeth Hospital (920-738-2000), 1506 Oneida Street, Appleton.

Theda Clark Regional Medical Center (920-729-3100), 130 Second Street, Neenah.

Children's Hospital of Wisconsin-Fox Valley (920-969-7900), 130 Second Street, Neenah.

✳ To See and Do

In Appleton

✦ ᵬ ↑ **The Building for Kids** (920-734-3226; buildingforkids.org), 100 West College Avenue. Open 9–5 Monday through Friday, 10–5 Saturday, noon–5 Sunday. This two-story downtown children's museum features a water table area, ball exhibit, play airplane and traffic control center, and a 45-foot tree with forts. Admission $5.

✄ ♿ ↑ **The History Museum at the Castle** (920-735-9370; myhistorymuseum .org), 330 East College Avenue, Appleton. Open 10–4 Monday through Saturday, noon–4 Sunday. Of the many items on display in this castle-like mansion, the Harry Houdini exhibit is likely the most popular. Aside from the historical and biographical information and artifacts here, the AKA Houdini exhibit shows visitors the secrets to his tricks. This created a firestorm within the magician community, because you're just not supposed to give away that information to the uninitiated. Nevertheless, fans think it's fun to try escaping from a straightjacket, pick a padlock, and break out of jail. $5 adults; $2.50 ages 5–17; children younger than 5, free.

✄ ♿ ↑ **Paper Discovery Center** (920-380-7491; paperdiscoverycenter.org), 425 West Water Street, Appleton. Open 10–4 Monday through Saturday. This is a science and history museum focused sharply on the paper industry. Makes sense that it's here, as that industry has been vital to the Fox Valley. Housed in a 19th-century paper mill along the Fox River, exhibits explore the paper-making process, the history and importance of the industry, and its future. The Paper Industry Hall of Fame is here, too, but the best part of all is that you get to make your own paper to take home. Adults $5; students $3.

✄ ♿ ↑ **Appleton Art Center** (920-733-4089; www.appletonartcenter.org), 111 West College Avenue, Appleton. Open 9–5 Monday through Thursday, 9–9 Friday, 10–4 Saturday. This 25,000-square-foot museum is devoted to promoting the visual

HONORING HARRY HOUDINI IN APPLETON

arts in the Fox Valley. See rotating touring exhibits as well as permanent collections. Adults $4, students $3, children younger than 10, free.

  ♿ ⛪ **Hearthstone Historic House Museum** (920-730-8204; focol.org/hearth stone/), 625 West Prospect Avenue, Appleton. Open 10–3:30 Wednesday through Friday, 11–3:30 Saturday. Tours begin every half hour. This 1882 Victorian mansion was the first home in the world to be lit by a hydroelectric central station. The house contains original light fixtures, switches, and accents. Exhibits pay homage to Thomas Edison, who developed the hydroelectric system. Adults $5; ages 5–17 $2.50; children younger than 5, free.

In Neenah and Menasha

  ♿ ⛪ **Barlow Planetarium** (920-832-2848; uwfox.uwc.edu/barlow), 1478 Midway Road, Menasha. Located on the campus of UW-Fox Valley, this planetarium offers regular programming in its 48-foot projection dome. Adults $7; children $5.

  ⛪ ♿ **Bergstrom-Mahler Museum** (920-751-4658; paperweightmuseum.com), 165 North Park Avenue, Neenah. Open 10–4:30 Tuesday through Saturday, 1–4:30 Sunday. This museum began with a bit of nostalgia on the part of one of the founders, Evangeline Hoysradt. Opened in 1959, today it holds more than 3,000 pieces of glasswork, including paperweights, Germanic glass, and contemporary works. Free.

In Oshkosh

EAA Airventure Museum (920-426-4818; airventuremuseum.org), 3000 Poberezny Road, Oshkosh. Open 8:30–5 Monday through Saturday, 10–5 Sunday. There's a big plane out front that's visible from US 41, so you won't miss it. Collections include more than 250 historic airplanes, 20,000 aviation artifacts, a kid's gallery, and the Pioneer Airport—a living museum that recreates the early days of human flight.

Paine Art Center and Gardens (920-235-6903; thepaine.org), 1410 Algoma Boulevard, Oshkosh. Open 11–4 Tuesday through Sunday. Touring art exhibits are displayed in this historic mansion. Outside, 20 different gardens and green spaces round out your visit. Adults $7; ages 5–12 $4; children younger than 5, free.

Oshkosh Public Museum (920-236-5799; oshkoshmuseum.org), 1331 Algoma Boulevard, Oshkosh. Open 10–4:30 Tuesday through Saturday, 1–4:30 Sunday. With collections totaling more than 250,000 objects covering natural history, art, Native American culturing, and more, this museum explores the history of Oshkosh and the Lake Winnebago region in general. Dating back to 1927, it's the state's second-oldest historical museum.

Menominee Park Zoo (920-236-5082; oshkoshzoo.org), Hazel Street, Oshkosh. Open 11–7 Monday through Friday, 10–7 Saturday and Sunday. This small zoo set in a city park has a few animals, such as wolves, goats, and prairie dogs.

✳ Outdoor Activities

Fin 'n' Feather Showboat Cruises (920-582-4305; fin-n-feathershowboats.com), 22 West Main Street, Winneconne. Schedule varies—check ahead. Take a cruise on the Wolf River in a traditional riverboat. The outfit offers sightseeing cruises, lunch and dinner cruises, and a Fourth of July fireworks cruise. (No better way to enjoy small-town fireworks than from a boat!) $19.95–31.95.

High Cliff State Park (920-989-1106), N7630 State Park Road, Sherwood. Open for day use 6–11 daily. At more than 1,000 acres, this is the only state park on Lake Winnebago. Features such as camping, playgrounds, and trails make this a fun park. The limestone cliffs—part of the Niagara Escarpment—forests, lakeshore, and effigy mounds make it unique. A state park vehicle sticker is required.

1000 Islands Environmental Center, (920-766-4733; 1000islandsenvironmental center.com), 1000 Beaulieu Court, Kaukana. With 300 acres of wooded land along the Fox River, this nature center boasts trails for hiking, skiing, and snowshoeing, and functions as habitat for countless birds.

Gardens of the Fox Cities (920-993-1900; gardensfoxcities.org), 1313 East Wizke Boulevard, Appleton. Open from dawn to dusk daily. Located at **Appleton Memorial Park**, the gardens are on 35 acres of land, and include the **Scheig Learning Center**. Free.

Gordon Bubolz Nature Center (920-731-6041; bubolzpreserve.org), 4815 North Lynndale Drive, Appleton. Open 8–4:30 Tuesday through Friday, 11–4 Saturday, 12:30–4 Sunday. This 775-acre nature preserve boasts eight miles of trails for hiking, skiing, or snowshoeing, plus a rustic log cabin for overnight rental. Hailed as a great spot for bird watching and prized for its white cedar forest, regular family programs are held regularly in the nature center. Skis and snowshoes can be rented onsite.

Mosquito Hill Nature Center (920-779-6433; www.mosquitohill.com), N3880 Rogers Road, New London. Trails open daylight hours except during deer-hunting season. Building open 8–4:30 Tuesday through Friday, 10–3 Saturday and Sunday. That's an off-putting name, but don't worry—the mosquitoes aren't any worse here than the rest of the state! Located along the Wolf River about 25 miles from Appleton, this 430-acre nature center boasts miles of hiking and ski trails, a gallery focused on nature art, and special events, but most unique is the **Butterfly House**, open 11–3 Wednesday, Saturday, and Sunday during July and August. Free/donation.

Lodging

Copper Leaf Boutique Hotel (920-749-0303; copperleafhotel.com), 300 West College Avenue, Appleton. Smack between the Fox Cities Performing Arts Center and the Appleton Art Center, this newer hotel boasts contemporary decor in warm, natural tones, in-room hot tubs, and an onsite spa, perfect for a relaxing, 30-minute massage. Rooms $99–299.

Radisson Paper Valley (920-733-8000; radisson.com/appletonwi), 333 West College Avenue, Appleton. Also downtown and in the midst of it all, the rooms here have recent updates with contemporary décor. On-site restaurants include the Vince Lombardi Steakhouse, which should suit fans of the Pack. Rooms $99-249.

Cambria Suites (920-733-0101; cambriasuites.com), 3940 North Gateway Drive, Appleton. This hotel has a contemporary, urban feel. Rooms are warmly decorated in earth tones and boast flat-screen televisions and stylish furnishings. There's also a nice pool and fitness area. Rooms $149–299.

Franklin Inn on Durkee (920-993-1711, appleton-wisconsin.com), 310 North Durkee, Appleton. Four rooms suit four different tastes—the sunny Petite Chateau Suite has a romantic French flair, the Sea Breeze Suite offers a tasteful homage to the tropics, the Primavera has a four-poster bed and elegant touches, and the Shangri-la has elegant touches. All of it is understated, so you won't feel like you're in a theme park. Full breakfast is served each morning. Rooms $119-209.

Bridgewood Resort (920-720-8000; bridgewoodresorthotel.com), 1000 Cameron Way, Neenah. The sizable rooms have contemporary furnishings, and there are special family suites with kids' rooms outfitted with toddler beds, bunk beds, and child-friendly decor. The indoor pool area has a kiddie pool with toys and a small slide, and the nine-hole golf course features watered fairways and greens. Rooms $130–188.

✷ Where to Eat

DINING OUT

In Appleton

Y ♿ **Black and Tan Grille** (920-380-4745; appleton.blackandtangrille.com), 300 West College Avenue, Appleton. Open for dinner daily. Housed in the **Copper Leaf Boutique Hotel**, the decor is upscale but casual, with lots of natural wood, and the menu features contemporary dishes such as Mediterranean chicken and vegetarian manicotti, although the restaurant is better known for its steaks. It has a decent wine list and lengthy martini menu, plus a host of nightcaps for rounding the night out. Dishes $22–38.

Y ♿ **Casa Blanca** (920-954-1010; casablancaappleton.com), 531 West College Avenue. Open 11–10 Monday through Saturday, noon–9 Sunday. Featuring Latin American cuisine from 27 countries, this is a popular downtown restaurant. The menu is split into meat, poultry, and fish sections, and dessert includes Pastel de Cuatro Leches. Inside, palm trees and seascape murals will put you in mind of the Caribbean. Dishes $21–35.

Y ♿ **Fratello's Waterfront Restaurant** (920-993-9087; supplerestaurant group.com/fratellos-appleton), 501 West Water Street, Appleton. Open for lunch and dinner daily. Fratello's was born in the Fox Valley in 1995, and today also livens up Milwaukee and Green Bay waterfronts. This restaurant is housed in a 1909 hydroelectric plant made of Cream City brick and offers a stunning view of the river. The menu has a little bit of everything, such as Thai shrimp noodles, roasted vegetable stromboli, and stone-fired pizza, plus lots of sandwiches, burgers, and traditional seafood and steak options. Vegetarian and gluten-free dishes are clearly marked on the menu. Lunch $10–15, dinner $15–30.

Y ♿ **Fin 'n' Feather Showboats** (920-582-4305; fin-n-feathershowboats .com), 22 West Main Street, Winneconne. Just west of Oshkosh, it was once a true Wisconsin supper club, but today this restaurant along the Wolf River blends slightly more contemporary tastes with the traditions of its roots. While you can order dishes such as a pecan-crusted chicken salad, a veggie sandwich, and Cajun pasta, the old favorites are still on the menu. So don't worry—this is still the place to get broasted chicken, chopped sirloin, and calf's liver and onions, all with a trip to the soup and salad bar. For the especially hungry, there are buffets for every meal, like the weekend dinner buffet with ribs, broasted chicken, buttered cod, and more. Lunch $5.49–11.99, dinner $11.99–20.99.

In Appleton

&b. **Frank's Pizza Palace** (920-734-9131) 815 West College Avenue. Open daily for dinner. This is the area's favorite pizza parlor, and it's been serving up thin-crust pies since 1955. Toppings are fresh and piled high to everyone's delight, and you get to watch the pizza chefs throw dough in the air. Fourteen-inch pie $12–23.

&b. **India Darbar** (920-560-4967; indiadarbar.com), 2333 West Wisconsin Ave, Appleton. Open for lunch and dinner Tuesday through Sunday. The extensive menu boasts kormas and curries in meat, fish, poultry, and vegetarian options, but the lunch buffet, with more than 100 items, is what brings the masses in. There's another location in Madison. Lunch buffet $7.95, entrees $10–13.

Ψ &b. **Koreana** (920-733-3205; the koreana.com), 201 West Northland Avenue, Appleton. Open for lunch and dinner Monday through Saturday. Popular for its sushi bar, this Asian fusion restaurant features Korean and Japanese dishes. The dinner menu boasts items such as bulgogi, tempura, and teriyaki, and the huge sushi menu includes traditional rolls, plus some that are deep fried. The atmosphere is casual and comfortable, good for just about anything. Entrees $10–15.

Ψ &b. **Apollon** (920-739-1122; www.apollonrestaurant.com), 207 North Appleton Street, Appleton. Open for dinner Monday through Saturday. Located downtown, this lovely eatery serves upscale Greek food that might surprise travelers who've been to one too many fast-food gyro spots. Dishes like spanakopita and pastitsio share space with filet mignon and chicken Florentine, so all diners should be pleased. Dishes $15.95–27.95.

Ψ &b. **Nakashima of Japan** (920-739-6057; nakashimas.com), 4100 Pine Street, Appleton. Open for dinner daily. This trendy Japanese restaurant features a large hibachi menu, a sushi menu complete with beginner's combo, and grill-your-own options. Kid's menu available. Dishes $10–20.

In Neenah and Menasha

Cy's Asian Bistro (920-969-9549), 208 West Wisconsin Avenue, Neenah. Open for lunch and dinner Monday through Friday, dinner Monday through Saturday. This cozy little Thai restaurant in downtown Menasha has a huge menu with every curry from sweet, red, and yellow, to native, five-star, and "evil." Pad Thai, spring rolls, and lemon grass soup are on the menu as well. Lunch $6.95–8.95, dinner $10.95–14.95.

&b. **Aspen Coffee and Tea** (920-886-1880; aspencoffee-tea.com), 1110 Midway Road, Menasha. Open for breakfast and lunch daily. This cozy but airy coffee shop is housed in a copy shop, of all places, and has an impressive stone fireplace, leather chairs for settling in, free WiFi, and Intelligentsia coffee. Aside from a good shot of espresso, you can pick up a sandwich such as the Vegetarian Roma or Turkey Moose, but the simple breakfast is where it's at. Get a breakfast panini, steel-cut oats, or yogurt. If you show up wearing pajamas, your choice among 40 cereals is on the house. Dishes less than $10.

In Oshkosh

&b. Ψ **Brooklyn Grill** (920-230-4477; brooklyngrill.com), 607 South Main Street, Oshkosh. Open for lunch and dinner daily. Brooklyn Grill is a 1920s gangster-themed bar and restaurant where the servers don fedoras. The food is pub grub—sandwiches and burgers—but the names of dishes are entertaining. Try the Five Finger Discount Tenders, the Al Capone (Chicago-style hot dog), or the "You Lookin' At Me" turkey club. Kids menu available. Dishes $7–12.

COFFEE AND SWEETS & **Brewed Awakenings** (920-882-9336; brewed awake.com), 107 East College Avenue, Appleton. Open daily. A casual spot for hanging out, checking your email, and fueling up, the best thing here isn't necessarily that strong cup of joe, but the homemade gelato bar. Blend the two afagato style for a real treat.

Ψ & **New Moon Coffee Cafe** (920.232.0976; newmooncafe.com), 401 North Main Street, Oshkosh. Open for all three meals daily. This cozy coffee shop in downtown Oshkosh serves a good cup of coffee, plus a handful of sandwiches and other cafe fare, as well as craft beers and wine. Evenings often feature live entertainment.

✳ Entertainment

In Appleton

& T **Fox Cities Performing Arts Center** (920-730-3760; foxcitiespac .com), 400 West College Avenue, Appleton. Construction on this state-of-the-art venue was completed in 2002, making it the most modern theater in the area. The main stage seats 2,100. The center brings in Broadway productions and other touring performers, comedians, dance companies, and more, and the schedule is full year-round.

Fox Valley Symphony (920-968-0300; foxvalleysymphony.com), 111 West College Avenue, Appleton. Founded in 1969, this symphony orchestra performs throughout the year at the **Fox Cities Performing Arts Center**, including a holiday pops concert.

FOX CITIES PERFORMING ARTS CENTER IN WAUSAU

✳ Selective Shopping

In Appleton

✦ ⬆ **Fox River Mall** (920-739-4100; foxrivermall.com), 4301 West Wisconsin Avenue. Open 10–9 Monday through Friday, 9–9 Saturday, 10–7 Sunday. This mall is the shopping hub of Northeastern Wisconsin, with more than 200 retailers.

✦ ⬆ **Fox River Antique Mall** (920-731-9699; foxriverantiques.com), 1074 South Van Dyke Road, Appleton. Open 10–6 daily. This is the state's largest antiques mall, with more than 165 dealers. A must-stop for fans of anything old.

Simon's Specialty Cheese (920-788-6311), 2735 Freedom Road (County Road N, just off US 41), Little Chute. Open 8–6 Monday through Friday, 8–5 Saturday, and Sundays in December. Simon's stocks more than 100 cheeses, all made in Wisconsin. Find cheese curds, gift packs, and chocolate cheese fudge to pack in a cooler and take home.

Kerrigan Brothers Winery (920-788-1423; kerriganbrothers.com), N2797 WI 55, Freedom. Open 9–5 Monday through Saturday, 10:30–3 Sunday. Using Wisconsin-produced cherries, apples, and cranberries, Kerrigan Brothers makes fruit wines right here in the Fox Valley. Tours and tastings are offered daily.

The Mill Boutique (920-954-6210; papercreations.com), 234 West Northland Avenue, Appleton. Open daily. Located at the Atlas Mill, the former site of a Kimberly-Clark papermaking facility dating back to 1878, this arts shop shares space with a coffee shop and the **Paper Industry Hall of Fame** (see listing under To See and Do). Find unique pottery, quilts, and other handcrafted items here.

The Olive Cellar (920-574-2361; the olivecellar.com), 277 West Northland Avenue, Appleton. Open Monday through Saturday. Like the Oilerie in Fish Creek and Vom Fass in Madison, here you can sample olive oils and balsamic vinegars stored in casks. The store also stocks specialty food items to go with your purchase. How about a blood orange olive oil or an 18-year-old balsamic vinegar?

Wilmar Chocolates (920-733-6182; wilmarchocolates.com), 1222 North Superior Street, Appleton. Open Monday through Saturday. Hand-dipped chocolates and other sweets draw people in to this corner shop. In business since the '50s, things don't look old-fashioned here, but the candy-making traditions are apparent with one bite.

In Neenah and Menasha

Mom and Pop Place (920-725-0488; momandpopplace.com), 117 West Wisconsin Avenue, Neenah. Open Monday through Saturday. This store stocks creative toys from companies such as Plan and Haba, as well as breastfeeding supplies, slings, and other items. To make life easy, there's an adjacent cafe that serves up a handful of sandwiches for mom and dad, smoothies, bakery, Alterra coffee, and kids' meals, all peanut-free. There's a play area for the kids, too, so you can actually eat.

Primitive Gathering (920-722-7233; primitivegatherings.us), 850 Racine Street, Menasha. Open Monday through Saturday. You'll find everything for needle arts here, including needles, kits, patterns, hand-dyed wool, historic reproduction fabrics, and everything else a knitter or stitcher could want.

In Oshkosh

✦ ⬆ **The Outlet Shoppes at Oshkosh** (920-231-8911; theoutlet shoppesatoshkosh.com), 3001 South

Washburn, Oshkosh. Open 10–9 Monday through Saturday, 10–6 Sunday. This outlet mall has more than 40 stores, including Gap, Motherhood Maternity, Nike, Jockey, and, of course, OshKosh B'Gosh.

& **Apple Blossom Books** (920-230-3395; appleblossombooks.com), 513 North Main Street, Oshkosh. Open 10–7 Tuesday through Friday, 10–4 Monday and Saturday. This colorful little bookshop stocks general used and new titles, with an emphasis on being family friendly. Hosts many kids' events.

Paper Tiger Book Store (920-231-0800; bookworldstores.com), 100-D City Center, Oshkosh. This independent Midwestern bookstore chain offers an impressive selection of titles, plus magazines, newspapers, and gifts.

Oaks Candy Corner (920-231-3660; oakscandy.com), 1206 Oregon Street, Oshkosh. Well-loved by visitors and locals alike, this candy shops history stretches back to 1890. No one can resist the tempting aroma of homemade chocolates. Be sure to pick up a Melty Bar, which is chocolate covered in chocolate.

Caramel Crisp & Cafe (920-231-4540; caramelcrispcafe.com), 200D City Center, Oshkosh. Open 7:30–7:30 Monday through Friday, 9–5 Saturday, 10–4 Sunday. This shop has served up delectable, buttery caramel corn for years, but now it also features a contemporary cafe with a small but complete lunch menu.

Dainty Daisies (920-233-6360; daintydaisies.com), 1606 Oregon Street, Oshkosh. Open 9–2:30 Thursday and Friday, 10–3 Saturday, or by appointment. In an age when brick-and-mortar shops are closing in favor of online retailers, it's refreshing that this one grew out of an Etsy shop. An outlet for the owner's handmade clothing and accessories, this shop also stocks vintage furniture, jewelry, and more.

Jambalaya Art Collective (920-312.3965; jambalayacoop.com), 413 North Main Street, Oshkosh. Hours vary, call ahead. This collective's gallery space works in all media from member artists, all of whom are local.

✴ Special Events

July: **Art in the Park**, Appleton City Park, Appleton. This one-day art fair boasts more than 200 artists from around the Midwest,

Late July/Early August: **EAA Airventure** (920-426-4800; airventure.org), Oshkosh. The Experimental Aircraft Association's annual week-long convention is held in Oshkosh each year—and everyone around the state knows it's happening, because more than 2,500 aircraft fly in for the fun. Everyone in Oshkosh knows when it's happening, too, because more than 500,000 people show up. Festivities include live music, outdoor aviation films, comedians, shopping, and more, plus an air show every afternoon for each of the seven days.

Door County

DOOR COUNTY

Visited by more than two million travelers each year, Door County's charm is certainly no secret; the year-round population of 27,000 swells to around 250,000 in summer, when the tourists make their way to the peninsula in search of fudge, cherry pie, and a little water recreation. Known by fans as the "Midwest's Cape Cod," Door County's sandy shores, simple architecture, and abundance of arts (not to mention cherries) bring couples, families, and groups of friends back year after year.

I mentioned shores. Located on Wisconsin's thumb, the Door Peninsula has the sandy beaches of the Green Bay on its west side, and rocky Lake Michigan shores on its east, totaling more than 300 miles of shoreline, complete with 10 lighthouses and nearly unlimited opportunities for fun on the water. Without question, this is a big draw to Door County, but it's certainly not the only one. After all, Wisconsin is hardly lacking in scenic lakefront. Door County's charm lies in its simple, small towns dotting the shoreline.

Sturgeon Bay is the largest of Door County's communities, home to roughly one-third of the county's year-round population. It's where the hospital is, and big-

WASHINGTON ISLAND

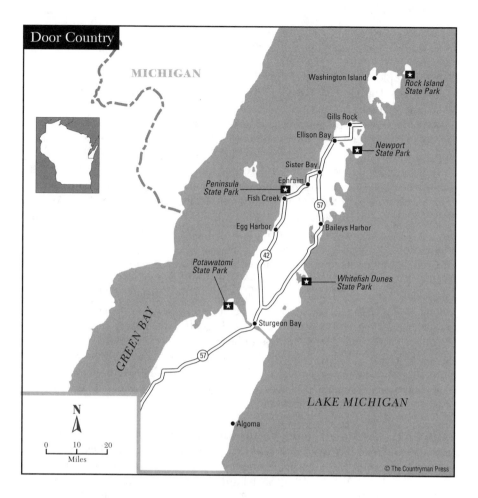

box discount stores, and while it's not quite the charming escape of its fellow northerly towns, there's a delightful historic district with all the shopping you expect from Door County. Covering ground between Green Bay and Lake Michigan, Sturgeon Bay's maritime history is self-explanatory, but just in case, check out the Door County Maritime Museum here.

Door County's 1800s development by white settlers is evident in the many historic and well-preserved buildings here. But long before Belgians and Scandinavians arrived, Native Americans made good use of the fruitful land and water here.

Heading north from Sturgeon Bay, you'll have to make a decision: Should you take WI 57, or WI 42? WI 57 travels east, along Lake Michigan, while WI 42 is along the bay. If that were the only difference, it would be a tough call. As it happens, the towns are all built up along the more moderate, western, bay side, along WI 42. The lake side is known as the "quiet side"; there just isn't the same sort of development. No shopping districts packed with tourists, no hubbub at all. What the lake side does have is the majority of the peninsula's lighthouses, beautiful parks, and plenty of peace. If you explore, you'll also find somewhat hidden artist studios and other special spots, as well as the center of the peninsula. Baileys Harbor is on the quiet side, home to the stunning Cave Point and some popular restaurants.

Most people, however, travel up WI 42, straight to the action. Going north, you'll hit Egg Harbor, Fish Creek, Ephraim, Sister Bay, Ellison Bay, and Gills Rock. The shopping hotspots are in Fish Creek and Sister Bay, but these villages all contain unique shops, galleries, and restaurants. It's no trouble at all to travel to the tip and back; it takes about 40 minutes each way, but you'll certainly be making stops. If you wish, you can hop a boat and head to Washington Island, a part of Door County a lot of people miss. Interesting to note, this is but one of 30 islands around the peninsula; it is the only one that's populated, however. It's different from anywhere else in Door County; different, really, from anything else in Wisconsin. Simply put, it's remarkably serene, with pristine lands and waters punctuating the island's removal from the rest of the state. It's a special place, perfect for a true escape.

Each season has its draw, too. Obviously, high season is summer, when the weather cooperates with everyone's plans to get outdoors, and the cherries are ripe for picking. But spring holds its own allure; that's when the cherry blossoms are in bloom. And fall, with all the trees and magnificent scenery, is popular with travelers seeking a glimpse of the colors as leaves begin to turn. Winter, undeniably, is the quietest time, and a huge number of businesses lock up for the season. Some do not, however, and Door County's beauty is appreciated by fans of snowshoeing and skiing. It makes an economical winter getaway, too—hotel rates are low, and many hotels offer romantic packages. Get a suite with a fireplace and buy a bottle of wine at one of the local wineries.

GUIDANCE The **Door County Visitor Bureau** (920-743-4456; doorcounty .com), 1015 Green Bay Road, Sturgeon Bay, is the official CVB for Door County, but there are numerous organizations and publications offering all kinds of information. Check, too, the **Washington Island Chamber of Commerce** (920-847-2179; washingtonislandchamber.com), 2206 West Harbor Road. You'll find information about the island not usually included in Door County information. In Sturgeon Bay, the **Sturgeon Bay Visitor and Convention Bureau** (920-743-6246; sturgeonbay.net), 36 South Third Avenue, offers information on the town most people breeze through on their way up the peninsula.

GETTING THERE *By Car:* There are two ways to get to the Door peninsula; the road less traveled is, indeed, the best. Instead of heading through Green Bay on WI 57, I heartily recommend traveling along the lake on WI 42, through Manitowoc County, Kewaunee, and Algoma. Not only is the scenery better, there are many shops and galleries along the way to whet your appetite for Door County.

GETTING AROUND There are site-seeing trolleys and that sort of thing, but you'll need wheels to really enjoy Door County. Part of the fun is traveling up and down the peninsula from town to town; you just can't do that without a vehicle. Biking around is a great option, too, and if you didn't bring your own, many hotels rent them.

MEDICAL EMERGENCY Call 911.

Door County Memorial Hospital (920-743-5566), 323 South 18th Avenue, Sturgeon Bay.

✳ To See and Do
MUSEUMS AND HISTORIC SITES

In Sturgeon Bay
✧ ♿ ❀ **Door County Maritime Museum** (920-743-5958; dcmm.org), 120 North Madison Avenue. Open daily. Like any maritime museum, this one has historic watercraft to check out, but it also includes exhibits exploring the area's ship-building history. Free admission.

♿ ❀ ⚑ **Door County Historical Museum** (920-743-5809; map.co.door.wi.us/museum), 18 North Fourth Avenue. Open daily May through October. A bit like your standard small-town museum, but exploring the history of the entire peninsula from early settlement to recent history, this museum includes a wildlife diorama. Free admission.

✧ **The Farm** (920- 743-6666; thefarmindoorcounty.com), 4285 WI 57. Open 9–5 daily Memorial day through Labor Day. Billed as a living rural museum, visitors get a chance to see and learn about family farm life in a very hands-on way. Pet pigs, milk goats, and otherwise get your fill of agricultural fun. Admission $7 adults, $3.50 kids 4–12, children younger than 4 free.

In Baileys Harbor

♿ ⚑ **Bjorklunden—The Boynton Chapel** (920-839-2216), 7590 Boynton Lane. Tours held June through August on Monday and Wednesday. Built in the Norwegian stavkirke style, the Boynton Chapel has 41 frescoes and numerous carvings inside. Tours $4.

In Fish Creek
⚑ **Historic Noble House** (920-868-2091; historicnoblehouse.org), 4167 WI 42. Open noon–5 June through October. Located right at the main intersection, the Historic Noble House once belonged to Fish Creek founding father Alexander Noble. Today it is restored to its original glory and contains many of its original furnishings. Adults $3; children $1.

In Sister Bay
Old Anderson House Museum (920-854-9242), WI 57 at Fieldcrest Road and Country Lane. Open 11–3 Saturday and Sunday from June through August. Tour a restored farmhouse and its associated buildings, with demonstrations on Saturdays. There's also a farmers' market here on Saturdays in summer, and other events throughout the season.

In Gills Rock
Door County Maritime Museum—Gills Rock (920-854-1844; dcmm.org), 12724 Wisconsin Bay Road. Open daily 10–5 from Memorial day through mid-October.

On Washington Island
Stavkirke (920-847-2341), 2206 West Harbor Road. Probably Wisconsin's best example of a traditional "stave" church, this one is a replica of one in Borgund, Norway. It's across the street from Trinity Evangelical Lutheran Church, which

LIGHTHOUSES

With 10 trusty beacons dotting its shores, Door County holds the distinction of having the most lighthouses in a single county anywhere in the U.S. Many of these remain in use by the U.S. Coast Guard, and only three of them are easily accessible to visitors, but that doesn't stop lighthouse fanatics from doing what it takes to see them all. For the less intrepid, the **Door County Trolley** lighthouse tour is the perfect option (see listing under Sturgeon Bay, To See and Do), but the **Door County Visitor Bureau** puts out a helpful brochure with all the information you'll need to plan out a tour yourself, including maps and history. An annual walk takes place each May; contact the **Door County Maritime Museum** (920-743-5958) for more information.

Here's a rundown of Door County's lighthouses:

Eagle Bluff Lighthouse (920-839-2377; eaglebllufflighthouse.org), 9462 Shore Road, Fish Creek. Tours run spring through fall. Find this historic lighthouse in Peninsula State Park (you'll need a state parks pass to get in, but daily passes are available at the entrance for a nominal fee) and take a narrated tour of the buildings and grounds. Adults $4, students $1, children younger than 6 free.

Cana Island Lighthouse, Baileys Harbor. Open 10–5 daily, May to November. Built in 1854, this lighthouse remains active and is accessible via a rocky causeway—while you won't be wading, you should still wear appropriate footwear. The keeper's house is open for a look-see, and those so inclined may climb to the top of the tower for an extra fee. $4 adults, $2 kids, $3 extra to climb.

Pottawatomie Light, Rock Island. It'll take up a whole day, but the light, and Rock Island, are worth the trouble. Hop a ferry to Washington Island, head across to Detroit Harbor, hop another ferry over to Rock Island, then hike about a mile to see Door County's oldest lighthouse. No admission to visit, but you will have to pay for transportation.

Pilot Island Lighthouse and **Plum Island Lighthouse**, off Washington Island. You can't visit these, but you will see them from the ferry on your way to Washington Island. Both constructed in the 1800s, these lights proved vital to helping vessels pass the treacherous waters of Death's Door. The islands have been neglected to some extent, and there's currently a push to protect both the buildings and the wildlife here.

STAVKIRKE ON WASHINGTON ISLAND

holds services here in the summer months. A prayer path guides you to the small church, where you can wander around inside and out.

Washington Island Farm Museum (920-847-2156), Jackson Harbor Road. Open daily in summer. Historic farm buildings were gathered from around the island to create the farm museum, focused on 19th-century rural life. Free admission, accepts donations.

Washington Island Archives (920-847-3072; washingtonisland-wi.gov/archives .htm), 910 Main Road. Open 1–4 Tuesday and Friday. Anyone with family ties to Washington Island or just an interest in the history of the area will find a wealth of information in the Washington Island Archives. The genealogy program alone has more than 12,000 entries.

✂ ♿ ☂ **Art and Nature Center** (920-847-2025; www.wianc.org), 1799 Main Road. Open daily. Serving as the cultural center of the island, the Art and Nature Center features the works of island artists, musical performances, and hands-on education about island nature. Adults $1, children younger than 11 free.

TOURS AND CRUISES

In Sturgeon Bay

Door County Fireboat Cruises (920-495-6454;www.doorcountyfireboatcruises .com), 120 North Madison Avenue. These narrated cruises offer a chance to relax and take in Door County's beauty on an original Chicago fireboat. Adult fare $18–30.

Door County Trolley Tours (920-868-1100; doorcountytrolley.com). Tours run June through October, with some additional seasonal runs. While most of the tours depart from Fish Creek, you can pick up the lighthouse tour and some seasonal tours in Sturgeon bay at the Door County Maritime Museum (920-743-5958; dcmm.org), 120 North Madison Avenue. Focusing on important and popular

ROCK ISLAND GETAWAY

Rock Island State Park (920-847-2235), 1181 Range Line Road, Washington Island. It takes two ferries to get here (one from the peninsula to Washington Island, then one over to Rock Island), and you can't take so much as a bike onto the island—this is a real getaway. As well as being a popular backpack camping spot, Rock Island features many unique and historic buildings for day-trippers to check out. Wisconsin's oldest lighthouse is here, as well as the many stone structures built by Chester Thordarson, who once owned the bulk of the island. Built, perhaps, to remind Thordarson of his homeland, the boathouse, great hall, and other structures here are remarkable. Also remarkable is the Pottawatomie Lighthouse, the oldest lighthouse in the area. Make a reservation with the state to secure a campsite if you plan to stay overnight. The **Karfi Ferry** (920-847-3322) departs from Jackson Harbor on Washington Island for Rock Island; it's an eight-mile trek from the end of Washington Island you'll arrive at to the end from which you'll depart for Rock Island, so be sure you have transportation.

aspects of Door County's culture and history, these tours are a great way to experience the peninsula. The Progressive Dinner Outing features a multi-course meal, each course at a different venue. Tours $13–73.

Wings Over Door County (920-743-6952; orionflightservices.com), 3538 Park Drive. Open daily. View the beautiful peninsula from the air. Wings Over Door County offers scenic air tours taking off from Sturgeon Bay, as well as plane rentals and charter flights. Tours $100–200.

In Baileys Harbor

Segway The Door Tours (920-376-0256; segwaythedoor.com), call for meeting location. A unique way to get out and see the sights up close, Segway The Door offers three different tours: Baileys Harbor, Peninsula State Park, and Washington Island. The Baileys Harbor tour cruises to lighthouses, the Ridges Sanctuary, and more, with views of Lake Michigan. Don't worry if you've never used a Segway before; you'll get training. Tours $74–89.

In Egg Harbor

Door County Kayak Tours (920-868-1400; doorcountykayaktours.com), 4690 Rainbow Ridge Court. Tours May through October. Offering a variety of excursions, including family friendly tours, fishing trips, and even yoga kayak tours, everybody down to the least-outdoorsy traveler will find something tempting in the brochure. $48–58 per person.

In Fish Creek

Classic Boat Tours of Door County (920-421-2080; classicboattours.com), 9145 Spring Road. Map out your own tour, including locations and duration, and have the boat to yourself. Up to six passengers are allowed in your group. It's not a huge tour boat, which is why you get such a customized itinerary. Rates per hour: Adults and kids older than 12, $25; ages 6–12, $12; 3–6, $6; children younger than 3, free.

Door County Trolley Tours (920-868-1100; doorcountytrolley.com), 9197 WI 42. Tours are offered June through October, with special seasonal tours in fall and winter. These trolley tours are popular and promise a great way to learn about Door County. Main tours are the lighthouse tour, the wine tour, and the scenic tour. Pick-up locations and times vary; be sure to call ahead. $13–54 per person.

In Ephraim

Stiletto Sailway Cruises (920-854-7245; stilettosailingcruises.com), 9993 WI 42, at South Shore Pier. Tours June through October. Operating seven catamaran cruises daily in summer, Stiletto takes you to lighthouses, bluffs, and some of the peninsula's islands. Tickets $28.

In Sister Bay

Bay Shore Outdoor Store Kayak Tours (920-854-7598; kayakdoorcounty.com), 2457 South Bay Shore Drive (WI 42). Open daily. Tours offered May through September. Aside from selling and renting all manner of outdoor gear, such as bikes, kayaks, skis, and snowshoes, this store offers a variety of kayak tours aimed at beginners, and private lessons. Try the mellow Sunset Tour, or one that takes a close look at beautiful Cave Point. Travel Green Wisconsin certified. Tours $38–58, lessons $75/two-hour session.

The Shoreline Charters (920-854-4707; shorelinecharters.net), 10733 North Bay Shore Drive. Tours offered April through October. These scenic tours aboard a comfortable passenger boat offer a relaxing way to see Door County's lighthouses, shipwreck sites, and coastline. Five tours depart from Sister Bay, and an additional three explore Death's Door and Washington Island, departing from Gills Rock. Adults $45–50, children $35–40.

On Washington Island

Bread and Water Kayaks (920-847-2400; breadandwater.us), 1275 Main Road. Tours operate in summer. Operating out of the Bread and Water cafe, three-hour tours are guided by kayaking expert Valerie Fons, who owns the business. Tours $65.

TRAIN TOURS Both the Cherry Train Tour (920-847-2039; cherrytraintours .com), 215 WI 42, Ellison Bay, and the Viking Tour Train (920-854-2972; island clipper.com), 12731 WI 42, Gills Rock, are little open-air trains pulled by trucks that hit major attractions on the island, then get you back to the ferry dock in as little as 90 minutes. Both tours make stops at **Schoolhouse Beach**, the **Double K Ostrich Farm**, and the **Farm Museum**. The **Cherry Train Tour** also stops at the **Art and Nature Center** and the **Stavkirke**, while the Viking Tour stops at **Den Norska Grenda** and **Mann's Mercantile**—both shopping stops. You'll miss out on a lot of the relaxation so intrinsic to the island, but if you just want to see what it's all about in an afternoon, this is the way to do it.

✴ Outdoor Activities

In Sturgeon Bay

⋗ **The Farm** (920- 743-6666; thefarmindoorcounty.com), 4285 WI 57. Open 9–5 daily Memorial day through Labor Day. See Green Space.

In Egg Harbor

⋗ **Plum Loco Animal Farm** (920-743-1617), 4431 Plum Bottom Road. Open

9:30–4:30 Thursday through Tuesday in summer, weekends in winter. This petting zoo offers a family-friendly break, with more than 60 animals to watch, pet, and feed, plus a play-farm and plenty of room to picnic. Adults $6.75; kids $3.75; younger than 3 free.

In Ephraim
Wisconsin Water Wings (920-854-9000; parasailrides.com), 9993 WI 42, at South Shore Pier. Open May through October. Here's a different way to view the scenery—parasailing over Eagle Harbor. You're in the air for less than 20 minutes, but it's 20 minutes you won't forget. Rides $50–90.

In Sister Bay
Bay Shore Outdoor Store Kayak Tours (920-854-7598; kayakdoorcounty.com), 2457 South Bay Shore Drive (WI 42). Rent or buy your outdoor gear here, or take one of the guided kayak tours for a more active way to enjoy the scenery.

WASHINGTON ISLAND
Overlooked Washington Island sits about seven miles across the Death's Door strait, but many visitors to Door County never make it there, preferring to stay behind in the more heavily populated towns on the peninsula. Too bad for them. Washington Island, rich with Icelandic heritage and untouched beauty, is a unique and unheralded secret Wisconsin getaway. It's not full of tourist traps and dense shopping districts like the rest of Door County. It has pleasant beaches, both rocky and sandy, woodlands, fresh air, and quiet. There is no industry here; the economy is largely dependent on tourism, with organic farming gaining ground, and the island's 700 year-round residents comprise a very self-sufficient community. It's a slower pace, to be sure, and a welcome one.

To get here, you'll need to hop on a ferry. A car ferry is operated by **Washington Island Ferry Line** (920-847-2546; wisferry.com), and departs from Northport Pier at Gills Rock; a passenger-only ferry called the **Island Clipper** (920-854-2972; islandclipper.com) leaves from the other end of Gills Rock (really, only a few minutes away). Once on the island, you'll want transportation. Attractions are spread out around the 22-square-mile island, so walking is not really feasible. If you choose not to bring your car, you can rent a car, moped, or bike rentals at Detroit Harbor, where you come ashore.

About that ferry ride. To get to Washington Island, you'll traverse Death's Door—so named because the wild currents created where the cold waters of Lake Michigan meet warmer Green Bay were responsible for many shipwrecks. (French explorer's originally called it Porte des Mortes.) While modern navigation systems and technology make the boat ride over undeniably safe, it's a rocky trip that will leave you with a strong under-standing of the strait's name.

⚔ **Double K Ostrich Farm** (920-847-3202), West Harbor Road. Open 10–5 daily. Tour this ostrich farm—a decidedly unique find on the island—and you'll see not only ostriches, but potbellied pigs, a camel, turkeys, sheep, and more in the petting zoo. Admission $1.

GOLF There are 11 golf courses Door County, suiting all levels of players. **Peninsula State Park Golf Course** (920-854-5791; peninsulagolf.org), 9890 Shore Road, Ephraim, offers an 18-hole course in the wooded park, along Eagle Harbor. The **Alpine Resort** (877-318-8773; alpineresort.com), 7715 Alpine Road, Egg Harbor, is another scenic spot, with 36 holes. On Washington Island, the **Deer Run Golf Course** (920-847-2017), 1885 Michigan Road, features both a regulation nine-hole course, plus an 18-hole mini-golf course. For more information on golfing in Door County, see the Door County Visitor Bureau website, doorcounty .com.

ORCHARDS AND WINERIES A visit to Door County wouldn't be complete with a stop at an orchard—after all, Door County is the nation's fourth-largest cherry producer. There are nearly fifty orchards around the peninsula, which means you won't have to look far to find one. Harvest season runs late July through August if you're looking to pick, and the trees blossom in May. In fall, it's time for apples.

In Sturgeon Bay

Von Stiehl Winery (920) 487-5208; vonstiehl.com), 115 Navarino Street. Open daily. The building that houses Von Stiehl—the state's oldest winery—began life in the 19th century as a brewery, of all things. Clearly, the celebration of a good drink runs deep here. Tours are conducted daily, but you can pop in for a free wine tasting any time.

⛃ **Cherry Lane Orchards** (920-856-6864; cherrylaneorchards.com), 7525 Cherry Lane, Forestville. Open in July for pick-your-own cherries, September weekends for pick-your-own apples. Call ahead. Plan to make your own pies, jams, and have a fun day in the orchard, filling your pail as the cherries fall off the tree into your hand. You can call ahead and have the orchard staff do the picking for you, but what fun is that?

⛃ **Choice Orchards Farm Market** (920-743-8980; choiceorchards.com), 4594 County HH. Open 9–5 daily from May through October. Get pre-picked cherries and apples, plus cider, baked goods, and other yummy treats in the market, then wander through the evergreen maze.

🍷 ⛃ **Simon Creek Vineyard and Winery** (920-746-9307; simoncreekwines .com), 5896 Bochek Road. Open daily. Smack-dab between WI 42 and WI 57, this winery is a favorite among visitors. This is the largest vineyard in Door County, at 30 acres, and free tours end with samples in the tasting room, where you can slip out onto the terrace for a view of the vineyard. Wines tend to be sweet, particularly the popular Door County Cherry.

In Egg Harbor and Carlsville

🍷 ⛃ **Door Peninsula Winery** (920-743-7431; dcwine.com), 5806 WI 42, Carlsville. Open daily. Offering mostly sweet, fruity wines made from Door County options (like apples and cherries), you can tour the winery and sample the wines for free.

🍷 ♿ **Stone's Throw Winery** (920-839-9660; stonesthrowwinery.com), 3382 County Road E, Egg Harbor. Open 10–5 daily. While most Door County wineries feature fruity wines made from the cherries on hand, Stone's Throw Winery makes nothing but grape wines. The grapes are brought from California, but the wines are made here. Take a tour and sample the offerings; the tasting room has a small dining menu, and there's live music occasionally.

In Fish Creek

🍷 ♿ **Orchard Country Winery and Market** (920-868-3479; orchardcountry.com), 9197 WI 42. Open Friday through Monday. Much more than a winery, you can get just about all the goodies you've come to Door County for—quarts of cherries, cherry pie, apple cider, and more. The winery is housed in an old dairy barn, and the entire grounds smacks of rural Wisconsin farm market, with cheery red and white buildings. Tour the winery and try samples of their offerings.

The Cherry Hut (920-868-3406), 8832 Hgwy. 42. Open daily in summer. There's a little bit of everything here, from Wisconsin cheese to Door County cherries, wines, pies, and more—including cherry salsas and grilling sauces. If you're short on time, this is your one-stop cherry shop.

✷ Even More to See and Do

🖍 **Egg Harbor Fun Park** (920-868-9417; eggharborfunpark.com), 7340 WI 42, Egg Harbor. Open daily Memorial Day through Labor Day. If the kids get bored with all the shopping and cherry picking, you can let them loose here. There's mini-golf, pizza, and an indoor arcade for rainy days.

🖍 **Pirate's Cove Adventure Golf** (920-854-4929; piratescove.net), Sister Bay. Open 9:30 AM–10 PM daily in summer. This national mini-golf chain is popular for a reason: The well-groomed, pirate-themed grounds offers plenty of fun for the whole family.

Sievers School of Fiber Arts (920-847-2264; sieversschool.com), Jackson Harbor Road, Washington Island. Open June through October. This school offers classes in all kinds of fiber arts—weaving, basket making, quilting, knitting and more, and there's a women-only dormitory on the grounds if you're taking a longer class. The shop has all the tools and materials you'll need for classes or your own projects, plus a large selection of books, patterns, and specialty fabrics and yarns. You can also pick up original works—everything from quilts to Christmas cards—made by students, faculty, and alumni.

✷ Green Space

Potawatomi State Park (920-746-2890; www.dnr.state. wi.us/org/LAND/parks/specific/Potawatomi), 3740 County Road PD, Sturgeon Bay. On the shores of Sturgeon Bay, this state park has two campgrounds and almost 10 miles of groomed, but not paved, trails—perfect for hiking or skiing. A 75- foot observation tower provides views across the bay. A state park admission sticker is required for vehicles.

🖍 ♿ **Whitefish Dunes State Park** (920-823-2400; www.dnr.state.wi.us/Org/land/parks/specific/whitefish/), 3275 Clark Lake Road, Jacksonport. Open 8–8 daily. At

WOODED SECLUSION IN FISH CREEK.

its simplest, this is a great beach. But ecological and historical significance make it much more than that, and in fact the park is listed on the National Register of Historic Places. There is evidence of eight separate cultures having occupied this land; stop in the Nature Center for archeology exhibits and more information. Recreated village sites offer glimpses of these cultures, while special hikes provide an education about the wildlife and geology of the area. These are the best dunes you'll find on the west side of Lake Michigan, which is rare indeed. A state park admission sticker is required for vehicles.

Cave Point County Park (920-746-9959), 5360 Schauer Road, Jacksonport. Open 30 minutes before sunrise–11 PM daily. Right next to **Whitefish Dunes State Park**, magnificent limestone bluffs and caves carved out by Lake Michigan's waves provide an amazing view and the major draw to this park—but holy cow, hang on to your kids, because there's no guard rail or barrier of any sort at the edge of the cliffs. Of course, that just makes the view better. Adventurous types can climb down for a closer view, while others enjoy a picnic with a little distance. This is a beautiful park—don't miss it.

The Ridges Sanctuary (920-839-2802; ridgessanctuary.org), 8270 WI 52, Baileys Harbor. Open dawn–dusk daily. More than 1,600 acres of preserved land here began with an effort to sustain native wildflowers and other endangered plants. Due to the narrow paths and fragile plants, hiking trails are for feet only; no bikes, strollers, or snowmobiles allowed. Admission $4.

✍ ♿ **Peninsula State Park** (920-868-3258; www.dnr.state.wi.us/org/land/parks/specific/peninsula), 9462 Shore Road. This state park has *everything*. Considered the most complete park in the state system, it's not hard to figure out why. Pitch a tent at one of the 468 campsites here, and you might never want to leave. Sure, there's hiking, a swimming beach, boundless beauty, an observation tower—all the usual things you go to a state park to find, but there's also an 18-hole golf course with a restaurant, an outdoor theater where the American Folklore Theatre performs family-friendly productions throughout summer, Eagle Bluff Lighthouse, and a nature center. Clearly, this state park is for camping as well as day use. A state park vehicle sticker is required.

Door Bluff Headlands, 12900 Door Bluff Park Road, Gills Rock. Completely undeveloped, this county park at the tip of the peninsula offers no facilities, just a few nature trails and undisturbed beauty. A stark contrast to the shopping mania that goes on in the more popular tourist spots, and good for a breather.

Newport State Park (920-854-2500), 475 County Highway NP, Ellison Bay. This quiet park offers nature trails, meadows, and forests to explore, plus a handful of campsites and an interpretive center. Eleven miles of sandy, Lake Michigan shoreline make it a perfect quiet escape. A state Park admission sticker is required for vehicles.

On Washington Island

Schoolhouse Beach, Town Line Road. There's no schoolhouse here anymore, but the name remains. This beach is pretty, with a shady park for picnicking and great swimming. The most interesting part, though, is that it has not sand, but smooth limestone rocks. That makes walking to the water a little difficult, but it's also amazing. The smooth rocks are protected; you'll be fined if you try to take one home.

Sand Dunes Beach, South Shore Drive. Follow the sandy trail past trees to the beach, and you'll think you've found your own slice of heaven. For reasons unfathomable to me, this beach is unpopular with islanders and visitors. Better for you—you'll have this soft, sandy Lake Michigan beach, marked by dunes and cattails, all to yourself. Plan to relax.

Mountain Park. In the middle of the island is Mountain Park, whose main draw is its lookout tower. Climb 180-some steps to the top, and you'll have an unmatched view of farmland, forest, and the waters around the island.

✳ Lodging

In Sturgeon Bay

Y ✿ ♿ **Bridgeport Resort** (920-746-9919; bridgeportresort.net), 50 West Larch Street. Not the most unique in terms of atmosphere, but the Bridgeport offers a great waterfront location with a variety of full suite layouts to choose from, making it a perfect place to bring the kids. There's an outdoor pool as well as an indoor splash park for little ones, along with a collection of board games and an adjacent Applebee's. $70–300.

Y ♿ **Westwood Shores Waterfront Resort** (920-746-4057; westwood shores.net), 4303 Bay Shore Drive. Another resort that's perfect for families, Westwood Shores has an indoor and outdoor pools, sauna and whirlpool, and modern amenities such as WiFi. The full one- and two-bedroom suites have water views. $80–240.

The Black Walnut Guest House (920-743-8892; blackwalnut-gh.com), 454 North Seventh Avenue. Comfortable and unique without being frilly or overdone, the four guest rooms all have fireplaces, hot tubs, and WiFi, but each room has its own personality. Continental breakfast comes to your

IT'S EASY TO FIND LODGING IN DOOR COUNTY.

door in a basket as late as 10 AM. Travel Green Wisconsin Certified. $99–155.

♿ **Chanticleer Guest House** (920-746-0334; chanticleerguesthouse.com), 4072 Cherry Road. The perfect B&B for people who want something a little different, yet wholly Wisconsin, the Chanticleer is comprised of the guest house, a renovated barn, and four cabins on three acres of land just outside of town. There's no common area, and you won't be bothered by a fussy innkeeper; this is a place to relax and enjoy. The grounds double as a working sheep farm, and there's a heated pool to take a dip in during summer. $120–350.

♿ **Quiet Cottage Bed & Breakfast** (920-743-4526; quietcottage.com), 4608 Glidden Drive. You're the only guest at this cute little cottage, but that doesn't mean you'll be left to your own devices. Innkeeper Debby Sween is ready to help you plan your stay or set up an appointment with the massage therapist, and full breakfast is served up with a view of the lake. Throw in the private beach and cozy fireplace, and you're set to relax. Travel Green Wisconsin certified. $180–240.

♿ **Reynolds House** (920-746-9771), 111 South Seventh Avenue. This Queen Anne-style mansion built in 1900 is carefully maintained, and the B&B is a consistent winner of awards and accolades by visitors and national publications. With proper common areas and breakfast served in an actual dining room, the Reynolds House offers a true B&B experience. The four guest rooms are named after apples and are decorated in a tasteful Victorian fashion (that's to say, the wallpaper is flowered, but won't hurt your eyes). $100–170.

♿ **Scofield House** (920-743-7727; scofieldhouse.com), 908 Michigan Street. The six rooms in this huge Victorian are decorated in keeping with the era; it's another traditional B&B with spacious rooms and modern amenities, including WiFi. Full breakfast is served in the dining room. $80–220.

&. **Little Harbor Inn** (920-743-3789; littleharborinn.com), 5100 Bay Shore Drive. Perched on the shores of Green Bay, all eight rooms have water views. The decor skews more nautical than flowery, which makes it unique in these parts. Each room has a fireplace, and four have whirlpools. Full breakfast is delivered to your door. $95–175.

In Baileys Harbor

&. **Inn at Windmill Farm** (920-868-9282; 1900windmillfarm.com), 3829 Fairview Road. Some would call this the real Door County. Off the beaten path, away from the bauble-filled tourist shops and hullaballoo, the innkeepers personify Door County's mystique; Ed Fenendael is a working artist and Frank Villigan's work is in catering and antiques. Vacationing artists will find this a perfect place to restore and rustle up some inspiration. The four guest rooms are tastefully decorated, without frills, and a full breakfast is served in the common dining room. $110–125.

&. **Blacksmith Inn on the Shore** (920-839-9222; theblacksmithinn.com), 8152 WI 57. The 15 lakeside rooms offer cozy, warm decor and modern amenities (iPod hookups!) in a quiet Baileys Harbor setting. Breakfast is made from local foods and served buffet-style for you to enjoy with others or take back to your room. Travel Green Wisconsin certified. $135–265.

&. **Journey's End Motel and Cabins** (920-839-2887; journeysendmotel .com), 8271 Journeys End Lane. These cute, inexpensive rooms and cabins offer a fantastic deal on the peninsula. Cabins sleep eight and feature a loft, fireplace, and full kitchen. They've been designed with energy efficiency in mind, helping to earn Journey's End its Travel Green Wisconsin certification. Rooms $50–90, cabins $90–175.

In Egg Harbor

♪ &. **The Newport Resort** (920-868-9900; newportresort.com), 7888 Church Street. A great choice for families, the Newport offers one- and two-bedroom suites with full kitchens and fireplaces, along with two pools, a hot tub, and a kids' play area. It's not a resort in the sense that you'd spend all your time here, but it does offer some great extras, such as bike rentals and a DVD library. The staff is friendly and happy to help you choose a restaurant. Check at the shoulders of high season—the Newport offers great deals. $80–259.

&. **The Ashbrooke** (920-868-3113; ashbrooke.net), 7942 Egg Harbor Road. The Ashbrooke has all the amenities of a typical Door County resort, but with five different styles of rooms to choose from—the decor is really surprising. Continental breakfast is served in the lobby, and there's also a pool, free WiFi, and a DVD library. Travel Green Wisconsin certified. $114–229.

Door County Lighthouse Inn B&B (920-868-9088; dclighthouseinn.com), 4639 Orchard Road. Perfect for lighthouse enthusiasts, you can choose from a variety of lighthouse tour packages to round out your stay. No, you're not staying in an actual lighthouse, but the rooms are decorated in a tasteful, nautical fashion and you might get to chat about lighthouses with fellow guests over breakfast. The four rooms are cozy and have private baths; cabin rentals offer an option for families. Rooms $120–180, cabins $1,075–1,200 weekly.

&. **The Feathered Star B&B** (920-743-4066; www.featheredstar.com), 6202 WI 42. Aside from the appeal of a renovated farmhouse and the cozy, quilt-themed decor, the Feathered Star is a find for anyone who's had a tough time finding a welcoming B&B. That's to say, the property is extremely wheelchair-accessible and barrier-free, pet-friendly, and even kid-friendly. Continental breakfast is served in the dining room, and salt- or sugar-free diets will be accommodated. $120–140.

Y & **Shipwrecked Inn** (920-868-2767; shipwreckedmicrobrew.com), 7791 Egg Harbor Road. This is for those who absolutely do not want to get away from it all. Basic rooms are right on top of the Shipwrecked Brewpub and Restaurant, which means you can shop the nearby stores, drink down a Shipwrecked Peninsula Porter or Cherry Wheat Ale with dinner, and wander up to bed, all without using your car. Shipwrecked is the only brewery in Door County, so if you're a fan of beer, you could do a lot worse than this. $60–119.

& **The Alpine Resort** (888-281-8128; alpineresort.com), 7715 Alpine Road. The Alpine's got a long history in Door County and remains its largest resort. Generations of families return for nostalgia and the resort's charm; there are tons of amenities and activities such as tennis courts and a private beach, and the Alpine has somewhat retained its character over the years. The onsite restaurant, The Hof, features German favorites such as wiener schnitzel and sauerbraten. Choose from the inn, cottages, or housekeeping homes. Rooms, $78–129; cottages, $102–205; housekeeping homes, $854–1,529 weekly.

In Fish Creek

Thorp House Inn and Cottages (920-868-2444; thorphouseinn.com), 4135 Bluff Lane. The inn functions as a bed & breakfast, while the cottages offer more privacy but no breakfast (they do have full kitchens), and tend toward the rustic. The Emma room at the inn features a whirlpool and sky-

light, but otherwise the accommodations are simple and charming. Simple, meaning there's no TV or phone in your room, and the antique furnishings are cozy and romantic but not overdone. Couple this with the fact that you're right in the heart of Fish Creek, within walking distance of shopping and fish boils, and you're in for a treat. Rooms $95–195, cottages $645–895 weekly, beach house $745–1,295 weekly.

The Whistling Swan (888-277-4289; whistlingswan.com), 4192 Main Street. Cheery, warm, and unfussy, the Whistling Swan is Door County's oldest inn, moved to Fish Creek across the ice from Marinette in 1907. Seven rooms in varying sizes all feature private baths, some with claw-foot tubs, but the deluxe rooms and suites have separate seating areas, too. Continental breakfast gets you going in the morning. Rooms $140–210.

& **The White Gull Inn** (920-868-3517; whitegullinn.com), 4225 Main Street. With 17 rooms, suites, and cottages to choose from, this darling, historic inn offers a great location near the action in Fish Creek. Breakfast in the restaurant is included, but you should stick around for dinner, too—one of Door County's favorite fish boils is here every weekend, and sometimes there's music, too. Rooms $155–220, suites $230–295, cottages $340–455.

& **Little Sweden** (920-868-9950; little -sweden.com), 8984 WI 42. Wherever you're staying in Door County, it's hard to drive past Little Sweden on WI 42 without feeling a pang of jealousy. The red peak of the clock tower and the rolling hills around the resort simply beckon you from the highway. It's a golf resort, but there's plenty for the non-golfer, too, both summer and winter. The two- and three-bedroom rentals have lots of room to move around in; if you're looking for a step

LITTLE SWEDEN

up from the run-of-the-mill hotels and resorts, this is the place to bring the family. Travel Green Wisconsin certified. $165–285.

Main Street Motel (920- 868-2201; mainstreetmoteldc.com), 4209 Main Street. As the name suggests, this motel is right on Main Street; in fact, it's in Founder's Square. It's the perfect place for anyone who wants cozy, simple accommodations without all the bells and whistles. After all—you're in Door County, why hole up in a resort? There's so much to do within walking distance, and you'll find the Main Street Motel the perfect place to retire at the end of the day. The decor is country, with patchwork quilts, and some rooms are themed—if you like teddy bears, there's a room for you, but you don't have to sleep with lovies if you don't want to. This is a great, affordable option for singles and couples who intend to spend more time exploring the Door than sitting in a hotel. $52–105.

✄ ♿ **Julie's Park Cafe and Motel** (920-868-2999; juliesmotel.com), 4020 WI 42. Just north of the hubbub of Main Street, and right at the entrance of Peninsula State Park, Julie's is charming and casual. An affordable option for families on the go, you can't go wrong with these clean, basic rooms. The adjacent restaurant offers something for everyone—see listing under Eating Out. $49–79.

The Hilltop Inn (920-868-3556; hill topinndc.com), 3908 County Road F. Just off WI 42, this inn is right near the action but secluded at the same time. Rooms include full kitchens, but with all the shops and dining right nearby, you might not need a stove. One- and two-bedroom suites mean plenty of room to relax after a day of exploring, or take a dip in the outdoor pool. Suites $199–209.

In Ephraim
French Country Inn (920-854-4001), 3052 Spruce Lane. A private residence from 1911 until 1984, this charming

inn still has a homey atmosphere. Cozy rooms and quiet are the draws here; there are no televisions, but there is a library if you need to kill some time. Usually, that's not a problem in Door County. A breakfast made of local and organic ingredients is served in the morning, and if there's a chill in the air, you can snuggle up by the large, stone fireplace. Minimum stays are required. $72–99.

Eagle Harbor Inn (920-854-2121; eagleharbor.com), 9914 Water Street. Near Ephraim's shopping district and Eagle Harbor, this nine-room inn offers cozy accommodations, an extended continental breakfast, and a serious bonus for a historic inn: a pool and spa. Houses on the property feature larger suites, and while breakfast is not included with those, you can purchase it for delivery. Travel Green Wisconsin certified. Rooms $98–205, suites $139–269.

Lodgings at Pioneer Lane (920-854-7656; lodgingsatpioneerlane.com), 9998 Pioneer Lane. Around the corner from **Wilson's Ice Cream Parlor**, this renovated historic building has charm to spare. Rooms are warm and tastefully decorated, each with its own style. Travel Green Wisconsin certified. $149–179.

In Sister Bay

Church Hill Inn (920-854-4885; churchhillinn.com), 2393 Gateway Drive. At this English-themed inn near shops and restaurants in Sister Bay, you can choose among 34 rooms, ranging from simple one-bed digs to huge suites with fireplaces and whirlpools. An honor bar in the style of an English pub and outdoor gardens and pool seal the deal. Buffet breakfast is served in the dining room. Rooms and suites $104–170.

Inn On Maple (920-854-5107; innonmaple.com), 2378 Maple Drive. Locat-ed in downtown Sister Bay, this 1902 building was originally a meat market on the first floor and a residence on the second. Today, a gift shop and the Gathering Room occupy the first level, and all the sleeping rooms are upstairs. While the inn retains its historic charm, updates have been made, such as the addition of private bathrooms. Rooms $85–120.

Woodenheart Inn (920-854-9097; woodenheart.com), 11086 Hgwy. 42. Choose one of five downright adorable rooms—one has a Door County cherry theme, another is decked out in apples—at this log home in the woods. Mornings get you a full breakfast. Rooms $95–134.

The Brodd's Little Cottage (920-854-2478; thelittlecottage.com), 2182 Seaquist Road. Open June through October. This one-bedroom cottage at the edge of a cherry orchard has 1930s charm and all the peace and relaxation you could want. The full kitchen means you can settle in here for a while to take advantage of the surroundings away from all the usual tourist hustle and bustle. It's a perfect getaway. $80 per night, $525 per week. Travel Green Wisconsin certified.

Little Sister Resort (920-854-4013; littlesisterresort.com), 10620 Little Sister Road. Open May through October. This secluded, family resort has amenities for everyone: swimming, kayak rental, a playground, dining. You can choose from a number of cozy cottages and chalets sprinkled around the resort. $57–92 per adult.

Birchwood Lodge (920-854-7195; birchwoodlodge.com), 337 WI 57. Unfussy and roomy, you get all the features of home with modern, full kitchens and more, plus a spa, sauna, pool, and bike rentals. The atmosphere is country, both inside and out (the building looks like a row of barns!), but it's not over the top. Travel Green Wisconsin certified. Lodge suites $145–245, farmhouse suites $264–356.

In Ellison Bay
Parkside Inn (920-854-9050; thepark sideinn.com), 11946 WI 42. Open April through November. If you'd like to spend a little less money than Door County usually requires, this is the place. While the room decor is a little generic, it's clean and comfy, and the grounds are attractive and well-maintained. Rooms $79–95.

On Washington Island
The Washington Hotel (920-847-2169; thewashingtonhotel.com), 354 Range Line Road. The culinary school and restaurant get all the attention, but the charming rooms above the dining area are a treat. These are simple accommodations—beds dressed with handmade quilts and organic linens and little more—you'll feel like you've traveled back in time. Originally meant to house ship captains while on the island, the hotel has been accurately restored. Nine rooms share two bathrooms, but those bathrooms, outfitted with steam showers, are so nice you won't mind. Travel Green Wisconsin certified. Rooms $119–280.

Shellswick's Cottages (920-847-2368), 581 Silver Birch Lane. Open summers. Islanders themselves, the Shellswicks offer two simple, charming waterfront cottages on Detroit. Spring Beach Cottage sleeps six and has everything you'll need for an extended stay, plus a great beachfront yard. Auntie Rose's cottage has been in the family since it was built in the early 1900s. This charming vacation home has two bedrooms and modern amenities, plus a fireplace for chilly nights. You couldn't ask for friendlier hosts than Betty and Leon Shellswick, and they know *everything* about the island.

Findlay's Holiday Inn (800-522-5469; holidayinn.net), 1 Main Road. This is not a Holiday Inn of global chain fame. Like everything on the island, it's a small operation—a mom and pop—and with that comes unique, low-tech charm. Accommodations here range from rustic to modern Scandinavian, but in all cases are simple and pleasant. $95–135.

Bread and Water (920-847-2400; breadandwater.us), 1275 Main Road. Travel Green Wisconsin certified. These cozy rooms adjacent to the cafe, with handmade quilts on the double beds, are perfect for a night before exploring. Grab breakfast in the cafe before you head out. Rooms $80–95.

Sunset Resort (920-847-2531; sunset resortwi.com), Old West Harbor Road. With a dozen simple guest rooms overlooking Green Bay, plus the serenity of the surrounding forestland, this resort takes advantage of Washington Island's quiet charm. Order Icelandic pancakes for breakfast in the dining room. Rooms $94–112.

Frog Hollow Farm (920-847-2835; froghollowfarm.com), N17 W1029 Jackson Harbor Road. Open summers. Located near Seivers School of Fiber Arts, Frog Hollow Farm is a B&B with options. The rooms are decorated simply and tastefully, and each offers something different. The Summer Parlor has a private entrance, canopy bed, and extra daybed for a guest or kid, and the Master suite also features extra sleeping space—rare among B&Bs. If you need a little more space, there's also a cabin to rent that sleeps six. Rooms $80–95, cabin $1,000 per week.

✳ Where to Eat

Dining in Door County once meant, primarily, traditional Wisconsin supper clubs and fish boils, and little more. These days, however, the variety in

THE WASHINGTON HOTEL ON WASHINGTON ISLAND

cuisines and price range is increasing; while it's still not a challenge to find meat and potatoes, more alternatives now exist, and the trend seems to be growing. You can now find everything from vegan dishes and veggie burgers to Mexican and Italian cuisine, plus all those fish boils and steak joints.

DINING OUT

In Sturgeon Bay

Y & **Trattoria dal Santo** (920-743-6100; trattoriadalsanto.com), 147 North Third Avenue. Open daily for dinner. Offering northern Italian dishes in a classy yet casual setting, dal Santo's menu isn't huge, but it is complete, with just the right range of options to satisfy picky groups. Seafood features prominently, but classics such as fettuccine Alfredo and lasagna do justice to the trattoria label. The wine bar offers a remarkable selection of vintages to pair with your meal, or simply enjoy. $10–20.

Y & **Sage Restaurant and Wine Bar** (920-746-1100; sagedoorcounty.com),

136 North Third Avenue. Open daily for dinner from Memorial Day to Labor Day; dinner Tuesday through Saturday the rest of the year. Another rare option for contemporary American cuisine, Sage offers everything from filet mignon to goat cheese and tomato ravioli. The interior looks a little like a Japanese restaurant, which is unusual for Door County to be sure. Live music on weekends. Entrees $18–38.

Y & **Nightingale Supper Club** (920-743-5593), 1541 Egg Harbor Road. Open for dinner Monday through Saturday. Like any proper Midwestern supper club, Nightingale offers a full array of meats and fish, including a Friday night fish fry, but this one includes a bar that makes ice cream drinks. A Grasshopper is just the thing to complete the experience! $10–20.

Y **The Mill** (920-743-5044), 4128 WI 42. Open for dinner Tuesday through Sunday from May to November, Wednesday through Sunday in winter. The Mill fits the bill for anyone searching for an old-school Wisconsin supper club, but with the obligatory Door County fish boil. Yes, the menu is heavy on seafood and steaks, but there's also a selection of pasta dishes and a kid's menu. Sundays bring chicken dinners, complete with all the fixins from mashed potatoes to coleslaw, and everything in between. $10–20.

In Baileys Harbor
Y Harbor Fish Market and Grill (920-839-9999; harborfishmarket -grille.com), 8080 WI 57. Open daily for all three meals. This restaurant is housed in a charming historic building with a casual upscale atmosphere. There are white tablecloths, yes, and the dinner menu has a finer dining edge to it (mainly seafood), but breakfast and lunch are right in line with everything else on the peninsula. In fact, breakfast and lunch offer so many options (from lox to quiche with plain ol' sandwiches and eggs), you'll have a tough time choosing which meal to have here. Breakfast $4.95–9.95, lunch $5.95–$10.95, dinner $18.95–$45.00.

In Egg Harbor
Y & Trio (920-868-2090), 4655 County Road E. Open daily for dinner. Closed winter. Trio is a great break from the steakhouses and supper clubs so common in these parts. Offering Italian dishes and French bistro fare in an upscale, contemporary setting, Trio makes a great choice for a low-key yet stellar meal. Dishes 12.95–19.95.

In Fish Creek
Y Mr. Helsinki (920-868-9898; mrhel sinki.com), 4164 Main Street. Open for dinner daily. Located on the main drag upstairs from Fish Creek Market (see listing under Selective Shopping), Mr. Helsinki's creative menu and contemporary atmosphere holds its own against the classic northern Wisconsin meat-and-potatoes joints. Try the fondue or dinner crepes, although if you

must, there are burgers here, as well. Dishes $9.95–14.95.

Y & Villaggio's (920-868-4646; villag gios-doorcounty.com), 4240 Juddville Road. Open daily for dinner. Villaggio's offers the homespun charm of its sister restaurant, **The Village Cafe**, as well at its high quality and satisfying portions. It's a little more upscale; you can get wine here, but it's casual enough for a relaxed dinner. Italian dishes such as pollo parmigiana and fettucini Alfredo rule the menu. Pick up a jar of Villagio's own marinara sauce, which is sold around town. Entrees $16–24.

Y & Whistling Swan (920-868-3442; whistlingswan.com), 4192 Main Street. Open daily for dinner. Offering contemporary fare with a French bent, this is the perfect place for white-tablecloth dining that's still casual enough for vacation. Dishes feature local foods and the menu goes well beyond the usual "up north" fare, but the options, such as angus beef rib eye and pancetta chicken breast, will satisfy. Entrees $23–35.

Y & C & C Supper Club (920-868-3412; ccsupperclub.com), 4170 Main Street. Open daily for dinner. This is a quintessential Wisconsin supper club, right down to the wood paneling, although the requisite salad bar is gone; it's among a dying breed. The menu is almost entirely steak and seafood, as is usual for a supper club, but also has a variety of salads and a huge appetizer menu. There's live music Friday and Saturday nights. Entrees $13.95–34.95.

In Sister Bay
Y Pasta Vino (920-854-7050), 10571 Country Walk Lane. Open daily for dinner. Charming and hidden, the way a lot of things are in Door County, Pasta Vino offers affordable Italian cuisine and a huge selection of wines in a casual setting. Dishes $10–20.

Waterfront (920-854-5491; jjs
waterfront.com), 10961 Bayshore
Drive. Open daily for dinner. Featuring homemade pasta and a seasonally
changing menu, Waterfront offers
more than just a great view at dinner.
One of only a handful of restaurants in
the area with a bent toward contemporary American cuisine, you'll find rib
eye on the menu, but also a willingness
to prepare vegetarian and vegan dishes. Dishes $25–38.

The Inn at Kristofer's (920-854-
9419; innatkristofers.com) 734
Bayshore Drive. Offering more spectacular water views in an elegant, stylish setting, Kristofer's is among the
more popular restaurants in Door
County, winning praise from local and
national media. It's contemporary cuisine that doesn't alienate the meat-
and-potatoes crowd, offering creatively
prepared meat and seafood options,
plus at least one vegetarian dish nightly. $25–36.

Sister Bay Bowl (920-854-
2841; sisterbaybowl.com), 10640 North
Bay Shore Drive. Open for dinner
daily, lunch Monday through Saturday.
A retro supper club that's been in the
family since supper clubs were a fresh
idea, this one serves up all the classics,
including big steaks, lots of seafood,
and even a kid's menu. Lunch (unusual
for a *supper* club) offers reasonably
priced sandwiches and specials. Lunch
$5–10, dinner $10–20.

In Ellison Bay

T. Ashwell's Fine Dining (920-
854-4306; www.tashwells.com), 11976
Mink River Road. Open nightly for
dinner, closed Tuesdays. Unusual
among Door County's finer dining, the
menu features organic and local foods,
a vegetarian tasting plate, and the
option to call ahead for dishes that
cater to special dietary needs. That
doesn't mean meat-and-potatoes diners

are left out, just that their pickier com-
panions can join them for a change.
Thursdays offer small-plate dining.
The menu is always changing, so check
ahead. Entrees $28–44.

EATING OUT

In Sturgeon Bay

Cafe Launch (920-746-8000), 306
South Third Avenue. Open daily for all
three meals. A storefront cafe in downtown Sturgeon Bay, Cafe Launch
offers a changing, but sizable, menu
with lots of sandwiches and tapas for
evenings. No espresso, but it offers
beer and a well-rounded wine selection. Dishes $5–8.

Blue Front Cafe (920-743-9218), 86
West Maple Street. Open for lunch and
dinner Tuesday through Saturday, Sunday for brunch. Focusing on seasonal
ingredients and whole foods, this cafe is
popular with locals and travelers alike.
Fish tacos are a hit, as is Sunday brunch,
and vegetarians will find plenty to eat
here. Service isn't speedy, but you're on
vacation, right? Entrees $10–20.

Door County Coffee and Tea
(920-743-8930), 5773 WI 42,
Carlsville. Door County Coffee's ubiquitous little golden packets of pre-
ground flavored beans make it easy to
forget there's an actual coffee shop and
roaster in Door County. There's a real
coffee shop here, and it serves homemade cheesecake as well. Less than $5.

In Baileys Harbor

Yum Yum Tree (920-839-2993),
8054 WI 57. Open daily for lunch and
dinner, May to October. It wouldn't be
a trip to Door County with an indulgent afternoon on a sugar high. The
Yum Yum Tree has your bases covered,
with ice cream and old-fashioned
candy-store goodies. Less than $5.

Espresso Lane Coffee Cafe (920-
839-2647), 8037 WI 57. Open daily for

breakfast and lunch. A charming coffee shop that offers everything from Belgian waffles to burgers, you can head off your latte withdrawal here. Less than $5.

Sandpiper Restaurant (920-839-2528; sandpiperfishboil.com), 8177 WI 57. Open daily for breakfast and lunch, Monday through Saturday for evening fish boil. Famous for its fish boil, the Sandpiper is also a popular breakfast spot because of its generous portions and a menu that reads like a greatest hits of classic American breakfast. $10–20

In Egg Harbor

☙ ♿ **The Village Cafe** (920-868-3342; villagecafe-doorcounty.com), 7918 WI 42. Open daily for breakfast and lunch. Closed in winter. The Village Cafe is a great place to take the family, picky eaters, or anyone looking for something a little different. Vegetarians will find three different veggie burgers here, but carnivores should try the creative sandwiches such as the Cherry Jack Wrap, a turkey sandwich loaded with Door County cherries and jack cheese. I've been known to eat here twice in one day. The interior is chock full of arts and crafts, all for sale. Take home a pie if you don't have room for dessert. Dishes $6.25–7.95.

♿ **The Bridge** (920-868-3221; the bridgedoorcounty.com), 7881 WI 42. Open daily for breakfast and lunch. Closed winter. The Bridge has a small sandwich menu and some odds and ends like granola and soup, but it's a well-rounded menu, and vegetarians will find plenty here. After lunch, check out the used books or art for sale. Travel Green Wisconsin certified. Sandwiches $6.95.

♿ **Door County Outpost Gallery and Cafe** (920-868-4321; doorcounty outpost.com), 4690 Rainbow Ridge Court. Open daily for breakfast and

lunch. Right in the middle of everything from shopping for natural goods to booking kayak tours, the Outpost Cafe offers simple breakfast and lunch, espresso drinks, and craft beer in an artsy setting, which I know is what I'm looking for when I'm here. Dishes $5–10.

♈ **Shipwrecked Brewpub** (920-868-2767; shipwreckedmicrobrew.com), 7791 Egg Harbor Road. Open daily for lunch and dinner. As you might expect, you'll find pub grub and seafood here—hardly a rare find in Door County, but here's the thing: Shipwrecked is the only brewery in Door County, so beer fans take note. Shipwrecked is also said to have ghosts—not one, but many. Watch out especially for Verna Moore; she's not scary, but her appearance predicts a mishap (hopefully not with your lunch!). Entrees $12.95–19.95.

Cupola Cafe (920-868-2354), 7836 WI 42. Open for breakfast and lunch daily May through October. This cute deli is perfect for a quick, inexpensive meal or snack—you can get sandwiches made to order here, or grab an ice-cream treat. Dishes less than $10.

In Fish Creek

Julie's Park Cafe (920-868-2999; juliesmotel.com), 4020 WI 42. Open daily for all three meals. Remarkably kid-friendly, the staff at Julie's won't bat an eye when you come in with a handful of hungry little ones. That's not to scare other diners—if they can, they seat families in their own little cove, away from the folks who don't think your kids are as cute as you do. What's more, Julie's has an enormous menu, with everything from seafood and meatloaf to vegan entrees (which are designated as such on the menu). Top it off with beer, wine, and espresso, and you really couldn't ask for more. Dishes $6.25–14.95.

DOOR COUNTY FISH BOIL

After cherries, the fish boil is Door County's most celebrated food. Begun as a cheap way to feed large numbers of lumberjacks who once populated the peninsula, if you visit Door County, you have to at least *watch* a fish boil, even if you're not interested in eating fish. It's almost more about the theatrics than the food. Spectators gather around a fire pit outside of a restaurant and watch as a boil master prepares your meal: stoking the flames, controlling the temperature by placing and removing boards around the pit, and telling decidedly corny jokes while explaining the process. The excitement comes when the "boilover" happens—the oils from the fish hit the fire and a spectacular flame shoots up, so get your camera ready. Once that's done, it's time to eat. The meal usually consists of locally caught whitefish boiled with potatoes, capped off with cherry pie, of course.

A FISH BOIL BOILS OVER

Blue Horse Bistro and Espresso (920-868-1471; bluehorsebistro.com), 4158 Main Street. Open daily for breakfast and lunch. Not exactly a bistro, Blue Horse is really a coffee shop, and it's my favorite place to get a jolt on the peninsula. The sandwich menu is short and sweet, with something for everyone, and the espresso drinks are made well. Check out the books for sale upstairs, or sit out on the deck—you can either gaze at the water or watch the hubbub on Main Street. Sandwiches $5–10.

Y & **Sonny's Pizzeria Bar and Grill** (920-868-1900; sonnyspizzeria.com), 3931 WI 42. A family friendly pizzeria by day, live music venue by night. Come here for pizza, chicken, or burgers, and wash it down with a beer—they've got more than 50 options. Then, follow dinner with dancing; reggae is popular here. $7–15.

♈ ♿ **Pelletier's** (920-868-3313; door countyfishboil.com), 4199 Main Street. Open for all three meals daily. Pelletier's, located in Founder's Square, might be Door County's most famous fish boil spot. And because of that, you might think it's all they do, but they actually have breakfast and lunch, too, and dinner (which includes a beverage and a slice of cherry pie) doesn't have to include whitefish. But the main draw is the fish boil, to be sure. Pelletier's puts on quite a show, and you'll be good and hungry after standing around waiting for the dramatic boil over. Entrees $10–15.

In Ephraim

♿ **Summer Kitchen** (920-854-2131), 10425 Water Street (WI 42). Open for all three meals in summer, hours and days vary in winter. Summer Kitchen is cute, with screened-in patios and indoor seating. There's a full menu, but you really should check out the soup bar, which features five soups and an array of breads daily. Dishes $7–15.

♿ **Chef's Hat Cafe** (920-854-2034), 3063 Church Street. Open daily for all three meals. Right in the historic downtown, you've got a great view of Eagle Harbor and the nearby shops. Chef's Hat is a charming and cozy cafe offering a creative and healthy menu and huge portions. Try the pear gorgonzola turkey wrap or the quesadilla with wild rice. You won't leave hungry. Dishes $7–15.

Wilson's (920-854-2041; wilsonsicecream.com), 9990 Water Street (WI 42). Open daily for lunch and dinner from May through October. No visit to Door County is complete without an ice-cream cone steeped in nostalgia. Wilson's has been here since 1906, and its real-deal retro appeal is hard to ignore. You can't miss it as you head north along WI 42; you'll nearly drive into it, it sits that close to the road. But the red-and-white-striped awnings ensure that you'll see it long before you're upon it. Everyone comes here for ice cream, but Wilson's has burgers and sandwiches, too. Burgers $5.25–7.75.

Old Post Office Restaurant (920-854-4034; oldpostoffice-doorcounty

C & C SUPPER CLUB

GOATS ON THE ROOF AT AL JOHNSON'S

.com), 10040 Water Street (WI 42). Open daily for breakfast, Monday through Saturday for evening fish boil. Right in the heart of Ephraim, along WI 42, the Old Post Office is housed in, yes, an early 1900s post office. Breakfast choices are outstanding, ranging from simple egg dishes to vanilla yogurt with granola and Door County cherries. Evening fish boils include all the proper theatrics, along with a boil master who makes fish jokes while you wait. Breakfast $3.75–8.25.

Good Eggs (920-854-6621), 9820 Brookside Lane. Open daily for breakfast. Here's a cheery breakfast place with a beachside theme befitting its location. The specialty is the breakfast wraps, tortillas stuffed with eggs, potatoes, veggies, and more, but Good Eggs also whips up great smoothies. Less than $10.

In Sister Bay
Al Johnson's (920-854-2626; aljohnsons.com), 10698 North Bay Shore Drive. Open daily for all three meals. Al Johnson's has Swedish pancakes with lingonberries and goats on the roof, which is enough for me. If you need more incentive, though, there's a full menu of sandwiches and entrees, both Swedish and American, and tons of breakfast options. Be sure to browse the gift shop before you leave. Sandwiches $6.75–8.95, entrees $10.95–19.50.

DC Deli (920-854-4514), 531 Bayshore Drive. Open daily for lunch and dinner from May to October. With more of a cafe feel to it than the name might suggest, Door County Deli offers up a limited but pleasing selection of soups and sandwiches, plus beer and wine. The prices are reasonable and there's plenty of patio seating for dining alfresco. Sandwiches $6.50–11.50.

Door County Ice Cream Factory & Sandwich Shoppe (920-854-9693; doorcountyicecream.com), 11051 WI 42. Open daily for lunch and dinner,

May through January. Here's a great, less-crowded alternative to Wilson's. The building has a long, if interrupted, history as a place for food and ice-cream treats, and today stands out as a great Door County stop. A wide range of sandwiches, including everything from a vegetarian to a Dagwood, plus pizza, soups, and more, make it a perfect lunch spot, but what you really want here is the ice cream. Sandwiches $6.99–8.99.

In Ellison Bay
Northport Pier Restaurant and Landing (920-854-9911), 215 WI 42. Open for all three meals daily in summer. Located at the car ferry dock at the tip of the peninsula, this restaurant is your last stop before you make the half-hour boat ride to Washington Island (or, conversely, your first stop once you get back). The menu is small, focused on breakfast, sandwiches, and seafood, plus a load of munchies, but the location is perfect if you're headed off shore. Breakfast and lunch less than $10, dinner $8–18.

DINING OUT

On Washington Island
Ⴘ **The Washington Hotel, Restaurant, and Culinary School** (414-847-2169; thewashingtonhotel.com), 354 Range Line Road. Located in a historic hotel that dates back to 1904, the Washington Hotel was restored to its original splendor in 2001. This is certainly the finest and most contemporary dining on the island, focused heavily on local and organic ingredients. Chef and owner Leah Caplan serves up a six-course menu from June through October. Dishes $5–30.

EATING OUT Ⴘ **Karly's Bar and Cellar Restaurant** (920-847-2655), Main Road. Open daily for lunch and dinner, closed winter. The Cellar Restaurant is in the basement of a bar, as you might expect from the name, but what it loses in ambiance is quickly made up for with friendly service and quality food. There's a regular menu, but specials feature local foods, such as pasta in morel sauce, that you just won't get every day or many other places. Though not a supper club, Karly's brings a proper relish tray with carrots, olives, and radishes before your meal—a nice welcoming touch that's at once classy and Northwoodsy. Dishes $10–20.

Findlay's Holiday Inn (800-522-5469; holidayinn.net), 1 Main Road. Open for breakfast and dinner daily. Breakfast is popular with both travelers and islanders (with homemade breads and jams, that's a given), and dinners feature all-you-can-eat fresh-caught whitefish twice weekly.

Ⴘ & **Ship's Wheel Restaurant** (920-847-2640; kapsmarina.com), at Kap's Marina, 234 Lobdell Point Road. Open daily for all three meals, closed in winter. There's a pleasing, breezy, tropical feel to this place that must be some feat to pull off. Offering tempting breakfast items such as Danish pancakes, skillets, and egg dishes, burgers (including veggie burgers), and an ostrich sandwich for lunch, and plenty of steaks and seafood for dinner, Ship's Wheel should please any hungry group just arriving on the island or awaiting a ferry. Chat with the owner or read from the trivia questions supplied to each table; whatever you do, you won't forget you're on an island. Entrees $10–20.

Red Cup Coffee House (920-847-3304), 1885 Detroit Harbor Road. A classic coffeehouse, with a more modern feel than perhaps anything else on the island. Strong coffee and a relaxed atmosphere allow you to chill for a bit. Browse Islandtime Books (see listing

BOILED LAWYERS

A sign on the window at **KK Fiske Restaurant** on Washington Island boasts "Fresh Lawyers," an advertisement that might seem at once odd and amusing to visitors. It doesn't take long to figure out that "lawyer" is the local name for a type of fish, and it's served up fresh daily here. The lawyer's proper name is burbot, and it's a fish that's found in northern lakes and streams. Because it doesn't hold up well to freezing, lawyers need to be cooked up right away after they're caught, making this a rare treat for seafood fans, and a reason to visit the island right there. It's an ugly fish, related to cod, and is often called "poor man's lobster" because of its flavor. Word on the island has it that the lawyer got its name because its fishy heart is located in its rear. That's what they say, not me!

You can get fresh lawyers at KK Fiske Restaurant & The Granary (920-847-2121), 1177 Main Road, Washington Island. Open daily for all three meals. KK Fiske is charming, rustic, and eclectic, but the best thing about the place is that owner Ken Koyen goes out daily and catches the fish he serves. And it's the island's only year-round restaurant serving all three meals.

K. K. FISKE RESTAURANT ON WASHINGTON ISLAND

under Selective Shopping) next door if you forgot some reading material.

Bread and Water (920-847-2400; breadandwater.us), 1275 Main Road. Light breakfast options and fresh baked goods make this cute, casual cafe a good bet. It's not the full breakfast or Icelandic pancake plate you'll get at other places in town, but it's quick and relaxed. Travel Green Wisconsin certified. Dishes less than $10.

✳ Entertainment

While Door County isn't exactly filled with a booming night scene—some areas roll up the sidewalks surprisingly early, and Ephraim is actually a dry town—there are plenty of bars where you can grab a pint, catch a play or live music, or take part in family friendly events.

Third Avenue Playhouse (920-743-1760; thirdavenueplayhouse.com), 239 North Third Avenue, Sturgeon Bay. Providing entertainment year-round, this performing arts center stages theatrical and musical productions, including childrens shows, in downtown Sturgeon Bay.

Door Shakespeare (920-839-2216; doorshakespeare.com), 7603 Chapel Lane, Baileys Harbor.

Begun as a spin-off of the popular American Folklore Theatre, Door Shakespeare stages a play or two each summer in the garden at Lawrence University's Bjorklunden Lodge.

Birch Creek Music Center (920-868-3763;), 3821 County Highway E, Egg Harbor. Open June through August. This summer music academy for teens puts on 32 concerts every summer, ranging from symphony to jazz. Performances take place in the Dutton Concert Barn.

American Folklore Theatre (920-854-6117; folkloretheatre.com), 10169

Shore Road, Fish Creek. Performing at the amphitheatre in **Peninsula State Park**, the American Folklore Theatre is a popular theater company that stages several musical comedies each summer. As summer winds down, performance are held at the Historic Ephraim Village Hall.

Peninsula Players (920-868-3287; peninsulaplayers.com), W4351 Peninsula Players Road, Fish Creek. Performances take place in the company's covered outdoor theater surrounded by cedar forest. The professional company stages five plays each summer, wrapping things up in October.

Door County Auditorium (920- 868-2728; dcauditorium.org), 3926 WI 42, Fish Creek. Bringing in local and national acts, this 750-seat auditorium hosts musicians and other performers throughout the year.

Island Players (920- 847-2689). This nonprofit community theater on Washington Island stages productions year-round at the Washington Island Recreation Center and other spots around the island. The state's smallest theater group, it sponsors other theatrical activities as well.

Skyway Drive-In Theatre (920-854-9938; doorcountydrivein.com), 3475 Highway 42, Fish Creek. Continuously running since 1950, if you grab a parking spot up front, you can use the speakers provided, otherwise go modern and tune in on your radio. There are fewer than 10 drive-ins left in the state—enjoy this one while you can.

Hands-On Art Studio (920-868-9331; handsonartstudio.com), 3655 Peninsula Players Road, Fish Creek. Open 10–6 daily, May through October; 10–5 Friday through Sunday, November through April. Known affectionately by many as the "Art Barn," because the original studio is in, well, a big, old, barn, this is the place for adults and kids to create art in all kinds of media. Friday nights, the studio is open 6:30 PM–10 PM for artists and would-be artists 21 and older, and there's food and drink.

Fred and Fuzzy's Waterfront Grill (920-854-6699), 10620 Little Sister Road, Sister Bay. Part of the Little Sister Resort, Fred and Fuzzy's is a popular, casual eatery with fantastic views and a relaxed atmosphere. Tuesday evenings feature live music.

   Sonny's Pizzeria Bar and Grill (920-868-1900; sonnyspizzeria.com), 3931 WI 42, Fish Creek. Among the few spots for dancing in Door County, you can grab pizza and beer here, too. $7–15.

Bayside Tavern (920-868-3441), 4160 Main Street, Fish Creek. Your best bet for a little nightlife, that being a few drinks and some live music.

✳ Selective Shopping

   The Flying Pig (920-487-9902; theflyingpig.biz), N6975 WI 42, Algoma. Open 9–6 daily May through October, 10–5 Friday through Monday, November through April. The Flying Pig is a little bit of everything—an edgy contemporary art gallery, coffee shop, gift shop, and garden center. If the giant flying pig on top of the building doesn't make you slam on your breaks as you travel WI 42, the outdoor garden displays will. If you travel through Algoma on your way to the peninsula (and I recommend that you do take this route), this is a perfect appetizer for your Door County shopping.

   Renard's Cheese (920-746-6626), 248 County Highway S, Algoma. Open Monday through Saturday. A family run cheese factory, this is a great place to stop for excellent cheese curds (yes, they squeak!), aged cheddar, and other dairyland goodies.

THERE ARE INTERESTING FINDS SHOPPING IN DOOR COUNTY.

In Sturgeon Bay

Small World Market (920-746-8820), 139 North Third Avenue. This little downtown shop focuses on fair trade and organic goods, from toys to tea. Green as can be, you'll feel good about shopping here.

& **Barn Door Quilts** (920-746-1544; barndoorquilts.com), 154 North Third Avenue. Open daily. Offering a huge selection of quilt fabrics, along with expertise and locally handmade quilts for sale, this place is a great stop for a hard-to-find or unique fabric.

Spin (920-746-7746), 108 South Madison Avenue. Open Monday through Saturday. Housed in a historic bank building, Spin is packed with all sorts of specialty yarns and books on needle arts. It will surely get your creative juices spinning.

In Baileys Harbor

Novel Ideas (920-839-1300; novel ideas-books.com), 8085 WI 57. Open daily in summer, Monday through Saturday in winter. This independent bookstore offers books for kids and grown-ups alike, plus novelty items and toys.

In Egg Harbor

Greens and Grains (920-868-9999), 7821 WI 42. Open 10–5 daily. This small but complete natural-foods store has everything a health conscious diner or vegetarian could want. Whether you're cooking a meal in your hotel or grabbing a snack before you go for a bike ride, this store is your best bet.

Made in Britain (920-868-1933; madeinbritainltd.com), 7828 WI 42. Open daily May through December, weekends January through April. Located in the Main Street Shops, a little mall on the east side of the highway, this store stocks all sorts of unique items imported from Britain. From London Underground signs to ales and

biscuits, the items are authentic and fun. The store has a huge selection of fruit curds, or butters, and you can sample them to your heart's content.

Maxwell's House (920-868-2989; maxwellshousedc.com), 7763 WI 42. Open daily in summer. A boutique on the main drag offering contemporary, stylish home goods and furnishings, it's fun to browse (and more fun to buy). Natural fiber rugs in trendy designs, and lots of eco-friendly choices, make this a great stop.

Door County Outpost Gallery and Cafe (920-868-4321; doorcountyout post.com), 4690 Rainbow Ridge Court. Open daily. Attached to a small eatery and coffee bar, the gallery here boasts paintings, pottery, jewelry and more.

Dovetail Gallery and Studio (920-868-3987; dovetailgallery.com), 7901 WI 42. Open Thursday through Friday. This gallery, appropriately enough, features egg art made by owner and artist Kathleen Beck. Beck also collects and display egg art from around the world, including a Fabergé Easter egg, plus an authenticated dinosaur egg, in the Egg Museum. The shop sells other art gifts, such as works from Seattle's Glass Eye Studio, and Door County's ubiquitous copper sprinklers and other garden art.

In Fish Creek

Door County Confectionary (920-868-3863; doorcountyconfectionery .com), 4191 Main Street, and other locations around Door County. Open daily in summer, winter hours are limited and vary by location. Stop in any of the locations for fudge, taffy, bark, and other delectable goodies; the scent will ensure you can't leave without a little red-and-white-striped bag of something sweet. A trip to Door County is not complete without a stop here.

Touch of the World (920-868-1734), 9424 Cedar Creek Street. Open daily in summer. Just off Main Street, this tiny import shop is not for the claustrophobic, because it's crammed full of imported clothing, jewelry, and gifts. It makes for great browsing, though, and the prices are good. There's more to see outside, too, including all sorts of lawn decor.

Fish Creek Kite Company (920-868-3769; fishcreekkites.com), 3903 WI 42. Open daily. Looking for something different to do? This shop is packed to the gills with all kinds of kites and similar objects (such as wind socks) to liven up a windy day. Browse stunt kites as well as basic ones; this shop stocks kites from around the world.

Hat Head (920-868-2371; gohathead .com), 4149 Main Street. Open 10–5 daily. Some hat stores leave me yawning, but this one is so stuffed with chapeaus that I couldn't help but linger. There are hats for men, women, and children, in every imaginable style. It's perfect when the summer sun catches you off guard—there are some reasonably priced options here, for sure—but it's also a great place to get a quality hat. Or a cheesehead, if you must.

Gallery 42 (920-868-4567; gallery fortytwo.com), 8499 WI 42. Open daily in summer. This contemporary art gallery caters to buyers looking for something to hang at home.

The Peninsula Bookman (920-868-1467; peninsulabookman.com), 4083 Main Street. Open 10–5 daily May through October, 10–5 Tuesday through Saturday November through April. Offers new and used books in all genres, plus a huge selection of Door County books, many of which are out of print. Browse, get a little peninsula history, and pick up something to read on the beach.

Top of the Hill Shops (shopping doorcounty.com), WI 42 and County Highway F. Store hours vary. This little outdoor mall at the north end of Fish Creek is a little bit away from the "downtown" Fish Creek shopping district, but it's not at all a long drive north on WI 42 to this fresh shopping spot. There are 23 stores here, selling everything from original art and custom-designed jewelry to designer kids' clothes and specialty imports.

The Oilerie, (800-310-2878; oilerie .com), 4083 Main Street. Open 10–5 daily. A foodie's heaven, this unique store offers more olive oils and balsamic vinegars than you can imagine. Some are spiced, flavored, or otherwise jazzed up; some are plain. All, however, are available for sample. The store also stocks pasta, snacks, and olive-oil body products. It's hard not to drop a lot of money here. A word of caution: They really, really don't want kids in the store.

Sunshine and Co. (920-868-3202), 4199 Main Street. Open daily in summer. Right next to Founder's Square, a brilliant lawn ornament might catch your eye as you stroll about with an ice-cream cone or fresh chunk of fudge. While it's hardly a challenge to find whimsical and unique garden accessories in Door County, there's something extra-friendly about this place. Maybe it's the name.

The Fish Creek Market (920-868-3351; fishcreekmarket.com), 4164 Main Street. Open daily. This smallish market offers all kinds of yummy breads, jams, specialty foods, and more, plus a great deli and bakery. Walking in is a culinary delight; your taste buds will be excited just to be here. Pick up snacks for later, or gifts for friends.

In Ephraim
Fine Line Designs Gallery (920-854-4343; finelinedesignsgallery.com), 10376 WI 42. Open daily May through November, weekends in winter.

Displaying the work of more than 80 artists on a sprawling estate, this gallery has indoor and outdoor exhibitions of original art, furnishings, gifts, and more.

City Farmer (920-854-7501), 10432 WI 42. Don't let the name—or the fact that the shop is housed in a restored barn—fool you. This place isn't about farming at all. Featuring English country furnishings and home goods, there's a lot to look at here. Outside, plenty of whimsical garden accessories are on display, just waiting for you to decide which to bring home.

Blue Dolphin House (920-854-4113; bluedolphinhouse.com), 10320 WI 42. Open 10–5 daily May through December, Thursday through Monday in winter. Blue Dolphin House has a little bit of everything for the home: kitchen gadgets, furnishings, designer linens, and more. Outside, the gardens are home to all manner of unique lawn decor, from birdbaths to furniture and fountains. The BDH Studio features fine art in various media.

In Sister Bay
Ecology Sports (920-854-5724; ecologysports.com), 10904 WI 42. Open 10–5 daily. Stocking all kinds of fashionable outdoor clothing and gear, if you plan to hit the trails in style, this is your place. Lines include Patagonia, North Face, and Ugg, and you can pick up a Sigg water bottle here, too. Be sure to take time to stop at Base Camp, the attached coffee shop, for a cup of joe and snack before you head out. Base Camp also rents gear, which makes it even easier. The building, by the way, is an old town hall, built in 1879.

&. **Book World** (920-854-4248; book worldstores.com), 326 Country Walk Road. Open daily. This independent Midwestern chain of bookstores began in Rhinelander and now has more than 40 stores in four states. Most are based

in small communities, like this one, and feature general books for all ages, plus a huge selection of magazines and regional titles.

Chelsea Antiques (920-854-4828; chelseabluewillow.com), 10002 WI 57. Open 10–5 daily in summer. A favorite among antiquers, this shop focuses on English and French pieces for the home. The attached Blue Willow Shop carries more home goods, plus works by Door County artists and even gourmet goodies.

In Ellison Bay
Linden Gallery (920-854-2487; lindensgallery.com), 12001 Mink River Road. Open daily May through October. This 6,000-square-foot gallery, somewhat away from everything else (but still right off WI 42), is an astounding find. Focused on Asian arts and antiques, there are beautiful pieces here that almost seem like they belong in a museum—but you can buy them (if you have enough money). Don't miss this one.

On Washington Island
Sievers School of Fiber Arts (920-847-2264; sieversschool.com), Jackson Harbor Road. Open June through October. The shop has all the tools and materials you'll need for classes at the school or your own projects, plus a large selection of books, patterns, and specialty fabrics and yarns. You can also pick up original works—everything from quilts to Christmas cards—made by students, faculty, and alumni.

Islandtime Books (920-847-2565), 1885 Detroit Harbor Road. Open daily May through October. This small, independent bookstore is right next door to Red Cup Coffeehouse (see listing under Eating Out), which makes a perfect combination. Though small, it's complete, and you'll find a broad selection of general and literary books here.

The shop also stocks local-interest titles, and brings in authors for events.

Den Norske Grenda (920-847-2030), 1176 Main Road. Open daily in summer. Who said there wasn't anything touristy on Washington Island? Goats on the roof, Scandinavian gifts, buildings that actually came here from Norway, plus fudge, bike rentals, and more—here it is!

✳ Special Events

January: **New Year's Parade**, downtown Egg Harbor. Brrr! This parade goes on no matter what it's like outside! It's a good excuse to break away from that cozy fireplace in your suite, though.

Polar Bear Swim, Jacksonport. New Year's Day. This is the only such plunge on the peninsula, so if you're inclined to jump into freezing Lake Michigan, here's your chance.

February: **Fish Creek Winter Festival**, Fish Creek. Putting to rest the notion that nothing goes on in Door County during winter, this three-day festival will warm anybody up. Take a dog-slide ride, or hop on the trolley for free, then check out local artwork and live music. There's even a kite festival.

March: **St. Patrick's Day Parade**, downtown Sturgeon Bay.

May: **Festival of Blossoms**, countywide. The activity starts to pick up, and this monthlong celebration cheers the cheery blossoms' arrival. Each community hosts its own festival.

Ellison Bay Spring Art Crawl, Ellison Bay. Check out what's going on at a number of galleries and art schools in the area.

Spring Arts and Crafts Fair, downtown Baileys Harbor.

Fine Art Fair, Sunset Park, Sturgeon Bay.

June: **Birding Festival**, Washington Island. Two-day event features guided tours and educational outings on both Washington Island and Rock Island.

Midsummer Music Festival, throughout the county. Classical and chamber music performed by professional groups several weeks each year.

Annual Steelbridge Songfest, throughout Sturgeon Bay. Each year, more than 100 bands and singer/songwriters from around the nation perform on 10 stages around town.

Fyr Bal Festival, downtown Ephraim. This two-day Scandinavian festival features traditional dance and music, crafts, fireworks, and more.

Olde Ellison Bay Days, downtown Ellison Bay. Music, arts, crafts, and more.

July: **Fourth of July** celebrations take place all over Door County. Sturgeon Bay offers music and food at Sunset Park before fireworks at dusk. Baileys Harbor hosts a parade in the morning, and fireworks at night, plus entertainment throughout the day. Gills Rock has live entertainment and evening fireworks on the water. On Washington Island, there's a fireworks display at dusk in Washington Island Ball Park. For something a little different, there's an arts and crafts fair, **Art on the Quiet Side**, in Jacksonport, and Fish Creek celebrates Independence day on July 5. Egg Harbor, on the other hand, shoots off its fireworks on July 3, although it still has a parade on the Fourth. Or, hop on a **Chicago Fireboat Cruise** to view a number of fireworks displays from the water.

FREE AND AL FRESCO

There's a free outdoor concert for nearly every day of the week in summer, which makes it very easy to find something to do. There are other free concerts sprinkled randomly throughout the summer; be on the lookout, or maybe you could just luck out.

Monday: **Monday Evening Concerts** in Ephraim are held in Harborside Park, 5 PM–7 PM June through August. Local musicians perform everything from jazz to country, and a number of the town's shops and galleries stay open late, as well.

Tuesday: **Concerts in the Park** are held at Noble Square in Fish Creek on Tuesday afternoons, 2:30–4:30.

Wednesday: Enjoy music ranging from jazz to folk at **Concerts in the Park** in Sister Bay, held at Beach Park Gazebo at 3 PM.

Thursday: Egg Harbor plays host to free concerts in **Harbor View Park** on Thursdays in July and August from 5 PM–6:30 PM. Area businesses stay open until 8 PM.

Saturday: Five jazz concerts in July and August start at 3 PM and are held at **Lakeside Park** in Jacksonport.

Sunday: **Concerts on the Waterfront**, Door County Maritime Museum, Sturgeon Bay. Free music by the bridge every Sunday, June through July.

Door County Folk Festival, held throughout the county. Five days of music and dancing from around the world, plus fish boils, kids activities, and more.

Jefferson Street Festival, Jefferson Street, Sturgeon Bay. A proper street festival, complete with strolling performers, live music, and more.

Summer Cherry Harvest Fest, Orchard Country Winery and Market, Fish Creek. Live music, free wine tastings, a pit-spitting contest, and activities for the kids.

Plein Air Festival, throughout Door County. More than 40 artists from near and far paint in the open air. Events are held throughout the week-long festival.

Carlsville Day, downtown Carlsville. The festivities kick off with a parade in the morning, and are followed by music, food, and more fun at **Dairy View Country Store** and **Door Peninsula Winery**.

August: **Classic Wooden Boat Show and Festival**, Door County Maritime Museum, Sturgeon Bay. See vintage boats and enjoy other family friendly events at this two-day festival.

Washington Island Music Festival, Trueblood Performing Arts Center, Washington Island. This 11-day festival brings in musicians from the Milwaukee Symphony Orchestra and other places to perform a series of concerts.

Peninsula Music Festival, Door County Auditorium, Fish Creek. Concerts performed by the Peninsula Music Festival Orchestra, a group consisting of musicians from around the country, are held three nights a week during this three-week festival.

Door County Fair, John Miles County Park, Sturgeon Bay. This four-day-long, traditional county fair has all the rides and foods-on-a-stick you'd expect.

Scandinavian Festival, Washington Island.

Door County Festival of the Arts, throughout the county. A weeklong festival dedicated to the arts (including literary and performing), there are events around the peninsula, capped off with the Visual Art Fair in Sister Bay.

Washington Island Fair and Parade, Community Center, Washington Island. Check out the crafts and food following a parade at noon.

Cherry Fest, Lakeside Park, Jacksonport. Here's your chance to gorge on Door County cherries (as though you haven't already been doing that). You'll also find music, crafts, and family friendly events, plus other kinds of food.

September: **Marina Fest**, downtown Sister Bay. Music, water ski shows, wooden boats, live music, and fireworks at dusk make up this one-day event.

A Kingdom So Delicious, throughout the county. Explore local foods on this three-week tour that brings you closer to the farm.

Jazz on Jefferson, Jefferson Street, Sturgeon Bay. There's live jazz all afternoon, and into the evening, plus other events all day long.

Belgian Kermiss Celebration, Camp Wabansi, Nemur. Enjoy a traditional Belgian harvest celebration, Kermiss, with authentic Belgian foods, including booyah, and music.

Autumn Fest, downtown Baileys Harbor. One-day event with live music, arts and crafts, and more.

October: **Art Day for Animals**, Hands-On Art Studio, Fish Creek. A traditional fall festival, with an arsty bent.

Pumpkin Patch Festival, Egg Harbor. Scarecrows and jack 'o lanterns abound at this two-day family festival.

Sister Bay Fall Festival, downtown Sister Bay. This three day festival has live music, juried art, and more.

November: **Sons of Norway Lutefisk and Meatball Dinner**, Bayview Lutheran Church, Sturgeon Bay. In case you've forgotten the area's Scandinavian roots, you can go try lutefisk at this annual dinner.

Egg Harbor Holly Days, Egg Harbor. A parade, Santa, and special deals from merchants throughout the village should get you in the proper holiday spirit.

Festival of Trees, Trueblood Performing Arts Center, Washington Island. Enjoy caroling and a silent auction.

December: **Christmas By The Bay**, Sturgeon Bay. Kids' activities, a parade, and brunch with Santa at this two-day holiday festival.

Northwoods

VILAS COUNTY

NORTHERN WISCONSIN

NORTHWOODS, WEST TO SUPERIOR
BAYFIELD, ASHLAND, HURLEY, SUPERIOR,
HAYWARD, AND ST. CROIX

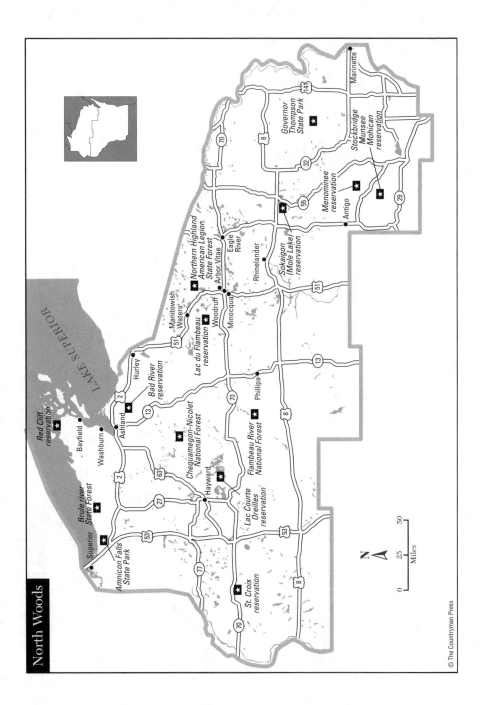

North Woods

LAKE SUPERIOR

Red Cliff
reservation

Bayfield

Washburn

Ashland

Bad River
reservation

Hurley

Brule river
State Forest

Superior

Amnicon Falls
State Park

Chequamegon-Nicolet
National Forest

Hayward

Lac Courte
Oreilles
reservation

St. Croix
reservation

Northern Highland
American Legion
State Forest

Manitowish
Waters

Lac du Flambeau
reservation

Woodruff

Minocqua

Arbor Vitae

Eagle
River

Rhinelander

Phillips

Flambeau River
National Forest

Sokaigon
(Mole Lake)
reservation

Antigo

Menominee
reservation

Governor
Thompson
State Park

Stockbridge
Munsee
Mohican
reservation

Marinette

N

0   25   50
Miles

© The Countryman Press

INTRODUCTION

When people say they're heading up north, it's usually assumed they'll be camping, fishing, boating, hunting, or hanging out at a private cabin—possibly all this and more. It's usually the case, because northern Wisconsin was made for outdoor recreation, all summer *and* winter long. Consider this: Forty-six percent of the state is forest, and most of that forest is in northern Wisconsin. It's green up there, all right. Narrow roads lined by towering pines are stunning and maybe a little disquieting—depends on your take—you're just so far from everything here. Your cell phone might not work, your dining options are somewhat limited, there's not a Starbucks in sight. And what if there were? The beauty of Northern Wisconsin is its remoteness; with the exception of Superior, the towns up here aren't much bigger than developed clearings in the woods, with less than 10,000 residents—most of them less than 2,000. They almost always have a small, historic downtown, and a coffee shop or two. This, mixed with cow-rich pastures to the south, is the image folks from out of state have of Wisconsin, either because it's all they've really seen, or because that's how the state is marketed—or both. It's hard to argue against it—northern Wisconsin is rural, rustic, and remote. That's why it's so popular.

Another draw to the area is the presence of Native American lands. Reservations dot the landscape here. Wisconsin has more reservations than any state east of the Mississippi River; there are nine Native American communities in northern Wisconsin alone. You'll find a handful of cultural centers and museums that explore Native American history, and they're worth a close look.

VILAS COUNTY
Including Minocqua, Arbor Vitae, Woodruff, Manitowish Waters, and Lac Du Flambeau

Some would say this is the "real" Northwoods, and you'll find plenty of marketing material to back that up. Graced by acres of forest numbering in the hundreds of thousands, plus thousands of lakes, rivers, streams, and creeks, it's no mystery why the Vilas County area is a popular spot for summer getaways—whether it's musky fishing, bird watching, mountain biking, or just relaxing. In winter, too, snowshoeing, skiing, and snowmobiling keep the visitors coming—after deer hunting season, that is. St. Germain and Eagle River, especially, are prime snowmobiling spots. In Minocqua, resorters and seasonal residents can take breaks from all that nature for a little frenzied shopping in the downtown blocks of boutiques and cafes; elsewhere, it's mainly about nature.

GUIDANCE Minocqua-Arbor Vitae-Woodruff Chamber of Commerce (715-356-5266; minocqua.org), 8216 WI 51.

Lac du Flambeau Chamber of Commerce (715-588-3346; lacduflambeauchamber.com), 602 Peace Pipe Road, Lac du Flambeau.

GETTING THERE *By Car:* From US/WI 51, travel north to Minocqua. From US/WI 51, US 47 heads west to Lac du Flambeau, US 70 to Arbor Vitae and St. Germain. Keep heading north to reach Manitowish Waters and Boulder Junction. After that, it's lots of winding, narrow roads lined with towering pines. Bring your GPS!

By Air: **Lakeland Airport** (715-356-4340), 1545 North Farming Road, Arbor Vitae, has two runways and a hangar to serve private plane needs.

GETTING AROUND Almost everyone will need a vehicle in these parts, without question, and likely did not get here without one.

MEDICAL EMERGENCY Call 911.

Howard Young Medical Center (715-356-8000), 240 Maple Street, Woodruff.

* To See and Do

MUSEUMS ♿ ☂ **George W. Brown, Jr. Ojibwe Museum and Cultural Center** (715-588-2355; lacduflambeaunation.com/depts/Museum.html), 603 Peace Pipe Road, Lac du Flambeau. Open 10–4 Monday through Saturday from May through October, 10–2 Tuesday through Thursday. Explores Ojibwe history and culture through multi-media displays and historical exhibits, including birch bark canoes, a French trading post, arts, and more. Tuesday evenings feature a pow-wow.

Wa-Swa-Goning Indian Village (715-588-2615), County Highway H, Lac du Flambeau. Open 10–4 Tuesday through Saturday from mid-June through August. Take a guided, historical tour on the Lac du Flambeau reservation; the village covers 20 acres along Moving Cloud Lake. Adults $8;ages 5–12 and older than 65 $6.

♿ ☂ **Minocqua Museum** (715-356-7666), 416 Chicago Avenue, Minocqua. Open 10–4 Monday through Friday from June through Labor Day. This is a cute little museum in Minocqua's main shopping area, with displays on the area's past. Good for a quick look. Free.

♿ ☂ **Vilas County Historical Museum** (715-542-3388; vilasmuseum.com), 217 Main Street, Sawyer. Open 10–4 daily from Memorial Day through September. See lots of artifacts from the area's past, including snowmobiles, typewriters, and vintage clothing.

♿ ☂ **Eagle River Historical Museum** (715-479-2396), 519 East Sheridan Street, Eagle River. Open 10–3 Tuesday through Friday, mid-May through mid-October.

♿ ☂ 🖍 **Northwoods Children's Museum** (715-479-4623; northwoodschildrens museum.com), 346 West Division Street, Eagle River. Open 10–5 Monday through Saturday, noon–5 Sunday. This hands-on kids' museum has common exhibits like a grocery store, construction area, and computers, but it also has a camping exhibit, pioneer cabin, fishing pond, displays about Wisconsin's birds, and other fun ways to learn about the area. $6.

♿ ☂ **Land O'Lakes Northern Waters Museum** (715-547-6979; landolakes history.org), County Highway B, Land O'Lakes. Open 11–3 Thursday through Saturday from June through August.

♿ **North Lakeland Discovery Center** (715-543-2085; discoverycenter.net), W215 County Highway W, Manitowish Waters. Open daily. This nature center is an official part of the **Great Wisconsin Nature and Birding Trail**, which means lots of opportunities to spy winged creatures as you bike and hike 13 miles of trails. There are programs and workshops all summer long, plus free guided nature hikes every other Wednesday in summer. Be sure to check out the bog boardwalk for a look at unusual vegetation, such as pitcher plant and pink lady slipper.

WINERIES ♿ 🍸 **Three Lakes Winery** (715-546-3080; www.cranberrywine .com), 6971 Gogebic Street, Three Lakes. Open daily. This winery produces fruit wines, including cranberry, strawberry, wild plum, kiwifruit, and elderberry—if you like 'em sweet, this is your place. Free guided tours are offered in summer, but tastings are available year-round.

Northwoods Wildlife Center (715-356-7400; northwoodswildlifecenter.com), 8683 Blumenstein Road, Minocqua. Open 10–4 Monday through Saturday in summer, seasonal hours the rest of the year. The center nurses between 700 and 1000 animals back to health each year. Guided tours are offered every half hour.

✳ Outdoor Activities

Holiday Acres Recreational Park (715-356-4400), 7994 US 51 South, Minocqua. Open 9–10 daily May through October. There's a little bit of everything here, including mini-golf, go-carts, and horses to ride.

Settlers Mill Adventure Golf (715-356-9797; settlersmillminocqua.com), US 51 South, Minocqua. Open daily in summer. Enjoy 18 holes of well-landscaped mini-golf and a treat of frozen custard when you're done.

Bearskin State Trail (715-536-8773), access points in Minocqua and in Oneida County at County Highway K and US 51. Once a railroad delivering the regions pine lumber to areas around the Midwest, today the path is popular for walking, biking, and in winter, snowmobiling.

Eagle River Area Guides (715-477-2248; eagleriverguides.com), 4315 Wall Street, Eagle River. Offers a fishing-guide service on the Eagle River Chain of Lakes—the world's largest inland chain, with 28 connected lakes in all. It's a great spot for chasing down walleye, bass, and musky.

& **Jim Peck's Wildwood Wildlife Park** (715-356-5588), US 70, Minocqua. Open daily in summer. There's a petting zoo, fishing pond, nature walks, and more, sure to delight kids.

✳ Green Space

& **Chequamegon-Nicolet National Forest** (715-362-1371; fs.fed.us/r9/cnnf/index.html). In all, the Chequamegon-Nicolet National Forest stretches over more than a million and a half acres in eleven northern Wisconsin counties. It's actually two forests combined into one; before 1993, there was the Chequamegon National Forest and the Nicolet National Forest. Today, the two are managed as a single entity, but they're still considered in terms of the Chequamegon side and the Nicolet side. The Chequamegon side spans Ashland, Bayfield, Sawyer, Price, Taylor, and Vilas counties, covering 858,400 acres.

Here's a stunning fact: The logging industry sparked by early European settlers in northern and central Wisconsin so thoroughly deforested the state that by the early 1900s—not that long ago, really—the trees had been cleared. During the Great Depression, the federal government took to restoring the forests with the help of Civilian Conservation Corps workers, and today we have woods again. The neat rows of towering pines in the northwoods are less than a century old. There is, of course, a mix of old growth—whatever managed to remain after most of the land was logged and farmed.

Visitors to the forest today can enjoy camping, hiking, skiing, kayaking, fishing, wildlife viewing—just about everything. The official visitor's center is a bit west of here in Ashland: **Northern Great Lakes Visitor Center** (715-685-9983; northerngreatlakescenter.org), 29270 County Highway G, Ashland. Open 9-5 daily. Not just a place to pick up brochures, this visitor's center offers an introduction to the entire area through interactive exhibits, archives, and programs. There's an observation tower here, too, as wells as nature trails.

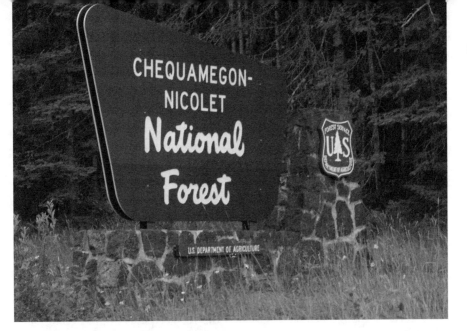

CHEQUAMEGON–NICOLET NATIONAL FOREST

& **Northern Highland-American Legion State Forest** (715-385-2704), 4125 County Highway M, Boulder Junction. The towering pines and chains of lakes in this forest cover 225,000 acres across three counties—Oneida, Vilas, and Iron. There are all manner of campgrounds here, including modern family sites and primitive, remote canoe sites, as well as some with accessible facilities. Canoeing is popular here, and most folks hop on the scenic Manitowish River, but it's far from the only option. If you're just spending the day here, there are trails and more trails for recreation: In winter, 400 miles of snowmobile trails and 70 miles of ski trails await. In summer, five nature trails, three hiking trails, and more than 30 miles of mountain biking should keep you busy. Also here is the Powell Marsh Wildlife Area, popular for hunting, but also its 1800-acre refuge.

Blackjack Springs Wilderness Area (715-479-2827; wilderness.net), Part of the National Wilderness Preservation System. Four miles of trails wend their way along Whispering Lake and the Blackjack Spring Ponds in this 5,800-acre forest.

✳ Lodging

& **The Waters of Minocqua** (715-358-4000; thewatersofminocqua.com), 8116 US 51, Minocqua. Spacious rooms and clean, rustic-themed decor make this a good match for the area. Rooms range from standard doubles to loft suites—plenty of room for the kids. There's a waterpark onsite—not enormous, but it should do the trick for anyone with a hankering to go down a slide. There's a pub, too, and

continental breakfast is included with stays. Travel Green Wisconsin certified. Rooms $89.99–369.

& **The Point Hotel and Suites** (715-356-4431; thepointeresort.com), 8269 US 51 South, Minocqua. Perched on Lake Minocqua and offering grand views, the Point is an upscale and almost perfect place to enjoy the area. Rooms offer tasteful, if bland, decor, with kitchens, balconies, free WiFi, and a little legroom. Outside, the property accesses a snowmobile trail, a putting green, boat slips, canoes and kayaks, and more, plus you can walk to the main shopping strip. Travel Green Wisconsin certified. Rooms $119–345.

& **The Beacons of Minocqua** (715-356-5515; thebeacons.com), 8250 Northern Road, Minocqua. This is a complete resort, with sports, summer activities, boat and bike rentals, and lots more. Lodging options include one- to three-bedroom condos and townhouses, log cabins set in the woods, and an equally peaceful cottage. The cabins and cottage will make you feel like you've bought your own piece of Northwoods real estate. $150–405.

& **Lake of the Torches Casino Resort** (800-258-6724; lakeofthe torches.com), 510 Old Abe Road, Lac du Flambeau. Owned by the Lac du Flambeau Band of Lake Superior Chippewa Indians, the hotel here has more than 100 rooms.

✳ Where to Eat

DINING OUT ☿ & **Mama's Restaurant** (715-356-5070; mamasrestaurant.biz), 10486 WI 70, Minocqua. Open for dinner daily. This is a popular spot for a night out. You can get everything from pizza and simple spaghetti to barbecued ribs and lobster tail here. Be sure to check out the Wednesday night Italian buffet. Dishes $10–48.

☿ & **Marty's Place North** (715-356-4335; martysplacenorth.com), 2721 US 51 North, Arbor Vitae. Open for dinner daily. Marty's is an old-school Northwoods Wisconsin supper club—dark but cozy, set in the woods, offering seafood, steaks, and pastas. Plan on a wait at the bar, because this is a popular place. Dishes $13–28.

☿ & **Bell Isle** (715-356-7444), 301 Front Street, Minocqua. Open daily for dinner. It advertises itself as a sports bar, but this restaurant on the main strip is popular with diners for its American fare. It's a good spot for Friday fish fry, followed by a few drinks and live music. Dishes $12.99–32.99.

☿ & **Pine Baron's** (715-543-8464; pinebarons.com), 149 County Road W, Manitowish Waters. Open for dinner daily. Another spot for a casual yet upscale night out, this one honors the tradition of the supper club—both the fare and the feel—but kicks it up a notch. Appetizers such as double-cream brie and Ma Uon make it clear this isn't a typical Northwoods restaurant. Dishes $14–40.

☿ & **Riverstone Restaurant** (715-479-8467; riverstonerestaurant.com), 219 North Railroad Street, Eagle River. Open for dinner daily, Sunday brunch. Here's upscale dining with a little creativity—a far cry from the steaks and potatoes you'll find almost everywhere else in northern Wisconsin. That's not to say this restaurant is lacking for steak; it's not. But it also has butternut squash ravioli, stone-fired pizza, artisan breads, and organic butter, plus an impressive wine menu. While not overtly subscribing to the locally sourced foods trend, plenty on the menu is, indeed, regional—in particular the artisan cheeses. Here's a Wisconsin dream menu: artisan cheese board to start, followed by the cheese and vegetable soup (there's beer in there, too!). Your main course is the Wisconsin Ethnic Sausages plate—that's sausages, plural, and it comes with potatoes, apples and kraut. Sunday brunch has among its offerings omelets, pasta, and a crêpe station. Dishes $14.99–28.99.

A MEAL TO DIE FOR

𐂷 ♿ **Little Bohemia Lodge,** Manitowish Waters. Open for breakfast and lunch Wednesday through Monday, dinner daily. Some places try to create an atmosphere of intrigue, harkening back to deliciously shady times and pretending they're more interesting than they are. Little Bohemia doesn't have to do a thing, because it actually *is* that interesting. This is the site of the infamous shootout between John Dillinger's gang and the FBI; it looks essentially the same as it did in the '30s, and even some of the bullet holes remain. Little Bohemia was also used as the film location for this scene in the Johnny Depp movie *Public Enemies,* and this summer the lodge expects to give tours, including Dillinger's (or Depp's, depending on your interests) room, timed with the release of the movie. Be sure to check out the small exhibit of artifacts Dillinger left behind.

Now, of course, for a lot of people up here, that's just an interesting side note. They come here not for the Dillinger, but for the food. The dining room—dark and classic Northwoods supper club—has a stunning view of Little Star Lake. The menu offers a range of seafood and steaks, plus a few pasta dishes such as fettuccini Alfredo and wild mushroom ravioli. For anyone here for the fun of it, though, there's Dillinger Medallions and a Baby-face steak sandwich, while breakfast offers Shoot'em up Pancakes, Gangster's Get-Away Breakfast, and Eggs Dillinger. Dishes $13–37.

LITTLE BOHEMIA

⅄ & **Outdoorsman Restaurant and Inn** (715-385-2826; outdoorsman restaurant.com), 10383 Main Street, Boulder Junction. Open for breakfast and lunch daily, dinner Tuesday through Saturday. Popular for its wide array of game dishes and creative entrees, this is a bit like the next step in the supper club evolution. It's *not* a supper club, but you do get a salad bar. With those kinds of details, plus an updated menu, this should suit just about everyone. Dishes $15–26.

EATING OUT

In Minocqua

& **Island Cafe** (715-356-6977; island cafeminocqua.com), 314 Oneida Street, Minocqua. Open for all three meals Thursday through Tuesday. This is a well-rounded and charming restaurant with a huge menu that includes American and Greek dishes, with plenty of vegetarian options, including veggie burgers. There are real burgers and meat dishes, too, so everyone ought to be happy. Dishes less than $10.

Life Spring, Minocqua (715-356-5405; headforthedome.com), 7578 Hgwy. 51 South, Minocqua. Open 7:30–5 Friday through Sunday in summer. This place is unique for several reasons. (1) It's housed in an old geodesic dome just south of town. (2) It has an associated antiques and folk-art shop, plus a natural-foods grocery. (3) The breakfast and lunch menu is entirely vegetarian. Stop by for healthy waffles, bean dishes, pizza, smoothies, lattes—or just a simple cup of Alterra coffee. Dishes less than $10.

⅄ & **Minocqua Brewing Company** (715-356-2600; minocquabrewing company.com), 238 Lakeshore Drive, Minocqua. Open for lunch and dinner Tuesday through Sunday. This brew pub serves sandwiches, burgers, and salads, plus a huge array of munchies like hot wings and deep-fried cheddar nuggets. Wash them down with one of the craft beers on tap. Dishes less than $10.

BRANDY OLD FASHIONED

The old-fashioned cocktail the Old Fashioned never really went out of style in Wisconsin. This mix of sugar, bitters, spirits, and soda has long been a staple at supper clubs, lounges, and holiday parties, and that's that. You might think that the love of this specific drink was enough to equal another Wisconsin quirk, but it gets better. Go anywhere else in the nation, and an Old Fashioned is made with whiskey. In Wisconsin, it's made with brandy. Not fancy-pants brandy, either; just brandy—usually Korbel. Manhattans are made with brandy here, too, and we don't know why. It is, perhaps, Wisconsin's greatest mystery, something state historians—both professional and amateur—have yet to agree on. Whatever the reason, it's a fact of Wisconsin cocktails—if you don't want brandy in your Old Fashioned, you'd better speak up. When ordering, it helps to mention what topper and garnish you want in your Old Fashioned, too—sweet or sour? Olives or cherries? Me? I'll have a brandy Old Fashioned sweet, with cherries. (I've got a sweet tooth, what can I say?)

♿ **Paul Bunyan's Northwoods Cook Shanty** (715-356-6270; paulbunyans.com), 8653 US 51 North, Minocqua. Open for all three meals daily. Just like the "famous" one in Wisconsin Dells, meals are served all-you-can-eat and family style at long tables, although there are smaller tables, too, good for smaller kids or folks who don't wish to socialize. Breakfast is a hit, with an endless supply of eggs, potatoes, pancakes, sausages, and warm, buttermilk doughnuts.

♿ **Polecat and Lace** (715-356-3335; polecatandlace.com), 427 Oneida Street, Minocqua. Open for lunch and dinner Monday through Saturday. Right in the downtown shopping district, the menu offers everything from simple sandwiches for lunch to pasta primavera, and even weinerschnitzel on the dinner menu. Dishes $10–25.

In Eagle River

♿ **Brew Moon** (715-479-1555; brewmooncoffeehouse.com), 113 South Railroad Street, Eagle River. Open 7–5 Monday through Saturday. Offering espresso drinks, homemade gelato, light breakfasts, and a great lunch menu with sandwiches, salads, soups, and quesadillas—including plenty of choices for vegetarians—Brew Moon is a great spot to refuel. There's free Wi-Fi, too, and a complimentary 10 minutes on the restaurant's computer, so you can check your email, if you need to. Dishes less than $10.

♿ **Soda Pops** (715-479-9424; soda-pops.com), 125 South Railroad Street, Eagle River. Open 11–10 daily in summer, shorter hours in winter. This is a retro soda fountain with a fun sandwich menu—you'll find a Spam sandwich, toasted cheese on a roll, and a crazy one with meatballs, cranberries, and sauerkraut, along with many more moderate sandwiches. Get a side of beer-battered cheese curds and a phosphate, then finish it off with a sundae.

POLECAT AND LACE

Dishes less than $10.

♿ **Joe's Pasty Shop** (715-369-1224; ilovepasties.com), 123 Randall Avenue, Rhinelander. Open 10–6 Tuesday through Friday, 8–3 Saturday. This is a popular stop for pasties—a hearty pastry filled with meats and veggies—in these parts. Most commonly found in Mineral Point as well as Upper Michigan, this one's a transplant from the U.P. Dishes less than $10.

❂ Entertainment

♿ **Scheer's Lumberjack Shows** (715-356-4050; scheerslumberjackshow.com), in Woodruff at WI 51 and WI 47. Shows late June through late August. Watch logrolling shows, axe throwing, speed carving, and more at this popular show celebrating the areas logging history.

&. ⊤ **Lake of the Torches Casino** (800-258-6724; lakeofthetorches.com), 510 Old Abe Road, Lac du Flambeau. Owned by the Lac du Flambeau Band of Lake Superior Chippewa Indians, the casino has about 800 slots, plus blackjack, poker, and bingo. Live entertainment is scheduled regularly.

&. ⊤ **Campanile Center For the Arts** (715-356-9700; campanilecenter .org), 141 Milwaukee Street, Minocqua. Hosts gallery shows, community theater, classes, and touring performers throughout the year.

✳ Selective Shopping

The Baker's House, Minocqua (715-356-0066), 201 West Milwaukee Street, Minocqua. Open daily. There are all kinds of irresistible cookies, breads, pies, and other pastries in this little shop just off the main drag. It's tiny and old-fashioned, which makes the goodies all the tastier. You can watch the bakers through the observation, and there's a little, low door where kids can get a free cookie.

&. **Dan's Minocqua Fudge** (715-356-2662), 521 Oneida Street, Minocqua.

Open daily. A perfect place to satisfy any sugar craving, this shop has homemade candies plus an old-fashioned ice-cream parlor, with all kinds of sundaes and sodas.

Anne-Marie's English Pottery and Gifts (715-356-1515; annmarie.com), 414 Oneida Street, Minocqua. Open daily in summer. A little bit tea shop, a little bit coffee shop, and a little bit gift shop, Anne-Marie's is a fun stop even if just to look around.

&. **The Country Store** (715-479-9226; ercandy.com), 116 Wall Street, Eagle River. Open daily. Everyone gets a fudge craving on vacation, and this store has the goods. It also carries nut brittles, saltwater taffy, and award-winning caramel corn.

&. **Three Lakes Winery** (715-546-3080; cranberrywine.com), 6971 Gogebic Street, Three Lakes. Open daily. This winery produces fruit wines, including cranberry, strawberry, wild plum, kiwifruit, and elderberry—if you like 'em sweet, this is your place. Free guided tours are offered in summer, but tastings are available year-round.

YOU CAN ALWAYS PICK UP QUILTS IN MINOCQUA.

&. **The Flour Sack** (715-479-7249; floursack.com), 348 West Pine Street, Eagle River. Open 8–6 Monday through Friday, 8–4 Saturday. There are all kinds of specialty foods here—lingonberries, sugar-free candies, gluten-free items, nuts, and more. You can also grab a sandwich for lunch here.

✳ Special Events

July: **Northwoods Art Tour**, various locations. This three-day tour of studios and galleries stretches from Mercer to Three Lakes. See artists at work, and the places they work. It's also a good chance to visit areas you might not otherwise.

Lac du Flambeau Indian Bowl Powwow 603 Peace Pipe Road, Lac du Flambeau. The Lac du Flambeau band of Ojibwe holds a powwow each year on July 4 along the shores of Long Interlaken Lake.

August: **Festival of Flavors**, Eagle River. This is a two-day event that's all about Wisconsin foods: artisan cheeses, apple wines—you name it, it's here to taste.

September: **Wisconsin Wife Carrying Championships**, Torpy Park, Minocqua. Men carry their wives through an obstacle course. The winner receives various prizes—like cranberries, bratwursts, and mustard—in quantities equal to the weight of his wife.

Beef-A-Rama, Minocqua. This annual event features live music, arts and crafts, a moo-calling contest, beef sandwiches, the Parade Of Beefs, and a 5K/10K fun run called the Rump Roast Run. Winners receive rump roasts.

Northwoods Art Tour, various locations. This three-day tour of studios and galleries stretches from Mercer to Three Lakes is held twice a year. Artists open their studios and let everyone in.

October: **Cranberry Fest**, Eagle River. Central Wisconsin is the state's largest producer of cranberries, but the northern communities grow a lot, too. Celebrate Wisconsin's abundance at this two-day festival featuring all kinds of cranberry breads, brats, and even the world's largest cranberry cheesecake. There are arts and crafts vendors, too.

Vilas County Fair, Eagle River. This is a typical county fair, with rides, music, animals, and foods on sticks, but it's a big one.

NORTHERN WISCONSIN: EAST TO THE UPPER PENINSULA

RHINELANDER, OCONTO, MARINETTE, AND SHAWANO

Edge toward Michigan's Upper Peninsula, and you'll find the home of the Nicolet side of the Chequamegon-Nicolet National Forest, numerous waterfalls, and the wild Wolf River. The Wolf River makes this area a whitewater rafting draw, but kayakers enjoy it, too. Marinette proclaims itself both "the real north" and "nature's waterpark." Whatever the case, this huge county is home to more than 12,000 acres of lakes, hundreds of miles of streams, three important rivers, a large cluster of waterfalls, and miles of trails.

GUIDANCE The **Rhinelander Chamber of Commerce** (800-236-4386; rhinelanderchamber.com), 450 West Kemp Street, Rhinelander, is right along US 8/WI 17. It's as worth a stop for a picture by the Hodag as it is for the information. **Marinette County Tourism** (800-236-6681; therealnorth.com), 601 Marinette Avenue, Marinette. Note that web address.

GETTING THERE *By Car:* US 8, WI 17, and WI 47 all cross Rhinelander; US 41, US 141, and US 8 head into Marinette; WI 29 heads into Shawano;
By Air: **Rhinelander/Oneida County Airport** (715-365-3416), 3375 Airport Road, Rhinelander. This is the largest airport in the area, but there's also **Crivitz Airport** (715-854-7075).

GETTING AROUND Northern Wisconsin necessitates a vehicle; you'll want a car.

MEDICAL EMERGENCY Call 911.
St. Mary's Hospital (715-361-2000), 2251 North Shore Drive, Rhinelander.
Bay Area Medical Center (888-788-2070), 3100 Shore Drive, Marinette.
Community Memorial Hospital (920-846-3444)855 South Main Street, Oconto Falls.

✳ To See and Do

 ⚘ **Forest County Potawatomi Cultural Center and Museum** (715-478-7478; potawatomimuseum.com), 5460 Everybody's Road, Crandon. Open 9–4 daily. The museum and library are home to a collection of Potowatomi artifacts, books, and periodicals on the Great Lakes Native American tribes. There's also a gift shop, and the center hosts language classes and workshops as well. Adults $3; ages 5–12 and older than 55, $1.

  Peshtigo Fire Museum (715-582-3244; peshtigofire.info), 400 Oconto Avenue, Peshtigo. Open 10–4:30 daily May through October. On October 8, 1871, Mrs. O'Leary's cow was blamed for setting Chicago ablaze; at the same time in northern Wisconsin, a fire raged so strongly, it is said to be the worst forest fire in U.S. history. More than 2,400 people died, and the town of Peshtigo was completely destroyed. This museum—housed in the first church built after the fire—is home to objects that survived the fire, as well as educational information. Outside, there is a mass grave for about 350 people who were never identified. Free.

  Menominee Indian Tribe Of Wisconsin Logging Museum (715-799-5258; menominee-nsn.gov), WI 47 and County Road VV, Keshena. Open 9–3 Tuesday through Saturday from May through October. Home to the world's largest collection of logging artifacts—more than 20,000 items—this museum is a careful reproduction of a typical 19th-century logging camp, common in northern Wisconsin. Adults $10; ages 10–15, $5.

  Camp Five Museum (715-674-3414; camp5museum.org), 5480 Connor Farm Road, Laona. Open Monday through Saturday from late June through August. A great way to learn about Wisconsin's logging history is to hop on the Lumberjack Steam Train and check out this extraordinary living museum. What makes it so unique is that it's the actual site of an 1890s lumber camp and 1914 farm (the farm still functions). You can tour the museum, farm, and forest, or take in a river tour, restaurant, gift shop, and guided nature walks. Plan on staying at least a couple hours. Adults $19; ages 4–12 $8; children 3 and younger, free.

⚘ **Langlade County Museum** (715-627-4464; langladehistory.com), 404 Superior Street, Antigo. Open 9:30–3:30 Wednesday through Saturday. This is a typical town historical museum documenting the area's past, but a little larger and broader. Aside from the usual array of industrial, Native American, and general historical artifacts, there's a sizeable research library and gift shop. Outside, check out the **Deleglise Cabin**—the preserved log cabin of Antigo's founder, Francis Deleglise, and the caboose next to the museum. Free.

✳ Outdoor Activities

Peshtigo River Trail This is an 11-mile trip down the Peshtigo River, popular for kayaking and canoeing. Most of it passes through Peshtigo Harbor State Wildlife Area.

Wildman Whitewater Ranch (715-757-2938; wildmanranch.com), N12080 Allison Lane, Athelstane. Open daily in summer. All kinds of adventure sports are offered here. Test your nerves rock climbing, whitewater rafting, or playing paintball. You can try more tranquil pursuits, too, such as kayaking on Caldron Falls Flowage or a relaxing float tubing the Menominee River. $15–50.

Big Smokey Falls Rafting (715-799-3359), WI 55, Keshena. Open daily in summer. Get an access permit from the Menominee Nation, then set your sights on this challenging portion of the Wolf River. Permit price includes shuttle service. $25.

Shotgun Eddy's (715-882-4461; shotguneddy.com), N2765 Hgwy. 55,White Lake. Open daily in summer. Offers whitewater rafting, tubing, and funyaking on the Wolf River. Levels range from somewhat calm to extreme. There's camping here for 10 bucks a night, and a gift shop selling maple syrup. Trips $20-65.

White Pines Family Fun Center (715-362-4653), 4380 WI 17, Rhinelander. Open daily Memorial Day through Labor Day. The center has go-carts, mini-golf, an arcade, and pizza, all of which should expend the kids' energy.

✴ Green Space

& **Chequamegon-Nicolet National Forest** (715-362-1371; www.fs.fed.us/ r9/cnnf/index.html). The Nicolet side spans Florence, Forest, Langlade, Oconto, Oneida, and Vilas counties, covering 661,400 acres.

Visitors to the forest can enjoy camping, hiking, skiing, kayaking, fishing, wildlife viewing—just about everything. The official visitor's center is at the **Florence Wild Rivers Interpretive Center** (888-889-0049; northerngreatlakescenter.org), 4818 Forestry Drive, Florence.

MARINETTE WATERFALLS Northern Wisconsin is home to numerous cascading falls; it's the payoff for a challenging hike. While the highest are located near Superior, Marinette County—the self-proclaimed waterfall capital of Wisconsin— has an impressive number of lovely falls. Fourteen waterfalls large and small make for a self-guided tour throughout the county, so plan on a couple days. Some of the

THE LAKES IN NORTHWOODS OFFER STUNNING VIEWS AND GREAT FISHING.

falls are found at **Veteran's Memorial Park** on Parkway Road, Crivitz; not far away is **Goodman Park** (715-732-7530), off Parkway Road, Silver Cliff; **Twelve Foot Falls Park** (715-735-6681), Twelve Foot Falls Road, Dunbar; and **Dave's Falls Park** (715-735-6681), WI 141, Amberg. There are many more to see, however. Pick up a guide and map from **Marinette County Tourism** (800-236-6681; therealnorth.com), 601 Marinette Avenue, Marinette. There are signs pointing to the waterfalls, too.

 ♿ **Peshtigo River State Forest** (715-757-3965), N10008 Paust Lane, Crivitz. The Wisconsin and Wolf rivers get all the attention for their rapids, but the Peshtigo River is no slouch, and the dams here generate electricity for the region. The forest is big—more than 9,000 acres stretched along 25 miles of river. Purchased in 2001, this is one of the state's newer forests. Right next door is **Governor Thompson State Park** (715-757-3979), a 2,800-acre spread with placid lakes and wild shoreline. Eventually, the park will include primitive camping, hiking trails, and picnic sites. A state park vehicle sticker is required.

Navarino Wildlife Area (715-758-6999; navarino.org), W5646 Lindsten Road, Shioction. This 15,000-acre area contains forest, wetlands, prairies, and gardens—perfect for hiking and nature viewing.

Oconto Marsh Refuge (888-626-6862), along the shores of Green Bay in Oconto. Among the largest wetlands on the west side of Green Bay, this 4,000-acre refuge is home to a large population of birds.

✳ Lodging

♿ ♿ **Holiday Acres Resort** (715-369-1500; holidayacres.com), 4060 South Shore Parkway, Rhinelander. The sprawling, 1,000-acre property is home to Lake Thompson, nature trails, restaurants, shopping, geocaching, an indoor pool, and lots more. You can rent basic rooms, cottages, even a six-bedroom home here. Rooms $99–149, cottages $119–329, vacation homes $3,689–4,699 weekly.

♿ **Konkapot Lodge** (715-787-4747; konkapot.com), W12635 County Road A, Bowler. Located right near the **North Star Mohican Casino**, if you're in the area for gaming, this is a convenient choice. The clean, rustic décor in the common areas fits well with the wooded surroundings. Rooms are basic, but sufficient, and include continental breakfast. $77–122.

♿ **Lauerman House Inn** (715-732-7800; lauermanhouse.com), 1975 Main Street, Marinette. It's a Victorian mansion, but most of the rooms are decorated in a casual, contemporary-meets-vintage style, with antiques and bright colors. Choose from among seven rooms, including two suites. Rooms $100–160.

✳ Where to Eat

DINING OUT ♿ ♿ **Lauerman House Restaurant** (715-732-7800; lauermanhouse.com), 1975 Main Street, Marinette. Open for lunch Monday through Friday, dinner Monday through Saturday. Enjoy upscale French fusion in this Victorian B&B. Guests get preferred seating, but it's worth a shot for a unique dinner in these parts. Dishes $20-40.

EATING OUT ♿ **Blue Bike Burrito** (715-735-9889; bluebikeburrito.com), 2020 Hall Avenue, Marinette. Open 11-7 Monday through Friday. As you might have guessed, this colorful cafe with bikes on the walls serves up Mexican fare. It's a short menu, but covers burritos, tacos, and fajitas. Dishes less than $10.

♿ ♿ **T & T Supper Club** (715-589-4111), 828 County Road N, Niagara. Open for dinner daily. This is an old-school supper club with traditional American fare. The twist here is the all-you-can-eat pasta. Dishes $8-28.

♿ ♿ **Brown Street Brewery** (715-369-2100), 16 North Brown Street, Rhinelander. Open daily for lunch and dinner. Among the area's only microbreweries, you can get pub grub here like burgers, pizza, wraps, and lots of munchies here. Dishes less than $10.

♿ ♿ **Farm Inn on Main** (715-524-4916), 123 North Main Street, Shawano. Open for all three meals daily. This cute, country café is everything Cracker Barrel wishes it could be. The homemade American fare is sure to suit everyone. Dishes $5–15.

✳ Entertainment

♿ ♿ **Potawatomi Northern Lights Casino** (715-473-2021; cartercasino.com), WI 32, Wabeno. One of the larger casinos in northern Wisconsin, this one has bingo, slots, blackjack, and more, plus accommodations.

♿ ♿ **North Star Mohican Casino** (715-787-3110; northstarcasinoresort.com), W12180 County Road A, Bowler. Bingo, slots, blackjack, and more. There's lodging and dining here, as well.

♿ ♿ **Crivitz Ski Cats** (715-854-7574), Lake Noquebay Park, Crivitz. This ski team has been performing acrobatic waterski stunts since 1964. Catch a free performance nearly every Wednesday and Saturday from mid-June through August.

HODAG

* Selective Shopping

Woodland Trail Winery (715-276-3668; catchwine.com), 17153 Big Hill Road, Lakewood. Nestled amongst the woods of the Nicolet National Forest, this winery produces both grape wines and fruit wines.

* Special Events

July: **Hodag Country Festival**, Rhinelander. Named for the grinning, Rhinelander-specific mythical creature—this area's own Loch Ness Monster, dating back to 1893, when a local named Eugene Shepard reported that he'd seen a beast with "the head of a frog, the grinning face of a giant elephant, thick, short legs set off by huge claws, the back of a dinosaur, and a long tail with spears at the end." Shepard later claimed to have killed the beast, and provided a photograph to the media to prove it. Eventually, Shepard admitted the whole thing was a hoax, but the name and mythology stuck. This a country music festival that draws around 40,000 people and big-name country acts each year.

August: **Menominee Nation Contest Powwow**, at the Woodland Bowl, Keshena. This annual contest draws participants from around the U.S. and Canada. The dances take place in a natural amphitheater on the Menominee reservation, and traditional foods and crafts are sale.

NORTHWOODS, WEST TO SUPERIOR

BAYFIELD, ASHLAND, HURLEY, SUPERIOR, HAYWARD, AND ST. CROIX

Pretty Bayfield might just be a postcard come to life. It's hard to imagine a more perfect resort town, with glistening waters, sea caves, islands, upscale resorts, a walkable downtown, and apple orchards within reach. Sure, other towns have at least a few of these, but Bayfield's remoteness makes it special. Sitting at the top of the state along Lake Superior, Bayfield is up there, all right, and has a very different feel than the rest of the Northwoods. The white wooden buildings, boutiques, and art galleries smack of a mini Door County, but it's not quite that, either (although they do throw fish boils up here). Sure, it's touristy, but even the most touristy shops feel a little more genuine than in other resort towns. The people here are friendly and excited to share their love of this picturesque, if sometimes chilly, town. It doesn't hurt that a large portion of the businesses are dedicated to green practices and sustainability, either.

MADELINE ISLAND FERRY

Outside of Bayfield, this region is marked by more majestic forests, countless lakes, and endless opportunities for recreation. The towns and cities—including industrial Superior—are less charming than Bayfield, but they all offer their own piece of Northern Wisconsin paradise.

GUIDANCE **Bayfield Chamber of Commerce and Visitor Bureau** (715-779-3335; www.bayfield.org), 42 S Broad Street, Bayfield.

Apostle Islands National Lakeshore Visitor Center (715-779-3397; nps.gov/apis) 415 Washington Avenue, Bayfield.

Superior-Douglas County Convention & Visitors Bureau (800-942-5313; visitsuperior.com), 205 Belknap Street, Superior.

Hurley Area Chamber of Commerce (866-340-4334; hurleywi.com).

GETTING THERE *By Car:* WI 13 heads to Bayfield, Washburn, and Ashland. US/WI 51 and WI 77 head straight for Hurley. From Hurley, you can catch US 2 west to 13. US 2/53 takes you to Superior, and from the west, take I-535. WI 77 and WI 63 cross Hayward.

GETTING AROUND You'll need a car to get around, although if someone plunked you down in Bayfield, you could do all right on foot. But since that probably won't happen, plan on driving.

MEDICAL EMERGENCY Call 911.

Memorial Medical Center (715-685-5500), 1615 Maple Lane, Ashland.

SMDC Health System (715-392-8281), 3500 Tower Avenue, Superior.

✳ To See and Do

& ⬥ **Madeline Island Museum** (715-747-2415; madelineislandmuseum .wisconsinhistory.org), 226 Colonel Woods Avenue, La Pointe. Open daily from June through August, weekends in May. The museum is contained within four historical buildings, plus newer ones. Among the older buildings is one used by the **American Fur Company** in 1835—a perfect place to view objects from the island's fur trade history. Adults $7; ages 5–17, $3.50; children younger than 5, free.

& ⬥ **Bayfield Heritage Center** (715-779-5958; bayfieldheritage.org), 100 Rittenhouse Avenue, Bayfield. Open 1–4 Tuesday through Saturday mid-June through mid-September. This small museum explores both the recent and distant past of the area.

& ⬥ **Bayfield Maritime Museum** (715-779-3925; apostleisland.com), 1536 First Street, Bayfield. Open 10–5 daily mid-June through mid-September. Naturally, Bayfield has a rich maritime history, and the museum covers it broadly, including displays on shipwrecks, commercial fishing, boatbuilding, and more. Adults $4.50; ages 6–12 $2.50; children younger than 6, free.

& ⬥ **Washburn Cultural Center** (715-373-5591; washburnculturalcenter.art .officelive.com), 1 East Bayfield Street, Washburn. Open 10–4 Monday through Saturday from May through December, 11–3 Monday through Saturday from

January through April. Housed in an 1890s brownstone bank, this museum houses a permanent art collection, temporary gallery hosting rotating shows, and historical displays.

&. **Northern Great Lakes Visitor Center** (715-685-9983; northerngreatlakes center.org), 29270 County Hgwy. G, Ashland. Open 9–5 daily. Not just a place to pick up brochures, this National Forest visitor center offers an introduction to the entire area through interactive exhibits, archives, and programs. There's an observation tower here, too, as well as nature trails. Free.

&. ⛨ **Richard I. Bong Veterans Historical Center** (715-392-7151; bongheritage center.org), 305 Harborview Parkway, Superior. Open 9-5 Monday through Saturday, noon-5 Sunday from late June through late October, 9-5 Tuesday through Sat-

---

SILVER STREET IN HURLEY

Hurley, at the top of the state, and butted up against Michigan, has a storied and seedy past: It was once a bastion of gambling and prostitution, frequented by the likes of John Dillinger and Al Capone for its, ahem, lively nightlife. Hurley refused to heed Prohibition, which increased its popularity among visitors. Today, the Silver Street district remains on the edge, if far less bawdy than it was in the '20s and '30s. Still, this town of barely 2,000 is home to upwards of 30 bars, and a cluster of strip clubs—like the Full Moon Saloon—remains along Hurley's main drag in the historic downtown. Of course, that's not all Hurley's about—it's more about waterfalls and snowmobiles than strip clubs, but its past sure is intriguing.

HURLEY'S SILVER STREET

urday the rest of the year. Honoring the life and career of Superior native and WWII fighter pilot Richard Bong, this center now serves as a historical museum and memorial to all veterans. $10.

↑ **A World of Accordions Museum** (715-395-2787; accordionworld.org), 1401 Belknap Street, Superior. Open 10–2 Monday through Wednesday. Although this museum didn't start out here—it started over in Duluth—it's safe to say any assemblage of squeezeboxes is right at home in Wisconsin. Museum owner Helmi Harrington has collected 1,000 of the instruments and put them on display. There's also a concert hall here (it's an old church), libraries, and more. Nominal donation.

Great Divide National Scenic Byway WI 77 cuts through the Chequamegon-Nicolet National Forest, offering you a look at these majestic woods from the comfort of your auto.

South of Lake Superior

&. ↑ **Fresh Water Fishing Hall Of Fame** (715-634-4440; freshwater-fishing .org), 10360 Hall of Fame Drive, Hayward. Open 9:30–4 :30 daily June through August, 9:30–4 May, September, and October. Don't confuse this for some run-of-the-mill oddball small-town museum. The museum's four buildings house more than 50,000 historical fishing artifacts, including lures and rods, but it's that giant musky outside that gets the attention. Nominal fee.

Forts Folle Avoine Historical Park (715-866-8890; theforts.org), 8500 County Road U, Danbury. Open 10–4 Wednesday through Sunday in summer. Built at the original site of two British fur trade businesses, today this land is a living museum that explores the history of the fur trade and Wisconsin's Native Americans. There are also hiking trails here, a gift shop, and more. Ages 13 and older, $7; 6–12, $5; younger than 6, free.

✳ Outdoor Activities

Brownstone Hiking Trail. This is an easy, 5-mile trail along the lakeshore. It starts in Bayfield near Maggie's Restaurant, and heads south.

Iron Bridge Nature Hiking Trail. Less than a mile, this trail heads uphill north from Bayfield's Broad Street, and promises a great view at the top.

Meyers Beach Hiking Trail. About 18 miles north of Bayfield off WI 13, this challenging lakeshore trail offers a look at the Apostle Islands and the shoreline's stunning sea caves.

Bayfield Bike Route (715-209-6864; bayfieldbikeroute.com), 251 Manypenny Avenue, Bayfield. Open Monday through Saturday in summer. This shop rents bikes by the day, half-day, and hourly. Pick up maps, route guides, or arrange a group ride.

Mount Ashwabay Ski Area (715-779-3227; mtashwabay.org), 32525 Ski Hill Road, Bayfield. Open Wednesday, Thursday, Saturday, and Sunday. Just south of Bayfield and a little west off WI 13, this ski area is popular for its downhill runs and winding, scenic trails. In summer, it's home to **Big Top Chitauqua** (see listing under Entertainment) and bike trails.

Hurley Waterfalls. There are 30 waterfalls in the Hurley area. Contact the **Hurley Area Chamber of Commerce** (715-561-4334; hurleywi.com), 316 Silver Street, Hurley, for a guide. They've even got GPS coordinates for Iron County waterfalls.

☀ Green Space

Brule River State Forest (715-372-5678), 6250 South Ranger Road, Brule. This 47,000-acre forest is popular for its paddling; check out **Brule River Canoe** (715-372-4983; brulerivercanoerental.com), 13869 US 2, Brule. Open 8–7 daily in summer. Hop on the river in a kayak or canoe, or take a guided trip on the 44-mile long Brule River. This outfit rents kayaks, canoes, wetsuits, and everything you need for your trip. The forest here features naturalist programs, five state natural areas, camping, trails, and eight miles of Lake Superior shoreline.

Wisconsin Point, off US 2 and Moccasin Mike Road. Part of the world's largest freshwater sandbar, once you get here you'll find a scenic outlook and the Wisconsin Point Lighthouse. Wave across the water at Minnesota; the other part of the sandbar is Minnesota Point. There are miles of sandy beach, and a wildlife area. Of note, too, is the marker announcing the 1700s Chippewa burial site here.

Patteson State Park (715-399-3111), 6294 WI 35, Superior. This park's biggest draw is its huge waterfalls—at 165 feet, the stunning Big Manitou Falls is the state's highest. There are plenty of places to view the falls, plus swimming in Interfalls Lake (it's not guarded, however, and you should take care to steer clear of the waterfalls). The park offers camping, guided hikes, and education at the **Gitche Gumee Nature Center**. A state park vehicle sticker is required.

Amnicon Falls State Park (715-398-3000), off County Highway U in Superior. Home to stunning waterfalls and an 1800s covered bridge, you can camp, bike, hike, and swim in this geographically remarkable park. A state park vehicle sticker is required.

THE WISCONSIN CONCRETE PARK

South of Superior

Wisconsin Concrete Park (800-269-4505; friendsoffredsmith.org), N8236 South Hgwy. 13, Phillips. Open daily. One of Wisconsin's wonderful outdoor folk art environments, the concrete-and-found-object sculptures here were constructed over 16 years by local tavern owner and retired lumberjack Fred Smith. Untrained in art, Smith built 237 pieces, including figures, animals, and scenes. Admission is free, but donations help ongoing restoration and maintenance.

Timm's Hill, off County Highway C and Rustic Road 62 in Price County. Follow the signs. Wisconsin's highest point, at 1,951 feet, is popular with hikers and cross-country skiers. Climb the observation tower to see what you can see.

Interstate State Park (715-483-3747), WI 35 at US 8. Like its name

THE APOSTLE ISLANDS

&. **Apostle Islands National Lakeshore** (715-779-3397), 415 Washington Avenue, Bayfield. Mainland visitors center open daily from the end of May through mid-October, Monday through Friday from October through May. Comprised of 21 islands and 12 miles of mainland shoreline on Lake Superior, this pristine getaway is one Wisconsin spots that might just be paradise. It's remote, and yet human history here stretches back to the 1400s, when the Ojibwe people called this home; the fishing and hunting has always been good. Later, the Jesuit explorers who first drew up maps of the area gave the sparkling isles their Biblical name, and European settlers followed, setting up fishing and logging camps here, as they did throughout northern Wisconsin. Today, the archipelago is all about nature and recreation. Fully 18 of the islands offer secluded camping, and all the islands plus the mainland portion contain hiking trails. Stockton Island alone has 23 campsites. (It also has the highest concentration of black bears in North America, so remember to keep your food sealed and the scraps out of your tent!) Kayaking, fishing, and boating offer endless opportunities, as well. Guided kayak tours are offered by **Living Adventure** (715-779-9503; livingadventure.com) and **Trek and Trail** (715-779-3595; trek-trail.com). For guided sailing, check out **Animaashi Sailing Company** (715-779-5468; animaashi.com).

Less outdoorsy visitors can enjoy the islands in a more casual way. The collection of historic lighthouses on the islands is stunning; **guided tours of the lighthouses** on four of the islands (Sand, Raspberry, Michigan, and Devils) are offered from June through September. Call 715-779-3397 to speak with park staff. **Apostle Islands Cruise Service** (800-323-7619; apostleisland .com) offers lighthouse cruises and its popular Grand Tour—a 55-mile cruise that hits pretty much everything. On the mainland, the rugged **Lakeshore Trail** offers views of the stunning sea caves that mark the shoreline.

Madeline Island is not part of the National Lakeshore, but it's the largest of the Apostle Islands, and the only one with year-round residents and businesses. Permanent residents total just more than 200; in summer, the population can reach 2,500. Although the island is open to commercial development, more than a third of it is wilderness preserves and parks. In La Pointe, Madeline Island's town, the **Madeline Island Historical Museum** (715-747-2415; madelineislandmuseum.wisconsinhistory.org), 226 Colonel Woods Avenue, features historical and new buildings. **Big Bay State Park** (715-747-6425), off Hagen Road, is here, with more than 2,000 acres of camping, fishing, bird-watching, snowshoeing, and more. There's a lovely, sandy beach, too.

suggests, this park has a counterpart in Minneapolis. It's Wisconsin's oldest park, established in 1900, and features camping, hiking, and swimming at Lake O' the Dalles. A state park vehicle sticker is required.

Turtle-Flambeau Flowage (715-769-3680; turtleflambeauflowage.com), off WI 51 near Mercer. With almost 19,000 acres of water to canoe and enjoy, there's a reason it's nicknamed "the crown jewel of Wisconsin." That's saying a lot, because there are a lot of jewels here. It's not just for boating, although musky fishers like it a lot; there's plenty of birding and trails, too.

✳ Lodging

♿ **Harbor's Edge Motel** (715-779-3962; harborsedgemotel.com), 33 North Front Street, Bayfield. With darling rooms and harbor views, you could do worse (and for much more money) than this. Choose from among basic rooms and larger suites, which have kitchenettes. Rooms $95–149.

♿ **Apple Grove Inn** (715-779-9558; applegroveinn.net), 85095 WI 13, Bayfield. Four country-themed rooms in this inn just south of Bayfield offer private baths, WiFi, and a full breakfast featuring locally sourced, organic foods. Stroll the adjacent apple orchards before you hit the Apostle Islands. Travel Green Wisconsin certified. Rooms $125–135.

♿ **Artesian House** (715-779-3338; artesianhouse.com), 84100 Hatchery Road, Bayfield. Open May through October. This contemporary bed & breakfast boasts four cozy guest rooms and lots of light. Travel Green Wisconsin certified. Rooms $115–135.

🍷 ♿ **Old Rittenhouse Inn** (715-779-5111; rittenhouseinn.com), 301 Rittenhouse Avenue, Bayfield. Catch a glimpse of Lake Superior from the wraparound porch on this Victorian mansion. Rooms range from cozy and snug to sprawling and lavishly decorated suites. Be sure to dine in the restaurant, which has received accolades from *Bon Appetit, Gourmet,* the *New York Times,* and others. Travel

HARBOR'S EDGE MOTEL

Green Wisconsin certified. Rooms $115–305.

♿ **Pinehurst Inn** (715-779-3676; pinehurstinn.com), 83645 WI 13, Bayfield. Five rooms in the Main House, built in 1885, and three in the adjacent Garden House, mean lots of options. Decor veers country and tasteful, with handmade quilts and cozy touches. The Garden House was built using sustainable building practices and features energy-efficient technologies and organic bedding. The Brownstone room in the Garden House has a three-sided fireplace. Full breakfast is served in the Main House. Travel Green Wisconsin certified. Rooms $115–190.

♿ **Seagull Bay Motel** (715-779-5558; seagullbay.com), 325 South Seventh Street, Bayfield. Just need a place to rest your head? This motel offers clean, basic rooms at a more affordable rate. But just because it's basic doesn't mean you're missing out—there's a view of the lake, and Madeline Island. Travel Green Wisconsin certified. Rooms $70–100.

♿ **The Bayfield Inn** (715-779-3363; bayfieldinn.com), 20 Rittenhouse Avenue, Bayfield. Eight contemporary rooms in this lakeside hotel feature basic modern amenities. Suites offer balconies and a little more leg room, or try one of four spacious condos. Travel Green Wisconsin certified. Rooms $95-450.

♿ **Cable Nature Lodge** (715-794-2060; cablenaturelodge.com), 20100 County Highway M, Cable. The clean, rustic appeal of these rooms let you experience the Northwoods from a cozy space. Room names pay homage to the surrounding environment, and the onsite Rookery Pub and Cafe boasts contemporary, healthy fare. Rooms $109–179.

✳ **Where to Eat**

DINING OUT ♈ ♿ **Old Rittenhouse Inn** (715-779-5111; rittenhouseinn .com), 301 Rittenhouse Avenue, Bayfield. Open for all three meals daily. The upscale fare in this Victorian inn has earned the restaurant accolades from national publications with its emphasis is on regional dishes and ingredients. The menu is always changing, but you might get something like the Rittenhouse apple-glazed pork chop. Dishes $20–40.

♈ ♿ **Wild Rice Restaurant** (715-779-9881; wildricerestaurant.com), 84960 Old San Road, Bayfield. Open daily for dinner from May through October. This sleek, upscale restaurant offers contemporary takes on traditional American fare, such as herbed duck breast and a New York strip with black-eyed pea ragout. Dishes $20–30.

EATING OUT

In Bayfield

♿ **Bayfield County Coffee Company** (715-779-9900; bayfieldcounty coffee.com), 39 South Broad Street. Open daily. It's right across the street from the Chamber of Commerce and visitor's center, so when you roll into town, it's a perfect first stop. Mitch Haycock will whip you up an iced coffee and offer a ton of great advice on the area. There's artwork and a little shopping here, too, so settle in and plan out your day. Travel Green Wisconsin certified. Less than $10.

♿ **Egg Toss** (715-779-5181), 41 Maypenny Avenue. Open daily. A popular spot for breakfast, you can enjoy your eggs or pastries on the deck before heading out for a day of adventure. Dishes less than $10.

♈ ♿ **The Groove Haus Bistro and Bar** (715-779-7004), 200 Rittenhouse

THE GROOVE HAUS BISTRO & BREW FEATURES LIVE MUSIC.

Avenue. Open daily for lunch and dinner. Get burgers, pizza, Mexican dishes, and seafood here, then enjoy live music in the bar at night. Dishes $7–14.

Big Water Cafe (715-779-9619), 117 Rittenhouse Avenue. Open daily. This is a traditional coffeehouse, where you can get your latte and sandwich. The focus is on local ingredients—milk comes from a nearby dairy—and organic, when possible, and there are loads of veggie options on the menu, such as the tofu curry wrap. The cafe also makes its own baked goods and hummus. Travel Green Wisconsin certified. Dishes less than $10.

South Shore Brewery and Deepwater Grille (715-682-4200; southshorebrewery.com), 808 West Main Street, Ashland. Open 11–10 daily, bar until 2 AM. The restaurants in this historic downtown building offer everything from pizza to sandwiches, but the craft brewery here stands out. Try one of the stouts or ales on tap. Dishes $9–27.

South of Lake Superior

Rookery Pub and Cafe (715-794-2062; cablenaturelodge.com/foodandspirits), 20100 County Highway M, Cable. Located at the **Cable Nature Lodge**, this is an uncommon option for vegetarian dishes and healthy fare. There's plenty of meat on the menu, so carnivores will be fine, but dishes such as curried bean curd and the "Friday Fish Un-Fry" will appeal to everyone else. Dishes $10–25.

Angry Minnow Bar and Restaurant (715-934-3055; angryminnow.com), 10440 Florida Avenue, Hayward. Open for meals 11–9 Tuesday through Saturday, drinks until bar time. The building, dating back to 1889, was originally the office of the North Wisconsin Lumber Company. Today, it's a microbrewery, serving up craft ales and stouts along with a selection of burgers, sandwiches, and creative dinner entrees. Dishes $7–20.

Coops Pizza Parloure (715-634-3027; coopspizza.com), 10588 California Avenue, Hayward. Open for lunch and dinner daily. There's also a location in Hudson. This is a good place to take the family, since there's a little bit of everything on the menu, not the least of which is pizza. There's a typical, rustic lodge appeal to the décor. Dishes $7–15.

✳ Entertainment

Big Top Chitauqua (715-373-5552; bigtop.org), 101 West Bayfield Street, Bayfield. Billing itself as the "Carnegie Hall Of Tent Shows," this non-profit venue boasts more than 70 nights of entertainment each summer. Regional and national acts play the 900-seat tent stage every year, and it takes its resident shows on the road around the Midwest. A one-hour radio program is recorded here, too, and distributed without charge to public radio in nine states.

Stagenorth and Stage Door Bar (715-373-1194; stagenorth.com), 123 West Omaha Street, Washburn. Bar open daily. Features live theater, music, dance, and film year round.

Lucius Woods Performing Arts Center (715-378-4272; lwmusic.org), Located in Lucius Woods Park on Upper St. Croix Lake, this outdoor theater offers live music all summer long. Make a day of it, and enjoy the park's 40 acres of nature trails, swimming beaches, and playgrounds.

Scheer's Lumberjack Shows (715-356-4050; scheerslumberjackshow.com), south of Hayward on County Road B. Shows late June through late August. See log-rolling, axe throwing, speed carving, and more at this popular show celebrating the area's logging history. There's also a lumberjack village to tour, a pancake house, and a gift shop.

Isle Vista Casino (715-779-3712; wisconsingaming.com), 88705 Pine Tree Lane, Red Cliff. Owned by the Red Cliff band of Lake Superior Chippewa, the games at Isle Vista include bingo, slots, blackjack, and more.

Bad River Casino (715-682-7121; badriver.com), US 2, Odanah, just east of Ashland. Owned by the Bad River band of Lake Superior Chippewa, the casino runs bingo, slots, blackjack games, and more. There's lodging here, as well.

St. Croix Casino (800-846-8946; stcroixcasino.com), at US 8 and WI 63 in Turtle Lake. Owned by the St. Croix Chippewa Indians of Wisconsin, this complex includes a casino with bingo, slots, blackjack, and more, as well as lodging and dining.

✳ Selective Shopping

Stone's Throw Pottery (715-779-5200; stonesthrowbayfield.com), 40 South Second Street, Bayfield. Open 9-6 daily. Not just pottery, Stone's Throw features functional art from a large number of local and regional artists. There's a pottery studio here, as well.

Donalee Designs (715-779-3374; donaleedesigns.com), 83150 WI 13, Bayfield. Open 10-6 daily May 15 through October 15. This is a working jewelry studio just south of Bayfield. Find unique, handcrafted silver and gold jewelry.

Chequamegon Books (715-373-2899), 2 East Bayfield Street, Washburn. Open 10–6 Monday through Saturday, 11–5 Sunday. This is a great indie new and used book store just south of Bayfield. Peruse the books, than grab a cup of coffee at the espresso bar.

Bayfield Bike Route (715-209-6864; bayfieldbikeroute.com), 251 Manypenny Avenue, Bayfield. Open Monday through Saturday in summer. This shop rents bikes by the day, half-day, and hourly. Pick up maps, route guides, or arrange a group ride.

Water Music Jewelry and Art (715-779-5262; watermusicjewelry.com) 13 South Second Street, Bayfield. Open Monday through Saturday.

Keeper of the Light (800-779-4487; keeperofthelight.net), 19 Front Street, Bayfield. Open daily in summer. This little shop is the place to buy your Apostle Islands souvenirs, from lighthouse replicas to books about the islands, and even pirate swords!

Gabriele's German Cookies and Chocolates (715-682-2114; gabrieles germansweets.com), 413 West Main Street, Ashland. Open Monday through Saturday. Stop in for traditional German sweets. There are usually 12 types of cookies and 12 types of chocolates in the house, and it's always changing, so you might want to make a couple stops.

✷ Special Events

May: **Chequamegon Bay Birding and Nature Festival**, Ashland. More than 100 activities and lessons keep birders busy during this three-day event.

August and September: **Apostle Islands Lighthouse Celebration**, Bayfield. Special lighthouse tours, plus arts and more, mark this annual event.

Scarecrow Festival and Orchard Tours The folks in Bayfield really goes wild for fall, and who can blame them? Late September is a perfect time to come see the fall colors, tour apple orchards, and go for a hay ride.

Oktoberfest, Rhinelander. A Wisconsin tradition—just about every town, or at least area, has one. This one's four days of polka, beer, and sausage, as well as arts and crafts, and more.

October: **Bayfield Apple Festival**, Bayfield. More than 50,000 people show up to sample the apple goodies, watch the Venetian Boat Parade, and peruse the arts and crafts vendors.

November: **Big Water Film Festival**, Stagenorth, Washburn. This three-day film festival brings recent independent film to the area.

Apostle Islands Dog Sled Race, Bayfield.

INDEX